Business and Professional Communication

Business and Professional Communication

Putting People First

Kory Floyd
UNIVERSITY OF ARIZONA

Peter W. Cardon
UNIVERSITY OF SOUTHERN CALIFORNIA

McGraw Hill Education

BUSINESS AND PROFESSIONAL COMMUNICATION: PUTTING PEOPLE FIRST

Published by McGraw-Hill Education, 2 Penn Plaza, New York, NY 10121. Copyright © 2020 by
McGraw-Hill Education. All rights reserved. Printed in the United States of America.
No part of this publication may be reproduced or distributed in any form or by
any means, or stored in a database or retrieval system, without the prior written consent of McGraw-Hill
Education, including, but not limited to, in any network or other electronic storage or transmission, or
broadcast for distance learning.

Some ancillaries, including electronic and print components, may not be available to customers outside
the United States.

This book is printed on acid-free paper.

1 2 3 4 5 6 7 8 9 LWI 21 20 19

ISBN 978-1-260-51449-0 (bound edition)
MHID 1-260-51449-8 (bound edition)

ISBN 978-1-260-24505-9 (loose-leaf edition)
MHID 1-260-24505-5 (loose-leaf edition)

Portfolio Manager: *Peter Jurmu*
Senior Product Developer: *Kelly I. Pekelder*
Marketing Manager: *Gabe Fedota*
Lead Content Project Manager: *Christine Vaughan*
Senior Content Project Manager: *Keri Johnson*
Senior Buyer: *Susan K. Culbertson*
Senior Designer: *Matt Diamond*
Content Licensing Specialist: *Jacob Sullivan*
Cover image: *©gobyg/Getty Images*
Compositor: *SPi Global*

All credits appearing on page or at the end of the book are considered to be an extension of the
copyright page.

Library of Congress Cataloging-in-Publication Data
Names: Floyd, Kory, author. | Cardon, Peter W., author.
Title: Business and professional communication: / Kory Floyd, University Of
    Arizona, Peter Cardon, University of Southern California.
Description: First edition. | New York, NY : McGraw-Hill Education, [2020] |
    Includes index.
Identifiers: LCCN 2018055794 | ISBN 9781260514490 (alk. paper)
Subjects: LCSH: Business communication. | Communication in management. |
    Communication in organizations.
Classification: LCC HF5718 .F595 2020 | DDC 658.4/5—dc23
LC record available at https://lccn.loc.gov/2018055794

The Internet addresses listed in the text were accurate at the time of publication. The inclusion of a website
does not indicate an endorsement by the authors or McGraw-Hill Education, and McGraw-Hill Education
does not guarantee the accuracy of the information presented at these sites.

DEDICATION

To the mentors who trained and nurtured us, and to the students who teach and inspire us.

—Kory Floyd
—Peter Cardon

ABOUT THE AUTHORS

Kory Floyd (left) and Peter Cardon (right)

Kory Floyd is a professor of communication at the University of Arizona. His research focuses on interpersonal communication in a variety of contexts, with particular focus on how positive communication contributes to well-being. He has written 15 books and over 100 scientific papers and book chapters on the topics of interpersonal behavior, emotion, nonverbal behavior, and health. He is a former editor of *Communication Monographs* and *Journal of Family Communication*. His work has been recognized with both the Charles H. Woolbert Award and the Bernard J. Brommel Award from the National Communication Association, as well as the Early Career Achievement Award from the International Association for Relationship Research. As an educator, he teaches courses on interpersonal communication, communication theory, nonverbal communication, and quantitative research methods. Professor Floyd received his undergraduate degree from Western Washington University, his master's degree from the University of Washington, and his PhD from the University of Arizona.

Peter Cardon is a professor of business communication at the University of Southern California. He also serves as the academic director of the MBA for Professionals and Managers Program. His research focuses on virtual team communication, leadership communication on digital platforms, and intercultural business communication. He has worked in China for three years and regularly takes MBA and other business students on company tours in China, South Korea, and other locations in Asia. He previously served as president of the Association for Business Communication, a global organization of business communication scholars and instructors. He is an active member of Rotary International, a global service organization committed to promoting peace, fighting disease, providing educational opportunities, and growing local economies.

BRIEF CONTENTS

A PEOPLE FIRST APPROACH

A rapidly evolving global workplace requires students to develop a variety of professional skills to succeed. Professional success often rests on the ability to listen, engender trust, adapt to cultural differences, and consider the perspectives of others.

To highlight these skills in professional settings, Kory Floyd and Peter Cardon adopt a **people first approach** that prioritizes quality workplace relationships.

Authentic Examples

Using dozens of authentic examples from the business world, *Business and Professional Communication: Putting People First* emphasizes how students can communicate in person and in virtual settings to develop meaningful, rich, and productive professional relationships in a technology-saturated world.

Perspective Taking

Unique to the market, this text includes a dedicated chapter focused on perspective taking, covering the processes of person perception; common perceptual errors; the self-serving bias and the fundamental attribution error; the self-concept; and the processes of image management. This chapter equips students to understand and pay attention to the perspectives of others.

Career Communication

Also unique to the market, this text includes a dedicated chapter focused on career communication, encouraging students to engage in networking and to consider the priorities and points of view of others as they seek employment and interact professionally.

Recurring *People First* Feature

Occurring in every chapter, the **People First** feature presents students with realistic scenarios that are sensitive, discomforting, or tricky to manage. It then teaches students how to navigate those situations effectively. Students are given concrete skills for preserving relationships with others as they encounter these difficult moments and conversations.

AN ONGOING FOCUS ON SKILL BUILDING, SELF-ASSESSMENT, AND CRITICAL THINKING

Throughout each chapter, students encounter opportunities to engage in skill building, self-assessment, and critical thinking:

- Each chapter includes **Sharpen Your Skills** features and end-of-chapter **Skill-Building Exercises** that identify particular communication skills and give activities for students to help build it them.

- Giving students the opportunity to analyze where they currently are with respect to a particular trait, **The Competent Communicator** feature allows students to self-assess a specific characteristic, trait, or tendency, and provides instructions for calculating and interpreting their scores.

- **Chapter Review Questions** at the end of each chapter stimulate critical thinking and reflection and can be used to spark interaction in the classroom or as writing assignments.

AN ENGAGING, NARRATIVE-BASED APPROACH

Chapters begin by presenting students with a narrative of a communication problem or dilemma, and then conclude by resolving that dilemma by referencing the principles throughout the chapter. Each chapter is illustrated with rich examples of real business communicators, which bring the principles to life for students. This interactive approach allows students to actively engage with the content instead of passively reading it.

Bringing It All Together

Students preparing to succeed in today's workplace require solid training in communication skills and principles, as well as experience applying them in realistic professional contexts.

Kory Floyd and Peter Cardon bring substantial and concrete business-world experience to bear in the product's principles, examples, and activities and ensure that the theories, concepts, and skills most relevant to the communication discipline are fully represented and engaged. The result is a program that speaks students' language and helps them understand and apply communication skills in their personal and professional lives.

Accolades from Our Reviewers

"This is the most student focused text that I have ever read. It deals with the real-world problems that students have to overcome in order to be successful in the course. There is no better text on the market."

—DR. BRADLEY S. WESNER, SAM HOUSTON STATE UNIVERSITY

"A perfect blend of business and communication expertise, written in an approachable tone, that uses real-world examples to enhance student engagement and learning."

—KELLY STOCKSTAD, AUSTIN COMMUNITY COLLEGE

"Full of rich, thoughtful, useful advice, up-to-date with the current job market. Easy to read, user-friendly. Not an organizational communication text . . . it is a performance enhancement text."

—JOHN CARL MEYER, UNIVERSITY OF SOUTHERN MISSISSIPPI

Students—study more efficiently, retain more and achieve better outcomes. **Instructors**—focus on what you love—teaching.

SUCCESSFUL SEMESTERS INCLUDE CONNECT

FOR INSTRUCTORS

You're in the driver's seat.

Want to build your own course? No problem. Prefer to use our turnkey, prebuilt course? Easy. Want to make changes throughout the semester? Sure. And you'll save time with Connect's auto-grading too.

65%

Less Time Grading

They'll thank you for it.

Adaptive study resources like SmartBook® help your students be better prepared in less time. You can transform your class time from dull definitions to dynamic debates. Hear from your peers about the benefits of Connect at **www.mheducation.com/highered/connect**

Make it simple, make it affordable.

Connect makes it easy with seamless integration using any of the major Learning Management Systems—Blackboard®, Canvas, and D2L, among others—to let you organize your course in one convenient location. Give your students access to digital materials at a discount with our inclusive access program. Ask your McGraw-Hill representative for more information.

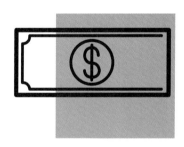

©Hill Street Studios/Tobin Rogers/Blend Images LLC

Solutions for your challenges.

A product isn't a solution. Real solutions are affordable, reliable, and come with training and ongoing support when you need it and how you want it. Our Customer Experience Group can also help you troubleshoot tech problems—although Connect's 99% uptime means you might not need to call them. See for yourself at **status.mheducation.com**

Effective, efficient studying.

Connect helps you be more productive with your study time and get better grades using tools like SmartBook, which highlights key concepts and creates a personalized study plan. Connect sets you up for success, so you walk into class with confidence and walk out with better grades.

> " I really liked this app—it made it easy to study when you don't have your textbook in front of you. "
>
> —Jordan Cunningham, Eastern Washington University

Study anytime, anywhere.

Download the free ReadAnywhere app and access your online eBook when it's convenient, even if you're offline. And since the app automatically syncs with your eBook in Connect, all of your notes are available every time you open it. Find out more at **www.mheducation.com/readanywhere**

No surprises.

The Connect Calendar and Reports tools keep you on track with the work you need to get done and your assignment scores. Life gets busy; Connect tools help you keep learning through it all.

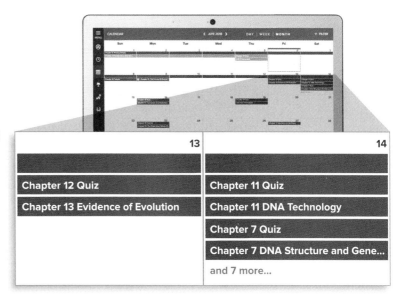

13	14
Chapter 12 Quiz	Chapter 11 Quiz
Chapter 13 Evidence of Evolution	Chapter 11 DNA Technology
	Chapter 7 Quiz
	Chapter 7 DNA Structure and Gene...
	and 7 more...

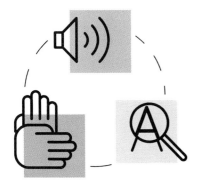

Learning for everyone.

McGraw-Hill works directly with Accessibility Services Departments and faculty to meet the learning needs of all students. Please contact your Accessibility Services office and ask them to email accessibility@mheducation.com, or visit **www.mheducation.com/about/accessibility.html** for more information.

ACKNOWLEDGMENTS

Few endeavors of any significance are achieved in isolation. There are always others who help us rise to—and exceed—our potential in nearly everything we do. We are delighted to acknowledge and thank those whose contributions and support are responsible for the book you are now reading.

First and foremost, we are grateful for the advice and input of the business and communication instructors who were kind enough to serve as reviewers for this text. Their contributions are invaluable, and we sincerely appreciate the time and energy they devoted to making this book as effective and user-friendly as possible.

Brock Adams, *Louisiana State University*

Gretchen Arthur, *Lansing Community College*

Benjamin Clark Bishop Jr., *Des Moines Area Community College*

Heidi Bolduc, *University of Central Florida*

Renee Brokaw, *University of Tampa*

Carolyn Cross, *Houston Community College*

Kathryn Dederichs, *University of St. Thomas*

Brandy Fair, *Grayson College*

Kristen A. Foltz, *University of Tampa*

Shelley Anne Friend, *Austin Community College*

Joseph Ganakos, *Lee College*

Karley A. Goen, *Tarleton State University*

Melissa Graham, *University of Central Oklahoma*

Rebecca Greene, *South Plains College*

Nancy Hicks, *Central Michigan University*

Kathy Hill, *Sam Houston State University*

Elaine Jansky, *Northwest Vista College*

Arthur Khaw, *Kirkwood Community College*

Jackie Layng, *University of Toledo*

Ronda Leahy, *University of Wisconsin, La Crosse*

Kirk Lockwood, *Illinois Valley Community College*

Donna Metcalf, *Greenville University*

John Meyer, *University of Southern Mississippi*

Dan Modaff, *University of Wisconsin, La Crosse*

Steven R. Montemayor, *Northwest Vista College*

Bev Neiderman, *Kent State University*

Kelly Odenweller, *Iowa State University*

Delia J. O'Steen, *Texas Tech University*

Aimee L. Richards, *Fairmont State University*

Shera Carter Sackey, *San Jacinto College*

Aaron Sanchez, *Arizona State University*

Sara Shippey, *Austin Community College*

Shavonne R. Shorter, *Bloomsburg University*

Michele Simms, *University of St. Thomas*

Richard Slawsky, *University of Louisville*

Ashly Bender Smith, *Sam Houston State University*

Ray Snyder, *Trident Technical College*

Sherry Stancil, *Calhoun Community College*

Kerry Strayer, *Otterbein University*

John Stewart, *University of South Florida, Sarasota-Manatee*

Kelly A. Stockstad, *Austin Community College*

Jenny Warren, *Collin College*

Rebecca Wells-Gonzalez, *Ivy Tech Community College*

Bradley S. Wesner, *Sam Houston State University*

Karin Wilking, *Northwest Vista College*

Julie A. Williams, *San Jacinto College*

Scott Wilson, *Central Ohio Technical College*

We could not ask for a better team of editors, managers, and publishers to work with than our team at McGraw-Hill. We are indebted to Anke Weekes, Kelly Pekelder, Gabe Fedota, Peter Jurmu, Christine Vaughan, Matt Diamond, Lisa Moore, and Sarah Blasco for the consistent, professional support we have received from each of them.

Elisa Adams is a development editor *par excellence.* She made nearly every word of this book more interesting, more relevant, and more compelling than it was when we wrote it. We have been exceedingly grateful for her insights, her humor, and her patience throughout this writing process.

Our students, colleagues, and administrators at the University of Arizona and the University of Southern California are a joy to work with and a tremendous source of encouragement. Undertaking a project of this size can be daunting, and it is so valuable to have a strong network of professional support on which to draw.

Finally, we are eternally grateful for the love and support of our families and friends. One needn't be an expert on communication to understand how important close relationships are—but the more we learn about communication, the more appreciative we become of the people who play those roles in our lives.

CONTENTS

Design elements: Title page image: ©gobyg/Getty Images

Business and Professional Communication

Learning Objectives

After reading this chapter, you should be able to do the following:

LO1.1 Summarize the six principles of communication.

LO1.2 Describe the principal elements of communication.

LO1.3 Illustrate the principles of effective communication in professional networks.

LO1.4 Explain credibility and identify the communication skills it embodies.

LO1.5 Summarize the characteristics of competent communicators.

CHAPTER 1

Communicating for Professional Success

Jaclyn and Elise walked to the front of the room to deliver their sales presentation. The ten potential customers in their audience were talking to one another and laughing loudly. Elise wondered when her headache would go away. As Jaclyn opened their PowerPoint document, she noticed it was an old version that was missing some critical information. Jaclyn whispered to Elise, "I don't have the right file. We'll have to present without the slides. At least we printed out the new ones. Let's get started, okay?"

Elise sighed in exasperation. She replied, "Why didn't you double-check the file? You can't keep doing this to me. We'll look really unprofessional without the slides."

Jaclyn responded, "It's not a big deal. The slides don't add much to our presentation anyway."

Elise reacted, "Are you joking? The slides have all the financial savings information I compiled. And then there's the product comparisons I put in there."

Jaclyn tried to give a reassuring smile. "Elise, we got this. Take a breath and get it together. We've done this dozens of times. We'll be fine without the slides. Let's stick to our parts and we'll be okay."

Jaclyn and Elise turned to face their audience. Each was upset with the other, and neither understood why her comments had only escalated their shared frustrations.

In professional relationships—in fact in virtually *all* relationships—our success and satisfaction rely heavily on our ability to communicate effectively. Sharing information, managing conflict, and understanding another's perspective are vital social skills, whether we are working with customers, colleagues, superiors, or subordinates.

We communicate every day of our lives, so it can be easy to think of communication as a natural, innate ability. In reality, however, you can probably easily remember instances in which your communication with others has been less than effective. Maybe you misunderstood your boss's instructions about a key project, causing you to make poor decisions. Perhaps your words or nonverbal behaviors unintentionally offended a potential customer, leading to a lost sale. As much as we may think of communication as intuitive, the truth is that it is a *skill,* one we must learn and practice in order to master.

LO1.1

Summarize the six principles of communication.

Understanding the Communication Process

Becoming an effective communicator begins with understanding what communication is and how it works. In this section, we'll explore six key principles that shape the way we think about communication in our lives. Then, we'll examine the way the communication process works and what its main elements are.

SIX PRINCIPLES OF COMMUNICATION

Communication serves many needs. It is governed by rules, comes in verbal and nonverbal forms, and has content and relational dimensions. It can also constitute metacommunication, and it derives its meaning from the people who use it. We look at each of the principles of communication next.

We use communication to meet many needs. Asking why we communicate may seem about as useful as asking why we breathe. But in fact we use communication to meet specific and ongoing needs. For one, communication helps us meet *relational needs,* which are our needs to form and maintain personal and professional relationships.[1] We all need some measure of social connection in our lives—whether at work, at home, at school, or online—and communication plays an essential role in establishing the quality and stability of our connections with others. Second, communication helps us meet *identity needs* by shaping the way we portray ourselves to others.[2] We might use formal, professional language to highlight our organized, efficient side during a job interview, but relaxed language and humor when socializing with co-workers.

Third, we use communication to fill our *informational needs,* by asking questions, gathering information, and sharing knowledge with the people around us.[3] These behaviors help us reduce our uncertainty about the world and give us the data and perspective we need to make good decisions. Finally, we use communication to serve our *instrumental needs,* which are our practical, everyday needs. Making travel arrangements, scheduling a Skype meeting with a client, and completing a self-evaluation at work are among the instrumental needs communication helps us meet.[4]

Communication is governed by rules. Rules tell us what behaviors are required, preferred, or prohibited in various social contexts.[5] Some rules for communication are **explicit rules**, meaning someone has clearly articulated them as direct expectations for communicative behavior. Perhaps your supervisor tells you specifically not to talk about your division's marketing strategies with anyone outside your company. Similarly, your college or university may have distributed explicit rules banning hate speech at campus events or in school publications.

Many communication rules, however, are **implicit rules**—rules that almost everyone in a certain social group knows and follows, even though no one has formally expressed them. In North American cultures, for instance, implicit rules about riding in elevators include, "Don't make eye contact with others while you're riding." Your workplace may also have an unspoken rule that it's impolite for employees to share salary information with one another. Even though implicit rules aren't posted anywhere or expressed in direct form, most people in a given group seem to know and follow them.

Communication comes in verbal and nonverbal forms.   How do we communicate with others? Much of the time, we rely on **verbal communication**, which is the use of words to communicate. Words are the building blocks of **language**, a structured system of symbols used for communicating meaning.[6] When we hear the term *verbal,* we usually think specifically of the words we speak to others. Spoken language is indeed a key aspect of verbal communication, but so are words that we write, text, or express through sign language. Anytime we use words to get our point across, we're engaged in verbal communication.

Many of the messages we exchange with others take the form of **nonverbal communication**, however, which includes those behaviors and characteristics that convey meaning without the use of words.[7] Whenever we frown to express anger, wave goodbye to an acquaintance, or touch a co-worker on the arm to convey sympathy, we are communicating our messages through our actions rather than through our words. Nonverbal communication is sometimes referred to as *body language* to reflect the idea that we can "talk" through our gestures, facial expressions, use of touch, and other behaviors. We will learn much more about both verbal and nonverbal communication in Chapter 3.

Communication has content and relational dimensions.   Nearly every verbal statement has a **content dimension**, which consists of the literal information being communicated by the message.[8] When you say to your supervisor, "I'm worried about next quarter's sales projections," the content dimension of your message is that you have concerns about the sales projections for the upcoming three months. When your officemate says, "The printer's out of paper again," the content dimension of the message is that you have no paper left.

There's more to messages than their literal content, though. Many messages also carry signals about the nature of the relationship in which they're shared. Those signals make up the **relational dimension** of the message. For instance, by telling your supervisor that you're worried about your sales projections, you may also be sending the message "I feel comfortable enough with you to share my feelings," or "I'd like your advice on improving my performance." Likewise, you might interpret your officemate's statement that you're out of printer paper as also saying "I'm sure you're aware of this, but I'm just reminding you," or perhaps "I'm irritated that you never replace the paper when it runs out." Even though these messages were never spoken, we often infer meanings about our relationships from the tone and manner in which they are made.

Some messages metacommunicate.   Communication is so important in our daily lives that we sometimes engage in **metacommunication**, which is communication about communication.[9] When we use phrases such as "Let me tell you what I think" and "Don't take this the wrong way," we are sending messages related to our other messages—that is, we're communicating *about our communication.* Usually, we do so to avoid misunderstanding and to provide listeners with greater clarity about our meaning.

We can also metacommunicate nonverbally. Suppose, for instance, that you're sitting in a meeting with your production team and a co-worker leans over to you, lowers her voice to a whisper, and cups her mouth with her hand, as though she's going to tell you a secret. That combination of nonverbal behaviors sends the message "What I'm about to say is meant for only you to hear." In other words, her nonverbal behavior metacommunicates her intentions to you. We often use nonverbal behaviors such as facial expressions and gestures to indicate how someone else should interpret our messages. For instance, we might smile and wink to indicate that we're being sarcastic or raise our eyebrows to signal that what we're saying is very serious.

People give communication its meaning.   Whenever we write or speak, we choose our words deliberately so we can say what we mean. Where does that meaning come from? On its own, a word has no meaning; it's just a sound or a set of marks on a piece of paper or a screen. A word is a **symbol**, or a representation of an idea, but the word itself isn't the idea or the meaning. The meaning of words—and many other forms of communication, such as gestures and facial expressions—comes from the people and groups who use them.

Almost all language is arbitrary in the sense that words mean whatever users of a language decide they mean. As a result, we cannot assume that other people automatically understand what we intend to communicate just because we ourselves understand what we mean. For instance, what is a mouse? If you had asked that question 40 years ago, the obvious answer would have been a small rodent that likes cheese and is chased by cats. Today, however, many people know a mouse as a pointing

Certain nonverbal behaviors metacommunicate the message "What I'm about to say is meant for only you to hear."

©Dave and Les Jacobs/Blend Images LLC

What is a robot? That depends on whom you ask.

Robot: *©Vitalii Tiahunov/123RF;* **Stoplight:** *©CORBIS/age fotostock*

device for navigating on a computer screen. As another example, what is a robot? In the United States, it can be a humanlike machine that performs mechanical tasks or a software that generates online spam. In South Africa, however, it's a traffic light. Those are just a few examples of how the meaning of a word depends on who is using it and how meanings can vary over time and across cultures.

As you can see, communication has several distinct characteristics. At its heart, however, communication is a *process*—that is, it is something we *do*. Let's take a closer look at the communication process in the next section.

ELEMENTS OF THE COMMUNICATION PROCESS

LO1.2

Describe the principal elements of communication.

Communication is a process that involves many core elements. As we'll see in this section, those include the message, senders and receivers, communication channels, context, noise, and feedback. These elements work together in a complex and dynamic way. A model of the communication process that includes these elements appears in Figure 1.1.

Communication is the creation and exchange of messages. As shown in Figure 1.1, the communication process begins with a **message**, which consists of verbal and/or nonverbal behaviors to which people give meaning.[10] Suppose you want to leave work early one day to attend a parent-teacher conference at your daughter's school, and you need to ask your supervisor, Janelle, for permission. Your message might be the question "Would it be all right if I leave work a little early today?"

Communication requires senders and receivers. When you formulate a message to convey to someone else—such as your question to Janelle—you act as the

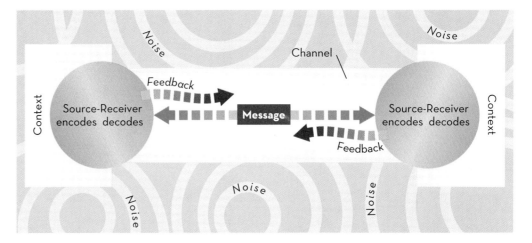

Figure 1.1

Model of the Communication Process

This model of the communication process recognizes that both people in a conversation are simultaneously senders and receivers.

sender, or the source of the idea. To express your message, you must **encode** it; that is, you must put your idea into the form of language or a nonverbal behavior that your supervisor can understand. When you ask her whether you can leave work early, she acts as the **receiver** of the message—the person who will **decode** or interpret it.

Communication occurs in multiple channels.   To convey your message, you must select a communication **channel**, a type of pathway. You might pose your question to Janelle face-to-face. Or you could send it in an email or text message, put a handwritten note on her desk, or leave a message on her voice mail. Those are all different channels through which you can express your message.

Communication is affected by context.   The channel you choose for asking your supervisor for time off—and her answer—may be affected by the **context**, or the physical and psychological environment in which your message is communicated. If others on your team have been unable to get to work due to bad weather, for instance, that aspect of the physical context may make Janelle hesitant to let you leave early, for fear the team won't have sufficient coverage. Similarly, if you worked overtime last week to help your team meet a major deadline, psychologically she may be inclined to repay your sacrifice by granting your request.

Communication includes noise and feedback.   During the communication process, there is likely to be some **noise**, which is anything that interferes with a receiver's ability to understand your message. The major types of noise are *physical noise* (such as background conversation in the room or static on the telephone line), *psychological noise* (such as other concerns distracting your supervisor that day), and *physiological noise* (such as experiences of fatigue or hunger). Any of these forms of noise could prevent Janelle from paying full attention to your question.

When you make your request, Janelle might nod to show she understands what you're saying, or she might frown slightly to indicate that she's considering whether to agree. These behaviors constitute **feedback**, which is a receiver's various verbal and nonverbal reactions to a message. By providing you such feedback, Janelle acts not as a passive recipient of your message, but as someone actively engaged in creating your conversation. Just as you are sending your message for Janelle to receive, she is also sending messages for you to receive and interpret. In that way, you are both acting as senders and receivers simultaneously.

CAREER TIP

Your ability to reach your goals and succeed in the workplace is profoundly affected by your communication skills. Warren Buffett, a legendary investor who spent several decades as the richest man in the world, admits he learned this lesson the hard way.

Buffett's extraordinary success can be traced to his passion for business from an early age. As a young boy, he delivered papers, sold popcorn and peanuts at baseball games, and started a used golf ball business and a pinball machine business. He regularly read financial publications, and when he filed his first income tax return, for $7 when he was 12 years old, he was astute enough to deduct the associated expenses of his bicycle and wristwatch. He purchased his first shares of stock for $120 at the age of 11.

Yet by his own admission Buffett was socially awkward and lacking in interpersonal communication skills. He didn't understand the importance of small talk and frequently offended those around him. A life-changing event occurred when he was denied admission to Harvard Business School because of his poor interview performance. He knew his business knowledge and experience were superior, but his interpersonal communication skills were not adequate for exceptional performance in the business world.

As his daughter later stated, "Once upon a time there was a slightly nerdish young man by the name of Warren Buffett, who, at the age of 20, was frightened to death to stand up in front of people and speak to them. Then he discovered Dale Carnegie's course on public speaking and it changed his life. Not only did he develop the courage and skill to speak in front of groups of people, he learned to make friends and motivate people. Warren considers his Carnegie education a life-changing event and the most important diploma he has ever received."

Warren Buffett
©Krista Kennell/Shutterstock

Buffett turned his weakness into strength and added excellent communication skills to his visionary knack for investing. Now acclaimed as one of the best business leaders and managers in the world, Buffett recently told a group of business students that effective communication skills can add $500,000 to their lifetime earnings and increase their earning power by 50 percent.

SOURCES: Shellenbarger, S. (2010, March 24). Before they were titans, moguls and newsmakers, these people were . . . rejected. *The Wall Street Journal*; Buffett, M., & Clark, D. (2009). *Warren Buffett's management secrets: Proven tools for personal success*. New York: Scribner; Warren Buffett interview hosted by Becky Quick. (2009, November 12). Warren Buffett and Bill Gates: Keeping America great. *CNBC Town Hall Event*, http://www.cnbc.com/id/33604479 (accessed November 19, 2009); Crippen, A. (2009, November 12). Warren Buffett's $100,000 offer and $500,000 advice for Columbia Business School students. *CNBC News*, http://www.cnbc.com/id/33891448 (accessed November 19, 2009).

Communication is dynamic. The communication process might seem straightforward and one-directional—that it consists of a simple flow of messages from one person to another. In reality, as Figure 1.1 illustrates, conversation can flow in multiple directions at once.[11] Suppose you're describing your company's services to a group of prospective clients. As you explain different service plans and their costs, you may be doing most of the talking. At one point in your presentation, however, you notice that your listeners have a confused look on their faces. You interpret that feedback as an indication that they don't understand what you're saying. You respond to that feedback by adding more detail to your explanation, and when your listeners begin to smile and nod, you take that behavior to mean they now understand you. Even though you're the one speaking, you are also receiving and responding to messages from your listeners, making everyone in the conversation simultaneously a sender *and* a receiver. This is an example of how the communication process is **dynamic**, or constantly changing and evolving as people send, receive, and interpret messages from multiple sources.

LO1.3

Illustrate the principles of effective communication in professional networks.

Communication in Professional Networks

The phrase *it's not* what *you know, but* who *you know that matters* reflects the idea that your success at work depends on cultivating strong professional networks. Thanks to forces such as globalization and improved communication technologies, communication in networks plays a more important role than ever before.

Savvy communicators—whom we'll refer to as *networkers* in this section—recognize distinctions between formal and informal professional networks and adapt their communication styles to support the goals of each. In addition, they understand how to build, develop, and tap into their broad professional networks.

NETWORKERS COMMUNICATE EFFECTIVELY IN FORMAL PROFESSIONAL NETWORKS

Much of our work on the job occurs in **formal professional networks**. These types of professional relationships—which might be found in a company department or on a work team—generally have clear lines of authority and reporting structures, shoulder standard sets of responsibilities, and require accountability to other members of the network. Communication in formal professional networks can be characterized as either downward, upward, or lateral/horizontal. **Downward communication** flows from superiors to subordinates,[12] **upward communication** from subordinates to superiors,[13] and **lateral** (or *horizontal*) **communication** among peers or colleagues with relatively equal positions in the organization.[14]

What happens in formal professional networks is often formal communication, including presentations, meetings, email messages, and résumés. Typically, **formality** is associated with protocols, rules, structure, and politeness. Many factors influence the degree of formality required, including the size of the organization, its culture, and the nature of workplace relationships. External communication—with people outside the organization such as customers, clients, and suppliers—tends to be formal. Within the organization, upward communication is usually the most formal, and lateral communication tends to be the least formal. How well you know others (familiarity) also has a strong impact on formality. As familiarity increases, formality typically decreases.

NETWORKERS COMMUNICATE EFFECTIVELY IN INFORMAL PROFESSIONAL NETWORKS

We also communicate at work via **informal professional networks**, which consist of voluntary professional connections—such as friendships we form with co-workers—rather than formal reporting structures. Although members of informal networks are not officially required to help one another, they often use these connections to get advice from experts, share contacts who could become clients, and set up informal mentoring and training.

Informal professional networks rely on **informal communication**, which is generally less bound by protocols, rules, structure, and politeness.[15] For example, *water cooler conversations* are the informal interactions in office hallways during which employees share social and professional information that might not be appropriate to discuss in formal meetings.

Effective networkers tap into the potential of informal professional networks to help reach their own and others' professional goals. They also learn to identify situations in which communication should be less formal, and they develop their own styles of informal communication to build professional relationships.

NETWORKERS EMPLOY MANY COMMUNICATION CHANNELS TO STAY CONNECTED TO THEIR NETWORKS

We all face dozens of channels when we communicate with others (including technology choices such as Twitter and Instagram). This variety is both a blessing and a

TECH TIP
Building Connections with Phone Calls

Smartphones have transformed business communication. Ironically, though, their increased use in our personal lives has actually led to a decline in voice calls. In fact, making calls is only the fifth-most used function of smartphones. However, business professionals continue to make both landline and mobile calls, with about half of all managers spending more than six hours per week on voice calls.[16] To become a more dynamic and savvy communicator, keep in mind the following guidelines for one-to-one calls in the workplace.

©wavebreakmedia/Shutterstock

- *Schedule and plan your phone calls.* Think ahead about your key discussion topics and points. Consider sending your conversation partner an invitation and agenda.
- *Open with a warm greeting and use your caller's name.* Calling others by name personalizes and elevates your communications with them.
- *After a brief light chat, direct the conversation to the issues at hand.* Most callers appreciate a few general comments to start, but you should get to the issues at hand within one to two minutes.
- *Apply the rules of active listening, and avoid multitasking.* Be eager to learn about the ideas of your conversation partner and ready to express your views as

well. Many professionals multitask during phone calls. Instead, make sure the call is your entire focus.
- *Close with appreciation.* You should nearly always express appreciation in closing. Say "thanks for taking the time to . . ." or "it's been great to get your ideas about . . ." to end on a warm note and pave the way for follow-up.
- *Follow up.* Sending a follow-up message within a few hours while the conversation is still fresh in your mind dramatically improves the likelihood that you will accomplish your shared objectives.

curse. Effective networkers carefully evaluate communication channels for their ability to enhance professional relationships and accomplish work. They recognize the benefits and drawbacks of these channels and learn the preferences of other members of their professional networks.

NETWORKERS BUILD BROAD PROFESSIONAL COMMUNICATION NETWORKS

Excellent networkers are *givers* rather than *takers*. They don't view networking as simply an instrumental activity. Rather, they take the initiative to share information and resources, and to support network members' personal and professional needs. Moreover, good networkers maintain a healthy balance between *strong ties* (close relationships) and *weak ties* (acquaintances) inside and outside their organizations.

Cultivating Credibility

Effective professionals understand that cultivating credibility is essential to communication. *Credible communicators* invest in building trust, developing rapport, listening actively, maintaining values and accountability, and knowing and adapting to their audience.

LO1.4

Explain credibility and identify the communication skills it embodies.

CREDIBLE COMMUNICATORS BUILD TRUST

Just 51 percent of employees trust senior management, and only 36 percent believe their company leaders act with honesty and integrity. Three-quarters report seeing illegal or unethical conduct at work in the past 12 months.[17] As future business managers and leaders, you will often find yourself in charge of employees who are accustomed to not trusting those in leadership positions.

Michael Maslansky, a leading corporate communications expert, and his colleagues have labeled this the **post-trust era**. People overwhelmingly view businesses as operating against the public's best interests, and the majority of employees view their leaders and colleagues skeptically. Maslansky says, "Just a few years ago, salespeople, corporate leaders, marketing departments, and communicators like me had it pretty easy. We looked at communication as a relatively linear process. . . . But trust disappeared, things changed."[18] You will often find yourself needing to establish credibility in this post-trust era.

CREDIBLE COMMUNICATORS DEVELOP RAPPORT

One of the best ways you can build trust is to develop rapport with colleagues, clients, customers, and others. **Rapport** is a sense of harmony, goodwill, and caring among people.[19] It is important at all stages of professional relationships. In first impressions, you gain trust more easily when others sense you are concerned about them. As professional relationships develop, if others believe you care about them, they will be more likely to trust you.

In the business world, caring implies understanding the interests of others, cultivating a sense of community, and giving to others with generosity. In the past, caring was seldom discussed as integral to business. Now, it is among the most important abilities for business leaders and managers. In fact, a recent study of business managers put it among the top 3 skills or abilities (from a list of 18) for managers of nearly any business discipline.[20]

CREDIBLE COMMUNICATORS LISTEN ACTIVELY

We all value being heard, and dozens of studies have shown that listening is ranked among the most important communication skills for job applicants to possess.[21] Listening builds trust, but it requires hard work. And it requires more than simply hearing. It calls for our full attention and the use of all our senses. In fact, great listeners respond physically to others. Research indicates that brain activity in excellent listeners mimics that of the speakers. In some cases, the listener's brain shows activity *before* the speaker's does. In other words, the best listeners anticipate how a speaker thinks and feels.[22]

Michael Hoppe of the Center for Creative Leadership has defined **active listening** as "a person's willingness and ability to hear and understand. At its core, active listening is a state of mind. . . . It involves bringing about and finding common ground, connecting to each other, and opening up new possibilities."[23] Because listening is so important to your success, you will read an entire chapter on listening later in the text. Meanwhile, for suggestions on using active listening in a potentially tense situation, see the "People First" box.

CREDIBLE COMMUNICATORS MAINTAIN INTEGRITY AND ACCOUNTABILITY

An essential part of gaining trust is demonstrating integrity and accountability. In a professional context, demonstrating integrity means staying true to commitments made to stakeholders and adhering to high moral and ethical values. Having accountability means taking responsibility for one's own actions. Integrity and accountability have always been important in business relationships, especially long-term, collaborative relationships, and they are becoming increasingly so.

PEOPLE **FIRST**

Actively Listening to an Angry Customer

IMAGINE THIS: You are working at a car rental counter at the airport when a customer approaches you to complain. She says your website listed the cost of her rental car at $39.95 per day, so she is frustrated about getting charged more than twice that amount. As you explain that taxes, insurance, and fuel fees account for the added costs, she accuses you of being dishonest and trying to cheat her. You get angry and consider calling security to have her escorted away.

Now, consider this: In your situation, it is natural to feel attacked. After all, the customer is blaming you when you know she was clearly shown the charges at the time of rental. You could respond to her anger with anger of your own, but a more constructive approach would be to listen actively and respond empathically.

- Begin by putting your own feelings aside and considering how you would feel if you were this customer. Have you ever felt cheated or taken advantage of by a business? If so, then you understand how this woman feels right now.

- Remember that it's not important whether you think her feelings are justified. All that matters in this moment is listening to her and identifying how she feels.

- Look for ways to communicate that you recognize the customer's feelings. Statements such as "I understand how frustrating this must be" convey your *empathy* for the other person's situation. Comments such as "I would feel the same way if I were in your situation" show that you are listening actively and can take her perspective.

Listening to the customer and recognizing her feelings may not, by itself, solve her problem. Communicating with empathy, however, can help you identify acceptable solutions because it lets you consider the situation from her point of view. Demonstrating that you are listening and paying attention to her feelings can also help keep the customer's emotions from becoming even more negative.

THINK ABOUT THIS:

How do you feel when others don't listen to you? In this situation, how can actively listening to the customer convey the message that you are putting her needs first? What mistakes might active listening help you avoid in this instance?

NOTE: For additional suggestions, see Geles, D. (2017, October 4). How to be mindful in an argument. *The New York Times*. Retrieved March 7, 2018, from https://www.nytimes.com/2017/10/04/well/mind/how-to-be-mindful-in-an-argument.html.

The Society for Human Resource Management espouses corporate values as the essence of business ethics. It defines business ethics as "organizational values, guidelines, and codes," and it emphasizes "behaving within those boundaries when faced with dilemmas in business or professional work."[24] Most organizations have created a written code of conduct or code of ethics to direct their members' behavior at work.

CREDIBLE COMMUNICATORS KNOW AND ADAPT TO THEIR AUDIENCES

Ultimately, effective communicators cultivate credibility by genuinely understanding and adapting to the needs, wants, and preferences of their audiences. These rare abilities to understand and adapt to others are what drive real connections between professionals. People trust us when they believe we try to understand them. As you read through this text, imagine yourself in real-life situations. Insert faces into scenarios. As you read about meetings, think about some of your real teammates at work and in school and how you might apply the principles in ways that support them. As you read about writing emails, imagine how the principles apply to real people you know.

LO1.5

Summarize the characteristics of competent communicators.

Characteristics of Successful Communicators

No one is born a successful communicator. Rather, like driving a car, playing a musical instrument, or writing a computer program, communicating successfully requires skills we have to learn and practice. That doesn't mean nature doesn't give some people a head start. Research shows that some of our communication traits—such as how sociable, aggressive, or shy we are—are partly determined by our genes.[25] No matter which traits we're born with, though, we still have to learn how to communicate competently and successfully.

COMMUNICATING COMPETENTLY

Think about five people you consider to be really good communicators. Who's on your list? Any of your friends or relatives? Teachers? Supervisors? Politicians or celebrities? Yourself? You probably recognize that identifying good communicators means first asking yourself what a good communicator is. Most scholars seem to agree that **communication competence** is the ability to communicate in ways that are *effective* and *appropriate* in a given situation.[26]

Competent communication is effective. Effectiveness describes how well your communication achieves its goals.[27] Suppose you want to persuade your co-worker to donate money to a shelter for abused animals. There are many ways to achieve that goal. You could explain how much the shelter needs the money and identify the many services it provides to animals in need. You could offer to help your co-worker with a project in exchange for his or her donation. You could even recite the times you have donated to causes that were important to your co-worker. No single communication strategy will be effective in all situations. Being an effective communicator means choosing the messages that will best meet your goals.

Competent communication is appropriate. Communicating appropriately means taking into account the implicit and explicit rules and expectations that apply in a social or professional situation. When communicating with customers online, for instance, it is polite to respond to their messages in a timely manner, show sensitivity to their concerns, and avoid letting conflicts escalate. If you violate those rules, customers may find your communication inappropriate.

Communicating appropriately can be especially challenging when you're interacting with people from other cultures, because many communication rules are culture-specific. What might be perfectly appropriate in one culture could be seen as inappropriate or even offensive in another.[28] For instance, if you are visiting a Canadian household and your hosts offer you food, it's appropriate to accept if you're hungry. In many Japanese households, however, it is inappropriate to accept until you have declined the food twice and your hosts have offered it a third time.

Communication competence, then, implies both effectiveness and appropriateness. Note that those are aspects of *communication*, not of people. Now let's ask whether *people* who are competent, successful communicators share any common characteristics.

Communicating appropriately can be especially challenging when you're interacting with people from different cultures.

©Image Source/Getty Images

CHARACTERISTICS OF SUCCESSFUL COMMUNICATORS

Look again at your list of five competent communicators. What do they have in common? Competence itself is situation-specific, so what works in one context may not work in another. However, successful communicators tend to have certain characteristics that help them behave competently in most situations. Table 1.1 presents six characteristics of competent communicators that this section discusses.

Successful communicators are self-aware. Successful communicators are aware of their own behavior and its effects on others.[29] Researchers call tapping into this awareness **self-monitoring**. People who are high self-monitors pay close attention to the way they look, sound, and act in social situations. In contrast, people who are low self-monitors often seem oblivious to both their own behaviors and other people's reactions to them. Self-monitoring usually makes people more competent communicators because it enables them to see how their behavior fits or doesn't fit in a given social setting. What's your level of self-monitoring? Check out "The Competent Communicator" box to find out.

Successful communicators are adaptable. It's one thing to be aware of your own behavior; it's quite another to be able to adapt it to different situations. Competent communicators are able to assess what is going to be appropriate and effective in a given context and then modify their behaviors accordingly.[30] That ability is important because what works in one situation might be ineffective in another.

Part of delivering a good speech, for instance, is being aware of the audience and adapting your behavior to your listeners. A competent communicator would speak differently to a group of senior executives than to a group of new hires, because one group has experience and expertise that the other does not. Competent communicators are also aware of generational and cultural differences that can influence what an audience finds engaging.

> **SHARPEN YOUR SKILLS**
>
> *Evaluating Competence*
>
> Identify a group of leaders from a business or school context, such as the managers at your company or the elected leaders of your student body. Based on what you have learned in this section, how would you rate each person's communication competence? What makes some individuals more competent than others? Try to identify specific skills, such as empathy and cognitive complexity, that distinguish one individual in your group from another. Then, consider how each person might improve his or her communication competencies. Share your thoughts in a brief report or blog post.

Table 1.1 **Six Characteristics of Competent Communicators**

Self-awareness	Ability to see how your behavior is affecting others
Adaptability	Ability to modify your behaviors as the situation demands
Cognitive complexity	Ability to consider a variety of explanations and understand a given situation in multiple ways
Empathy	Skill at identifying and feeling what others around you are feeling
Emotional intelligence	Ability to understand, express, and manage emotions, and to use emotion to facilitate thought
Ethics	Ability to treat people fairly, communicate honestly, and avoid immoral or unethical behavior

Are You a High Self-Monitor?

One of the ways to improve your communication ability is to think about how you communicate now. Each "The Competent Communicator" box in this book will help you do so by letting you assess a given communication skill or tendency. For instance, we've just seen that self-monitoring is one of the characteristics of competent communicators. How high a self-monitor are you? Read each of the following statements, and indicate how accurately it describes you by assigning a number between 1 ("not at all") and 7 ("very much").

1. ____ I sometimes show different aspects of my personality to different people.

2. ____ I suspect I would be good at acting.

3. ____ When I've said something inappropriate, I can usually tell from the listener's reaction.

4. ____ I notice how others react to my behavior.

5. ____ I can modify my behavior to meet the expectations of any situation I'm in.

6. ____ I'm good at reading people's emotions through their eyes.

7. ____ Most of the time, I can tell when someone is lying to me.

8. ____ Sometimes I am not the person I appear to be.

When you're finished, add up your scores and write the total on this line: ____. The ranges below will help you see how high your self-monitoring is right now.

- 8–23: Self-monitoring is a skill you can work on, as you are doing in this class.
- 24–39: You are a moderate self-monitor, with a good sense of self-awareness. Continued practice will strengthen that skill.
- 40–56: You are a high self-monitor, which often makes your communication more effective.

Your score on this quiz—and on each quiz in this book—reflects only how you see yourself at this time. If your score surprises you, take the quiz again later in the course to see how studying communication may have changed your assessment of your communication abilities.

SOURCE: Adapted from Lennox, R. D., & Wolfe, R. N. (1984). Revision of the self-monitoring scale. *Journal of Personality and Social Psychology, 46,* 1349–1364.

Successful communicators are cognitively complex. Suppose you see your co-worker Annika coming toward you in the hallway at work. You smile and get ready to say hi, but she walks right by as if you're not there. How would you interpret her behavior? Maybe she's mad at you. Perhaps she was concentrating on something and didn't notice anyone around her. Or maybe she did smile and you just didn't see it.

The ability to consider a variety of explanations and understand a given situation in multiple ways is called **cognitive complexity**. As communication scholar Brant Burleson explained, cognitive complexity is a valuable skill because it helps you avoid jumping to the wrong conclusion and responding inappropriately.[31] Someone with little cognitive complexity might feel slighted by Annika's behavior and ignore her the next time they meet. In contrast, someone with higher cognitive complexity would remember that behaviors do not always mean what we think. That person would be more open-minded, considering several possible interpretations of Annika's behavior and remembering that his or her perception could always be mistaken.

Successful communicators practice empathy. Successful communicators practice **empathy**, the ability to be "other-oriented" and understand other people's

FOCUS ON ETHICS
To Tell or Not to Tell?

You have just started a new position in the human resources department of the financial services company where you and your close friend Mahesh both work. Your supervisor asks you to familiarize yourself with the company's active HR files to make yourself aware of ongoing HR actions on which she may require your assistance. In doing so, you discover that two other employees have filed a confidential complaint against Mahesh for harassment, and the human resources department is investigating. You realize that Mahesh could lose his job, and as his friend, you feel you should warn him because he is about to make an offer on a house. However, you also know you are bound by strict confidentiality rules that would make warning him inappropriate. You fear that no matter what you do, you will lose either your job or your friendship.

CONSIDER THIS: What ethical obligations do you have to your employer in this instance? What ethical obligations do you feel to your friend? Is there a way to encourage Mahesh to modify his behavior without violating any confidentiality rules?

thoughts and feelings.[32] When people say "Put yourself in my shoes," they are asking you to consider a situation from their perspective rather than your own. Empathy is an important skill because people often think and feel differently than you do about the same situation. You saw the idea of empathy being applied to a potentially tense situation earlier in this chapter in the "People First" box.

As another example, suppose you want to ask your manager for a one-week extension on a marketing report you have been assigned to complete. You might think, "What's the big deal? It's only a week." To your manager, though, the extension might mean that she would be unable to complete her work in time for her family vacation. If your situations were reversed, how would you feel? An empathic person would consider the situation from the manager's perspective and then choose his or her behaviors accordingly.

Successful communicators are emotionally intelligent. **Emotional intelligence** refers to a person's ability to "perceive and accurately express emotions, to use emotion to facilitate thought, to understand emotions, and to manage emotions for emotional growth."[33] People with high emotional intelligence are aware of their own emotions as well as those of others, and they think deliberately about their emotions when choosing how to act. Business managers with high emotional intelligence are more effective at influencing others, overcoming conflict, showing leadership, collaborating in teams, and managing change. People sometimes refer to a person's level of emotional intelligence as his or her **EQ**, which stands for *emotional quotient,* a play on the more familiar term "IQ," or *intelligence quotient.*

Successful communicators behave ethically. Finally, successful communicators are ethical communicators. **Ethics** guides us in judging whether something is morally right or wrong. Ethical communication, then, generally dictates treating people fairly, communicating honestly, and avoiding immoral or unethical behavior. That can be easier said than done, because people often have very different ideas about right and wrong. What may be morally justified to one person or one culture may be considered unethical to another. Successful communicators are aware that people's ideas about ethics vary. However, they are also aware of their own ethical beliefs, and they communicate in ways that are consistent with those beliefs.

The more we consciously think and learn about the communication process, the better we can help others and ourselves communicate in professional environments. Here's a quick review of the chapter.

LO1.1 Summarize the six principles of communication.

- We use communication to meet relational, identity, informational, and instrumental needs.
- Communication is governed by explicit and implicit rules.
- Communication comes in verbal and nonverbal forms.
- Communication has content and relational dimensions.
- Some messages metacommunicate.
- People give communication its meaning.

LO1.2 Describe the principal elements of communication.

- The creation and exchange of messages
- Senders and receivers
- Multiple channels
- Context, noise, and feedback
- Communication dynamics

LO1.3 Illustrate the principles of effective communication in professional networks.

- Formal networks involve clear lines of authority and reporting structures, standard sets of responsibilities, and accountability to other members of the network.

- Informal networks involve voluntary professional associations rather than formal reporting structures.
- Downward communication is communication initiated from superiors to subordinates.
- Upward communication is communication initiated from subordinates to superiors.
- Lateral communication is communication among peers or colleagues with relatively equal positions.

LO1.4 Explain credibility and identify the communication skills it embodies.

- Credibility is the extent to which others perceive us to be competent and trustworthy.
- Credible communicators build trust.
- Credible communicators develop rapport.
- Credible communicators listen actively.
- Credible communicators maintain values and accountability.
- Credible communicators know and adapt to their audiences.

LO1.5 Summarize the characteristics of competent communicators.

- Successful communicators are self-aware.
- Successful communicators are adaptable.
- Successful communicators are cognitively complex.
- Successful communicators practice empathy.
- Successful communicators are emotionally intelligent.
- Successful communicators behave ethically.

When we last saw them in the opening scenario, Jaclyn and Elise were growing increasingly frustrated with each other. We don't know much about their relationship or their history of working together. Using communication principles, however, we can make sense of why their conversation seemed to be on a downward spiral, leading them both to an unsuccessful presentation.

Jaclyn and Elise are likely bringing very different relational, identity, information, and instrumental priorities to their conversation. Jaclyn appears to focus on *informational* needs, such as asking about printout content,

and *instrumental* needs, such as moving to a plan B without the slides. In contrast, Elise appears to focus on *relational* needs, such as mentioning Jaclyn is hurting the team, and *identity* needs, such as suggesting they won't come across as professional. The two continue to carry out their conversation without noticing the differing needs and priorities of the other.

They're also not attuned to the communication process. Each creates competing messages (Jaclyn thinks "we're okay without the slides"; Elise thinks "this is a disaster without the slides"), continues to repeat her messages with each statement, and avoids listening to or recognizing the other's message. They are likely affected by *physical noise* (their audience members talking and laughing), *psychological noise* (their frustrations with each other, the stress of presenting and not having the slides), and *physiological noise* (Elise's headache).

It also appears that neither Jaclyn nor Elise is displaying much *self-awareness, adaptability,* or *emotional intelligence* in this situation. With a small audience of potential customers who seem to be enjoying one another's company, Jaclyn and Elise can probably spare a few more minutes to listen to each other and make a presentation plan that matches both of their needs and priorities.

KEY TERMS

active listening   12

channel   8

cognitive complexity   16

communication competence   14

content dimension   5

context   8

decode   8

downward communication   10

dynamic   9

emotional intelligence   17

empathy   16

encode   8

EQ (emotional quotient)   17

ethics   17

explicit rules   4

feedback   8

formal professional networks   10

formality   10

implicit rules   4

informal communication   10

informal professional networks   10

language   5

lateral (horizontal) communication   10

message   7

metacommunication   5

noise   8

nonverbal communication   5

post-trust era   12

rapport   12

receiver   8

relational dimension   5

self-monitoring   15

sender   8

symbol   6

upward communication   10

verbal communication   5

CHAPTER REVIEW QUESTIONS

1. Define and give examples of relational needs, identity needs, informational needs, and instrumental needs that communication can help us meet. LO1.1

2. What is the difference between an explicit rule and an implicit rule? What are examples of explicit and implicit communication rules that you might encounter, or have encountered, in the professional world? LO1.1

3. What is the defining characteristic of verbal communication? LO1.1

4. What makes a form of communication nonverbal? Why do we sometimes call nonverbal communication *body language*? LO1.1

5. Come up with a statement that you might say to a supervisor and explain how its content dimension and relational dimension might differ. LO1.1

6. What is metacommunication, and how do people metacommunicate with one another? LO1.1

7. Give examples of various communication channels you might use when sending a message in the workplace. LO1.2

8. What types of noise are we likely to encounter in a professional environment? Are they physical, psychological, or physiological? LO1.2

9. What does it mean to say that communication is dynamic? How can two people in a conversation be both senders and receivers simultaneously? LO1.2

10. With whom might we have downward communication, upward communication, and lateral communication in the workplace? What are the differences among these? LO1.3

11. In what ways does communication differ in formal and informal professional networks? LO1.3

12. What does it mean to say that excellent networkers are *givers* rather than *takers*? LO1.3

13. What do networkers do to make their communication successful? How can you adopt the same strategies to improve your own communication? LO1.3

14. What is meant by the term *post-trust era*? LO1.3

15. Why is building rapport advantageous? What are some behaviors that help establish rapport? LO1.4

16. What makes listening *active* listening? Why is active listening valuable? **LO1.4**

17. How is effective communication different from appropriate communication? **LO1.5**

18. What is meant by the term *self-monitoring*? What are the advantages of being a high self-monitor? A low self-monitor? **LO1.5**

19. In what ways are competent communicators adaptable? What does it mean to adapt to your audience? **LO1.5**

20. Define cognitive complexity and explain why it is advantageous in a professional setting. **LO1.5**

21. What is empathy? What does it mean to communicate empathically? **LO1.5**

22. Why is emotional intelligence (also called EQ) valuable? **LO1.5**

23. What is required to make communication *ethical* communication? **LO1.5**

SKILL-BUILDING EXERCISES

Violating Implicit Rules (LO1.1)

Implicit communication rules are never taught or verbalized, yet people seem to know and follow them anyway. Often, implicit rules become explicit only when they have been violated and others react. Describe a situation you have encountered at work or in school when someone said or did something that violated an implicit rule, and then respond to the following questions:

- What was the implicit rule?
- How did the person violate it?
- How did others react when that happened?
- After the violation, was the rule verbalized, such that it became an explicit rule? If so, how was it verbalized (orally, in writing, etc.)?

Identifying Miscommunication (LO1.2)

Miscommunication is prevalent because communication has a symbolic aspect and because different people can interpret the same words in different ways. Report on an experience in which someone interpreted your words differently than you intended, or in which you did the same with someone else. Was the miscommunication eventually resolved? If so, how did the parties ultimately come to understand each other? If they did not, why not? Share your answers in a brief report.

Examine Personal Credibility (LO1.4)

Think about a specific professional context, and respond to each of the following questions. For the context, you can use a current or previous job, or a professional or student activity in which you participated. Ideally, you will select a context with challenging cooperation issues.

- How much do/did others trust you in this situation?
- How credible are/were you in terms of competency, caring, and character (in the perceptions of others)?
- Do you think you are/were being perceived inaccurately in any ways? Why?

- Have you done or did you do anything that may have broken trust in any way?
- Have you kept or did you keep your word in all your agreements?
- List three things you need to do or should have done better to establish your credibility.

Gather Information from Websites about Business Ethics (LO1.5)

Read at least three blogs or articles about trust and/or ethics from a reputable organization or other source. Choose an issue that interests you, and in four to five paragraphs, summarize key findings related to that issue. Consider the following options for gathering information:

- Ethics & Compliance Initiative (ECI) (www.ethics.org)
- Institute of Business Ethics (www.ibe.org.uk)
- Society of Corporate Compliance and Ethics (www.corporatecompliance.org)
- *Business Ethics* magazine (http://business-ethics.com)
- International Business Ethics Institute (www.business-ethics.org)
- Edelman Trust Barometer (www.edelman.com/trust-barometer)

Content and Relational Dimensions of Messages (LO1.1, LO1.2)

Suppose your supervisor says to you, "I love it when you text me at 6:30 in the morning." What is the content dimension of that message? What are some various ways in which you could describe the relational dimension of that message? Which verbal or nonverbal cues would you pay attention to when deciding how to interpret the relational dimension accurately?

Communication Needs (LO1.1, LO1.2)

Consider a common communication context in the professional world, such as making a sales presentation, attending a team meeting, or socializing with co-workers after work. Describe how each of the various types of communication needs might be relevant to people in that situation. Then, articulate how people might use communication to meet each of those needs in that context.

Learn More about Carnegie Training (LO1.1, LO1.5)

By his own admission, billionaire businessman Warren Buffett lacked the interpersonal skills necessary for success. That began to change when he discovered Dale Carnegie's training program for public speaking and communication skills. Discover Carnegie's principles for enhancing interpersonal interactions and building high-performance teams by visiting www.dcarnegietraining .com/resources/dale-carnegie-principles. In a short essay or blog post, explain each of the three principles and give examples of how you can foster those skills in your own life.

Handling Ethical Quandaries (LO1.4, LO1.5)

Ethical quandaries—situations for which more than one possible response could be ethically justified—are common in the business world. Consider a quandary such as discovering that a favorite co-worker is conducting personal business on company time or has taken credit for someone else's work. Interview three to five people who work in different professions or industries, asking them whether they have ever encountered a similar situation and what they think is the most ethical response (and why). Share your findings in a brief report or blog post.

ENDNOTES

1. Hall, J. A., & Davis, D. C. (2017). Proposing the Communicate Bond Belong theory: Evolutionary intersections with episodic interpersonal communication. *Communication Theory, 27*, 21–47.

2. Sinigaglia, C., & Rizzolatti, G. (2011). Through the looking glass: Self and others. *Consciousness and Cognition, 20*, 64–74.

3. Kashian, N., & Walther, J. B. (2016). Does uncertainty reduction facilitate the perceptual disconfirmation of negative expectancies in computer-mediated communication? *Journal of Media Psychology, 30*, 139–149.

4. Kenrick, D. T., Griskevicius, V., Neuberg, S. L., & Schaller, M. (2010). Renovating the pyramid of needs: Contemporary extensions built upon ancient foundations. *Perspectives on Psychological Science, 5*, 292–314.

5. Richards, J. C., & Schmidt, R. W. (2013). *Language and communication*. New York, NY: Routledge.

6. Deutscher, G. (2006). *The unfolding of language: An evolutionary tour of mankind's greatest invention*. New York, NY: Henry Holt & Co.

7. Matsumoto, D., & Hwang, H. C. (2016). The cultural bases of nonverbal communication. In D. Matsomoto, H. C. Hwang, & M. G. Frank (Eds.), *APA handbook of nonverbal communication* (pp. 77–101). Washington, DC: American Psychological Association.

8. Watzlawick, T., Beavin, J., & Jackson, D. (1967). *The pragmatics of human communication*. New York, NY: Norton.

9. Proust, J. (2016). The evolution of primate communication and metacommunication. *Mind & Language, 31*, 177–203.

10. See, e.g., Cho, H. (Ed.). (2012). *Health communication message design: Theory and practice*. Los Angeles, CA: Sage.

11. Barnlund, D. C. (1970). A transactional model of communication. In K. K. Sereno & C. D. Mortensen (Eds.), *Foundations of communication theory* (pp. 83–102). New York, NY: Harper & Row.

12. Altinöz, M. (2008). An overall approach to the communication of organizations in conventional and virtual offices. *International Scholarly and Scientific Research & Innovation, 2*, 627–633.

13. Tourish, D., & Robson, P. (2006). Sensemaking and the distortion of critical upward communication in organizations. *Journal of Management Studies, 43*, 711–730.

14. Bartels, J., Peters, O., de Jong, M., Pruyn, A., & van der Molen, M. (2010). Horizontal and vertical communication as determinants of professional and organisational identification. *Personnel Review, 39*, 210–226.

15. Newman, A. H. (2014). An investigation of how the informal communication of firm preferences influences managerial honesty. *Accounting, Organizations and Society, 39*, 195–207.

16. Cardon, P. W. (2016, April 23). *The role of leadership communication and emotional capital in driving internal social media use*. Presentation at the Association for Business Communication Southeast/Midwest Regional Conference, St. Louis, MO.

17. Covey, S. R. (2006). *The speed of trust*. New York, NY: Free Press.

18. Maslansky, M. (2010). *The language of trust*. New York, NY: Prentice Hall. Quote is from p. 6.

19. Miles, L. K., Nind, L. K., & Macrae, C. N. (2009). The rhythm of rapport: Interpersonal synchrony and social perception. *Journal of Experimental Social Psychology, 45*, 585–589.

20. Caring was listed as *consciousness* in a survey of important skills and abilities for business managers in the following study: Graduate Management Admission Council. (2014). *Alumni perspectives survey: 2014 survey report*. Reston, VA: Author.

21. *Fast Company*. (2015, February 23). Why listening might be the most important skill to hire for. Retrieved March 7, 2018, from https://www.fastcompany.com/3042688/why-listening-might-be-the-most-important-skill-to-hire-for.

22. Hasson, U. (2010, December). I can make your brain look like mine. *Harvard Business Review*, 32–33.

23. Hoppe, M. H. (2006). *Active listening: Improve your ability to listen and lead.* Greensboro, NC: Center for Creative Leadership. Quote is from pages 6 and 12.

24. Society for Human Resource Management. (2018). Retrieved from https://www.shrm.org/pages/default.aspx.

25. Eid, M., Riemann, R., Angleitner, A., & Borkenau, P. (2003). Sociability and positive emotionality: Genetic and environmental contributions to the covariation between different facets of extraversion. *Journal of Personality, 71,* 319–346; Porsch, R. M., Middeldorp, C. M., Cherney, S. S., Kraphol, E., van Beijsterveldt, C. E., Loukola, A., . . . Bartels, M. (2016). Longitudinal heritability of childhood aggression. *American Journal of Medical Genetics, 171,* 697–707.

26. Spitzberg, B. H., & Cupach, W. R. (2011). Interpersonal skills. In M. L. Knapp & J. A. Daly (Eds.), *The Sage handbook of interpersonal communication* (4th ed., pp. 481–524). Thousand Oaks, CA: Sage.

27. Spitzberg, B. H. (2013). (Re)introducing communication competence to the health professions. *Journal of Public Health Research, 2,* 126–135.

28. See Collier, M. J. (2015). Intercultural communication competence: Continuing challenges and critical directions. *International Journal of Intercultural Relations, 48,* 9–11.

29. Lou, H. C. (2015). Self-awareness—an emerging field in neurobiology. *Acta Paediatrica, 104,* 121–122.

30. Hwant, Y. (2011). Is communication competence still good for interpersonal media: Mobile phone and instant messenger. *Computers in Human Behavior, 27,* 924–934.

31. Bodie, G. D., Burleson, B. R., Holmstrom, A. J., McCullough, J. D., Rack, J. J., Hanosono, L. K., & Rosier, J. G. (2011). Effects of cognitive complexity and emotional upset on processing supportive messages: Two tests of a dual-process theory of supportive communication outcomes. *Human Communication Research, 37,* 350–376.

32. Dimberg, U., Andréasson, P., & Thunberg, M. (2011). Emotional empathy and facial reactions to facial expressions. *Journal of Psychophysiology, 25,* 26–31.

33. Brackett, M. A., Mayer, J. D., & Warner, R. M. (2004). Emotional intelligence and its relation to everyday behavior. *Personality and Individual Differences, 36,* 1387–1402. Quote is from p. 1389.

Learning Objectives

After reading this chapter, you should be able to do the following:

LO2.1   Explain culture and co-cultures.

LO2.2   Identify primary forms of human diversity.

LO2.3   Explain the major cultural dimensions.

LO2.4   Describe behavioral strategies for adapting to cultural norms and customs.

LO2.5   Illustrate ways of engaging diversity in an ethical manner.

LO2.6   Demonstrate communicating with cultural proficiency.

CHAPTER 2

Culture, Diversity, and Global Engagement

Jason Romano was on his first overseas business trip, waiting in the lobby of his Seoul, Korea, hotel for Jae Kim to pick him up for meetings. Jason and Jae had emailed back and forth for the past few weeks, but Jason was worried. He had specifically notified Jae in their emails that he needed an "accessible" hotel room, yet the room Jae had reserved was a standard one. Would Jae arrive with a vehicle that could hold his wheelchair and comfortably accommodate him?

A Korean man strolled over to Jason. He appeared to be around thirty and was dressed in a stylish suit and perfectly polished shoes. He gave a slight bow and said, "Good morning! Welcome to Korea! You must be Mr. Romano."

"Oh, yes, that's right. Hello, Jae!"

Jae appeared slightly confused. "I thought you would be older, Mr. Romano. You must only be in your twenties or thirties. How old are you?"

Jason was surprised to get a question about his age. "Well, actually, I'm 28 years old. Jae, can you tell me where we'll hold our meetings today and how we'll get there?"

Jae responded, "We have a full day ahead of us. We'll start with a tour of one of our new facilities. Then, we'll get some Korean BBQ. You'll meet our president and his team at lunch. Then, we'll drive for a view from the mountains. Next, we'll go to our offices to meet with some of the engineers. This evening, we'll hold a banquet with some other members of the team. We have prepared everything for you."

Jason watched Jae summon a beautiful Mercedes-Benz sedan, which did not look like it could accommodate his wheelchair. In addition to his concerns about the hotel room and the car, Jason also wondered why Jae seemed so formal and stuffy. Were all Koreans like that? And he felt the day's agenda seemed overwhelming and likely uncomfortable. Why wasn't Jae concerned about his comfort after a long trip?

We live in a wonderful time when we can readily work with people of many backgrounds. Not only do diverse teams and workplaces produce better performance, but our efforts to be inclusive emotionally reward and enrich us.

LO2.1

Explain culture and co-cultures.

Appreciating Culture and Human Diversity

Success in the business world—and in many areas of life—requires us to communicate effectively with people whose backgrounds and experiences are different from our own. Developing this ability starts with appreciating the influences of culture and human diversity. In this section, we will see that people vary in their cultures and co-cultures; their race, ethnicity, and nationality; their socioeconomic status; their disability status; their sex, gender, and sexuality; their religion; and their generational identity.

CULTURE AND CO-CULTURE

We use the term *culture* to mean all sorts of things. Sometimes we connect it to a place, as in "Italian culture" and "New England culture." Other times we use it to refer to an ethnic or a religious group, as in "African American culture" or "Jewish culture." We also speak of "deaf culture" and "the culture of the rich." What, exactly, makes a culture?

Although the word *culture* can have different meanings, we define **culture** as the totality of learned, shared symbols, language, values, and norms that distinguish one group of people from another. That definition tells us that culture isn't a property of countries or ethnicities or economic classes. Rather, it's a property of *people*. We can refer to groups of people who share the same culture as **societies**.

When you contemplate your own culture, you may think first of the country in which you were born and raised, considering yourself to belong to, say, U.S. or

Many people feel that occupational groups, such as this group of computer developers, constitute co-cultures.

©Hero Images/Getty Images

Mexican or Chinese culture. At the same time, if you enjoy comic books, vintage cars, or skateboarding, you may notice that the people who share your interest appear to share particular customs, vocabulary, and ways of thinking. Researchers use the term **co-cultures** to refer to groups of people who share values, customs, and norms related to mutual interests or characteristics besides their national citizenship.[1] When you consider all the different groups with which you identify, you may realize you belong to many different cultures at once.

RACE, ETHNICITY, AND NATIONALITY

LO2.2
Identify primary forms of human diversity.

People often confuse a person's culture with his or her nationality or racial or ethnic background, but these are all *different* aspects of a person's identity. Culture is a set of norms, values, and practices we learn from the people who raised us. It is often, but not necessarily, related to our **nationality**, which is our status as a citizen of a particular country. For example, Elsa was born in Sweden but has lived in the United States for much of her life, so although her nationality is Swedish, she identifies with U.S. culture.

We can think of **ethnicity** as our perception of our ancestry and heritage. Matías considers himself Hispanic, for instance, because he identifies with the language, customs, rituals, and history of his Nicaraguan ancestors, even though he is a U.S. citizen and also identifies with aspects of U.S. American culture. People's ethnicity is not dictated by the nationalities or experiences of their ancestors; it depends instead on the characteristics of their heritage with which they identify, and how strongly they do so.

The concept of **race** refers to differences in sets of physical characteristics—such as bone structure and the color of skin, hair, and eyes—that have often been presumed to have a biological or genetic basis. The U.S. Census—a nationwide survey of the U.S. population conducted every ten years by the federal government—asks people to report which race or races they identify most strongly with, choosing from among several categories. The racial categories offered in the most recent U.S. Census, taken in 2010, appear in Table 2.1.[2]

Of all these descriptors—race, ethnicity, and nationality—race has been the most controversial. Although racial differences in physical characteristics are sometimes argued to have a biological or genetic basis, the scientific evidence for such a basis has been relatively weak, except for skin color.[3] In the past, racial differences were also presumed to influence personality, intelligence, or competence, and these arguments were used to justify various forms of discrimination against particular racial groups. Such arguments unfortunately still influence people's perceptions and behaviors today, even though there is no scientific evidence for racial differences in personality or intellectual ability.[4]

SOCIOECONOMIC STATUS

A person's **socioeconomic status** (also referred to as SES) is a measure of his or her financial and social position relative to that of others. SES is typically assessed by comparing a person's income, education, work experience, and occupation to those of other people in that person's group or community. People with more extensive educations, more prestigious careers, and/or higher incomes than their peers are considered to be of high socioeconomic status, a designation often associated with also having greater power, privilege, and access to resources. In comparison, low SES can

Table 2.1 **Racial and Ethnic Categories and Subcategories in 2010 U.S. Census**

Category	Subcategories, if Relevant
Asian	Chinese Japanese Filipino Korean Asian Indian Vietnamese Other Asian
American Indian or Alaska Native	
Black or African American	
Hawaiian or Pacific Islander	Native Hawaiian Samoan Guamanian or Chamorro Other Pacific Islander
Hispanic origin	Mexican, Mexican American, Chicano Puerto Rican Cuban Another Hispanic, Latino, Spanish origin
White	
Some other race	

Source: U.S. Department of Commerce. (2010). *United States Census 2010 official form.* Washington, D.C.

result from a lack of access to education or other opportunities; it is often associated with poorer mental and physical health, as well as reduced life expectancy.

DISABILITY STATUS

Progressive employers not only comply with ADA laws and regulations, they create inclusive environments for those with physical and mental disabilities.

©*Image Source/Getty Images*

People also differ in their physical and mental capabilities. Some have sensory impairments, such as blindness or deafness. Some require crutches, a walker, or a wheelchair to get around, and others cope with physical disfigurements or deformities as a result of birth defects or later injuries. Still other people face cognitive limitations, such as those associated with autism—a psychological disorder characterized by impaired communication and social skills—or dyslexia—a learning disability that affects reading and writing ability.

In the United States, the Americans with Disabilities Act (ADA) prohibits employers from engaging in unjustified discrimination based on a person's disability status.[5]

For example, a restaurant may not refuse to hire a job applicant with a physical or cognitive disability if such a disability would not prevent that applicant from doing his or her job. The law also requires employers to provide reasonable work accommodations to employees with disabilities, such as installing ramps and elevators accessible to workers who are wheelchair users, and it also requires facilities and services—such as a post office or an airline—to provide similar accommodations to members of the public.

SEX, GENDER, AND SEXUALITY

Diversity also includes the influences of sex, gender, and sexuality. **Sex** is a genetic variable that determines whether someone is born male, female, of another sex, or of an indeterminate sex. It is different from **gender**, which is a social and psychological variable that characterizes a person's identity as feminine, masculine, or androgynous (a combination of masculine and feminine traits). Sex and gender often coincide; children born male are often socialized to think, communicate, dress, and behave in masculine ways, whereas female children are often taught to develop feminine traits. Although sex is a function of the combination of chromosomes we inherit from our biological parents, gender is acquired through our social and cultural experiences. Consequently, some girls grow up developing stereotypically masculine traits—such as a tendency toward assertiveness and competition—and some boys develop stereotypically feminine traits—such as empathy and a desire to nurture.

Sexuality (also called *sexual orientation*) describes the sex or sexes to which a person is romantically or sexually attracted. Although some argue that sexuality is more accurately described as a point along a continuum than as a group or category, researchers typically distinguish four broad categories of sexuality. *Heterosexuality* means being physically and romantically attracted to people of the other sex. Several studies have confirmed that the majority of adults in most societies have experienced mostly heterosexual attraction and have engaged in primarily heterosexual behavior.[6] *Homosexuality* refers to romantic and sexual attraction to members of your own sex. Homosexual males are typically referred to as "gay," and female homosexuals are commonly called "lesbian." People who are *bisexual* have romantic and/or sexual attraction to both women and men. They are not necessarily attracted to both equally, nor do they usually maintain long-term relationships with partners of either sex. Finally, people who are *asexual* have little interest in sex whatsoever. This orientation is fairly uncommon, characterizing less than 1 percent of U.S. adults, according to one study.[7]

Some people experience conflict between the sex they were born and the sex they feel they should be. For instance, a person may see herself as male even though she was born genetically female. The term *transgender* describes individuals who experience such conflict.[8] Some transgender people choose only to dress and represent themselves as members of the other sex. Others use hormone therapy or sex-reassignment surgery to bring their physical body in line with their self-image.

RELIGION

Both within the United States and around the world, populations differ greatly in terms of their religious beliefs and traditions. In 2017, the Pew Research Center analyzed thousands of censuses, surveys, and population registers to understand better the nature of religious diversity around the globe. Their report estimates that 84 percent of the world's population identifies with a particular religious tradition. Specific percentages of various religious affiliations appear in Table 2.2, which shows that Christianity is the most common affiliation, followed by Islam, nonreligious, Hinduism, and Buddhism.

The Pew report finds that Hindus, Christians, and Muslims tend to live in countries where they are the predominant religious group, whereas members of other religious groups live in countries where they are in the minority. The median ages of Muslims (24 years) and Hindus (27 years) are the lowest, whereas median ages are 30 for Christians, 36 for Buddhists, and 37 for Jews.[9]

Table 2.2 **Percentage of the Global Population Representing Various Religious Groups**

Religious Affiliation	Percentage of World Population
Christianity	31.2
Islam	24.1
No religious affiliation	16.0
Hinduism	15.1
Buddhism	6.9
Folk religions	5.7
Other religions	0.8
Jewish	0.2

Note: Folk religions include African traditional religions, Chinese folk religions, Australian aboriginal religions, and Native American religions. Other religions include Sikhs, Jains, Bahai's, Shintoists, Taoists, Wiccans, Zoroastrians, and other faiths.

Source: Pew Research Center/The Pew Forum on Religion & Public Life. (2017, April). The changing global religious landscape: Babies born to Muslims will begin to outnumber Christian births by 2035; people with no religion face a birth dearth. Washington, D.C.

Many religious followers, such as these Muslim employees, observe religious traditions in the workplace.

©Bloomberg/Getty Images

Religion is an important characteristic of diversity because it influences so many aspects of people's lives. These include food and clothing choices, occupational options, political preferences and voting behaviors, use of technology, and marriage and parenting practices, among others.

GENERATIONAL IDENTITY

Finally, people's communication behaviors often vary according to the values, experiences, and demands of the era in which they grew up. To understand the people with whom you are communicating, therefore, consider their generational identities. Researchers find important differences in the values and attitudes of

- *Post-Millennials* (or Gen Zers), born after 2000
- *Millennials* (or Gen Yers), born between 1980 and 2000
- *Generation Xers* (or Gen Xers), born between 1965 and 1979

- *Baby Boomers,* born between 1945 and 1964
- *Silvers,* born before 1945

As one example in industrialized societies, generational identity can make a difference when you are using communication technology or social media to interact. Younger individuals, who have grown up with smartphones and constant Internet access, have no problem texting, tweeting, or using Snapchat, behaviors that are often less familiar to older individuals. Research also finds that younger workers, such as millennials, have a strong need to receive frequent positive feedback about their work, whereas their more senior counterparts may find such behavior unnecessary or even annoying. People with different generational identities also evidence different attitudes about social issues, which can be important to take into account when creating communication products such as advertising messages.

In the United States, where a person grew up—the region, or rural, semi-urban, or urban settings—often instills lifelong norms and values.

©shotbydave/Getty Images

OTHER ELEMENTS OF IDENTITY AND DIVERSITY

The elements of identity and diversity we have discussed are among the most important, yet they are certainly not comprehensive. Professionals hold identities in many groups and generally adopt some of the shared values and norms of these groups. Regional differences may impact communication. Phrases such as *Southern hospitality* or a *New York minute* often reflect distinct approaches to working with others and getting things done. Similarly, professionals who grew up in rural, suburban, and urban areas often gain lifelong attitudes and behaviors related to sense of community, pace of life, and communication patterns. Occupational groups often hold distinct ways of approaching work. For example, engineers and marketers are often socialized into distinct ways of discussing, approaching, and solving problems. Even companies have distinct cultures, which are influenced by many factors, including industry and size. For example, a small tech start-up in Silicon Valley likely has a markedly different culture than that of a large, established bank in New York City. The longer people work in companies, the more they adopt the ways of doing things in those organizations. These are just a few of the many additional ways of understanding identity and diversity in the workplace.

Cultures and co-cultures; race, ethnicity, and nationality; SES; disability status; sex, gender, and sexuality; religion; and generational identity are not the only ways in which people and groups differ from one another, but they are among the most potent influences on our communication behavior. While we have focused on distinctions among these various groups and identities, it's always worth remembering that similarities often outnumber differences among these groups.

Conducting Business on a Global Scale

If you have ever had difficulty communicating with someone whose culture or background is different from your own, you have experienced the challenge of overcoming cultural differences in communication. Understanding how culture affects the way we think and act, and then practicing various ways of adapting to others' cultural norms and customs, can help you accomplish effective professional communication on a global scale.

LO2.3

Explain the major cultural dimensions.

IDENTIFYING THE WAYS CULTURES VARY

Understanding and communicating successfully with people from other cultures depends on understanding the specific ways in which cultures vary from one another. Dutch social psychologist Geert Hofstede has pioneered the study of cultures and cultural differences. His work suggests that at least five specific cultural differences influence the way people interact.

Cultures can be individualistic or collective.   According to Hofstede, cultures differ in how much emphasis they place on individuals rather than on groups. In an **individualistic culture**, people believe their primary responsibility is to themselves. They value self-reliance and the idea that people should "pull themselves up by their own bootstraps"—that is, help themselves instead of waiting for others to come to their aid. Children are raised hearing messages such as "Be yourself," "You're special," and "There's no one else in the world who's just like you." Research shows that the United States, Canada, Great Britain, and Australia are among the most individualistic societies in the world.[10]

In contrast, people in a **collectivistic culture** are taught that their primary responsibility is to their families, their communities, and their employers.[11] Their focus is on taking care of the needs of the group rather than the individual. People place a high value on duty and loyalty and see themselves not as unique or special but as a part of the group or groups to which they belong. Among the Kabre of Togo, for instance, individuals try to give away many of their material possessions in order to build relationships and benefit their social groups. Collectivistic cultures include North and South Korea, Japan, and many countries in Africa and Latin America.

The degree to which a culture is individualistic or collectivistic can affect communication behavior in several ways. For example, many people feel anxious when they have to give a speech, but especially in collectivistic societies, where people are taught to blend in rather than to stand out. Asserting yourself and standing up for yourself are valued in individualistic cultures, but pressure to adopt these norms can cause embarrassment and shame for people in a collectivistic culture.

Culture can be low- or high-context.   If you have traveled much, perhaps you have noticed that people in various parts of the world differ in how direct or explicit their language is. You may have spent time with people from both low- and high-context cultures, with *context* referring here to the broad set of factors surrounding every act of communication.

In a **low-context culture**, people are expected to be direct, to say what they mean, and to use language that is specific and concrete. They value expressing themselves, sharing opinions, and trying to persuade others to see things their way.[12] They appreciate agreements that are explicit in their meaning and that avoid ambiguity—such as specifically worded contracts—and they generally expect others to live up to their word. The United States is a low-context society, as are Canada, Israel, and most northern European countries.

In comparison, people in a **high-context culture**—such as South Korea and the cultures of Native Americans and the Māori of New Zealand—are taught to speak in a much less direct way. Maintaining harmony and avoiding offense are more important than expressing your true feelings.[13] Speech is more ambiguous, and people convey much more of their meaning through subtle behaviors and contextual cues, such as facial expressions and tone of voice.

Differences between communicative contexts reveal themselves in the ways in which people handle criticism and disagreement.[14] In a low-context culture, a supervisor might reprimand an irresponsible employee openly, to make an example of the individual. The supervisor would probably be direct and explicit about the employee's shortcomings, the company's expectations for improvement, and the consequences of failing to meet those expectations. In a high-context culture, however, the supervisor probably wouldn't reprimand the employee publicly for fear of putting the employee to shame, causing him or her to "lose face." Criticism is more likely to take place in private. The supervisor would also likely use more ambiguous language to convey what the employee was doing wrong, "talking around" the issue instead of confronting it directly.

Cultures differ in power distance. Cultures also differ from one another in the degree to which power is distributed within society. Several types of assets can give someone power, including money or other valuable resources, education or expertise, age, popularity, talent, intelligence, and experience.

In democratic societies such as the United States and western European nations, people believe in the value of equality among the sexes and other social groups. The belief that all individuals are equal and that no one person or group should have excessive power is characteristic of a **low-power-distance culture**. The United States and Canada fall in that category, as do Israel, New Zealand, Denmark, and Austria.[15] People in low-power-distance societies are raised to believe that although some individuals are born with more advantages (such as wealth or fame), no one is inherently better than anyone else. That doesn't necessarily mean people in those societies *are* treated equally, only that they value the idea that they *should be*.

Power is distributed less evenly in a **high-power-distance culture**. Certain groups, such as members of the royal family or the ruling political party, have great power, and the average citizen has much less. People in high-power-distance societies are taught that certain individuals or groups deserve more power than others, and that respecting power and privilege is more important than promoting equality. Mexico, Brazil, India, Saudi Arabia, and the Philippines are all high-power-distance societies.[16]

Power distance affects many aspects of communication. For example, individuals in a low-power-distance society are often taught that it is their right—even their responsibility—to question authority. It's not unusual for them to ask "Why?" when a parent or teacher tells them to do something. In contrast, individuals in a high-power-distance society learn to obey and respect those in power, such as parents and teachers, without question.[17]

That difference is also evident in individuals' relationships and communications with their employers. Workers in a low-power-distance culture value *autonomy*— freedom of choice about the way they do their jobs—as well as opportunities to influence decisions that affect them. They might provide their input, for example, through

Cultural dimensions, such as individualism/collectivism and power distance, influence how much professionals in various societies speak up and directly critique one another's ideas in meetings.

©Rawpixel.com/Shutterstock

union representatives or employee satisfaction surveys. In contrast, employees in a high-power-distance culture are used to having little or no say about how to do their jobs. Instead, they expect their employers to make the decisions and are more likely to follow those decisions without question.

Cultures differ in uncertainty avoidance. Humans have a natural tendency to avoid unfamiliar and uncomfortable situations. In other words, we generally dislike uncertainty—in fact, uncertainty causes many of us a good deal of stress.[18] Not all cultures find uncertainty to be problematic to the same degree, however. Rather, cultures vary in what Hofstede called **uncertainty avoidance**, or the extent to which people try to avoid situations that are unstructured, unclear, or unpredictable.[19]

Individuals from cultures that are highly uncertainty-avoidant are drawn to people and situations that are familiar, and they are relatively unlikely to take risks for fear of failure. They are also uncomfortable with differences of opinion, and they tend to favor rules and laws that maximize security and reduce ambiguity. Argentina, Portugal, and Uruguay are among the countries whose cultures are the most uncertainty-avoidant.

In contrast, people in uncertainty-accepting cultures are more open to new situations and more accepting of people and ideas that are different from their own. They take a "live and let live" approach, preferring as few rules as possible that might restrict their behaviors. Societies with cultures that are highly accepting of uncertainty include Hong Kong, Jamaica, and New Zealand.

Hofstede determined that U.S. culture is more accepting than avoidant of uncertainty, but it is closer to the midpoint of the scale than many countries are. Co-cultures within the United States, however, vary in their tolerance of uncertainty. Amish communities—which adhere to strict guidelines regarding dress, behavior, and the use of modern technology—are often highly uncertainty-avoidant. In comparison, actors, singers, and other artists may have a high tolerance for uncertainty if it facilitates their creativity.

Cultures can be masculine or feminine. We usually use the terms *masculine* and *feminine* when we're referring to people. Hofstede suggested that we can also apply those terms to cultures.[20] In a highly **masculine culture**, people tend to cherish stereotypically masculine values, such as ambition, achievement, and the acquisition of material goods. They also value sex-specific roles for women and men, preferring that men hold the wage-earning and decision-making positions (such as corporate executive) while women occupy the nurturing positions (such as teacher or homemaker). Examples of masculine cultures are Austria, Japan, and Mexico.

In a highly **feminine culture**, people tend to value nurturing behavior, quality of life, and service to others, all stereotypically feminine qualities. They also tend *not* to believe that women's and men's roles should be strongly differentiated. In a feminine culture, therefore, it is not unusual for a man to care for children or for a woman to be her family's primary wage earner. Employers in most feminine cultures also provide new mothers and fathers with more paid parental leave than do employers in masculine cultures, so that those parents can focus their attention on their new infants. Examples of feminine cultures are Sweden, Chile, and the Netherlands.

According to Hofstede's research, the United States has a moderately masculine culture. U.S. adults tend to value sex-differentiated roles—although not as strongly as Austrians, Japanese, and Mexicans do—and they place a fairly high value on stereotypically masculine qualities such as achievement and the acquisition of resources.

Individualism, context, power distance, uncertainty avoidance, and masculinity/femininity are among the most potent ways in which people's cultural background influences the way they interact socially. To communicate successfully with people from a variety of backgrounds, however, it is useful to know how to adapt to their norms and customs.

CAREER TIP

Did you know Mark Zuckerberg, CEO and founder of Facebook, speaks Chinese? He started learning it nearly ten years ago. Zuckerberg travels often to China to meet politicians, business professionals, and even students, and he's used his language skills to make speeches in Chinese to a variety of audiences.

Zuckerberg has strong business reasons for cultivating relationships in China. For now, Facebook is blocked in China (it has been since 2009), and he clearly hopes it can enter the Chinese market at some point. His earnest efforts to learn more about the Chinese and their culture through its language have opened many opportunities for him to

meet important Chinese officials and executives. While he may not have helped Facebook gain access to the Chinese market quite yet, Zuckerberg serves in a variety of influential roles in China, including as a board member for Tsinghua University (one of China's most prestigious universities).

Zuckerberg explained why he's invested so much time learning Chinese: "There are three reasons I decided to learn Chinese. The first, my wife is Chinese. Her grandmother can only speak Chinese. When I told her in Chinese I was going to marry Priscilla, she was very shocked. Then I want to study Chinese culture. The third: Chinese is hard and I like a challenge!"

Like Zuckerberg, you can benefit from learning another language for a variety of reasons. It gives you many insights into the way people of other cultures think. It helps you appreciate the richness of other cultures. It fosters tremendous goodwill with others. And you may find yourself in situations where your language ability allows smoother communication than relying solely on English.

SOURCES: Leibowitz, G. (2017, February 2016). Mark Zuckerberg is learning Chinese. Here's why you should, too. *Inc.com*. Retrieved from https://www.inc.com/glenn-leibowitz/mark-zuckerberg-is-learning-chinese-heres-why-you-should-too.html; Snyder, B. (2014, October 23). Why Facebook's Mark Zuckerberg spent years learning Mandarin Chinese. *NBC News* Retrieved from https://www.nbcnews.com/tech/social-media/why-facebooks-mark-zuckerberg-spent-years-learning-mandarin-chinese-n232266; Moore, M. (2014, October 24). How good really is Mark Zuckerberg's Mandarin? *The Telegraph*. Retrieved from http://www.telegraph.co.uk/technology/mark-zuckerberg/11182575/How-good-really-is-Mark-Zuckerbergs-Mandarin.html.

Mark Zuckerberg speaks to Chinese university students.

©Stringer/AP Images

ADAPTING TO CULTURAL NORMS AND CUSTOMS

In today's global marketplace, opportunities abound to interact with people from different cultures—and the ability to do so effectively is highly valued. In this section, we will explore strategies for adapting to another culture's social customs, norms for touch and proximity, expected level of formality, time orientation, gender roles, and tolerance for conflict.

Social customs dictate expected behaviors. Communication makes use of several social customs—patterns of behavior considered traditional and meaningful in interpersonal interactions—and these vary considerably from culture to culture. One example is a greeting custom. Most Americans are used to shaking hands with someone they are greeting, so they may be surprised to learn that this custom is not universal. In Japan, for instance, the custom is to bow to someone you are greeting, with longer and lower bows reserved for those who are most respected. People in Thailand place their palms together in front of their faces and bow their heads when greeting others, a behavior known as the *wai*. Kissing someone on each cheek is a common greeting behavior in Europe, the Mediterranean and Middle East, and Latin

LO2.4

Describe behavioral strategies for adapting to cultural norms and customs.

In most Asian cultures, various forms of bowing are appropriate greetings.

©Jennifer Lam/Shutterstock

America. Men in traditional Bedouin tribes greet each other by rubbing noses, and in Tibet it is considered polite to show your tongue when greeting someone. Certain co-cultures also have specific greeting customs, such as the way members of the military salute one another.

Another social custom valued in many cultures is gift giving. Business transactions are often punctuated by the sharing of gifts, which can help establish trust, goodwill, and a sense of community. Cultures vary in the types of gifts they consider appropriate, however. A nice bottle of wine or cognac may be welcomed by a Japanese colleague, for instance, but would be considered taboo in Saudi Arabia, where alcohol consumption is prohibited. A leather portfolio might make a lovely gift in Great Britain, but not in India, where many people consider cows to be sacred. Even the giving of flowers relies on cultural customs, because countries vary in the types, colors, and even numbers of flowers they consider appropriate as gifts. When doing business with people from other cultures, knowing their social customs regarding greetings and gift giving can aid your interactions and reduce the likelihood of causing offense.

Societies vary in levels of touch and proximity. Culture also plays a large role in the way people negotiate touch and personal space. People in a **high-contact culture** usually stand or sit fairly close to one another and touch one another frequently. Many Latin American, southern European, and Middle Eastern cultures are classified as high-contact. In contrast, people in a **low-contact culture** keep greater amounts of personal space between themselves and touch one another less frequently.[21] Some Asian and Scandinavian cultures are examples of low-contact cultures. Many communication researchers also classify the United States as a fairly low-contact culture.[22] In one study that observed customers at a fast-food restaurant, touch researcher Tiffany

Members of some cultures, such as these Brazilians, are known for preferring closer proximity and touching more frequently in professional and social situations.

©JAG IMAGES/Getty Images

Field found that adolescents in France (a high-contact culture) touched each other substantially more often during a 20-minute period than did U.S. adolescents.[23]

Anthropologist Edward T. Hall discovered that people in Western cultures observe four spatial zones, or levels of personal distance, when interacting with one another.[24]

- **Intimate distance**, which ranges from 0 to approximately 1½ feet, is the zone we willingly occupy with only our closest and most intimate friends, family members, and romantic partners.
- **Personal distance**, which Hall defined as extending from 1½ to about 4 feet, is the distance we typically maintain with other friends and relatives.
- **Social distance**, which ranges from about 4 to 12 feet, is used with customers, casual acquaintances, and others whom we don't know very well to convey more formal, impersonal interaction.
- Finally, **public distance** typically applies when someone is giving a speech or performing in front of a large audience. The purpose is to keep the presenter far enough away from the group that he or she is comfortable and visible to everyone. Public distances are usually 12 to 25 feet or greater, depending on the circumstance.

When conducting business cross-culturally, you may encounter others whose norms for touch or distance are substantially different from your own. One customer might stand closer to you or touch you more often than you expect, while a customer from a different culture may keep her distance. You may tend to interpret their behaviors through the lens of your own cultural expectations, thinking of one as overly friendly or overbearing and the other as standoffish or aloof. But understanding *their* cultural norms for proximity and touch can help you interpret and respond to their behaviors more appropriately.

Formality expectations differ between cultures. Americans, as well as Canadians and Australians, often prefer to interact with one another in relatively informal ways, such as by observing casual-dress days at work and using one another's first names. They find such informality comfortable and believe it contributes to a friendlier and more relaxed work environment.

People in many other cultures find such informality inappropriate and off-putting, however, especially when conducting business.[25] In Germany, Egypt, and Mexico, referring to others by their titles—such as Ms., Mr., or Dr.—is considered a sign of respect, at least until they invite you to interact on a first-name basis.[26]

Another cultural difference in formality shows up in interactions with strangers. Few in the United States are dismayed when strangers strike up a conversation on an airplane, for instance, or in line for a movie. In some cultures, however, addressing someone you don't know makes that person uncomfortable. When U.S.-based retailer Walmart began opening stores in Germany, it was advised not to hire greeters—commonly seen in its U.S. stores—because German customers would find it awkward to be greeted by a stranger when entering the business.[27] Understanding and matching the level of formality expected by colleagues and customers from other societies can help business and professional interactions succeed.

Societies vary in their norms and expectations concerning the use of time. Some societies—such as the Swiss, the German, and often the U.S. society—have a **monochronic** concept of time, which means they view time as a commodity. People in these cultures save, spend, fill, invest, and waste time as though it were tangible. They treat time as valuable, believe "time is money," and talk about making time and losing time. This orientation affects several social behaviors. People who think of time as valuable hate to waste it. Therefore, they expect meetings and classes to start on time, and if that doesn't happen, they are willing to wait only so long before

Adapting to Time Management

Interview someone whose career depends heavily on maintaining a tightly managed schedule (such as a person in the travel or broadcast industries). Ask how he or she has managed or would manage a customer or co-worker who took a polychronic approach to time management.

leaving. They also place a high value on punctuality and expect others to show up when they say they will.[28]

In contrast, societies with a **polychronic** orientation—which include Latin America, the Arab part of the Middle East, and much of sub-Saharan Africa—conceive of time as more holistic and fluid and less structured. Instead of treating time as a finite commodity we must manage properly to avoid wasting it, people in a polychronic culture perceive it more as a never-ending river, flowing infinitely into the future. In societies with a polychronic time orientation, schedules are more fluid and flexible. In Pakistan, for instance, if you're invited to a wedding that begins at 4:30 in the afternoon and you arrive at 4:25, you will most likely be the first one there. A bank or restaurant may open not at a specified time—as expected in a monochronic society—but whenever the owner or manager decides to open.[29] Being aware of a culture's time orientation allows you to adjust your observance of time—and your expectations about other people's punctuality—accordingly.

Behavior is influenced by gender roles.   Around the world, societies differ greatly in their expectations about gender-appropriate behavior, particularly of women. Especially in highly masculine cultures, women are often perceived as less powerful than men and as less likely to be experts or decision makers. Some societies expect women to be subservient to their fathers or husbands and routinely restrict their access to education, the political process, and even the ability to drive. In business transactions, men in such cultures may overlook their female colleagues, preferring to interact and negotiate only with other men. In contrast, many other societies observe little difference in their expectations for gender-appropriate behavior, including in the business world. Women and men in those cultures are perceived and treated according to their expertise, achievements, and competence, rather than their biological sex or psychological gender.

One way in which gender-role differences are often especially visible is in a culture's norms for dress. In business transactions, a suit is often expected for both women and men, but people in some cultures adopt other styles of dress. Arab businessmen, for instance, may prefer wearing a *thawb,* a typically light-colored ankle-length garment with long sleeves. Women in Islamic countries usually cover their hair when in public, and some may cover their faces entirely.

Societies differ in their tolerance for conflict.   Earlier in this chapter, you read about the difference between individualistic cultures—those in which people are taught to focus on their own lives—and collectivistic cultures—those in which people are taught to focus on their groups and communities. This difference can influence, among other things, how comfortable people are with engaging in conflict. People in an individualistic society—such as the United States—are expected to express their conflict and work toward resolving it. During a business negotiation, for example, parties may be explicit about which aspects of an offer they accept and which ones they reject, and they may rely on elements of the legal system—such as a court or a mediator—to help them reach resolution. The emphasis in such a culture is typically on settling the conflict, even if that means one party wins and the other loses.

Collectivistic cultures emphasize preserving social harmony rather than winning. People are taught to be more indirect when they handle disagreements. In some Asian cultures, for instance, businesspeople are hesitant to say *no*—even if they mean *no*—for fear of causing offense. They may also try to soften the blow of criticism or bad news in order to avoid embarrassing people, especially in front of others. Their

Reem Al Zarouni, an accomplished entrepreneur and fashion designer, wears a hijab or veil in most professional settings.

©Al Otaiba Inmaa

PEOPLE **FIRST**

Engaging with Ideas That Offend You

IMAGINE THIS: Your new officemate is from the Middle East, and his cultural background is strongly masculine. He believes, among other things, that women belong in the home, not the workforce. He is friendly enough, but he quietly criticizes women who work outside the home, including some in your own company. You want to be welcoming, but you feel uncomfortable because your own ideas about women are substantially different.

Now, consider this: The two of you eat together in the company cafeteria from time to time, and you wonder about the pros and cons of expressing your own beliefs about women in the workforce. Is there a way to be true to your beliefs while also validating your officemate as a person?

- Remember that you are entitled to your ideas about gender and equality. The issue isn't whether you can take a position different from your officemate's, but whether and how to communicate about your beliefs in a way that won't damage your working relationship.

- Your position is likely informed by your cultural values, so be mindful that your officemate's is too. You can certainly think your position is the preferred one,

but be careful about concluding that it is the only valid way to think.

- If you choose to discuss your differing ideas with your officemate, it may help to start by expressing curiosity rather than condemnation. Instead of simply telling him you disagree, ask him how he came to believe the way he does about women's roles. Rather than saying, "I think you're wrong," you might say, "I imagine you've met people who think differently than you do on this issue."

Behaving politely and expressing curiosity may feel like implicitly endorsing your officemate's ideas about women. Instead, however, this approach conveys *mindfulness* by acknowledging that his position is informed by his cultural values, just as yours is. You can hold different values without condemning your officemate as wrong.

> **THINK ABOUT THIS:**
>
> Have you worked or gone to school with people whose beliefs about social issues are strongly different from yours? What have you done in the past that has allowed you to maintain a positive relationship with them despite your differences?

objective may still be to prevail in the conflict, yet their strategy for doing so emphasizes social harmony over overt conflict.

When negotiating with people from other cultures, it helps to pay attention to their tolerance and expectations for conflict. If you were taught to engage in conflict directly, that strategy might work well when dealing with others who have the same expectation, but it can quickly backfire and cause offense with audiences that are more conflict-avoidant.

Addressing Diversity in an Ethical Manner

LO2.5

Illustrate ways of engaging diversity in an ethical manner.

Addressing diversity from an ethical perspective means asking *what we should do* in the workplace to make our professional environments more inclusive and fair for all. Many organizations hire diversity teams (often led by a chief diversity officer) to help their organizations realize the potential of their diverse workforces while ensuring equal opportunity for their employees and other stakeholders. All professionals should consciously think about ways to draw out the best in all their colleagues, and taking a diversity perspective helps accomplish this goal and facilitate rich and rewarding communication as well.

HONORING YOUR OWN CULTURAL VALUES

It's often easier to appreciate the cultural values and diverse backgrounds of others when we consciously recognize our own. The ability to articulate our own values and the impacts they have on our behavior is rare—after all, most people act on their values without much thought. Often, we can best identify and articulate our own values after encountering cultures with different ones.

Among Americans, a relatively low power distance is a point of pride for most citizens. The idea that people are—or should be—equal is wrapped up in many people's sense of patriotism and manifests itself in calls for more equal rights. In the workplace, the idea that anyone can succeed or rise to the top is a reflection of low power distance. The use of first names rather than titles, willingness to give your opinion when it differs from the boss's, and the casual approach to workplace conversations all are grounded in an egalitarian approach to work. It's appropriate for people to feel proud of this egalitarian approach and actively encourage it.

RESPECTING THE CULTURAL VALUES AND DIVERSE BACKGROUNDS OF OTHERS

Respecting the cultural values of others is often challenging when they differ significantly from our own. Try to understand the legitimate reasons for those values and adapt your behavior to other cultures as appropriate. After all, cultural values generally feel natural, appropriate, and even right to members of those cultures.

For example, members of lower-power-distance cultures could easily view cultures with higher power distance as nonegalitarian or unfair. Instead, understand the underlying values and historical reasons that make higher power distance reasonable or legitimate. Recognize that members of higher-power-distance cultures feel more comfortable with status differences because they *value* age, seniority (including length of time in employment), educational attainment, orderly decision making, and even trusted and dependable social connections.

SEEING CULTURES AND DIVERSITY AS AN OPPORTUNITY TO LEARN AND GROW

We live in an amazing time to learn and grow from people of other cultures and diverse backgrounds. We can work, socialize, and meet people of many backgrounds and enjoy unprecedented access to information about people of diverse backgrounds. However, many people spend most of their time with people similar to themselves and access only information that supports their own views of the world. As you actively seek to learn and grow from others who are different than you, you'll find that you are a better team member and a better leader in the workplace.

As a college student, you are in a stage of life that gives you unique opportunities to acquire cross-cultural experiences, including studying abroad, learning a language, developing friendships with international students on campus, and taking an interest in and learning about a particular culture. One of the best ways to gain an in-depth understanding is to take an inquisitive approach—ask how other cultures view knowledge; how they reason and approach problems; how they work, worship, and view the world; how they view time; and so on. You might even consider watching some films, television shows, documentaries, news, and other video of the culture. It's increasingly easy to access video of other cultures, such as television shows, documentaries, and news. You can observe many aspects of the culture in context with visual and auditory cues.

RECOGNIZING THE INDIVIDUALITY OF OTHERS

Although a diversity perspective can help you understand why people think, feel, and communicate in certain ways, nearly all people of all backgrounds like to be

TECH TIP
Read, Listen, and Learn from a Diversity of Online Sources

Used wisely, social media give you many ways to read, listen, and learn about your company, your industry, and your discipline. One key to effective learning is to rely on a diversity of reputable sources, so you avoid trapping yourself in an echo chamber. *Social reading platforms* (such as LinkedIn Pulse, Digg Reader, and Flipboard) help you weed out less relevant information and efficiently access information to develop your knowledge and skills. To make the best use of these platforms, consider the following strategies:

• *Identify the 10 to 20 sources most helpful to you.* You'll likely need to experiment over time to identify the best mix of information. Follow professionals with diverse perspectives (inside and outside your company), companies of interest (including competitors), and news sources related to your professional interests and expertise (set up as RSS feeds to important periodicals and thought leaders).

• *Use hashtags and topical searches to track information important to you.* Using automated searches wisely allows you to get relevant information for your professional interests. You can use a variety of platforms such as Tweetdeck to automate this process.

• *Take time to read the most important articles and posts.* Most online readers are skimmers. Skimming is important to quickly extract key ideas. You will learn more deeply and be more informed if you set aside at least a few hours per week for dedicated, comprehensive reading of key articles and posts in your subject area. Commit to taking enough time to process this information well.

• *Recognize and praise the contributions of others.* Make sure to like and compliment the well-developed content of others. Many of your colleagues and other contacts will greatly appreciate your thoughtful, specific praise. They'll also likely return that appreciation when you post your own content.

treated as individuals. Our identities may be tied to various groups, yet regardless of our cultures, we all still like be known for our unique personalities, interests, skills, abilities, and contributions. As a communicator, you'll often find it helpful to understand others' diverse backgrounds. Yet you'll connect and collaborate most effectively as you learn about the distinctive and admirable traits and interests of people on an individual level.

Studying abroad provides rare opportunities to immerse yourself in and learn from other cultures.

©andresr/Getty Images

LO2.6

Demonstrate communicating with cultural proficiency.

Communicating with Cultural Proficiency

Communicating with cultural proficiency means developing skills and traits that help us collaborate more effectively with people of different cultural and identity backgrounds. It calls for a deep awareness of other cultures and graceful adaptation to their communication preferences. Here are some ways you can develop these skills.

CULTIVATE CULTURAL AWARENESS

Developing strong cross-cultural relationships requires a learner mind-set. With the learner mind-set, you expect that members of other cultures possess unique types of knowledge and approaches to problem solving that will be helpful for achieving your shared business goals. You rely on their being full partners in the decision-making process. An example of someone who adopts this learning mind-set is Henry Paulson, the former CEO of Goldman Sachs (1999–2006) and a former United States Treasury Secretary (2006–2009). He now runs the Paulson Institute, which has a mission to "strengthen U.S.-China relations and to advance sustainable economic growth and environmental protection in both countries."[30] Many of Paulson's major achievements in private and public life involved deals with China. With over 70 business trips to China, he constantly initiated contacts with important Chinese politicians and executives, learned as much as he could about these Chinese partners, traveled widely around the country to learn about each region, and picked up basic Chinese language skills.[31] As you focus on awareness of other cultures, make sure you take Paulson's approach and find the admirable aspects that you can adopt into your own worldview and values.

PRACTICE PERSPECTIVE TAKING

There are many prisms with which to see the point of views of others, and several strategies are helpful. Get in the habit of asking nonjudgmental, open-ended questions and listening carefully to the responses of others. In business, you often don't have time to experience other cultures completely before engaging in long-term relationships and transactions. In these situations, find trusted members of these cultures who can advise you. Spend time asking them questions about how your cultural counterparts are perceiving and experiencing the business process.

AVOID CULTURAL CENTRISM

We naturally develop **stereotypes**, or generalizations, to try to understand the attitudes and behavior of people we do not know, especially those of different cultures. It is an attempt by the brain to group and categorize in complex situations. Stereotypes can make interactions less complicated since they serve as a starting point for understanding the motives and values of others. For example, people may have a stereotype of tax accountants as credible, professional, and detail-oriented. This allows them to go to a tax accountant's office assuming the professional will help them and provide excellent service. Similarly, people who work across cultures often form stereotypes about how members of that culture communicate and approach work problems. These stereotypes can be productive as long as they are only a starting point, they are flexible, and they are primarily positive.[32]

Stereotyping about cultures can also be counterproductive and even hurtful when it emerges from **cultural centrism**—the belief that your own culture is superior and the correct lens from which you judge other cultures. Cultural centrism leads to two types of stereotypes: projected cognitive similarity and outgroup homogeneity effect.[33]

FOCUS ON ETHICS
Cultural Centrism

Gretchen's position at the nonprofit organization where you both work requires extensive travel, and on her first trip to the southern Africa, Gretchen found herself put off by some of the cultural practices she encountered. Many people kissed her on the lips when they met her for the first time. Strangers sat uncomfortably close to her on public buses, and their closeness bothered her even more because few seemed to use deodorant. Some of the men she interacted with had multiple wives, and some took their children to witch doctors when they got sick. "What a messed-up culture," she said to you upon her return. On one hand, you recognize that Gretchen's statement is culturally centric, because it judges another's cultural practices as inferior to her own. On the other hand, you feel a little relieved you didn't have to make the trip yourself.

CONSIDER THIS: Many people believe their cultural values and traditions are the *right* values and traditions for everyone. Is that idea unethical, or is it just human nature to feel that way? Is there an ethical difference between *thinking* this way and *acting* on those thoughts?

Projected cognitive similarity is the tendency to assume others share your cultural norms and values. This occurs when we project own cultural norms and values to explain the behaviors we see in others. Take the case of an American interviewing a Japanese man for a new position. The Japanese man might downplay his own achievements and give credit to the teams he has worked with, honoring Japanese norms of modesty and collectivism. The interviewer, based on the American cultural lens, may think the man lacks self-confidence and initiative. The Japanese applicant, by contrast, is most likely displaying Japanese norms and values associated with modesty, politeness, and collectivism.

Outgroup homogeneity effect is the tendency to think members of other groups are all the same. Psychologically, this approach minimizes the mental effort needed to get to know people of other groups. Practically speaking, it is counterproductive to developing effective working relationships with members of other cultures. The reality is that all cultures contain a lot of diversity—individuals of many backgrounds, worldviews, interests, and approaches to life.

Negative stereotyping can also easily emerge from popular culture forms like films, television shows, and music. Research has shown that television depictions of particular cultural groups as criminal, cruel, backward, or dishonest affect viewers' stereotypes of those cultures.[34] News stories about the political relationships between countries, used as a lens for understanding others, often lead to unjustified negative stereotyping. Also be aware of stereotypes that others may have about you. Members of other cultures often form stereotypes about people from the United States based on news stories and popular culture.

ADAPTING TO CHANGING CULTURAL NORMS AND EXPECTATIONS

All cultures change, usually over years and more often decades. For example, American business culture has increasingly moved to a more team-based approach

Communicating with Cultural Competence

Communicating competently across cultures is a skill most of us can improve. How culturally competent are you? Read each of the following statements, and indicate how much it describes you by assigning a number between 1 ("not at all") and 7 ("very much").

1. ____ I have confidence that I can deal well with people from different cultures.

2. ____ Before I interact with someone from a new culture, I ask myself what I hope to achieve.

3. ____ I can alter my expressions when a cultural encounter requires it.

4. ____ I am certain I can make friends with people from other cultural backgrounds.

5. ____ I modify the way I speak when it will help someone from another culture understand me.

6. ____ I can adapt to the lifestyle of a different culture quite easily.

7. ____ I change the way I act when a cross-cultural encounter requires it.

8. ____ I am confident I can deal with a cultural situation that's unfamiliar.

When you're finished, add up your scores and write the total on this line: ____. The ranges below will help you see how high your cultural competence is right now.

- 8–22: Cultural competence is a skill you can work on, and this class will help you do so.
- 23–38: You are moderately good at cultural competence already. Continued practice will strengthen that skill.
- 39–56: You are highly culturally competent, which often makes your communication more effective.

SOURCE: Adapted from Earley, P. C., & Mosakowski, E. (2004, October). Cultural intelligence. *Harvard Business Review, 82*(10), 139–146.

over the past few decades, taking a slightly more collectivist orientation. As you learn about other cultures, recognize that they too are constantly shifting. It's often in cultures undergoing rapid economic development that norms and expectations change the most quickly. For example, China's rapid economic development over the past 30 years has been remarkable and unprecedented for a country of its size. As Chinese have grown more prosperous, more individualistic and more low-context communication patterns have become part of their business culture.

CHAPTER WRAP-UP

You will have many opportunities to work across cultures and enjoy diversity in the workplace. Here's a quick review of the chapter.

LO2.1 Explain culture and co-cultures.

- Culture is the totality of learned, shared symbols, language, values, and norms that distinguish one group of people from another.
- Co-cultures are groups of people who share values, customs, and norms related to mutual interests or characteristics besides their national citizenship.

LO2.2 Identify primary forms of human diversity.

- Race, ethnicity, and nationality
- Socioeconomic status
- Disability status
- Sex, gender, and sexuality

- Religion
- Generational identity

LO2.3 **Explain the major cultural dimensions.**

- Individualism and collectivism
- Low- and high-context cultures
- Power distance
- Uncertainty avoidance
- Cultural masculinity and femininity

LO2.4 **Describe behavioral strategies for adapting to cultural norms and customs.**

- Social customs
- Touch and proximity
- Formality
- Time orientation
- Gender roles

LO2.5 **Illustrate ways of engaging diversity in an ethical manner.**

- Honor your own cultural values.
- Respect the cultural values and diverse backgrounds of others.
- See cultures and diversity as an opportunity to learn and grow.
- Recognize the individuality of others.

LO2.6 **Demonstrate communicating with cultural proficiency.**

- Cultivate cultural awareness.
- Practice perspective taking.
- Avoid cultural centrism.
- Adapt to changing cultural norms and expectations.

A LOOK BACK

Now, let's return to the opening scenario. Jason Romano has traveled to Korea for meetings. He is frustrated with his host, Jae Kim, who seems to have neglected requested accommodations for Jason's physical challenges. Yet, Jason likely misinterprets a variety of signals and relies on incorrect stereotypes.

Jason wonders why Jae keeps calling him "Mr. Romano." He even thinks Jae is "formal and stuffy." Yet Jae's use of titles is more likely a sign of respect from a culture that is higher in *power distance* and in which *formal, high-context communication* (titles, expensive clothes and vehicles) project status and garner respect. When Jason wonders whether all Koreans act this way, he commits a blunder common when working across cultures: *outgroup homogeneity effect*, which is the tendency to think members of other cultures are all the same.

One likely reason Jae didn't reserve a room that could accommodate Jason's physical challenges is he didn't understand the term *accessible*. While this term is often used for hotel rooms that accommodate people with disabilities, even many Americans are not familiar with the term. It may be especially difficult for a non-native English speaker to understand what is meant by an "accessible" room.

Jason also likely misinterprets Jae's motives for the agenda he has outlined. The day's activities, which include a lot of socializing and getting to know people in Jae's company, are consistent with a *collectivist* orientation. When he wonders why Jae isn't more accommodating to him, Jason is falling back on projected cognitive similarity, the tendency to assume others have the same norms and values as your own cultural group. In this case, he thinks Jae should act from Jason's own *individualistic* orientation by giving him more time and privacy during the day.

KEY TERMS

CHAPTER REVIEW QUESTIONS

1. What is culture? What do we mean when we call culture "a property of people"? **LO2.1**

2. How is a culture different from a society? How is it different from a co-culture? **LO2.1**

3. What does it mean to identify an individual's nationality, ethnicity, and race? **LO2.2**

4. In what ways do socioeconomic status and disability status affect people culturally? **LO2.2**

5. How are sex, gender, and sexuality related to each other? How are they different? **LO2.2**

6. To what extent do various religious traditions or age groups qualify as different cultures? **LO2.2**

7. Why might knowing whether someone is from an individualistic or collectivistic culture be beneficial for professional communication? **LO2.3**

8. Would you characterize your own cultural background as low-context or high-context? How do you know? **LO2.3**

9. How are power distance, uncertainty avoidance, and cultural masculinity/femininity relevant for business communication? **LO2.3**

10. Which social customs are important for your own culture? Why would failing to observe social customs in another culture be problematic? **LO2.4**

11. Do you consider your own culture to be high-contact or low-contact? How does it feel to interact with people whose cultural norms for touch and proximity are highly different from your own? **LO2.4**

12. Define and give an example of each of Edward T. Hall's four spatial zones. **LO2.4**

13. How do you see formality observed in your own cultural practices? **LO2.4**

14. What is the difference between a monochronic and a polychronic culture? **LO2.4**

15. Why is it valuable to understand the gender roles and tolerance for conflict of a culture in which you are doing business? **LO2.4**

16. What does it mean to recognize diversity in an ethical manner? **LO2.5**

17. Why is it important to recognize people both as individuals and as members of cultural groups? **LO2.5**

18. How can we cultivate cultural awareness? **LO2.6**

19. Why is it useful to practice perspective taking? **LO2.6**

20. What is cultural centrism, and why is it problematic? How is cultural centrism reflected in projected cognitive similarity and the outgroup homogeneity effect? **LO2.6**

21. Which stereotypes do you think others hold about you? Of those, which ones describe you inaccurately? Do any describe you accurately? **LO2.6**

SKILL-BUILDING EXERCISES

Interview Professionals from Several Generations (LO2.2)

Interview at least two professionals from at least two generations. Ask them about their views of similarities and differences between professionals of different generations. Consider asking questions such as the following:

- Do you see people of various age groups using technology differently at work? How? (Consider asking specifically about texts, voice mail, email, social media, and so on.)

- What are some differences in word choice between generations?

- Do employees of different generations approach meetings differently? How?

- Do they view business etiquette and formality differently? How?

- What do you think co-workers of different generations can learn from each other? How can they do so?

- What do you see as the main similarities across generations in your field?

Write a short report of your findings. Conclude with three recommendations for working effectively across generations.

Analyze the Cultural Dimensions of a Country (LO2.3)

Choose a country of interest to you. Using Hofstede's cultural dimensions (www.hofstede-insights.com/product/compare-countries), analyze the country in terms of the following:

- Individualism and collectivism
- Power distance
- Cultural masculinity and femininity
- Uncertainty avoidance

In conclusion, describe five communication practices you think may be key when working with members from this country.

Analyze the Etiquette of a Business Culture (LO2.4)

Choose a country of interest to you. Go to a website about differences in etiquette (one such website is: www.ediplomat.com/np/cultural_etiquette/cultural_etiquette.htm). Read all the information about this country's business culture and then do the following:

1. Write about the five most intriguing aspects of the culture.
2. Write about the five norms of etiquette you would observe when interacting with members of this culture.
3. Choose three relevant cultural dimensions (from Hofstede's list) and explain how they probably affect business etiquette in this country.
4. Write five questions about business etiquette you would like to ask a person from the country you chose.

Read News Stories Written by and for Members of Another Culture (LO2.3, LO2.4, LO2.5, LO2.6)

Read three online newspaper articles from a country of interest. Go to these websites:

- www.world-newspapers.com
- www.onlinenewspapers.com
- www.refdesk.com/paper.html

After reading the three articles, write the following for each:

1. *Bibliographic information:* article author, article title, newspaper name, date/edition, pages, web address if available.
2. *Summary:* a short summary of the article.
3. *Cultural lessons:* a paragraph describing one or two aspects of culture illustrated by the article.
4. *Implications for business communication:* a paragraph about how these aspects of the culture matter when conducting business with members of this culture.

Read a Magazine Article about Global Business (LO2.3, LO2.4, LO2.5, LO2.6)

Read a magazine article about global business that includes issues about cross-cultural differences. Consider the following online sources for an article:

- www.bloomberg.com/europe
- www.bloomberg.com/asia
- www.bloomberg.com/middleeast
- www.bloomberg.com/africa
- www.time.com/business
- http://money.cnn.com/news/world

After reading the article, write the following:

1. *Bibliographic information:* article author, article title, magazine name, date/edition, pages, web address if available.
2. *Summary:* a short summary of the article.
3. *Cultural lessons:* a paragraph describing one or two aspects of culture illustrated by the article.
4. *Implications for business communication:* a paragraph about how these aspects of the culture matter when conducting business with members of this culture.

Interview a Professional with International Experience (LO2.3, LO2.4, LO2.5, LO2.6)

Interview someone you know who has worked extensively with members of other cultures. Spend an hour or two asking this person about his/her experiences. Report what this person had to say about five of the following areas:

- Adapting to new etiquette norms
- Using preferred communication channels
- Working in teams
- Conducting meetings
- Resolving differences of opinion
- Negotiating
- Adapting to cultural values and norms
- Adjusting to living in another country (if applicable)
- Resolving conflicts or disagreements
- Persuading others

Interview an International Student (LO2.3, LO2.4, LO2.5, LO2.6)

Interview an international student at your university. Report what the person has to say about his/her home culture. Consider topics such as the following:

About the student's home country:

- Business practices
- Popular entertainment
- Prevalent ideas about U.S. culture
- Changes occurring in the culture

About the student's experience in the United States:

- Challenges in adapting to the food
- Experiences making friendships with Americans
- Experiences working in teams with American students

- Experiences working with American professors
- Observations about American culture

Conclude your report with three recommendations for people doing business with members of your fellow student's culture.

ENDNOTES

1. E.g., Rudick, C. K., Sollitto, M., Claus, C. J., Sanford, A. A., Nainby, K., & Golsan, K. B. (2017). Comparing Hispanic-to-white co-cultural communication at four-year, public Hispanic serving and predominately white institutions. *Communication Reports, 30,* 104–115.

2. United States Census Bureau. (n.d.). Race. Retrieved from https://www.census.gov/topics/population/race.html.

3. See, e.g., Berardesca, E., Mariano, M., & Cameli, N. (2017). Biophysical properties of ethnic skin. In N. A. Vashi & H. I. Maibach (Eds.), *Dermatoanthropology of ethnic skin and hair* (pp. 27–33). New York, NY: Springer; Erbele, I. D., Lin, F. R., & Agrawal, Y. (2016). Racial differences of pigmentation in the human vestibular organs. *Otolaryngology—Head and Neck Surgery, 155,* 479–484.

4. Gillborn, D. (2016). Softly, softly: Genetics, intelligence and the hidden racism of the new geneism. *Journal of Education Policy, 31,* 365–388.

5. ADA National Network. (n.d.). What is the American Disabilities Act (ADA)? Retrieved from https://adata.org/learn-about-ada.

6. Savin-Williams, R. C., Joyner, K., & Rieger, G. (2012). Prevalence and stability of self-reported sexual orientation identity during young adulthood. *Archives of Sexual Behavior, 41,* 103–110; Savin-Williams, R. C., & Vrangalova, Z. (2013). Mostly heterosexual as a distinct sexual orientation group: A systematic review of the empirical evidence. *Developmental Review, 33,* 58–88.

7. Poston, D. L., & Baumle, A. K. (2010). Patterns of asexuality in the United States. *Demographic Research, 23,* 509–530.

8. Norton, A. T., & Herek, G. M. (2013). Heterosexuals' attitudes toward transgender people: Findings from a national probability sample of U.S. adults. *Sex Roles, 68,* 738–753.

9. Pew Research Center/The Pew Forum on Religion & Public Life. (2012, December). *The global and religious landscape: A report on the size and distribution of the world's major religious groups as of 2010.* Washington, DC: Author.

10. Becker, M., Vignoles, V. L., Owe, E., Brown, R., Smith, P. B., Easterbrook, M., . . . Yamakoğlu, N. (2012). Culture and the distinctiveness motive: Constructing identity in individualistic and collectivistic contexts. *Journal of Personality and Social Psychology, 102,* 833–855.

11. Hofstede, G. (2001). *Culture's consequences: Comparing values, behaviors, institutions, and organizations across nations* (2nd ed.). Thousand Oaks, CA: Sage.

12. Kittler, M. G., Rygl, D., & Mackinnon, A. (2011). Beyond culture or beyond control? Reviewing the use of Hall's high-low-context concept. *International Journal of Cross Cultural Management, 11,* 63–82.

13. Stahlin, W. A., Harris, P., & Kinkela, K. (2014, January). Increasing your cultural awareness. *Global Conference on Business & Finance Proceedings, 9,* 177–182.

14. Chua, E. G., & Gudykunst, W. B. (1987). Conflict resolution styles in low- and high-context cultures. *Communication Research Reports, 4,* 32–37.

15. Ramaswami, A., Huang, J.-C., & Dreher, G. (2014). Interaction of gender, mentoring, and power distance on career attainment: A cross-cultural comparison. *Human Relations, 67,* 153–173.

16. Hofstede, G. (2001). *Culture's consequences: Comparing values, behaviors, institutions, and organizations across nations* (2nd ed.). Thousand Oaks, CA: Sage.

17. Yook, E. L., & Albert, R. D. (1998). Perceptions of the appropriateness of negotiation in educational settings: A cross-cultural comparison among Koreans and Americans. *Communication Education, 47,* 18–29.

18. Heereman, J., & Walla, P. (2011). Stress, uncertainty and decision confidence. *Applied Psychophysiology and Biofeedback, 36,* 273–279.

19. Minkov, M., & Hofstede, G. (2014). A replication of Hofstede's uncertainty avoidance dimension across nationally representative samples from Europe. *International Journal of Cross Cultural Management, 14,* 161–171.

20. Hofstede, G., & Hofstede, G. J. (2010). *Cultures and organizations: Software of the mind* (3rd ed.). New York, NY: McGraw-Hill.

21. Andersen, P. A. (2011). Tactile traditions: Cultural differences and similarities in haptic communication. In M. Hertenstein & S. J. Weiss (Eds.), *The handbook of touch: Neuroscience, behavioral, and health perspectives* (pp. 351–372). New York, NY: Springer.

22. Andersen, P. A. (2012). The basis of cultural differences in nonverbal communication. In L. A. Samovar, R. E. Porter, & E. R. McDaniel (Eds.), *Intercultural communication: A reader* (11th ed., pp. 293–312). Boston, MA: Wadsworth.

23. Field, T. (1999). American adolescents touch each other less and are more aggressive toward their peers as compared with French adolescents. *Adolescence, 34,* 753–758.

24. See Matsumoto, D., Frank, M. G., & Hwang, H. S. (Eds.). (2013). *Nonverbal communication: Science and applications.* Thousand Oaks, CA: Sage; Hall, E. T. (1963). System for notation of proxemic behavior. *American Anthropologist, 65,* 1003–1026.

25. E.g., Zhu, Y. (2001). Comparing English and Chinese persuasive strategies in trade fair invitations: A sociocognitive approach. *Document Design, 2,* 2–17.

26. Boone, L. E., & Kurtz, D. L. (2014). *Contemporary business* (16th ed.). New York, NY: Wiley.

27. Knorr, A., Lemper, A., Sell, A., & Wholmuth, K. (2003). *Why did Wal-Mart fail in Germany?* Bremen, Germany: Institute for World Economics and International Management.

28. Hall, E. T., & Hall, M. R. (1990). *Understanding cultural differences: Germans, French, and Americans.* Boston, MA: Intercultural.

29. Burgoon, J. K., Guerrero, L. K., & Floyd, K. (2010). *Nonverbal communication.* Boston, MA: Pearson.

30. Paulson Institute. (2018). About the Paulson Institute. Retrieved from http://www.paulsoninstitute.org/about/about-overview/] Paulson.

31. Wharton Business School. (2016, April 12). Why the U.S. should engage more deeply with China. Retrieved from http://knowledge.wharton.upenn.edu/article/henry-paulson-on-engaging-with-china/.

32. Verluyten, S. P. (2007). *Cultures: From observation to understanding.* Leuven, Belgium: ACCO.

33. Neuliep, J. W. (2009). *Intercultural communication: A contextual approach.* Thousand Oaks, CA: Sage; Dimnik, T., & Felton, S. (2006). Accountant stereotypes in movies distributed in North America in the twentieth century. *Accounting, Organizations and Society, 31,* 129–155.

34. Cardon, P. W. (2010). Using films to learn about the nature of cross-cultural stereotypes in intercultural business communication courses. *Business Communication Quarterly, 73*(2), 150–165.

Learning Objectives

After reading this chapter, you should be able to do the following:

LO3.1 Indicate the most important characteristics of language.

LO3.2 Outline the ways in which language can enhance or diminish credibility.

LO3.3 Practice methods of fostering effective verbal communication.

LO3.4 Explain the primary nonverbal communication channels.

LO3.5 Formulate strategies for improving nonverbal interpretation and expression skills.

CHAPTER 3

Verbal and Nonverbal Messages

Elijah, a customer service specialist in his first full-time position, entered his boss Jeremy's office for his first performance review. He sat down with a mostly expressionless face, but inside he felt terrified as he glanced at Jeremy sitting behind his desk.

"Well, the good news is we're going to keep you!" Jeremy said with a large smile. "Your performance has been above average, but let's talk about some ways you can better hit your targets."

"Okay," replied Elijah.

Jeremy continued, "You take too much time to resolve customer disputes. It's true your customers tend to give you high marks. We want you to keep the customers just as happy, but you need to take less time to do it. Do you have any ideas?"

"Well, I guess I could, um, spend less time in chit-chat. Maybe I could bring in a supervisor sooner on the toughest customers. If I could get my average time to resolution down by two minutes, do you think that would be okay?"

Jeremy leaned back in his chair. "You know, you just need to get as efficient as possible. We always need to focus on doing more with less."

Twenty minutes later, after more of the same back-and-forth conversation, Elijah thanked Jeremy for his advice but left the office feeling dejected and confused. Jeremy closed the door behind him, satisfied that Elijah would improve his time-to-resolution rates.

When we communicate with others, our goal is not simply to exchange words and gestures. It's to create *meaning,* and that is often more complicated than it seems. In the performance review, Elijah and Jeremy took part in the same conversation, yet they left it with quite different perceptions. Jeremy felt satisfied that his objectives had been met, but Elijah felt baffled and down. How could the same conversation have had such different meanings for them?

To understand why, consider that humans use a wide range of symbols, usually simultaneously, to communicate. Some of those symbols are the words we speak and write. Others are behaviors such as facial expressions, gestures, touch, and the way we use time and space, which convey meaning without the use of words. With so many words and behaviors to pay attention to, perhaps it is little wonder that we sometimes misunderstand one another.

The more we know about language and nonverbal communication, the better equipped we are to avoid misunderstandings and accomplish our goals.

LO3.1

Indicate the most important characteristics of language.

How People Use Language

Abraham Lincoln was reportedly fond of asking people, "How many legs does a dog have if you call its tail a leg?" Many replied that if you call a dog's tail a leg, then a dog has five legs. How would you respond? Lincoln's answer was that dogs have only four legs, because calling a tail a leg doesn't make it one.

Some would say the former U.S. president was correct and that simply changing the way we talk about an object doesn't change the nature of the object itself. Others, however, would observe that Lincoln's assessment was incorrect, and that words have only the meanings we choose to assign them. Thus, the term *leg* means what it does only because English language speakers give that meaning to it—so, if we call a tail a leg, it is therefore a leg. Lincoln's riddle illustrates one reason why it is so important for us to understand language: we use words to refer to objects, events, ideas, and other entities in the real world, but most words have only the meanings that we, as the users of a language, give them.

What is language in the first place? **Language** is a structured system of symbols, in the form of words, used for communicating meaning. You can probably think of many objects and behaviors that symbolize meaning. A smile often symbolizes happiness, whereas a red traffic light symbolizes the need to stop your car. You might wave to say "hello" and shrug your shoulders to indicate "I don't know." Although facial expressions, traffic lights, and gestures all symbolize meaning, none qualifies as language. Why? The answer is that language is characterized by the use of a specific type of symbol: words.[1]

Words are the building blocks of language and verbal communication. As we'll see in this chapter, we use them to represent ideas, observations, feelings, and thoughts. Words—whether we speak them, write them, or express them through the use of sign language—can have a profound influence on the way we relate to others. In this section, we'll explore the nature of language and then examine some of its most important connections to credibility.

THE NATURE OF LANGUAGE

When we consider the nature of language, we discover that language is symbolic, is governed by rules, has layers of meaning, and varies in clarity.

Language is symbolic.   When we say language is symbolic, we mean that each word represents a particular object or idea but does not constitute the object or idea itself. For example, the word *computer* represents an electronic device for storing and processing data. The word itself is not the object, though; it merely symbolizes it.

Words are the building blocks of language.

©mindscanner/Shutterstock

One way to understand that language is symbolic is to remember that different languages have different words for the same object. The English word *computer,* for instance, is *tölva* in Icelandic, компютър in Bulgarian, *ríomhaire* in Irish, and *máy vi tính* in Vietnamese. Those are completely different symbols, but they all represent the same concept: a computer.

As technology advances we often acquire new words—and new meanings for older words. The use of computer-mediated communication, for instance, has added new terms to our everyday conversations, such as *blog* and *email,* and generated new meanings for existing words such as *web, crash,* and *tweet.* As digital technology continues to develop, new words will likely be added to our vocabulary to help us communicate about it.

Language is governed by rules.   If language is symbolic and the meanings of words can change over time, then how do we all understand one another? The answer is that every language is governed by rules.

You already know many of the rules that frame your native language. Even if you can't explain them, you usually notice when they're violated. To a native speaker of English, for instance, the statement "I filled the coffeemaker with water" sounds correct, but "I filled water into the coffeemaker" does not. This is why, when you learn a new language, you don't learn just the words; you also learn the rules that make the words work together to convey meaning.

Researchers distinguish among four different types of language rules:

- **Phonological rules** deal with the correct pronunciation of a word, and they vary from language to language. In French, for example, the proper way to pronounce *travail* is "trah-VYE." According to English phonological rules, however, the word looks as though it should be pronounced "trah-VALE."

American Sign Language uses different syntactic rules than spoken English.

©Juan Aunion/Shutterstock

- **Syntactic rules** govern the order of words within phrases and clauses. The question "What is your name?" makes sense to an English speaker because the words are in the proper order. To ask the same question in American Sign Language, we would sign "your – name – what?"
- **Semantic rules** dictate the meaning of individual words. When you hear the word *lawyer*, for instance, you think of an attorney, not a paper mill or an iPad or a Caribbean vacation. It's a semantic rule that connects *lawyer* with *attorney* and not with any of those other meanings.
- **Pragmatic rules** help us interpret statements. Depending on the context and the speaker's tone, you might think someone who says, "Nice to meet you," really is happy to meet you, or you might infer that he or she is just being polite. If the speaker's tone is sarcastic, you might even infer that he or she is *unhappy* to meet you.

Language has layers of meaning. The literal meaning of a word—the way a dictionary defines it—is called its **denotative meaning**. The denotative meaning of *home*, for instance, is "a shelter used as a residence." The word may also remind you of "a place where I feel safe, accepted, and loved" or "a space where I am free to do whatever I want." Those are examples of the word's **connotative meaning**, the ideas or concepts the word suggests in addition to its literal definition.

To illustrate the relationship between words and their denotative and connotative meanings, psychologist Charles Ogden and English professor Ivor Richards developed the *semantic triangle* (see Figure 3.1).[2] In its three corners, the semantic triangle portrays three elements necessary for identifying the meaning in language. The first element is the *symbol*, the word being communicated. In the second corner is the *reference*, the word's connotative meaning. Finally, there's the *referent*, the word's denotative meaning.

If several listeners hear the same word, they might attribute to it the same denotative meaning but different connotative meanings. For instance, if you hear the word *euthanasia*, the word itself is the symbol, and its referent (or denotative meaning) is a medically assisted death. To one listener, the word evokes images of a merciful end to someone's pain and suffering. To another, it evokes images of homicide. Still other listeners think of an unfortunate but sometimes justified component of the death experience.

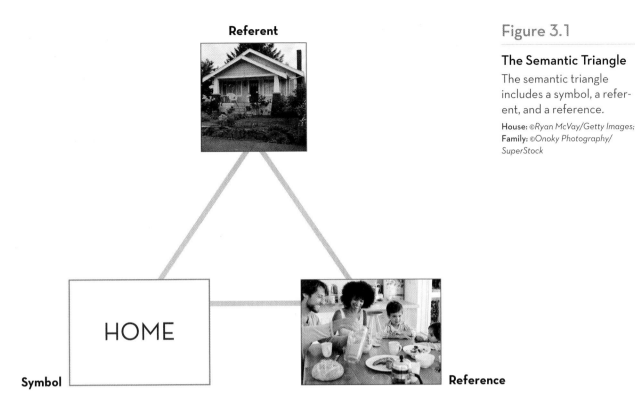

Referent

Symbol

HOME

Reference

Figure 3.1

The Semantic Triangle

The semantic triangle includes a symbol, a referent, and a reference.

House: ©Ryan McVay/Getty Images; **Family:** ©Onoky Photography/ SuperStock

Language varies in clarity. Clara is driving her assistant Josh to an appointment with a client, but only Josh knows the way. As they approach an intersection, they have the following conversation:

Clara: *I need to turn left at this next light, don't I?*

Josh: *Right.*

Which way should Clara turn? Was Josh saying Clara was correct in anticipating a left turn, or was he telling her to turn right instead of left? We don't really know, because Josh has used **ambiguous language** by making a statement that we can interpret to have more than one meaning.

A certain amount of ambiguity is inherent in our language. In fact, according to the *Oxford English Dictionary,* the 500 most frequently used words in the English language have an average of 23 different meanings each. The word *set* has so many different meanings—nearly 200, more than any other English word—that it takes the *Oxford English Dictionary* 60,000 words to define it![3] As a verb, for example, *set* can mean to prepare a table or to mount a precious stone in a ring; as a noun, it can mean a collection of items that belong together or a collection of scenery and furniture used in a play.

One reason language varies in clarity is that some words are more concrete than others. A word that is *concrete* refers to a specific object in the physical world, whereas a word that is *abstract* refers to a broader category or organizing concept of objects. According to English professor Samuel Hayakawa, words can be arrayed along a "ladder of abstraction" that progresses from more abstract to more concrete.[4]

Figure 3.2 gives an example of Hayakawa's ladder of abstraction. At the top is a reference to all living beings, which is a broad, abstract category. As we move down the ladder, the words become more concrete, referencing all animals and then all mammals, all primates, all *Homo sapiens,* and all males before reaching the most concrete reference to a specific individual.

Figure 3.2

Hayakawa's Ladder of Abstraction

Words are arrayed along a continuum of concrete to abstract in Hayakawa's ladder of abstraction.

Ladder: ©Gerville/Getty Images

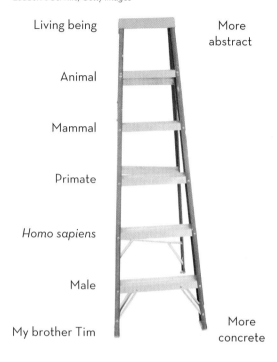

Living being

More abstract

Animal

Mammal

Primate

Homo sapiens

Male

My brother Tim

More concrete

LO3.2

Outline the ways in which language can enhance or diminish credibility.

LANGUAGE AND CREDIBILITY

Our ability to achieve our goals is affected by the credibility our language use gives us. **Credibility** is the extent to which others perceive us to be competent and trustworthy. Some speakers have credibility on certain topics because of their training and expertise. For instance, if you want to know how to make a great latte, you'll probably trust your barista more than your lawyer.

Whatever our training or credentials, however, our words can portray us as confident, trustworthy communicators, or they can make us appear unsure of ourselves. In fact, several specific forms of language can enhance or diminish our credibility.

Clichés diminish credibility. **Clichés** are words or phrases that were novel at one time but have lost their effect due to overuse. When corporate leaders recommend "thinking outside the box" or politicians promise to "make a difference," they may lose credibility with their audiences because those phrases are clichés that can make speakers sound out of touch.

Dialects can enhance or diminish credibility. **Dialects** are language variations shared by people of a certain region or social class. For instance, whether you call a soft drink a "soda," a "pop," a "Coke," or something else depends largely on where you grew up. Different regions of the United States, including New England, the South, the Midwest, and the West Coast, sometimes use different terms to describe the same concept or object, such as a soft drink, and these are differences in their dialects.[5]

Defamation harms credibility. **Defamation** is language that harms a person's reputation or gives that person a negative image, and it comes in two forms. The first, **libel**, refers to defamatory statements made in print or some other fixed medium, such as in a photograph or on a website or blog. The second, **slander**, is a defamatory statement made aloud, within earshot of others. In professional settings, defamatory language can harm not only a person's credibility but also his or her livelihood.

FOCUS ON ETHICS

Defamation When the Accusation Is True

In the example from the text, Erin circulated a false rumor to discourage people from doing business with Jerome's law firm. Because Erin's accusation was made up, it clearly qualified as defamation if it harmed Jerome's reputation. Now suppose Jerome *had* been investigated by his state bar association but had been cleared of all charges. Erin spreads the rumor that he was investigated but doesn't mention that he was cleared. Her accusation is therefore true—it is simply incomplete and potentially misleading. Nonetheless, it has the intended effect of driving business away from Jerome's law firm and toward hers.

CONSIDER THIS: Is it ethical for Erin to point out that Jerome has been investigated, given this is technically true? Is she ethically obligated to mention that he was acquitted of all charges?

Suppose Erin wants to open a law office in a small town where Jerome already operates one. To discourage potential clients from doing business with Jerome's firm, Erin circulates a false rumor that Jerome is being investigated by the state bar association for ethics violations. That statement is defamatory because it harms Jerome's reputation and credibility. When Erin is found to have made this untrue claim, her credibility suffers as well.

Loaded language can affect a person's credibility.   **Loaded language** consists of words with strongly positive or negative connotations. Such words are also called *trigger words,* because their connotations can act like a trigger for listeners by setting off intense emotional responses. Consider, for instance, the ongoing national debate about private ownership of firearms. Those who oppose tighter restrictions typically speak out against "gun control," which seems to imply the government is telling people what to do, whereas advocates of tighter restrictions often speak in favor of "violence prevention," which implies proactive efforts to reduce unnecessary violence. Unsurprisingly, opinion polling shows that speaking in favor of "gun violence prevention" generates significantly more enthusiasm and agreement from listeners than speaking in favor of "gun control."[6]

In summary, language is symbolic, is governed by rules, has layers of meaning, and varies in clarity. Many forms of language are also intimately tied to our credibility. In the next section, we will explore specific strategies for harnessing the power of language and fostering effective verbal communication.

Fostering Effective Verbal Communication

LO3.3
Practice methods of fostering effective verbal communication.

To improve your verbal communication, you can separate opinions from factual claims, speak at an appropriate level for your audience, own your thoughts and feelings, and use powerful—rather than powerless—language.

SEPARATE OPINIONS FROM FACTUAL CLAIMS

A **factual claim** makes an assertion that we can verify with evidence and show to be true or false, such as "I work at an engineering firm." An **opinion** expresses a personal judgment or preference that we could agree or disagree with but that is not true or false in an absolute sense, such as "I work at the best engineering firm ever." Competent communicators know how to keep opinions and factual claims separate in verbal communication, which is challenging when we're dealing with strong opinions on emotionally heated issues.

Suppose you and several co-workers are discussing an upcoming election. Half of you prefer Candidate C and the other half prefer Candidate L. One of your co-workers makes the following statements:

- "Candidate C has more experience in government." That is a factual claim because we can show it to be true or false by comparing the candidates' records.
- "Candidate L is a better choice for our future." That is an opinion because it expresses a value judgment (this candidate is *better*), which we cannot objectively validate.
- "Candidate C is immoral." This is an opinion because the truth of the claim depends on your co-worker's morals. Morals are subjective; therefore, the statement can't be proved true or false in an absolute sense.
- "Candidate L accepted bribes." This is a factual claim because it is possible to examine the evidence to discover whether it is true.

How good are you at distinguishing opinions from factual claims? Check out "The Competent Communicator" box to find out.

Distinguishing Opinions from Factual Claims

The ability to separate opinions from factual claims is an essential skill for effective business communication. How well can you spot the difference? Read each of the following statements. Assuming nothing more than what the statement tells you, indicate whether you think the statement is an opinion or a factual claim by placing a checkmark in the appropriate column.

		Opinion	Factual Claim
1.	New York is a better place to work than Chicago.	_____	_____
2.	Apple Computer Company was founded in 1976.	_____	_____
3.	Emotional appeals are more persuasive than logical appeals.	_____	_____
4.	Capitalism is immoral.	_____	_____
5.	Selling pizza has a higher profit margin than selling hamburgers.	_____	_____
6.	Companies should not do business with corrupt governments.	_____	_____
7.	The government should tax corporations at a higher rate.	_____	_____
8.	Amazon's Jeff Bezos is the world's richest man.	_____	_____
9.	Millennials know more about social media than Gen Xers.	_____	_____
10.	The airline industry should offer more flight options.	_____	_____

Statements 1, 4, 6, 7, and 10 are all opinions. Statements 2, 3, 5, 8, and 9 are all factual claims (whether they are true is a different issue). How well did you do?

As you develop this skill, keep two principles in mind.

- First, *opinions are opinions whether you agree with them or not.* If you believe Prezi is better than PowerPoint, you might be inclined to call that statement a fact. It isn't, though. It is still a statement of opinion because it expresses an evaluation or preference.

- Second, *factual claims are factual claims whether they are true or not.* If you think it's untrue that men talk more than women do in the workplace, you might be inclined to call that statement an opinion, but it isn't. Regardless of whether it is true, it is still a factual claim because it expresses something that can be verified as either true or false by evidence.

Although it's probably more difficult to separate opinions from factual claims when you feel strongly about an issue, that's often when it is most important to do so. Instead of telling others that their positions on sensitive issues are right or wrong, state whether you agree or disagree with them. That language expresses your own position and acknowledges that different—even contradictory—opinions may also exist.

When you feel strongly about an issue, that's when it is often most difficult—yet most important—to separate opinions from factual claims.

©LightFieldStudios/Getty Images

SPEAK AT AN APPROPRIATE LEVEL

Another part of being an effective verbal communicator is knowing how simple or complex your language should be for your audience. A competent instructor, for instance, knows to use simpler language in an introductory course than in an advanced course because students in each class will have different levels of understanding. When you use language that is too complex for your listeners, you are *talking over their heads.*

The opposite error is *talking down* to people, or using language that is inappropriately simple. Speakers often do this by mistake. If a speaker uses overly simple language on purpose, however, listeners feel patronized, disrespected, or even insulted.

Speaking at an Appropriate Level

Select a topic about which you know quite a bit, and imagine you are presenting it to two different groups. Write one paragraph representing how you would explain it to people who also have a sophisticated understanding of it. Write a second paragraph representing how you would explain it to people who know nothing about it. Then, in a blog or journal entry, describe how you used language differently in each paragraph.

OWN YOUR THOUGHTS AND FEELINGS

Suppose that when your marketing manager doesn't understand you, she typically says "You're not being clear," but when you don't understand her, she says "You're not paying attention." By using that language pattern, your manager blames you for misunderstandings but takes no responsibility for her own role in the communication process. The real problem may be that she is not paying attention herself or is not using clearly understandable language.

Good communicators take responsibility for their thoughts and feelings by using I-statements rather than you-statements. An **I-statement** claims ownership of what a communicator is feeling or thinking, whereas a **you-statement** shifts that responsibility to the other person. Instead of saying "You're not being clear," your marketing manager might say "I'm having a hard time understanding you." Rather than saying to a colleague "You're making me mad," you might say "I'm angry right now." Table 3.1 provides examples of you-statements and I-statements.

I-statements don't ignore the problem; instead, they allow the communicator to claim ownership of his or her feelings. That ownership is important, because it acknowledges that the individual controls how he or she thinks and feels. Remember that other people can't control our thoughts and feelings unless we let them. Effective communicators therefore speak in ways that acknowledge responsibility for and ownership of the ways they feel and think.

USE POWERFUL LANGUAGE

Many years of research have established that, on average, people of higher status use more powerful forms of speech than do those of lower status.[7] For instance, people

Table 3.1 Examples of You-Statements and I-Statements

You-Statement	I-Statement
You're making me mad.	I'm mad right now.
You're not listening to me.	I'm feeling ignored.
You don't know what you're doing.	I don't think this task is getting done correctly.
You hurt my feelings.	My feelings are hurt.
You're not making any sense.	I'm having trouble understanding you.

CAREER TIP

Sheryl Sandberg

©Krista Kennell/Shutterstock.com

Sheryl Sandberg has contributed immensely to the rapid growth of technology. She served as a vice president of global sales at Google from 2001 to 2008 and became chief operating officer at Facebook in 2008. Several years ago, she wrote the book *Lean In: Women, Work, and the Will to Lead* to help women succeed in the workplace.

Much of Sandberg's advice in *Lean In* is about helping women avoid using powerless language. Sandberg points out, for instance, that women are more likely to share credit rather than state their individual contributions, give feedback by stating strengths first and then suggesting improvements, avoid verbal opposition, and offer compliments. Generally, women are more likely to be indirect with subordinates and speak less in meetings to avoid sounding bossy. In fact, women who are more assertive and speak up more often are judged more negatively (by both men and other women), whereas men are judged more positively for these same actions.[8]

Of course, you can easily find men who use powerless language more often than women. You can also find many situations in which doing so improves teamwork and collaboration. As you notice how various language patterns—including disclaimers, hedges, tag questions, and other forms of powerless language—contribute to listeners' judgments about power and status, you can begin to alter unfair perceptions of others and contribute to a fairer work environment for yourself and your colleagues.

whose expertise or position give them authority interrupt more frequently, give more directions, and express more opinions.[9] Those behaviors are characteristic of what researchers call **powerful speech**, a style of speaking perceived as active and assertive.[10]

In comparison, according to linguists such as Deborah Tannen and Robin Lakoff, lower-status individuals are more inclined to use **powerless speech**, a style of speaking that is perceived as passive and timid.[11] Powerless speech is characterized by disclaimers, hedges, tag questions, hesitations, intensifiers, and formal address terms.

Disclaimers are statements, usually offered at the beginning of a message, that express a speaker's uncertainty, such as "I could be wrong about this, but. . . ." **Hedges** are words that introduce doubt into a speaker's message, such as "I guess I feel we should. . . ." **Tag questions** at the end of a statement ask for listener agreement, such as "Okay?" and "Don't you agree?" **Hesitations** are terms that introduce pauses into speech, such as "um" and "well." **Intensifiers** are words such as "very" and "really" that heighten the importance of other words. Finally, **formal address terms** indicate the listener is of higher status than the speaker, such as "Sir" and "Ma'am."

Credibility is enhanced when the use of hedges and tag questions is low, and messages that use hedges[12] or tag questions[13] generate less favorable responses than those that do not. Sometimes, however, less-powerful speech may be advisable. In one study, when speaking to a highly interdependent group—one that must work together to accomplish a task—speakers were seen as having higher status when they used powerless speech than when they used powerful speech, perhaps because it implied greater willingness to work with the group.[14]

Language is a powerful tool for communicating in a variety of settings. But much of what we communicate to others is conveyed not with words but with nonverbal behaviors, which we explore next.

Channels of Nonverbal Messages

LO3.4

Explain the primary nonverbal communication channels.

Not all communicating is accomplished with words. In fact, we convey much of the meaning we share in social and professional interaction through our nonverbal behaviors. **Nonverbal communication** consists of those behaviors and characteristics that express meaning without the use of words. As we'll discover in this section, nonverbal communication comes in a variety of forms, or channels. Those channels are the face and eyes, movement and gestures, touch behaviors, vocal behaviors, the use of space and distance, physical appearance, the use of time, and the use of artifacts.

THE FACE AND EYES

It is difficult to overestimate the role of **facial displays**, or facial expressions, in nonverbal communication. Indeed, according to the *principle of facial primacy*, the face communicates more information than any other channel of nonverbal behavior.[15] That communication power is especially evident in three important functions of facial displays: revealing identity, signaling attractiveness, and expressing emotion.

1. *Identity.* First, the face is the most important visual cue humans use to identify one another.[16] This is the reason we don't display photos of our loved ones' hands, legs, or feet—we display pictures of their faces.

2. *Attractiveness.* Second, the face plays a large role in determining attractiveness. Two especially influential properties are *symmetry*, the similarity between the left and right sides of your face, and *proportionality*, the relative size of your facial features. Research shows that faces are judged as more attractive the more symmetrical and proportional they are.[17]

3. *Emotion.* Finally, our facial muscles give us the ability to express hundreds of different emotions— from happiness, surprise, and determination to anger, fear, sadness, and disgust.

According to the principle of facial primacy, the face communicates more information than any other nonverbal channel.

©Plush Studios/Blend Images LLC

Just as facial behavior communicates more than any other nonverbal channel, the eyes communicate more than any other part of the face. Thus we treat **oculesics**, the study of eye behavior, as a separate nonverbal channel. Eye contact plays a role in several important types of interaction, for example. We use it to signal interest in someone and to infer that someone is interesting to us. We use it to gain credibility and to come across as sincere or trustworthy. We use it to persuade others, as well as to signal that we are paying attention and understanding what others are saying. We can even use eye contact when we want to intimidate someone or take a dominant or authoritative position in a group discussion.

Another eye behavior with communicative value is pupil size. The pupil is the dark spot in the center of each of your eyes, which you can see in a mirror. Your pupils control how much light enters your eyes. In darker environments they dilate, or open wider, to take in all available light. In brighter environments they contract, or become smaller, to avoid taking in too much light at once. What communication researchers find interesting, however, is that your pupils also dilate when you look at someone you find physically attractive and when you feel arousal—whether it is a positive response, such as excitement, or a negative response, such as anxiety or fear.

In addition, many people experience pupil dilation when they are attempting to deceive others. Watching the way a person's pupils react can therefore tell us something about the individual's honesty. For suggestions on how to take a people-first approach when you suspect someone is lying, take a look at the "People First" box.

MOVEMENT AND GESTURES

When you're feeling confident, you hold your head high and walk with smooth, consistent strides. When you're nervous, you probably walk more timidly, stealing frequent glances at the people around you. Your *gait,* or the way you walk, is one example of the way your body movements can communicate various messages about you to others, such as "I feel proud" or "I feel scared." The study of movement, including the movement of walking, is called **kinesics**.

Now consider how you use your arms and hands to communicate. Perhaps it's to wave at your co-worker when you see her in the parking lot. Maybe it's to hold up two fingers to signal that you want two soft drinks with lunch. The use of arm and hand movements to communicate is called **gesticulation**. Research indicates that most people—even those who are born blind—use gestures even before they begin speaking.[18]

PEOPLE **FIRST**

When You Think Someone Is Lying

IMAGINE THIS: During your lunch break at work, you stop by the ATM and withdraw $300, which you put in an envelope in your desk drawer at work. At the end of the day, you open the drawer and discover the money is missing.

Now, consider this: You mention the missing cash to your officemate. He says "That's weird" and "I wonder what happened to it," but his voice sounds higher and more stressed than normal, and he appears jittery and nervous. Although his words suggest he knows nothing about the missing money, his nonverbal communication leads you to think otherwise. Before simply accusing him of stealing your money, however, consider the following:

- Just because you perceive that your officemate may be lying to you, that doesn't necessarily mean he is. The average person's ability to detect deception is quite poor, so it is easy to be wrong when trying to spot a lie.

- Even if your officemate is engaging in nonverbal behaviors consistent with deception—such as fidgeting and speaking in a higher-pitched voice—those aren't foolproof cues. He may be feeling anxious or nervous for some other reason entirely.

- If you are convinced your officemate is lying, raise your suspicion with him calmly. Instead of pointing your

finger and saying "You're a liar," ask "Are you telling me the truth?" and explain why you believe he isn't. Give him a chance to admit his deception—and if he does, give him a chance to explain why he did what he did.

- If your officemate is adamant about his innocence, you may be unlikely to resolve the issue in that conversation. Rather than continue to accuse him, say that you hope he is telling you the truth because it will be hard to trust him again if you find out he lied.

Most of us feel very uncomfortable when we believe someone is lying to us, especially if we have a positive relationship with that person. If that happens to you, remember that your suspicions may be unfounded and that it helps to give people the benefit of the doubt. If the other person truly has lied, that may harm your relationship in the short term—but over time, he or she may be able to regain your trust.

THINK ABOUT THIS:

Have you ever been certain someone was lying to you, only to discover later that he or she was telling the truth? If so, what verbal or nonverbal behaviors made you convinced the person was trying to deceive you? Do you find it difficult to forgive people who have lied to you in the past?

TOUCH BEHAVIORS

Even before an infant can see, hear, taste, or smell, his or her skin can respond to stimuli in the environment. Touch is the first sense to develop and the only one without which we cannot survive. No matter how we may cherish our other senses, it is entirely possible to live without being able to see, hear, taste, or smell. Without touch, however, we would constantly be susceptible to wounds, burns, frostbite, and other potentially life-threatening forms of injury.

Touch can play a critical role in conveying several forms of meaning, and **haptics** is the study of the way we use touch to communicate. Touches that convey affection or aggression, and that serve to provide care, may be more important in close personal relationships than in business and professional settings. More commonly observed at work are *ritualistic touches,* meaning forms of touch we enact as part of a custom or tradition. For instance, when North American adults shake hands with each other, the behavior is part of a greeting ritual and does not convey any particular meaning about the relationship (the way that, say, holding hands would). Touch can also express power and control by influencing other people's behavior. The host of a reception may put his hand on a guest's back to guide her in a certain direction, or a police officer may hold a suspect to the ground while applying handcuffs.

Touch can be used to exercise power over another person. In the workplace, this behavior can constitute sexual harassment.

©richyrichimages/Getty Images

VOCAL BEHAVIORS

Perhaps you have a high, breathy voice or a deep, booming one. Maybe you usually talk very fast or loudly. Perhaps you have an accent that indicates to others where you grew up. And there are times when you speak with a particular tone in your voice, to suggest that you are irritated, amused, or bored. Those and other characteristics of the voice are referred to, collectively, as **vocalics**. Vocalics are also called *paralanguage* (meaning "beside language") to indicate that they go along with the words we speak to convey meaning.

Some people are surprised to learn that the voice is a channel of nonverbal communication. After all, we speak with our voices, and spoken communication is verbal, right? That statement is true, but the only verbal aspect of spoken communication is what we say—the words themselves. Everything else about your voice, including the characteristics listed in Table 3.2, is nonverbal.

THE USE OF SPACE AND DISTANCE

When we interact socially, we constantly negotiate our use of space. That negotiating process becomes particularly apparent when our personal space is limited, such as in a crowded elevator or on a full airplane. Many of us find such situations uncomfortable, but why? The scientific study of spatial use, known as **proxemics**, tells us that we each have a preferred amount of personal space we carry like an invisible bubble around us. The amount of personal space we prefer depends on our temperament, the situation we are in, and our level of familiarity with those around us.

Table 3.2 **Characteristics of the Voice**

Characteristic	Definition and Explanation
Pitch	An index of how high or deep your voice sounds. On average, women's voices have a higher pitch than men's voices, and adults have deeper voices than children.
Inflection	Your variation in pitch. Voices that have a lot of inflection are usually described as expressive; those with little inflection are said to be monotone.
Volume	How loud or quiet your voice is. Most of us alter our volume as the social context demands, such as by speaking quietly during a meeting and more loudly at a crowded reception.
Rate	How fast or slowly you speak. The average adult speaks at a rate of approximately 150 words per minute, but we might speak faster when we're excited or slower when we're unsure of ourselves.
Filler words	Nonword sounds such as "umm" and "er" that people often use to fill the silence during pauses. If we have to pause while speaking—such as to remember a piece of information—we sometimes use filler words to indicate that we intend to continue speaking.
Pronunciation	How you combine vowel and consonant sounds to say a word. For example, how would you pronounce the word *victuals*? Although it looks as though it should be pronounced "VIK-TULES," the correct pronunciation is "VITTLES."
Articulation	How clearly you speak. Also known as *enunciation*. People who mumble their words demonstrate poor articulation; those whose words are clear and easily understandable are good articulators.
Accent	A pattern of pronouncing vowel and consonant sounds that is representative of a particular language or geographic area. Everyone speaks with an accent—even you—although we typically notice only accents that are different from our own.
Silence	The absence of sound. We frequently use silence to convey meaning in conversations. For instance, we may become silent when we are unsure how to respond to a question or when we have said as much as we wish to about a topic.

Sources: Tse, A. C.-Y., Wong, A. W.-K., Ma, E. P.-M., Whitehill, T. L., & Masters, R. S. W. (2013). Influence of analogy instruction for pitch variation on perceptual ratings of other speech parameters. *Journal of Speech, Language, and Hearing Research, 56,* 906–912; Wolvin, A., & Coakley, C. (1996). *Listening.* Dubuque, IA: Brown & Benchmark.

Recall from Chapter 2 that people in Western cultures use four different spatial zones, or levels of personal distance, when interacting with one another.[19] *Intimate distance,* which ranges from 0 to 1½ feet, is the zone we willingly occupy only with our closest and most intimate friends, family members, and romantic partners. With other friends and relatives, we typically maintain a *personal distance,* which extends from 1½ to about 4 feet. With customers, casual acquaintances, or others whom we don't know very well, we observe a *social distance.* Social distance ranges from about 4 to 12 feet and indicates that interactions are more formal and less personal. Finally, we typically use *public distance* when giving a speech or performing in front of a large audience, in order to ensure our safety and visibility to the crowd. Public distances are usually 12 to 25 feet or greater, depending on the circumstance.

PHYSICAL APPEARANCE

Society places extraordinary importance on physical appearance. Whether we intend to or not, we make all sorts of judgments about people based on their looks. In particular, we have a strong predisposition to attribute positive qualities to physically attractive people, a tendency that researchers refer to as the **halo effect**. In other words, when a person *looks* good, most of us subconsciously assume he or she *is* good. Indeed, research has shown that we think attractive people are friendlier, more competent, and more socially skilled than less attractive people.[20]

Those perceptions translate into some real advantages for attractiveness. For instance, attractive people have higher self-esteem and more dating experience than less attractive people.[21] We are also nicer to and more cooperative with attractive people and more lenient toward attractive criminal defendants.[22] Physically attractive job candidates are often seen as more desirable than less attractive ones,[23] and more attractive managers earn more money than less attractive managers, whether male or female.[24] Much as we may like to claim otherwise, most of us are strongly influenced by physical appearance when making assessments about other people.

Some aspects of personal appearance—such as your height and eye color—are relatively fixed. Others, however, are easily changeable, and far from being trivial, the attention people pay to their clothing and appearance makes a difference in the way others perceive them, the way they are evaluated socially, and their success in their careers. Even clothing color makes a difference—one study found that female wait staff received higher tips when wearing red than any other color.[25]

THE USE OF TIME

Chronemics is the way we use time. You might not immediately think of time usage as nonverbal behavior, but the way we give (or refuse to give) our time to others can send them important messages about what we value and how we feel about them. When we spend our time looking at our smartphones, for instance, instead of talking to the people we are with, we imply that our phones are more important than those people.

Our use of time also sends messages about power. When you visit someone in a position of power over you, such as your supervisor, it is not uncommon to be kept waiting. However, you would probably consider it bad form to make a more powerful

TECH TIP
Leading Online Conferences

In the working world, it is increasingly common to participate in and even lead online conferences. People in some professions spend 20 hours per week or more interacting with others online. Common online conference platforms include Google Hangouts, Zoom, and Skype. Online conferences require you to pay attention to a variety of verbal messages and nonverbal cues. Consider the following tips:

- *Practice using the technology before the conference.* If you haven't used a platform before, make sure to practice a few times before a consequential online conference.

- *Send participants information about the technology so they can be prepared.* When the first several minutes of an online conference are consumed by participants trying to figure out the technology, the meeting rarely turns out to be productive or engaging.

- *Use your webcam effectively.* Carefully position your webcam so you are speaking directly to your listeners. Maintain direct eye contact as much as possible so that other participants can see your interest level and understand your nonverbal cues. If you're in your home office, dress professionally and make sure you have good lighting and a clean background.

- *Start the call with purpose and take charge.* Many professionals will judge the importance of a call within the first few minutes. Unless you get people interested and engaged quickly, some will tune out and start multitasking.

- *Keep everyone engaged throughout the conference.* As much as possible, make sure everyone takes frequent turns in the conversation. You can lose engagement from others much more quickly in an online setting than in person.

person wait for you. Indeed, the rule seems to be that the time of powerful people is more valuable than the time of less powerful people.

THE USE OF ARTIFACTS

Artifacts are the objects and visual features within our environment that reflect who we are and what we like. One office you routinely visit, for instance, may be plush and opulent, with an oak desk, leather furniture, soft lighting, and expensive paintings on the walls. Another may be plain and basic, featuring a metal desk and chairs, fluorescent lighting, and bare walls. What messages might those different artifacts send you about the occupants of those two offices?

Many corporations have designed their work spaces with open areas and minimal walls to maximize collaboration and visibility among employees. Some people find such spaces intimidating, however—especially those with introverted personalities who prefer quiet over continuous interaction. To serve their needs—and those of employees who simply desire private spaces in which to conduct sensitive business—Michigan-based furniture company Steelcase has begun designing office spaces intended to be cozy and to invite calm self-reflection. The company's designs are based on large-scale workplace surveys in which 95 percent of employees reporting wanting a greater sense of privacy at work.[26]

As the "Tech Tip" box explains, certain nonverbal behaviors, such as eye contact and personal appearance, are especially important to consider when conducting online meetings and conferences. To conclude this chapter, let's look at some useful strategies for using nonverbal communication effectively.

LO3.5

Formulate strategies for improving nonverbal interpretation and expression skills.

Improving Your Nonverbal Communication Skills

In the CBS comedy series *The Big Bang Theory,* Sheldon Cooper is a theoretical physicist at Caltech who has two doctoral degrees and is at the top of his profession but is inept in most social situations. He does not understand the rules of politeness and has little ability to interpret other people's emotions. He maintains a social network, but even his closest friends find him annoying and difficult to be around. In all, Sheldon is a particularly unskilled nonverbal communicator.

He would be well advised to read this section, in which we will explore some ways of improving two particular types of nonverbal communication skills: interpreting nonverbal communication and expressing messages nonverbally.

INTERPRETING NONVERBAL COMMUNICATION

People use nonverbal communication to express many types of messages, including those related to emotions and attitudes, power and dominance, persuasion, and deception. An important skill for communicators, therefore, is the ability to decode, or interpret, the nonverbal behaviors of others. That ability requires two separate but interrelated skills, sensitivity to others' nonverbal messages and the ability to decipher their meaning.

Be sensitive to nonverbal messages. When your co-worker grimaces after learning the team has to work late for the third night in a row, or your client has an excited tone when talking about his children's successes in school, do you notice those nonverbal emotion cues? Sensitivity to nonverbal behaviors is essential because we can't interpret messages unless we first take note of them. Although research indicates that some of us are naturally more nonverbally sensitive than others, it is possible to increase our nonverbal sensitivity through mindful awareness—that is, by tuning in closely to what's happening around us.[27] When you're interacting with someone, try these approaches:

- Pay particular attention to facial expressions. Remember that the face communicates more emotion than all other nonverbal channels.
- Notice tone of voice and body movements. These are particularly relevant for signaling dominance and deception.

Decipher the meaning of nonverbal messages. If you notice a young man smiling as he interacts with another person, it might mean he's happy. Or he might be persuading a customer to make a purchase, comforting a peer who has just shared bad news, or flirting.[28] If you notice him speaking loudly, it might mean he's excited, but he could also be angry, surprised, or talking with someone who has a hearing disability.

Paying attention to body movement can aid your interpretation of others' nonverbal behaviors.

©Hero Images/Getty Images

The second interpretive skill, therefore, is accurately deciphering the meaning of the nonverbal behaviors others enact. This means taking the behavior to mean what the sender intended.[29] Suppose that while you are describing your grandmother's failing health, your co-worker Vanessa squeezes your hand to convey her support. If you take her behavior as a gesture of support, you have accurately deciphered her nonverbal message. If you take it to mean she's trying to persuade you or is interested in you romantically, however, you have deciphered her message inaccurately.

To improve your skill at deciphering nonverbal messages, try the following strategies:

- Consider both the social situation and the nonverbal behaviors the sender is enacting. If you notice a man in your

Charades is a game that can improve both your interpretation and expression skills.

©Image Source/Getty Images

office crying, your first instinct might be to conclude he is sad. Perhaps you also notice, however, that he is surrounded by smiling people who are hugging him and patting him on the back. You even hear him laugh, although tears are running down his face. Armed with these additional pieces of information, you might take his crying to mean that he is happy or relieved rather than sad.

- Keep in mind that cultural differences sometimes influence the meaning of a nonverbal message—particularly for gestures and eye behaviors. Using the thumbs-up gesture or failing to make eye contact while talking with someone can have different meanings in different cultures. The more you learn about cultural variation in nonverbal behavior, the more accurately you will be able to decipher it.

- When you are unsure how accurately you've deciphered someone's nonverbal message, ask. Let's say you're relating the details of a new product to a client and her facial expression suggests confusion. Instead of assuming you've deciphered her expression accurately, you might ask her directly, "Did my description make sense?" If she replies that she found it confusing, you can explain the product again, using simpler language. If she instead replies that she is developing a headache, you know the expression you deciphered as confusion was actually expressing discomfort. Asking is a way to check your interpretation of someone's nonverbal message and make sure you have deciphered it correctly.

As you practice your sensitivity and deciphering skills, you should be able to improve your ability to interpret the meaning of nonverbal behaviors.

EXPRESSING NONVERBAL MESSAGES

Some of us are good at interpreting the nonverbal behaviors of others but not particularly good at expressing ourselves nonverbally. Yet as we have seen, we communicate more information nonverbally than verbally. If you're skilled at expressing nonverbal messages, you'll therefore be able to communicate with others more effectively and more efficiently than someone who is less skilled.

Some people are naturally more expressive, charismatic, and outgoing than others,[30] but we all can improve our ability to express nonverbal messages. To heighten yours, try the following ideas:

- Spend time with highly expressive people. Some researchers have suggested that we can learn how to become more nonverbally expressive by being around extroverted and charismatic people.[31] We've also learned that highly expressive people are attracted to certain professions, which include teaching and lecturing, acting and singing, politics, sales, diplomacy, customer service, counseling and therapy, and religious ministry.[32] Each of these requires an ability to communicate clearly and competently with others, which is served by being nonverbally expressive.

- Take part in games and activities that exercise your nonverbal expression skills. A good example is charades, the game in which you act out a word or phrase without speaking while members of your team try to guess what it is. Another example is role playing, in which you realistically act out the roles of characters in a specific but hypothetical situation.

CHAPTER WRAP-UP

By understanding, evaluating, and adjusting verbal and nonverbal messages, we improve our professional relationships. Here's a quick review of the chapter.

LO3.1 Indicate the most important characteristics of language.

- Language is symbolic.
- Language is governed by rules.
- Language has layers of meaning.
- Language varies in clarity.
- Language influences credibility.

LO3.2 Outline the ways in which language can enhance or diminish credibility.

- Clichés are words or phrases that were novel at one time but have lost their effect due to overuse.
- Dialects are language variations shared by people of a certain region or social class.
- Defamation is language that harms a person's reputation or gives that person a negative image.
- Loaded language comprises words with strongly positive or negative connotations.

LO3.3 Practice methods of fostering effective verbal communication.

- Separate opinions from factual claims.
- Speak at an appropriate level.
- Own your thoughts and feelings.
- Use powerful language appropriately.

LO3.4 Explain the primary nonverbal communication channels.

- The face and eyes
- Movement and gestures
- Touch behaviors
- Vocal behaviors
- The use of space and distance
- Physical appearance
- The use of time
- The use of artifacts

LO3.5 Formulate strategies for improving nonverbal interpretation and expression skills.

- Interpreting nonverbal communication benefits from being sensitive to nonverbal messages and practicing deciphering their meaning.
- Expressing nonverbal messages benefits from spending time with highly expressive people and taking part in games and activities that exercise your expression skills.

A LOOK BACK

Now, let's return to the opening scenario. Elijah is a relatively new customer service specialist who feels dejected after talking to his boss Jeremy. Jeremy, already in a position of power, uses verbal and nonverbal language to emphasize his power. He is assertive in his comments, jokes about Elijah keeping his position (implying his own authority to fire), and nonverbally separates himself from Elijah by sitting behind a desk. Elijah contributes to the power difference because he uses a lot of powerless language, including hedges ("I guess . . ."), hesitations ("um"), and tag questions ("is that okay?").

Even though Jeremy asserts his power, he loses credibility in Elijah's eyes. He gives unclear guidance, equivocates (doesn't respond directly to Elijah's specific question about reducing time-to-resolution rates by two minutes), uses loaded language ("hitting a target" is a phrase that is positive to some people as goal-driven language but negative to others who associate it with impersonal approaches to business), and relies on empty clichés ("we need to do more with less"). It's likely that Elijah feels dejected because he now believes his professional opportunities are even more dependent on Jeremy, yet Jeremy does not provide credible mentorship or support.

KEY TERMS

ambiguous language 55	gesticulation 62	opinion 57
artifacts 66	halo effect 64	phonological rules 53
chronemics 65	haptics 63	powerful speech 60
clichés 56	hedges 60	powerless speech 60
connotative meaning 54	hesitations 60	pragmatic rules 54
credibility 56	I-statement 59	proxemics 63
defamation 56	intensifiers 60	semantic rules 54
denotative meaning 54	kinesics 62	slander 56
dialects 56	language 52	syntactic rules 54
disclaimers 60	libel 56	tag questions 60
facial displays 61	loaded language 57	vocalics 63
factual claim 57	nonverbal communication 61	you-statement 59
formal address terms 60	oculesics 61	

CHAPTER REVIEW QUESTIONS

1. What is the defining characteristic of language? If waving to say "hello" and shrugging your shoulders to indicate "I don't know" symbolize meaning, why don't these behaviors qualify as language? LO3.1

2. What does it mean to say that language is symbolic? LO3.1

3. Define and give examples of phonological, syntactic, semantic, and pragmatic rules for language. LO3.1

4. How is a word's denotative meaning different from its connotative meaning? LO3.1

5. Ogden and Richards's semantic triangle contains three elements: the symbol, the reference, and the referent. What does each element represent? LO3.1

6. In what ways can ambiguous language be problematic? LO3.1

7. What does it mean to say that some words are more concrete than others? LO3.1

8. How are clichés, dialects, defamation, and loaded language tied to credibility? LO3.2

9. How is libel different from slander? LO3.2

10. What is the difference between an opinion and a factual claim? Why is it necessary to distinguish between them? LO3.3

11. How can you avoid "talking down" to people? How can you avoid "talking over their heads"? LO3.3

12. Why is using I-statements more effective than using you-statements? LO3.3

13. Which forms of language are characterized as powerless? **LO3.3**

14. Under what circumstances is using powerless speech advantageous? **LO3.3**

15. What makes communication nonverbal? **LO3.4**

16. What does the principle of facial primacy tell us about nonverbal behavior? **LO3.4**

17. How are kinesics and gesticulation different from each other? **LO3.4**

18. What makes a touch ritualistic? **LO3.4**

19. What are the primary elements of vocalics? **LO3.4**

20. What is the halo effect, and how does it influence communication? **LO3.4**

21. Chronemics is associated with two particular kinds of messages; identify and give an example of each. **LO3.4**

22. What do we communicate through our use of artifacts? **LO3.4**

23. In what ways can people improve their ability to interpret nonverbal messages? **LO3.5**

24. How can people improve their ability to express nonverbal messages? **LO3.5**

SKILL-BUILDING EXERCISES

That Was So Yesterday: Identifying Clichés (LO3.2)

In a small group, brainstorm a list of five to ten phrases you view as clichés. Identify the intended meaning of each, and discuss why it has become worn-out or lost its meaning. When you hear these phrases today, what impression do they give you of the speaker? Finally, consider a better, more contemporary way to express the meaning of each cliché.

Violating Language Rules (LO3.3)

Alone or as part of a team, collect magazine and newspaper ads and articles, online ads, and/or photos of billboards that violate one or more of the four language rules (phonological, syntactic, semantic, and pragmatic). For each, identify the violation and the way it affected the meaning of the message. Did you find any examples in which violating the rule actually makes the meaning clearer than observing it? Why or why not?

Nonverbal Observations and Assumptions (LO3.5)

Pair with a student you do not know well. Without speaking to each other, write down ten observations and ten corresponding assumptions about each other (she has a ring on her left ring finger = she must be married). After you have both finished, exchange your lists and read the observations and assumptions that were made about you. Are they accurate? Why or why not? Discuss what you each learned about the way you present yourself nonverbally.

Practicing Nonverbal Encoding Skills (LO3.5)

Ask your instructor to generate a list of situations in which employees commonly find themselves, such as being late for a meeting, stressed about a deadline, nervous before a big presentation, or disappointed at losing a bid. With your fellow students, select one situation and act it out nonverbally for the rest of the class, as if you were playing charades. Ask the other students to identify the situation, and then to name the specific nonverbal behaviors you used that helped them arrive at their impression.

Denotative vs. Connotative Meanings (LO3.1, LO3.2)

Ask your instructor to identify ten common words from the working world (such as *desk, finance, boss, market*). Write down the first meaning for each that comes to mind. After all students in the class have completed their definitions, compare your lists and separate denotative and connotative meanings. Afterward, discuss any differences you saw in the connotations these words had for you.

Nonverbal Culture Shock (LO3.4, LO3.5)

Assemble in a small group and ask each student to share an experience in which the norms or expectations for nonverbal communication were unfamiliar. Perhaps it was on a job site where people were using unfamiliar gestures to communicate, or at a gathering where silence was expected. It may even have been while traveling in a foreign country and trying to understand a different culture's way of communicating. Did the unfamiliarity lead to misunderstanding? How did each student adapt?

You and I: Approaching Conflict with You-Statements and I-Statements (LO3.2, LO3.3)

Gather in a small group and have your instructor assign you a scenario about a conflict (for instance, your supervisor gave you an unfair evaluation; or, you left your lunch in the office refrigerator and your co-worker ate it). Act out a conversation in which you attempt to address the conflict using you-statements; then act out the conversation again using I-statements. As a group, discuss how the two approaches might have different effects on conflict resolution.

ENDNOTES

1. Deutscher, G. (2006). *The unfolding of language: An evolutionary tour of mankind's greatest invention.* New York, NY: Henry Holt & Co.

2. Ogden, C. K., & Richards, I. A. (1927). *The meaning of meaning: A study of the influence of language upon thought and of the science of symbolism* (2nd ed.). Orlando, FL: Harcourt Brace.

3. Set. (2018). In *Oxford English Dictionary*. Retrieved March 8, 2018, from https://en.oxforddictionaries.com/definition/set.

4. See Leviton, L. C. (2015). Evaluation practice and theory: Up and down that ladder of abstraction. *American Journal of Evaluation, 36,* 238–242; see also Hayakawa, S. I., & Hayakawa, A. R. (1991). *Language and thought in action.* San Diego, CA: Harcourt.

5. West, E. (2018, January 14). 25 words that have different meanings across the United States. *Lifehack.* Retrieved March 8, 2018, from https://www.lifehack.org/articles/lifestyle/25-words-that-have-different-meanings-across-the-united-states.html.

6. Shapiro, A. (2013, February 26). Loaded words: How language shapes the gun debate. *It's All Politics: Political News from NPR.* Retrieved June 20, 2017, from http://www.npr.org/sections/itsallpolitics/2013/02/26/172882077/loaded-words-how-language-shapes-the-gun-debate.

7. Kalbfleisch, P. J., & Herold, A. L. (2006). Sex, power, and communication. In K. Dindia & D. J. Canary (Eds.), *Sex differences and similarities in communication* (2nd ed., pp. 299–313). Mahwah, NJ: Lawrence Erlbaum Associates.

8. Ignatius, A. (2013, April). Now is our time. *Harvard Business Review,* 84–88; Sandberg, S. (2013). *Lean in: Women, work, and the will to lead.* New York, NY: Knopf; Sandberg, S., & Grant, A. (2015, January 12). Speaking while female. *The New York Times,* https://www.nytimes.com/2015/01/11/opinion/sunday/speaking-while-female.html.

9. Mehl, M., & Pennebaker, J. (2002, January). *Mapping students' natural language use in everyday conversations.* Paper presented at the third annual meeting of the Society for Personality and Social Psychology, Savannah, GA.

10. Hosman, L. (2015). Powerful and powerless speech styles and their relationship to perceived dominance and control. In R. Schulze & H. Pishwa (Eds.), *The exercise of power in communication: Devices, reception and reaction* (pp. 221–232). London, England: Palgrave Macmillan.

11. Tannen, D. (1990). *You just don't understand: Women and men in conversation.* New York, NY: HarperCollins; Lakoff, R. (1975). *Language and woman's place.* New York, NY: Harper & Row.

12. Durik, A. M., Britt, M. A., Reynolds, R., & Storey, J. (2008). The effects of hedges in persuasive arguments: A nuanced analysis of language. *Journal of Language and Social Psychology, 27,* 217–234.

13. Hosman, L. A., & Siltanen, S. A. (2011). Hedges, tag questions, message processing, and persuasion. *Journal of Language and Social Psychology, 30,* 341–349.

14. Fragale, A. R. (2006). The power of powerless speech: The effects of speech style and task interdependence on status conferral. *Organizational Behavior and Human Decision Processes, 101,* 243–261.

15. Knapp, M. L., Hall, J. A., & Horgan, T. G. (2013). *Nonverbal communication in human interaction* (8th ed.). Boston, MA: Cengage.

16. Faerber, S., Kaufmann, J., & Schweinberger, S. (2015). Early temporal negativity is sensitive to perceived (rather than physical) facial identity. *Neuropsychologia, 75,* 132–142.

17. Fink, B., Neave, N., Manning, J. T., & Grammer, K. (2006). Facial symmetry and judgments of attractiveness, health and personality. *Personality and Individual Differences, 41,* 491–499.

18. Iverson, J. M., Tencer, H. L., Lany, J., & Goldin-Meadow, S. (2000). The relation between gesture and speech in congenitally blind and sighted language-learners. *Journal of Nonverbal Behavior, 24,* 105–130.

19. Matsumoto, D., Frank, M. G., & Hwang, H. S. (Eds.). (2013). *Nonverbal communication: Science and applications.* Thousand Oaks, CA: Sage.

20. Zebrowitz, L. A., & Franklin, R. G. (2014). The attractiveness halo effect and the babyface stereotype in older and younger adults: Similarities, own-age accentuation, and older adult positivity effects. *Experimental Aging Research, 40,* 375–393.

21. Bale, C., & Archer, J. (2013). Self-perceived attractiveness, romantic desirability and self-esteem: A mating sociometer perspective. *Evolutionary Psychology, 11,* 68–84.

22. Desantts, A., & Kayson, W. A. (1997). Defendants' characteristics of attractiveness, race, and sex and sentencing decisions. *Psychological Reports, 81,* 679–683.

23. Watkins, L. M., & Johnston, L. (2000). Screening job applicants: The impact of physical attractiveness and application quality. *International Journal of Selection and Assessment, 8,* 76–84.

24. Judge, T. A., Hurst, C., & Simon, L. S. (2009). Does it pay to be smart, attractive, or confident (or all three)? Relationships among general mental ability, physical attractiveness, core self-evaluations, and income. *Journal of Applied Psychology, 94,* 742–755.

25. Guéguen, N., & Jacob, C. (2014). Clothing color and tipping: Gentlemen patrons give more tips to waitresses in red clothes. *Journal of Hospitality & Tourism Research, 38,* 275–280.

26. Zeiger, M. (2014, June 3). Steelcase and Susan Cain design offices for introverts. Retrieved July 14, 2017, from http://www.fastcodesign.com/3031341/steelcase-and-susan-cain-design-offices-for-introverts.

27. Bänzinger, T., Scherer, K. R., Hall, J. A., & Rosenthal, R. (2011). Introducing the MiniPONS: A short multichannel version of the Profile of Nonverbal Sensitivity (PONS). *Journal of Nonverbal Behavior, 35,* 189–204.

28. See, e.g., Bartlett, M. S., Littlewort, G. C., Frank, M. G., & Lee, K. (2014). Automatic decoding of facial movements reveals deceptive pain expressions. *Current Biology, 24,* 738–743.

29. Riggio, R. E. (2005). The Social Skills Inventory (SSI): Measuring nonverbal and social skills. In V. Manusov (Ed.), *The sourcebook of nonverbal measures: Going beyond words* (pp. 25–34). Mahwah, NJ: Lawrence Erlbaum Associates.

30. Ilies, R., Curşeu, P. L., Dimotakis, N., & Spitzmuller, M. (2013). Leaders' emotional expressiveness and their behavioural and relational authenticity: Effects on followers. *European Journal of Work and Organizational Psychology, 22,* 4–14.

31. Kramer, A. D. I., Guillory, J. E., & Hancock, J. T. (2014). Experimental evidence of massive-scale emotional contagion through social networks. *Proceedings of the National Academy of Sciences, 111,* 8788–8790.

32. Liu, M. W., & Guan, Y. (2014). Consumer compliance in face-to-face interactions: The role of sensitivity and expressiveness. *Advances in Consumer Research, 42,* 584–585.

Learning Objectives

After reading this chapter, you should be able to do the following:

LO4.1   Justify the importance of listening effectively.

LO4.2   Summarize the stages in the HURIER model of listening.

LO4.3   Differentiate and illustrate informational listening, critical listening, and empathic listening.

LO4.4   Analyze barriers to effective listening in social interactions.

LO4.5   Implement strategies for improving informational, critical, and empathic listening skills.

CHAPTER 4

Listening and Learning

Janice and Antoine run a solar panel installation business together. This morning they received an email from Freddy, a customer who had panels installed nearly two years ago. Now Freddy is demanding free repair of "improperly installed panels." Janice and Antoine discussed what to do.

"This is a ridiculous claim. I'll reply and tell him we can examine the panels and fix any problems at our regular fee," said Janice. Janice was thinking about the fact the installation occurred about two years ago, yet the warranty was only for one year.

"But we should be careful about our response," said Antoine. "Freddy probably feels like we can do a quick fix and that it would be easy for us to do without cost."

"It doesn't matter how he feels. The warranty doesn't cover this. I'll email him and let him know our standard fees."

"Well, we want to find ways to show goodwill and make sure he's happy with our services."

Janice and Antoine continue to disagree. They may not realize their approaches to listening are making matters worse.

Like Janice and Antoine, many of us believe we're better at listening than we actually are. Anyone can listen, but the ability to listen *well* is less common. In the professional world, however, effective listening can make the difference between success and failure in a wide range of contexts. Therefore, it pays to attend to your listening ability and to sharpen your listening skills.

LO4.1

Justify the importance of listening effectively.

Effective Listening and Learning

You can take classes to become a better speaker or a better writer, but few schools offer courses on improving listening skills. Yet if you are like most people, you spend much more time listening than you do speaking, writing, or engaging in other communicative behaviors. That's one reason why listening effectively is such a valuable skill.

WHAT IS LISTENING?

Listening is one of the most important skills in business and professional communication, yet many people find effective listening hard to define. When someone says, "You're not listening to me!" what exactly does he or she mean?

We can think of **listening** as the active process of making meaning from another person's spoken message.[1] Several details about that definition are important to note. First, listening isn't just about **hearing**, which is the sensory process of receiving and perceiving sounds—listening is about creating meaning from what you hear. It is about *attending* to someone's words, or paying attention well enough to understand what that person is trying to communicate. Second, listening is an active process. That means it isn't automatic; you have to *make* yourself listen to someone.

Even if people are hearing the same message, they may construct different meanings for it, an indicator that they are listening differently. For instance, you might listen to your colleague's description of his new officemate and conclude that he finds her competent and likable. After listening to the same description, however, your supervisor might conclude that your colleague feels threatened by his officemate's intelligence and self-confidence. In this instance, you and your supervisor heard the same description, but you each listened to it differently.

Finally, listening deals with spoken messages. We certainly pay attention to written messages, as well as to nonverbal messages, which influence our interpretation of people's behaviors. But we can engage in listening only when someone is speaking.

We have different listening styles. Researchers have identified four distinct listening styles, each consisting of a different set of attitudes and beliefs about listening.[2] People can use any or all of them, depending on the situation; however, most of us have one primary style that we use most often. Here is a brief overview of each style.

- **People-oriented style**, as the name suggests, is attuned to finding common interests with others and discerning their emotions and interests. For instance, when Palik listens to his customers, he tries to understand what they are thinking and feeling so he can relate to them effectively.
- **Action-oriented style** looks for organization and precision. An action-oriented listener likes neat, concise, error-free presentations. For example, Monica approves her interns filling her in on the week's activities in a clear, straightforward way and gets frustrated when she can't understand them.
- **Content-oriented style** hones in on intellectual challenges. Someone with a content-oriented style likes to attend to details and think things through. Ben really enjoys listening to political commentators, for instance, because they make him think about his own social and political views.
- **Time-oriented style** emphasizes efficiency. Someone with a time-oriented style prefers conversations that are quick and to the point. As an emergency room

physician, for example, Emma relies on quick, short reports of a patient's condition from paramedics and nurses, and she gets impatient when they take more time than is necessary.

Each style has strengths and weaknesses, so none is inherently better than the others. If you are primarily a people-oriented listener, for example, you're likely to get to know other people well, but you might not be able to work as efficiently as a time-oriented listener. Action-oriented listeners might do best in majors that emphasize clarity and precision, such as engineering and computer science, whereas content-oriented listeners might prefer majors with greater ambiguity and room for debate, such as art and political science.

Regardless of your primary listening style, research demonstrates that we adopt different styles for different situations. For instance, you might prefer a time-oriented style when you're in a rush but a people-oriented style when you're visiting loved ones. Similarly, you might adopt a content-oriented style when listening to your professor give a lecture but an action-oriented style when listening to the evening news.[3] What's your primary listening style? Check out "The Competent Communicator" box to find out.

Listen effectively.   If you are listening to someone speak, that doesn't automatically mean you are listening *effectively*. Effective listening requires listening with the conscious and explicit goal of understanding what the speaker intends to communicate. You might never know for certain whether you have understood a speaker's meaning *exactly* as he or she intended. If you're listening with the goal of understanding as best you can, however, then you're listening effectively.

As we will consider in this chapter, several barriers make effective listening challenging, and different situations call for different types of listening. Understanding those dimensions of listening can help each of us improve our ability to listen effectively.

THE IMPORTANCE OF LISTENING EFFECTIVELY

How much of your day do you think you spend listening? In one study, researchers Richard Emanuel and colleagues found that college students spent more time listening than doing any other communication activity. As depicted in Figure 4.1, participants spent 54 percent of their waking hours listening.[4] In contrast, they spent only 17 percent of their time reading, 16 percent speaking, and 11 percent writing. Other studies have found similar results, at least with college students, suggesting that most of us spend a similar percentage of our communication time listening.[5]

Suppose your employees don't listen when you tell them the alarm they will soon hear signals a fire drill, not a real fire. Some might panic at the sound of the alarm, and some might injure themselves as they rush frantically from their workspaces. Now suppose your manager doesn't listen to the staff's warnings about problems with the company's equipment. As a result, a critical production line breaks down, stalling operations for a week.

These examples illustrate how consequential effective listening can be at work. After analyzing 625 business and professional publications to see which communication skills businesses value most, researchers found that listening was among the most important.[6] And a recent survey of employers showed that listening skills were the second most important skill from a list of 20 skills. Listening skills were considered more important than presentation skills, quantitative analysis, innovation and creativity, technology skills, and written communication, among others.[7] In other research, listening also topped the list of the most important communication skills in families and personal relationships.[8] Being a good listener is vital to just about every social and personal bond we have.[9]

Yet many of us overestimate our listening abilities. In one study, employees rated their managers' listening skills, and managers rated their own listening skills. Roughly 94 percent of corporate managers who were identified as poor listeners by employees rated themselves as "good" or "very good" at listening, and not a single one rated him- or herself as "poor" or "very poor."[10] There appears to be very little association, in other words, between how good *we* think we are at listening and how good *others* think we are.[11]

Exactly what do we *do* when we're listening, however? We'll explore that question in the next section.

Stages and Styles of Effective Listening

Until now, we've been talking about listening as though it were a single activity. In truth, listening *effectively* has several stages, all equally important.

STAGES OF EFFECTIVE LISTENING

Judi Brownell, an expert on listening, developed the *HURIER model* to describe the six stages of effective listening, outlined in Table 4.1.[12] The stages, from whose first letters the model is named, are hearing, understanding, remembering, interpreting, evaluating, and responding. We don't necessarily have to enact those stages in order; sometimes listening effectively requires us to go back and forth among them. Nonetheless, when we listen effectively, those are the behaviors we adopt. Let's look at each.

Hearing is physically perceiving sound. Hearing, the physical process of perceiving sound, is where listening begins. Yet, as we've seen, we can certainly hear someone without listening to that person. Hearing without listening is common

Figure 4.1

Percentages of Time Spent Communicating in Various Ways

©Kristy-Anne Glubish/DesignPics

Source: Emanuel, R., Adams, J., Baker, K., Daufin, E. K., Ellington, C., Fitts, E., & Okeowo, D. (2008). How college students spend their time communicating. *International Journal of Listening, 22,* 13–28.

LO4.2

Summarize the stages in the HURIER model of listening.

Table 4.1 HURIER Model of Effective Listening

Brownell's model suggests that effective listening has six elements, represented by the acronym HURIER.

Hearing	Physically perceiving sound
Understanding	Comprehending the words we have heard
Remembering	Storing ideas in memory
Interpreting	Assigning meaning to what we have heard
Evaluating	Judging the speaker's believability and intentions
Responding	Indicating that we are listening

when we're tired or uninterested in what a person is saying, or when we're hearing multiple voices at once, as in a crowded restaurant. However, we can't really listen effectively to someone unless we can first hear the person.

The sensory task of hearing may be difficult for individuals with hearing impairments. Some read lips, and others use sign language to communicate. For individuals without hearing problems, though, hearing is the first step in effective listening.

Understanding is comprehending the words we have heard.   It's not enough simply to hear what someone is saying—you also have to understand it. That means comprehending the meanings of the words and phrases.[13] If someone is speaking in a language you don't understand, you might be able to hear, but you won't be able to listen effectively. The same is true when you hear technical language or jargon with which you're unfamiliar: even if the speaker is speaking your language, you can't effectively listen if you do not understand the words. If you're uncertain whether you understand, the most effective course of action is usually to ask the person questions so you can check your understanding.

Remembering is storing ideas in memory.   The third stage of the HURIER model of effective listening is remembering, or being able to store something in your memory and retrieve it when needed.[14] Remembering what you hear is critical for business and professional communication, not least because it can help you avoid awkward situations. For instance, you might have had the embarrassing experience of running into a co-worker or customer whose name you can't remember.

As a student, you probably test your memory skills on an ongoing basis. Research shows that most people can recall a mere 25 percent of what they hear—and even then, they remember only about 20 percent of that fraction accurately.[15] The average person is not especially good at remembering. Fortunately, short-term memory is a skill you can practice and improve.

Mnemonics are tricks that can aid our short- and long-term memory. They come in several forms. If you've ever studied music, for instance, perhaps you learned the lines of the treble staff—EGBDF—by memorizing the phrase, "Every good boy does fine." You might also develop rhymes to help you remember certain rules, such as the spelling convention "*I* before *E*, except after *C*." Another mnemonic device treats an acronym as a word, as Brownell's effective listening model does by inventing the word *HURIER*. Research suggests that using mnemonic devices can significantly enhance our memory of what we hear.[16]

Yet another effective way to remember what you hear is to take notes. Most colleagues feel honored and respected when you take notes during your conversations and meetings. Make sure to take high-level notes, focusing on main themes, questions you need to answer, assumptions you want to test, and action items.[17]

Taking notes is an important way to remember what you hear from others.

©Anton Gvozdikov/123RF

Interpreting is assigning meaning to what we have heard.   Besides hearing, understanding, and remembering, an effective listener must interpret the information he or she receives. *Interpretation* is the process of assigning meaning to information that has been selected for attention and organized. This process has two parts. The first part is paying attention to all the speaker's verbal and nonverbal behaviors so you can assign meaning to the person's message. Suppose your associate Maya says, "This is pretty good work!" Based on her facial expressions and tone of voice, you might interpret her message as sincere—meaning that Maya thinks the work *is* good—or as sarcastic—meaning she thinks the work is subpar. Those are very different interpretations of Maya's message, even though her words are the same.

The second part of interpreting is signaling your interpretation of the message to the speaker. If you interpret Maya's statement as sincere, you might smile and say appreciate her recognition of your work. If you interpret it as sarcastic, however, you might laugh or respond with an excuse. Signaling, in other words, not only lets the speaker know we're following along with the message; it also allows us to check our interpretation.

Evaluating is judging the speaker's believability and intentions. The next step in the HURIER process is assessing the value of the information we've received, a process called *evaluating.* Several things happen at this stage. First, you're judging whether the speaker's statements are accurate and true. You might base those judgments on what you already know, or you might seek out information that verifies or challenges their accuracy. Second, you're separating factual claims from opinions. As explained in Chapter 3, opinions assert *what should be* whereas factual claims assert *what is,* and each statement calls for a different type of response. Finally, you're considering the speaker's words in the context of other information you have from that speaker, such as his or her actions or previous statements. For instance, the speaker might be making a different claim today than he or she made last week, which would call the accuracy of the claim into question. All those processes help you to be an active, engaged listener rather than a passive recipient of information.

Responding is indicating that we are listening. The last stage of effective listening is responding, or indicating to a speaker that we are listening. We sometimes refer to this process as "giving feedback." We respond both verbally and nonverbally using a variety of strategies.

Below are seven types of listening responses you might use, in order from the most passive to the most active strategies:[18]

- *Stonewalling:* Silence and a lack of expression on your face often signal a lack of interest in what the speaker is saying.
- *Backchanneling:* Facial expressions, nods, vocalizations such as "uh-huh," and verbal statements such as "I understand" and "that's very interesting" let the speaker know you're paying attention.
- *Paraphrasing:* Restating in your own words what the speaker has said shows you understand.

Your expressions often impact others' perceptions of how well you're listening.

©Antonio Guillem/123RF

- *Empathizing:* Conveying to the speaker that you understand and share his or her feelings on the topic demonstrates empathy.
- *Supporting:* Expressing your agreement with the speaker's opinion or point of view is the supportive strategy.
- *Analyzing:* Explaining your opinion or describing your experience provides your own perspective on what the speaker has said.
- *Advising:* Communicating advice to the speaker about what he or she should think, feel, or do is the most active feedback strategy.

Your choice of response may depend on the situation. For instance, if you are listening to a friend who has just lost her favorite uncle to cancer, empathizing and supporting responses are probably the most fitting. Stonewalling, backchanneling, or paraphrasing might make it seem as though you don't care about your friend, whereas analyzing or advising might seem insensitive. In contrast, if you're listening to a client who is wondering how she can make the most of her stock portfolio, analyzing and advising are probably called for.

To summarize, the stages of effective listening are hearing, understanding, remembering, interpreting, evaluating, and responding. (Keep in mind that mnemonic word *HURIER*.) According to Brownell's model, those stages characterize effective listening no matter why we are listening in the first place. As you probably know, we listen to others for several different reasons. We'll take a close look at three of the most common types of listening next.

LO4.3

Differentiate and illustrate informational listening, critical listening, and empathic listening.

TYPES OF LISTENING

When we talk about different *types* of listening, we're referring to the different *goals* we have when we listen to other people. Learning, evaluating, and empathizing aren't necessarily exclusive; sometimes we listen with more than one goal in mind. But when we distinguish among types of listening, we are considering our *primary* listening goal at that time.

Informational listening is used when learning.   Much of the listening you do in class or at work is **informational listening**, or listening to learn. Whenever you watch the news or listen to driving directions or pay attention to your manager's remarks during a sales meeting, you're engaged in informational listening.

Informational listening is one of the most important ways we learn. It is also a relatively passive process because we're simply taking in information. Although we may be listening effectively and even taking notes, we are listening primarily to learn something new rather than to critique what we're hearing or support the person saying it.

Critical listening is used for analyzing.   When our goal is to evaluate or analyze what we're hearing, we are engaged in **critical listening**. You listen carefully to a marketing pitch to see whether you want to buy the product being described. You listen to a political speech to evaluate the merits of a senator's ideas. You listen critically to your mother's description of her recent medical appointment to determine how worried she is about the results of her blood test.

Listening critically doesn't necessarily mean criticizing what you're hearing. Instead, it means analyzing and evaluating the merits of a speaker's words. Critical listening is therefore a more active, engaging process than informational listening. It requires not only taking in information but also evaluating and judging it.

Empathic listening is used for understanding the speaker.   The most challenging form of listening is often **empathic listening**, which occurs when you are trying to identify with the speaker by understanding and experiencing what he or she is thinking or feeling.[19] When talking to a colleague who has just lost a parent unexpectedly, you can use empathic listening to give comfort and support.

Effective empathic listening requires two separate skills. The first, *perspective taking,* is the ability to understand a situation from another's point of view.[20] The second skill, *empathic concern,* is the ability to identify how someone else is feeling and to experience those feelings yourself.[21] When listening to a client describing his recent diabetes diagnosis, for instance, you can practice perspective taking by imagining how he must feel and sharing in those emotions.

Empathic listening is different from *sympathetic listening,* which is feeling sorry for another person. If your neighbors lost their young grandson to leukemia, for instance, you might be able to sympathize with them even if you can't truly understand their grief. With empathic listening, however, the goal is to understand a situation from the speaker's perspective and to feel what he or she is feeling. Listening empathically can be a challenge, because our own perceptions can cause us to focus on how *we* would be feeling in the same situation, when our goal is to understand the *speaker's* feelings.

The goal of empathic listening is to understand the feelings of others.

©Monkey Business Images/ Shutterstock

Other types of listening exist. Informational, critical, and empathic listening aren't the only types of listening. *Inspirational listening* is listening to be inspired by what someone is saying, such as when we're taking in a sermon or a motivational speech. *Appreciative listening,* which is listening for pure enjoyment, is what we do when listening to someone tell a funny story or sing one of our favorite songs. When it comes to interacting with others, however, informational, critical, and empathic listening are among the most common and most important types.

Overcoming Barriers to Successful Listening

LO4.4

Analyze barriers to effective listening in social interactions.

For most people, life moves fast. This is especially the case in today's workplace. With tight deadlines, more information than ever, and involvement in more teams than ever, today's professionals face many challenges to successful listening. In this section, we examine several obstacles to effective listening.

NOISE

How many different stimuli are competing for your attention right now? How about when you're at work, where your boss, customers, and co-workers may all be trying to talk to you at once? Anything that interferes with your ability to encode or decode a message is called **noise**. In the context of listening, noise is anything that distracts you from listening to what you wish to listen to. That distraction could be *physical noise,* which consists of actual sound, or *psychological noise,* which is anything else we find distracting.

Most of us find it tougher to listen to a conversational partner when there are other sounds in the environment, such as loud music or other people talking.[22] These are examples of physical noise. However, it isn't just sound that can distract us. If we're hungry or tired, or if we're in an especially hot or cold environment, those influences qualify as psychological noise because they also distract us and thus reduce our ability to listen effectively.

When faced with such distractions, focus your attention on your conversational partner and listen intently to what he or she is saying. That strategy requires being conscious of noise in your environment and identifying the factors that are drawing your attention away from your conversation. If you can eliminate or ignore these, such as by turning off your music or disregarding your ringing cell phone, you will better focus attention on your partner. If you're being distracted by noise you can't ignore or reduce, it may be best to reschedule your conversation for a time when fewer stimuli are competing for your attention.

PSEUDOLISTENING AND SELECTIVE ATTENTION

At one time or another, you've probably pretended to pay attention to someone when you weren't really listening, a behavior called **pseudolistening**. When you

---

TECH TIP
Avoiding Digital Distractions

Great listeners know how to focus completely on their conversational partners. Consider experimenting with the following tips to help you identify how to become more productive and a better listener in your professional environment:[23]

Check digital messages just four to five times each day at designated times. Unless your job calls for it (or your boss demands it!), try not to check your messages more often than every 45 minutes. Consider taking some interruption-free periods during the day exclusively devoted to email and other online tools so you can concentrate on communicating with others. For example, you might schedule 30 minutes to an hour at 8 a.m., 11 a.m., 1 p.m., and 4 p.m. each day for this purpose.

Wean yourself off checking your mobile devices constantly. Some professionals get anxious if they don't check their phones every 15 minutes or even more frequently. A variety of anxieties, such as FOMO (fear of missing out) and FOBO (fear of being offline), drastically cut our productivity and ability to listen to others. Consciously extending the time before you next check your devices can dramatically improve your effectiveness at other tasks.

Develop strategies to manage your inbox and other incoming digital messages. Experiment with various ways of reading your email. Common strategies include LIFO (last in, first out), reverse chronological, and inbox zero. LIFO, a top-down reading of your inbox, is the most common and helps you deal with your most current emails. Older messages sometimes cover issues that have been worked out already, but the risk is that you may read and respond to a more current message without the context needed from prior messages. The reverse chronological method solves this problem by ensuring you see the original messages first. It also responds to people in the order they sent messages to you. Yet, you may also expend time reading and responding to issues that have already been addressed or resolved. Inbox zero is a strategy of immediately taking action on every email and getting your inbox to empty by the end of each session.

Turn off message alerts. Alerts can distract you and reduce your focus on your colleagues and immediate tasks at hand. Some professionals put their phones in airplane mode for portions of the day when they need to focus on others.

Reply immediately only to urgent messages. When you reply immediately to nonurgent messages, you set a precedent, letting others form an expectation that you can be interrupted at any time for any reason.

Effective listeners and productive professionals are keenly aware of the influences of selective attention and information overload.

©somethingway/Getty Images

are pseudolistening, you use feedback behaviors that make it *seem* as though you're paying attention, even though your mind is elsewhere. A variation of pseudolistening is paying **selective attention**, which means listening only to what you want to hear and ignoring the rest.[24] In her job as an insurance adjustor, for instance, Sue-Ann receives an evaluation from her supervisor every January. Most of her supervisor's comments are positive, but some suggest ways in which Sue-Ann could improve. The problem is, Sue-Ann doesn't listen to those suggestions. Instead, she listens selectively, paying close attention to her supervisor's praise but only pretending to listen or pseudolistening to his critiques.

People engage in pseudolistening and selective attention for many different reasons. Think about your own experiences. Maybe you're bored with what a speaker is saying, but you don't want to seem rude. Maybe you don't understand what you're hearing, but you're embarrassed to say so. Perhaps you're paying attention to something else while someone is talking to you, or maybe you simply don't like what is being said. Whatever the reason, pseudo-listening and selective attention are not only barriers to effective listening; they can also be a source of frustration for those you're pretending to listen to, because (as you probably know from your own experience) people are often aware when others aren't listening to what they're saying.

Pseudolistening is not only a barrier to effective listening; it can also be an unethi-cal behavior. Check out the "Focus on Ethics" box to understand how.

INFORMATION OVERLOAD

A third barrier to effective listening is **information overload**, the state of being over-whelmed by the huge amount of information we take in every day. We talk to peo-ple, watch television, listen to the radio, surf the Internet, get text messages, thumb through magazines, read newspapers and books, check email, and take in a variety of notices and advertisements. At times, the sheer volume of information we have to attend to can seem overwhelming. When it is, we find it hard to listen effectively to new information.

Consider how many advertising messages you see or hear on a daily basis. We view ads on television, in magazines and newspapers, on billboards, on people's clothing, in junk mail, and in movie previews. We receive ads on our smartphones, hear them on the radio, and find them in product inserts. They are visible at gas pumps, at auto-mated teller machines, on banners flying behind airplanes, and on the stickers we peel off apples and other fruits. We also receive them in the form of email spam and pop-up announcements on the Internet.

Information overload might seem like a product of the digital age, as massive amounts of information have become so easily and immediately available at the touch of a key. In fact, the term *information overload* was coined in 1970 by sociologist Alvin Toffler, in a book discussing the downsides of rapid technological change.[25] People were experiencing the distracting effects of information overload long before computer-mediated communication was widely used.

One of the biggest problems with information overload is that it can interrupt our attention. If you're emailing an important client, for instance, your ability to pay attention to her messages can be compromised repeatedly by each new radio adver-tisement you hear and each new pop-up ad you see. In fact, the average U.S. adult is exposed to about 360 advertising messages each day.[26] Each might seem small

FOCUS ON ETHICS

Merely Pretending to Listen

As a human resources professional, you are used to employees in your company sharing with you their private concerns about their colleagues. Your co-worker Marlene confides that some of her supervisor's recent behaviors have been making her uncomfortable. Although you care about Marlene's well-being in the workplace, you are distracted by a growing list of tasks you have to accomplish before the upcoming three-day weekend. As a result, you nod along and pretend to listen to what Marlene is describing, even though your mind is elsewhere. She leaves believing you have listened and heard her concerns, although by the end of the day, you don't recall very much of what she has said.

CONSIDER THIS: Is it ethical to give Marlene the false impression that you are listen-ing to her? Have you, in effect, deceived her by pseudolistening? To what risks have you exposed her by not paying better attention to her concerns?

and inconsequential when considered individually, but when you think about their effects on the entire population over time, they become a significant distraction. One analysis estimated the annual productivity loss to U.S. companies of unnecessary interruptions from information overload to be a staggering $650 billion.[27]

GLAZING OVER

A fourth reason effective listening is challenging is that we think so much faster than we speak. Most people are capable of understanding up to 600 words per minute, but the average person speaks fewer than 150 words per minute.[28] That gap leaves a lot of spare time for the mind to wander, during which we can engage in what researchers call **glazing over**, or daydreaming.

For instance, Rochelle picks up her young daughter and son at school every afternoon, and during the drive home the children describe what they did that day. Although she listens to them, Rochelle allows her mind to wander as they talk. She thinks about the productivity report she's preparing at work and ponders her grocery list. Because her children speak more slowly than she can listen, and because their reports of school activities are similar every day, Rochelle often glazes over when listening to them.

Glazing over is different from pseudolistening, which, as you'll recall, means only pretending to listen. When you're glazing over, you actually *are* listening to the speaker. It's just that you're allowing your mind to drift while doing so.

Glazing over can lead to at least three different problems. First, it can cause you to miss important details. In your communication course, for instance, you might fail to hear a critical piece of information about the term paper assignment. Second, glazing over might lead you to listen less critically than you normally would. For example, if your mind is wandering while you're listening to a salesperson describe the terms of a car loan, you might not realize the deal isn't as good as it seems. Finally, you can appear not to be listening even though you are. In those instances, you can come across as inattentive or dismissive. An effective listener will work to keep his or her focus on what the speaker is saying, instead of daydreaming or thinking about other topics.

REBUTTAL TENDENCY

Regan has recently started work as a customer service representative for an electronics retailer, but his first two weeks have not gone well. He knows he should listen nonjudgmentally to customers as they describe their frustrations with the products they bought and then offer assistance and advice. Instead, he begins arguing with customers in his mind while they're still speaking and jumps to conclusions about what they have done wrong. He has formulated his response even before they've stopped talking.

Regan is enacting a **rebuttal tendency**, the propensity to debate a speaker's point and formulate a reply while that person is still speaking.[29] According to research by business professor Steven Golen, the tendency to think about how you're going to respond to a speaker, arguing with the speaker in your mind, and jumping to conclusions before the speaker has finished talking are all barriers to effective listening.[30] There are two reasons why.

SHARPEN YOUR SKILLS

Listening Rather Than Responding

Have a conversation with someone about a topic on which you disagree. During your talk, focus your attention on what the other person is saying rather than on how you're going to respond. Check your ability by repeating the person's claims back to him or her after your conversation.

First, the rebuttal tendency requires mental energy that should be spent paying attention to the speaker. That is, it's difficult to listen effectively when all you're thinking about is how to respond. The second reason is closely related: because you're not paying close attention to the speaker, you can easily miss some of the details that might change your response in the first place. Regan had that very experience when a woman returned a wireless Internet router she was having trouble installing. Regan concluded too quickly that she hadn't followed the instructions, and he got sidetracked thinking about what he was going to say in response. Consequently, he didn't hear the customer say that she'd already had a technician guide her through the installation procedure and advise her that the router was defective. If Regan had heard that important detail, he could have exchanged the product efficiently and sent the customer on her way. Instead, he spent 10 minutes telling her to do what she had already done, leaving her feeling frustrated.

PEOPLE **FIRST**

Responding to Being Called "Closed-Minded"

IMAGINE THIS: Some co-workers are circulating a petition to place a referendum on the ballot in an upcoming state election. Several of your co-workers have signed it, but when you discover what the referendum is about, you realize you are fundamentally opposed.

Now, consider this: Because you don't support the referendum, you respectfully decline to sign the petition. Instead of respecting your right to do so, some of your co-workers get angry and call you closed-minded. Naturally, you feel attacked and somewhat defensive. As you consider how to respond to their comment, bear in mind the following:

- Remember that when people say, "You're being closed-minded," often what they mean is, "You should agree with me." Most of us like to believe we make sound, well-informed decisions, so when other people disagree with us, it is easier to call them closed-minded than to consider their reasons for thinking differently. Your co-workers may simply be frustrated that you hold a different position than they do.

- Ask yourself honestly whether you are open to considering all sides of the issue the referendum is about. You may feel that the strongest evidence supports your position, but are you open to being persuaded? Being open-minded doesn't mean you should take a position you don't believe is well supported. It does mean you recognize the possibility that your position may be wrong, and you are open to changing your mind if better arguments or evidence comes along.

- Your co-workers may be so strongly committed to their belief that no possible arguments or evidence could change their mind. In that case, putting people first means agreeing to disagree for the sake of maintaining a positive working relationship with one another.

Few of us enjoy being called closed-minded, and even fewer recognize closed-mindedness in ourselves. It is always worth considering honestly whether we are open to the possibility of changing our minds about an important issue. When two people are closed-minded about each other's ideas, however, it helps if they accept the differences between their perspectives instead of trying to change each other's mind.

THINK ABOUT THIS:

When do you tend to think of others as closed-minded? How do you usually react when others use that term to describe you? Why do you suppose it is so difficult to recognize closed-mindedness in ourselves?

CLOSED-MINDEDNESS

Another barrier to effective listening is **closed-mindedness**, the tendency not to listen to something with which we disagree.[31] Perhaps you know people whom you would describe as closed-minded: they typically refuse to consider the merits of a speaker's point if it conflicts with their own views. Many people are closed-minded only about particular issues, not about everything. For example, as an educator, Bella prides herself on being open to diverse opinions on a range of topics. When it comes to her religious beliefs, however, she is so thoroughly convinced of their merits that she refuses even to listen to ideas she doesn't already accept. It's as if Bella is shutting her mind to the possibility that any religious ideas besides her own can have value. Many of her teaching colleagues find this reaction off-putting. It prevents Bella not only from learning more about their religious traditions but also from teaching others about her beliefs, because she refuses to talk about religion with anyone who doesn't already share her views.

Bella should remember that we can listen effectively to people even if we disagree with them. As the Greek philosopher Aristotle (384–322 B.C.) wrote: "It is the mark of an educated mind to be able to entertain a thought without accepting it." When we refuse even to listen to ideas with which we disagree, we limit our ability to learn from other people and their experiences. If you find yourself feeling closed-minded toward particular ideas, remind yourself that listening to an idea doesn't necessarily mean accepting it.

COMPETITIVE INTERRUPTING

Normal conversation is a series of speaking "turns." You speak for a while, and then you allow another person to have a turn, and thus the conversation goes back and forth. Occasionally, though, people talk when it isn't their turn. There are many reasons people interrupt. Sometimes they want to express support or enthusiasm for what the other person is saying ("Yeah, I agree!"); sometimes they want to stop the speaker and ask for clarification ("Wait, I'm not sure what you mean"); and sometimes they talk out of turn to warn the speaker of an impending danger ("Stop! You're spilling your coffee!").

For some people, however, interrupting can be a way to dominate a conversation. Researchers use the term **competitive interrupting** to describe the practice of using interruptions to take control of the conversation. The goal is to make sure you get to speak more than the other person does and that your ideas and perspectives take priority. You can probably think of people who engage in that behavior—individuals with whom you feel you "can't get a word in edgewise." Although research shows that most interruptions *aren't* competitive, talking with a competitive interrupter can be frustrating.[32] Some people respond by becoming competitive themselves, turning the conversation into a battle of wits; others simply withdraw from the interaction. Some studies suggest that on average, men interrupt more often than women, although other studies have found no sex difference in the use of interruptions.[33]

Table 4.2 summarizes the barriers to effective listening. Bear in mind that with training and practice, most of us can improve our abilities to listen well, as we'll consider next.

Some professionals use competitive interrupting to dominate conversations.

©fizkes/Shutterstock

CAREER TIP

Melanie Whelan is the CEO of SoulCycle, a chain of fitness studios in North America, who has helped the company rapidly grow from 7 locations to 74 locations. Whelan says the most exciting moment in her career came when the chain's Washington, DC, location opened and then first lady Michelle Obama came to take a class.[34]

Whelan is clear about her view of leadership style: "Great leaders are great listeners." She believes the key to active listening is asking questions: "You have to ask a lot of questions and you have to really listen to the answers. Don't be thinking about the next question, and don't be thinking about what you're having for lunch. Really listen, because in every answer there are at least three more questions you want to be asking."[35]

Whelan points out that when asking questions, you have to be comfortable with silence.[36] People often need time to collect their thoughts before responding. If you are uncomfortable with silence after asking a question, you may start talking too soon and inadvertently miss the opportunity to hear what others are thinking.

Melanie Whelan
©Taylor Hill/Getty Images

Table 4.2 **Barriers to Effective Listening**

Noise	Anything that distracts you from listening to what you wish to listen to
Pseudolistening	Using feedback behaviors to give the false impression that you are listening
Selective attention	Listening only to points you want to hear, while ignoring all other points
Information overload	Being overwhelmed with the large amount of information you must take in every day
Glazing over	Daydreaming when you aren't speaking or listening during a conversation
Rebuttal tendency	Propensity to argue inwardly with a speaker and formulate your conclusions and responses prematurely
Closed-mindedness	Refusal even to listen to ideas or positions with which you disagree
Competitive interrupting	Interrupting others to gain control of a conversation

LO4.5

Implement strategies for improving informational, critical, and empathic listening skills.

Honing Your Listening and Learning Skills

Fortunately, effective listening is a skill rather than an innate ability, so it is possible to improve through education and practice. In this section, we'll look at various strategies for boosting your skills in informational, critical, and empathic listening.

BECOME A BETTER INFORMATIONAL LISTENER

When you engage in informational listening, your goal is to understand and learn from the speaker's message. For instance, you might be participating in a videoconference about saving for retirement or asking a marketing manager over Skype about your most recent sales figures. How can you make the most of those opportunities?

Separate what is and isn't said.   One important strategy for improving your informational listening skills is to beware of the tendency to "hear" words or statements that aren't actually said. Think about the last time you saw a TV commercial for a pain reliever, for instance. A common tactic for advertisers is to claim that "nothing is more effective" than their product. What do you learn from hearing that statement? In other words, how would you restate the message in your own words?

The advertisers are hoping you "hear" that their particular pain reliever is the strongest one available—but all they said is that nothing is *more effective,* which could mean several other products are *just as effective* as theirs. When you are engaged in informational listening, practice being aware of what is actually being said rather than inferring something else.

Perhaps the most effective way to determine whether you have understood a speaker's message is to paraphrase it. As we saw earlier in the chapter, paraphrasing means restating a speaker's message in your own words in order to clarify its meaning.

Let's suppose that after completing your last sales call of the day, you and your co-worker Dean have the following exchange:

1. **Dean:** *I think we should swing by that new barbecue place on the way home.*
2. **You:** *You want to pick up some dinner?*
3. **Dean:** *Yeah, I'm starving.*

You conclude that Dean is implying he's hungry and wants to get some food, but that isn't actually what he said. To check your understanding, you therefore paraphrase his statement by putting it into your own words. Because you understood his statement correctly, he replies by confirming your interpretation.

If you paraphrase a statement in a way that changes its meaning, most speakers will reply by correcting your understanding. Let's say the exchange with Dean goes like this:

1. **Dean:** *I think we should swing by that new barbecue place on the way home.*
2. **You:** *You want to pick up some dinner?*
3. **Dean:** *No, I want to see if my friend Blake is working tonight.*

In that instance, your interpretation of Dean's statement was inaccurate. By paraphrasing his statement, you invited him to correct your understanding, and he did. Paraphrasing is a simple but very efficient way to determine whether you have correctly separated what a speaker has and has not said.

Avoid the confirmation bias.   The *confirmation bias* is the tendency to pay attention only to information that supports our values and beliefs, while discounting or ignoring information that doesn't.[37] This tendency becomes a problem for listening when it causes us to make up our minds about an issue without paying attention to all sides. Suppose you're turning to talk radio for perspective on U.S. immigration policies. If you favor a conservative approach to immigration laws, including deportation of illegal immigrants, then you may consider a politically conservative commentator to be a more credible source than a politically liberal commentator. If your preference is for a more liberal immigration policy, including a guest-worker program, then you'll probably listen more to what a liberal commentator has to say. In either case, by seeking a perspective that already aligns with your point of view, you prevent yourself from hearing alternative viewpoints.

Good informational listeners are aware, however, that their beliefs are not necessarily accurate. Thus, another strategy for improving your informational listening skills is to ask yourself whether you have listened to all sides of an issue before you form a conclusion—or whether, instead, you are simply avoiding information that would lead you to question your beliefs.

Listen for substance more than style. The psychological principle called the *vividness effect* is the tendency of dramatic, shocking events to distort our perceptions of reality.[38] We watch news coverage of a deadly terrorist attack, for instance, and we worry about being killed by terrorists ourselves, even though the average person's likelihood of dying in a terrorist attack in the United States is about 1 in 20 million.[39] In one Gallup poll, 63 percent of U.S. parents surveyed thought a shooting at their child's school was likely, even though according to the FBI only 3.3 percent of all violent crimes occur in schools.[40]

We can experience much the same problem during informational listening if we focus only on what's most vivid. Let's say the sales pitch you heard yesterday included dramatic stories and flashy PowerPoint slides you found highly entertaining, but today's sales pitch was comparatively dry. You shouldn't conclude that the flashy presentation contained better information or that you necessarily learned more from it. Being a good informational listener means being able to look past what is dramatic and vivid to focus on the *substance* of what you're hearing. That skill starts with being aware of the vividness effect and remembering that vivid experiences can distort your perceptions. The next time you go through a dramatic event or listen to a particularly engaging speaker, ask yourself whether you are listening and paying attention to accurate information rather than being swayed by drama or charisma.

BECOME A BETTER CRITICAL LISTENER

Many interpersonal situations require you to assess the reliability and trustworthiness of what you're hearing. Here are three ways to hone that ability.

Be a skeptic. Being a good critical listener starts with being skeptical of what you hear. *Skepticism* is a method of questioning whether a claim is well supported by evidence; it isn't about being cynical or finding fault. Being skeptical means setting aside your biases and being willing to be persuaded by the merits of the argument and the quality of the evidence. A good critical listener doesn't accept claims blindly but questions them to see whether they are valid.[41]

Suppose your co-worker Faith has come up with a business opportunity, tells you about her plan, and asks you to consider investing in it. Poor critical listeners might make their decision based on how they feel about Faith or how excited they are at the prospect of making money. If you're a good critical listener, though, you'll set aside your feelings and focus on the merits of Faith's idea. Does she have a sound business plan? Is there a genuine market for her product? Has she budgeted for advertising? Did she explain how she would use your investment? Being a critical listener doesn't mean criticizing her plans—it means evaluating them to see whether they make sense.

Evaluate a speaker's credibility. Besides analyzing the merits of an argument, a good critical listener pays attention to the credibility of the speaker. As we've seen, *credibility* refers to the reliability and trustworthiness of someone or something. All other things being equal, you can generally presume that information from a credible source is more believable than information from a noncredible source.

What makes a speaker more or less credible? One quality is expertise. It makes more sense for us to trust medical advice from a physician than from a professional athlete, for instance. For the same reason, it doesn't make sense to trust a physician for legal or financial advice.

It's sometimes easy to confuse *expertise* with *experience.* Having experience with something may give a person credibility in that area, but it doesn't necessarily make the individual an expert. Consider Hannah, a small business owner. In the course of running her business, Hannah has become a very experienced supervisor for the many employees and interns she has overseen, so she has sufficient credibility to give advice to other business owners insofar as she can draw on her many experiences. Yet Hannah isn't an expert on management, because her only source of credibility is her individual experience. For example, she isn't a recognized authority on human resource management issues, nor does she have a degree in business.

Conversely, people can be experts on topics and areas with which they have no direct personal experience. As a board-certified obstetrician and gynecologist, Tyrell is an expert on pregnancy and women's health, even though, as a man, he has not personally experienced a pregnancy or a disease to which only women are vulnerable. Similarly, Young Li is an outstanding marital therapist who has helped countless couples even though she has never married. How can a man be a good obstetrician and a single person be a good marital therapist? The answer is that they draw on their training and expertise to help others, not just on their individual experiences.

Another characteristic that affects a speaker's credibility is bias. If a speaker has a special interest in making you believe some idea or claim, that bias tends to reduce his or her credibility. For instance, if a tobacco company executive claimed publicly that smoking has health benefits, a good critical listener would be highly skeptical because the executive is a biased source. Some biases, like this one, might be obvious, but sometimes you have to dig below the surface to evaluate someone's credibility. For example, you might be intrigued to hear about a research report claiming that using your cell phone while driving does not increase your risk of being in a collision. You might assume the study was conducted by a reputable source, such as a research team at a major university, and that assumption would enhance the report's credibility in your mind. You decide to investigate further, however, and you discover that the study was funded by a group that lobbies on behalf of the telecommunications industry. Given its purpose, such a group would have a vested interest in research results favorable to cell phone use. That doesn't necessarily mean the study's conclusions are wrong. It does mean, though, that you should be more skeptical when thinking about them.

Understand probability. Evaluating the merits of a claim means speculating about the likelihood that the claim is true. Such speculation can be tricky, however, because we sometimes confuse what's possible with what's probable and what's probable with what's certain. An event or fact is *possible* if there's even the slightest chance, however small, that it might be true. In contrast, to be *probable,* a statement has to have greater than a 50 percent chance of being true. Finally, a statement is *certain* only if its likelihood of being true is 100 percent and nothing less.

Consider a claim such as "I can survive without water for a week." There's a possibility that assertion could be true, but the likelihood is extremely small. The claim certainly isn't probable, and a good critical listener wouldn't treat it as though it were.

The statement "I will get married someday" is not only possible, it's also probable, because a very large majority of people marry at least once in their lives. Is that claim therefore certain? No, because there's a chance, however small, that it might not happen. For a claim to be certain, there can be *absolutely no chance* that it isn't true. A claim such as "I will die someday" is certain, because every living being eventually dies. Good critical listeners understand the differences among possibility, probability, and certainty. They bear in mind that a claim that something is possible isn't necessarily worth believing.

BECOME A BETTER EMPATHIC LISTENER

Within our relationships, a common goal for listening is to provide empathy and support. You can become a better empathic listener by adopting these strategies.

Listening nonjudgmentally is the foundation for empathic listening.

©Image Source/Getty Images

Listen nonjudgmentally.   When we listen to learn, and especially when we listen to evaluate, we often make judgments about the information we're taking in. But good empathic listening is about being open-minded and nonjudgmental.

Two strategies are particularly helpful here. First, listen without interrupting. Being empathic means letting the other person say what he or she needs to say without jumping into the middle of the message. Fight the urge to interrupt, and simply listen. Second, think twice before offering unsolicited advice. When other people tell us their problems, our tendency is often to respond with advice on solving those problems.[42] A good empathic listener remembers that people aren't always looking for advice—they often just want someone to listen to them.

Acknowledge feelings.   Empathizing is about understanding how someone else is feeling and trying to relate to those feelings. It's *not* the same as sympathizing, which is feeling sorry for the other person. An important strategy for good empathic listening, therefore, is to acknowledge a speaker's feelings and allow him or her to continue expressing them.

We do so by responding to speakers with *continuer statements,* phrases that identify the emotions a person is experiencing and allow him or her to communicate them further. In contrast, it is important to avoid *terminator statements,* phrases that fail to acknowledge a speaker's emotions, shutting down his or her opportunity to express them. After listening to a co-worker describe her worries about her daughter's illness, for instance, empathic listeners can use continuer statements, such as "That must make you feel very uncertain" and "I can imagine how scary this must be" to convey to the co-worker that they understand and appreciate her feelings. Listeners with less empathic ability will be more likely to use terminator statements, such as "I'm sure the doctors are doing everything they can" and "You just need to give this some time." Those types of responses imply to the co-worker that her feelings are unimportant and discourage her from continuing to speak about them.

In one study, researchers, with permission, recorded nearly 400 conversations between advanced cancer patients and their oncologists and listened for times when patients expressed negative emotions such as sadness, fear, and anxiety. When those moments arose, doctors replied with continuer statements only 22 percent of the time. Younger physicians were more likely than older ones to use continuers, and female physicians were more likely than male doctors to do so.[43] That doesn't mean oncologists lack empathy. Rather, it illustrates that they may have trouble communicating their empathy through emotionally supportive listening responses, which are particularly important for individuals struggling with a terminal illness such as advanced cancer. To help doctors demonstrate empathy, medical schools are increasingly providing formal training in empathic listening.[44]

Communicate support nonverbally.   When you're listening rather than speaking, your nonverbal behaviors convey your interest, understanding, and empathy. Perhaps the most important nonverbal behavior in this situation is eye contact. If you allow yourself to be distracted by your environment, you can convey the message that you aren't really listening. Other important empathic behaviors are your use of facial expressions and touch. A reassuring smile and a warm touch can make people feel you understand, support, and empathize with them.[45]

CHAPTER WRAP-UP

Listening is among the most valuable communication skills, yet few professionals and managers consciously develop their listening skills. Here's a quick review of the chapter.

LO4.1   Justify the importance of listening effectively.

- Most people adopt one of four main listening styles: people-oriented style, action-oriented style, content-oriented style, or time-oriented style.

LO4.2   Summarize the stages in the HURIER model of listening.

- The stages of effective listening (the HURIER model) include hearing, understanding, remembering, interpreting, evaluating, and responding.

LO4.3   Differentiate and illustrate informational listening, critical listening, and empathic listening.

- Information listening focuses on learning something new rather than to critique what we're hearing.
- Critical listening focuses on evaluating or analyzing what we're hearing.

- Empathic listening focuses on are trying to identify with the speaker by understanding and experiencing what he or she is thinking or feeling.

LO4.4   Analyze barriers to effective listening in social interactions.

- Barriers to listening include noise, pseudolistening, selective attention, information overload, glazing over, rebuttal tendency, closed-mindedness, and competitive interrupting.

LO4.5   Implement strategies for improving informational, critical, and empathic listening skills.

- Become a better informational listener by separating what is and isn't said, avoiding the confirmation bias, listening for substance more than style.
- Become a critical listener by being a skeptic, evaluating a speaker's credibility, understanding probability.
- Become an empathic listener by listening nonjudgmentally, acknowledging feelings, communicating your support nonverbally.

A LOOK BACK

Now, let's return to the opening scenario. We can see that Janice and Antoine have very different listening styles. Janice appears to have an *action-oriented listening style*, whereas Antoine appears to have a *people-oriented listening style*. Janice immediately recognizes an action to take, which is logical and precise based on their warranty policy. Janice is so convinced she is correct that she thinks about her next response to Antoine before he's finished what he's saying. We saw that this is a common non-listening behavior called the *rebuttal tendency* we're all guilty of from time to time. Antoine demonstrates a people-oriented listening style with a focus on the feelings of their customer. He even uses *continuer statements* that are intended to open conversation about the customer's feelings. By contrast, Janice uses a *terminator statement* to remove any discussion of the customer's feelings from the conversation. If Janice and Antoine can recognize their different listening styles, they'll develop solutions together much more quickly.

action-oriented style   76
closed-mindedness   88
competitive interrupting   88
content-oriented style   76
critical listening   82
empathic listening   82

glazing over   86
hearing   76
information overload   85
informational listening   82
listening   76
noise   83

people-oriented style   76
pseudolistening   83
rebuttal tendency   86
selective attention   84
time-oriented style   76

CHAPTER REVIEW QUESTIONS

1. What is the definition of listening? LO4.1

2. How is listening different from hearing? LO4.1

3. In what ways are the people-oriented, action-oriented, content-oriented, and time-oriented listening styles different? Which listening style best characterizes you? LO4.1

4. Why is effective listening so advantageous? LO4.1

5. Identify and define each of the six stages of the HURIER model of effective listening. LO4.2

6. What are mnemonic devices, and why are they useful? LO4.2

7. What are seven strategies for responding to what someone has said? Which of these is the most active strategy, and which is the most passive? LO4.3

8. How are informational, critical, and empathic listening similar? How are they different? LO4.3

9. What is the difference between perspective taking and empathic concern? LO4.3

10. How is empathic listening different from sympathetic listening? LO4.3

11. Besides informational, critical, and empathic listening, in what other forms of listening do we engage? LO4.3

12. How are physical and psychological noise different? LO4.4

13. In what ways can you avoid digital distractions? LO4.4

14. Compare and contrast pseudolistening and selective attention, and explain how each is a barrier to effective listening. LO4.4

15. What is information overload? How new a phenomenon is it? LO4.4

16. Why do people engage in "glazing over"? LO4.4

17. How does the rebuttal tendency interfere with effective listening? LO4.4

18. What does it mean to be closed-minded? LO4.4

19. What makes an interruption "competitive"? LO4.4

20. Which barriers to effective listening are the most common for you? LO4.4

21. What does it mean to "separate what is and isn't said"? Why is that good advice for becoming a better informational listener? LO4.5

22. What are the confirmation bias and the vividness effect, and why are they important to avoid? LO4.5

23. What does it mean to be skeptical? LO4.5

24. As an aspect of credibility, how is experience different from expertise? LO4.5

25. What does it mean to have bias? LO4.5

26. How are possibility, probability, and certainty different? LO4.5

27. In what ways can you become a better empathic listener? How does using continuer statements instead of terminator statements help you in that effort? LO4.5

SKILL-BUILDING EXERCISES

Evaluate Your Non-Listening Behaviors (LO4.4)

Which barriers to listening are most difficult for you? Choose three of the following barriers to listening: noise, pseudolistening, selective attention, information overload, glazing over, rebuttal tendency, closed-mindedness, and competitive interrupting. Then, for each of your chosen barriers, explain why you struggle with this barrier and how you can improve.

Describe the Listening Skills of an Excellent Listener and a Poor Listener (LO4.1, LO4.2)

Think of two people with whom you have worked at school or work—one an excellent listener and the other a poor listener. Describe and contrast these two individuals in terms of their ability to listen based on the HURIER model. Explain how each person made you feel as he or she listened, or didn't listen, to you. Explain two or three ways in which you want to emulate the excellent listener in the workplace.

Assess Your Listening Skills (LO4.2, LO4.4)

Think about how well you listen in *high-pressure* environments or when you're busy. Explain how well you do at each of the following elements of listening: hearing, understanding, remembering, interpreting, evaluating, and responding. For each stage of listening, evaluate your abilities and tendencies and think of strategies to help you improve.

Listening and Caring (LO4.3, LO4.4, LO4.5)

Tachi Yamada, a former president of the Bill & Melinda Gates Foundation's Global Health Program, recently said this:

> A second key lesson was from a doctor named Marcel Tuchman. He was the most compassionate person I have ever met in my life—I mean, full of human kindness. And every time he met somebody, you had the sense that he cared more about them than anything else in the world. So what I learned from him is that when you actually are with somebody, you've got to make that person feel like nobody else in the world matters. I think that's critical. So, for example, I don't have a mobile phone turned on because I'm talking to you. I don't want the outside world to impinge on the conversation we're having. I don't carry a BlackBerry. I do my e-mails regularly, but I do it when I have the time on a computer. I don't want to be sitting here thinking that I've got an e-mail message coming here and I'd better look at that while I'm talking to you. Every moment counts, and that moment is lost if you're not in that moment 100 percent.[46]

Based on Yamada's comments and your own experiences, answer the following questions:

1. What do you think Yamada means by the statement, *"that moment is lost if you're not in that moment 100 percent"*? How does this relate to listening? Do you think this is a reasonable expectation in the workplace?
2. What kinds of electronic gadgets and communication tools can take focus away from a conversation? What are some principles for making sure these gadgets and tools are not distracting?
3. Do you believe kindness is an important principle of listening and communicating in business? Can kindness be developed? How?

Write a Listening Journal (LO4.2, LO4.3, LO4.4, LO4.5)

For a length of time specified by your instructor (one week, two weeks, one month), write daily in a journal about your listening skills. Each day, describe one interaction you had and discuss whether you actively listened. Explain how well you did at each of the following listening stages: hearing, understanding, remembering, interpreting, evaluating, and responding. For each of these interactions, describe the nonverbal behavior of others and the nonverbal behavior you exhibited to show your interest. Also, analyze how effectively you asked questions. Conclude your daily journal with a summary of lessons you have learned and five goals for improving your active listening.

Group Listening Exercise (LO4.2, LO4.3, LO4.4, LO4.5)

Form groups of three. You will complete this exercise three times, with each person rotating roles each time. The roles are asker, listener, and observer. Choose a time period (two to five minutes) to complete the exercise. The asker will choose a topic to learn about from the listener (e.g., professional interests, reasons for choosing major, challenges at work or in school right now). The asker will devote the time to learning about the other person through asking questions. The observer will take notes about how effective the asker's asking, listening, and nonverbal communication skills are. Once the exercise is complete, the observer will facilitate a three- to five-minute debriefing by explaining his/her observations and asking both the asker and the listener about their observations.

ENDNOTES

1. Beard, D., & Bodie, G. (2015). Listening research in the communication discipline. In P. J. Gehrke & W. M. Keith (Eds.), *A century of communication studies: The unfinished conversation* (pp. 207–233). New York, NY: Routledge.

2. Watson, K., Barker, L. L., & Weaver, J. B., III. (2012). The Listening Styles Profile (LSTP-16): Development and validation of an instrument to assess four listening styles. *International Journal of Listening, 9*(1), 1–13.

3. Bodie, G. D., & Worthington, D. L. (2010). Revising the Listening Styles Profiles (LSP-16): A confirmatory factor analytic approach to scale validation and reliability estimation. *International Journal of Listening, 24,* 69–88.

4. Emanuel, R., Adams, J., Baker, K., Daufin, E. K., Ellington, C., Fitts, E., . . . Okeowo, D. (2008). How college students spend their time communicating. *International Journal of Listening, 22,* 13–28.

5. Dindia, K., & Kennedy, B. L. (2004, November). *Communication in everyday life: A descriptive study using mobile electronic data collection.* Paper presented at the annual conference of the National Communication Association, Chicago, IL; Barker, L., Edwards, R., Gaines, C., Gladney, K., & Holley, F. (1980). An investigation of proportional time spent in various communication activities by college students. *Journal of Applied Communication Research, 8,* 101–109; Hargie, O., Saunders, C., & Dickson, D. (1994). *Social skills in interpersonal communication* (3rd ed.). New York, NY: Routledge.

6. Waldeck, J., Durante, C., Helmuth, B., & Marcia, B. (2012). Communication in a changing world: Contemporary perspectives on business communication competence. *Journal of Education for Business, 87,* 230–240.

7. Graduate Management Admission Council. (2017). *Corporate recruiters survey: 2017 survey report.* Reston, VA: Author.

8. See Vangelisti, A. L. (Ed.). (2012). *Handbook of family communication* (2nd ed.). New York, NY: Taylor & Francis.

9. See, e.g., Park, J.-K., Chung, T.-L., Gunn, F., & Rutherford, B. (2015). The role of listening in e-contact center customer relationship management. *Journal of Services Marketing, 29,* 49–58; Jagosh, J., Boudreau, J. D., Steinert, Y., MacDonald, M. E., & Ingram, L. (2011). The importance of physician listening from the patients' perspective: Enhancing diagnosis, healing, and the doctor-patient relationship. *Patient Education and Counseling, 85,* 369–374.

10. Brownell, J. (1990). Perceptions of effective listeners: A management study. *Journal of Business Communication, 27,* 401–415.

11. Carrell, L. J., & Willmington, S. C. (1996). A comparison of self-report and performance data in assessing speaking and listening competence. *Communication Reports, 9,* 185–191.

12. Brownell, J. (2017). *Listening attitudes, principles, and skills* (6th ed.). Boston, MA: Pearson.

13. Mar, R. A. (2011). The neural bases of social cognition and story comprehension. *Annual Review of Psychology, 62,* 103–134.

14. See Janusik, L. A. (2007). Building listening theory: The validation of the conversational listening span. *Communication Studies, 58,* 139–156.

15. Benoit, S. S., & Lee, J. W. (1986). Listening: It can be taught. *Journal of Education for Business, 63,* 229–232.

16. Gross, A. L., Parisi, J. M., Spira, A. P., Kuelder, A. M., Ko, J. Y., Sacynski, J. S., . . . Rebok, G. W. (2012). Memory training interventions for older adults: A meta-analysis. *Aging & Mental Health, 16,* 722–734.

17. Nawaz, S. (2017, March 24). Become a better listener by taking notes. *Harvard Business Review blog.* Retrieved from https://hbr.org/2017/03/become-a-better-listener-by-taking-notes.

18. Tice, M., & Henetz, T. (2011). Reading between the turns: Social perceptions of turn-taking cues in conversation. *Journal of the Acoustical Society of America, 130,* 2443.

19. Floyd, K. (2014). Empathic listening as an expression of interpersonal affection. *International Journal of Listening, 28,* 1–12.

20. Bernhardt, B. C., & Singer, T. (2012). The neural basis of empathy. *Annual Review of Neuroscience, 35,* 1–23.

21. O'Brien, E., Konrath, S. H., Grühn, D., & Hagen, A. L. (2013). Empathic concern and perspective taking: Linear and quadratic effects of age across the adult life span. *Journal of Gerontology B: Psychological Sciences & Social Sciences, 68,* 168–175.

22. Sarampalis, A., Kalluri, S., Edwards, B., & Hafter, E. (2009). Objective measures of listening effort: Effects of background noise and noise reduction. *Journal of Speech, Language, and Hearing Research, 52,* 1230–1240.

23. Rosen, L., & Samuel, A. (2015, June). Conquering digital distraction. *Harvard Business Review,* 110–113.

24. Gazzaley, A., & Nobre, A. C. (2012). Top-down modulation: Bridging selective attention and working memory. *Trends in Cognitive Science, 16,* 129–135.

25. Toffler, A. (1970). *Future shock.* New York, NY: Random House.

26. Media Dynamics, Inc. (2014, September 22). Adults spend almost 10 hours per day with the media, but note only 150 ads. *Media Matters,* 1–2.

27. Bhasin, K. (2012). This is how information overload destroys your productivity. Retrieved July 18, 2017, from http://www.businessinsider.com/infographic-how-information-overload-affects-you-in-the-workplace-2012-2.

28. Wolvin, A. (2011). *Listening and human communication in the 21st century.* New York, NY: Wiley Blackwell.

29. Neal, K. L. (2014). *Six key communication skills for records and information managers.* Oxford, England: Elsevier.

30. Golen, S. (1990). A factor analysis of barriers to effective listening. *International Journal of Business Communication, 27,* 25–36.

31. Masicampo, E. J., & Baumeister. R. F. (2012). Committed but closed-minded: When making a specific plan for a goal hinders success. *Social Cognition, 30,* 37–55.

32. Nelson, A., & Brown, C. D. (2012). *The gender communication handbook: Conquering conversational collisions between men and women.* San Francisco, CA: Wiley.

33. Redeker, G., & Maes, A. (1996). Gender differences in interruptions. In D. Slobin, J. Garhardt, A. Kyratzis, & J. Guo (Eds.), *Social interaction, social context, and language* (pp. 579–612). Mahwah, NJ: Lawrence Erlbaum Associates.

34. Hutcheson, S. (2017, June 2). How I became a CEO: Melanie Whelan of SoulCycle. *USA Today.* Retrieved from http://college.usatoday.com/2017/06/02/how-i-became-a-ceo-melanie-whelan-of-soulcycle.

35. Bryant, A. (2015, December 17). Melanie Whelan of SoulCycle: Find the questions in every answer. *New York Times.* Retrieved from https://www.nytimes.com/2015/12/20/business/melanie-whelan-of-soulcycle-find-the-questions-in-every-answer.html.

36. Bryant, A. (2015, December 17). Melanie Whelan of SoulCycle: Find the questions in every answer.

The New York Times. Retrieved from https://www.nytimes
.com/2015/12/20/business/melanie-whelan-of-soulcycle-
find-the-questions-in-every-answer.html.

37. Kassin, S. M., Dror, I. E., & Kukucka, J. (2013). The forensic
confirmation bias: Problems, perspectives, and proposed
solutions. *Journal of Applied Research in Memory and
Cognition, 2*, 42–52.

38. Guadagno, R. E., Rhoads, K. V. L., & Sagarin, B. J. (2011).
Figural vividness and persuasion: Capturing the "elusive"
vividness effect. *Social Psychology Bulletin, 37*, 626–638.

39. Bailey, R. (2011, September 6). How scared of terrorism
should you be? Not very. You are four times more likely
to be killed by a lightning bolt than by a terror attack.
Reason.com. Retrieved June 22, 2017, from http://reason
.com/archives/2011/09/06/how-scared-of-terrorism-
should.

40. Federal Bureau of Investigation. (2015). Crime in
schools and colleges. *FBI Uniform Crime Reports*.
Retrieved July 18, 2017, from https://ucr.fbi.gov/nibrs/
crime-in-schools-and-colleges.

41. Snyder, L. G., & Snyder, M. J. (2008). Teaching critical
thinking and problem solving skills. *Delta Pi Epsilon
Journal, 50*, 90–99.

42. Tannen, D. (1990). *You just don't understand: Women and men
in conversation*. New York, NY: Ballantine.

43. Pollak, K. I., Arnold, R. M., Jeffreys, A. S., Alexander, S.
C., Olsen, M. K., Abernethy, A. P., . . . Tulsky, J. A. (2007).
Oncologist communication about emotion during visits
with patients with advanced cancer. *Journal of Clinical
Oncology, 25*, 5748–5752.

44. Boodman, S. G. (2015, March 15). How to teach
doctors empathy. *The Atlantic*. Retrieved from https://
www.theatlantic.com/health/archive/2015/03/
how-to-teach-doctors-empathy/387784.

45. Floyd, K. (2006). *Communicating affection: Interpersonal
behavior and social context*. Cambridge, England: Cambridge
University Press.

46. Bryant, A. (2010, February 2017). Talk to me. I'll turn off my
phone. *The New York Times*. Retrieved from https://www.
nytimes.com/2010/02/28/business/28corner.html.

Learning Objectives

After reading this chapter, you should be able to do the following:

LO5.1 Illustrate how selection, organization, and interpretation occur during perception.

LO5.2 Explain the reasons why people commit perceptual errors.

LO5.3 Differentiate self-serving bias and fundamental attribution error.

LO5.4 Explain how the nature of self-concept is partially subjective.

LO5.5 Describe three pathways through which self-concept can shape communicative behavior.

LO5.6 Identify the ways in which image management is collaborative, involves the management of multiple identities, and is complex.

CHAPTER 5

Perspective Taking

Liz sat in the breakroom with Caleb, a close colleague. "I'm so frustrated with Aisha. We just missed our deadline with a client because she took too much time creating the graphics. By the time she gave them to me, I had only one day to finish the updates to our website. With all the meetings that were scheduled that day, there was no way for me to finish in time. Aisha simply doesn't care when we miss these deadlines."

Caleb replied, "Don't worry about it. It's not your fault—you always get the job done unless one of the graphics designers drops the ball. Graphics designers worry more about getting awards than about giving the clients what they want."

We have an ongoing need to make sense of other people. Especially when they act in ways that are surprising or disappointing—as Aisha did by taking so long to create graphics for Liz—our natural tendency is to come up with explanations for their behaviors. Liz explained Aisha's behavior by perceiving that Aisha doesn't care when deadlines are missed, whereas Caleb perceived that all graphics designers—including Aisha—are more interested in winning accolades than in pleasing their clients.

We come up with perceptions about other people, and even about ourselves, all the time. What's more, many of us assume our perceptions are accurate reflections of reality, and we communicate on the basis of those perceptions without recognizing that they may be inaccurate or incomplete. Liz and Caleb may be correct in perceiving that Aisha doesn't care about their deadlines or their satisfaction with her work—but they may also be wrong. As we'll discover in this chapter, our perceptions of people, including ourselves, are susceptible to a wide range of influences that can distort their accuracy. Before we act on the basis of our perceptions, therefore, it is critical to recognize that we don't always see things the way they are.

How We Perceive Others

Before going on a job interview, applicants may practice introducing themselves, prepare answers to anticipated questions, and consider clothing options to refine their look. As we'll discuss later in this book, all these preparations are worthwhile because they help you put your best self forward. Job candidates may be disappointed, however, to learn that interviewers often make up their minds about someone within the first few minutes.[1] Although that may seem too short a period to make a serious hiring decision, research indicates that people are surprisingly accurate at evaluating others after very brief periods of time. In fact, some studies have shown that our impressions and evaluations of others can be more accurate if we have less—rather than more—information to go on.[2]

We form these impressions and evaluations by engaging in **perception**, the process of making meaning from what we experience in the world around us. We notice physical experiences—such as fatigue, body aches, and congestion—and perceive that we are ill. We notice environmental experiences—such as cold air, wind, and rain—and perceive that a storm is under way. When we apply the same process to people,

In both personal and professional settings, we have an ongoing need to make sense of others.

©XiXinXing/Alamy Stock Photo

we engage in *interpersonal perception,* which helps us make meaning from our own and others' behaviors.[3]

As social beings, we are constantly engaged in interpersonal perception. Although our perceptions may seem to take shape instantaneously, we will find in this section that they actually form in stages, although quickly. We will also see that several factors can influence the accuracy of our perceptions, including culture, stereotypes, primacy and recency effects, and perceptual sets.

PERCEPTION IS A PROCESS

LO5.1

Illustrate how selection, organization, and interpretation occur during perception.

We usually select, organize, and interpret information so quickly and subconsciously that we think our perceptions are objective, factual reflections of the world. Suppose you had a conflict this morning with an intern you are training, and throughout the day he failed to respond to your text messages reminding him to post an update about your charity donation drive on your organization's Facebook page. You might believe he is ignoring you because he is not replying. However, you have created your perception based on the information you *selected* for attention (he doesn't respond), the way you *organized* that information (he is angry about your conflict), and the way you *interpreted* it (he's ignoring you).[4] In fact, you might also perceive that he is having an extremely busy day or that he left his cell phone in his car. The perception you form depends on which pieces of information you attend to, how you organize them in your mind, and how you interpret their meaning.

As Figure 5.1 shows, selection, organization, and interpretation are the three basic stages of perception. Let's examine each in turn.

Selection is the first stage. Perception is initiated when one or more of your senses are stimulated. You hear a customer placing her order in a store. You see a puppy chewing on an old tennis ball. You smell a co-worker's cologne. Those sensory experiences of hearing, seeing, and smelling can prompt you to form perceptions.

Your senses are constantly stimulated by events in your environment, but it's impossible to pay attention to all these stimuli at any given moment.[5] Instead, you engage in **selection**, the process by which your mind and body help you isolate certain stimuli to pay attention to. For example, you notice that your officemate left the lights on all night, but you overlook that he brought you lunch when you were overwhelmed with work. Clearly, the information we attend to influences the perceptions we form, although we don't necessarily make conscious choices about what to ignore.

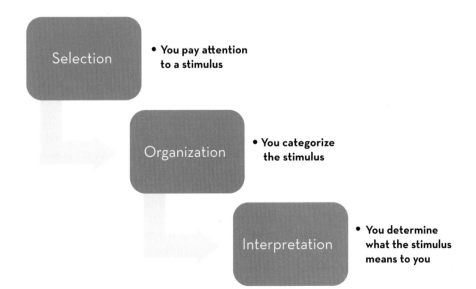

Figure 5.1

Three Stages of Perception

Perception occurs in three stages: selection, organization, and interpretation.

- Selection • You pay attention to a stimulus
- Organization • You categorize the stimulus
- Interpretation • You determine what the stimulus means to you

How, then, does selection occur? Research indicates that three characteristics make a given stimulus more likely to be selected for attention.

First, being unusual or unexpected makes a stimulus stand out.[6] You might not pay attention to people talking loudly in a restaurant, but in the library the same loud conversation would grab your attention because it is unusual there. Second, repetition or frequency makes a stimulus stand out.[7] For example, you're more likely to remember television commercials you've seen repeatedly than those you've seen only once. Third, the intensity of a stimulus affects how much you take notice of it. You are more aware of strong odors than weak scents, and of bright and flashy colors than dull and muted hues.[8]

How do we avoid becoming overwhelmed by so much sensory information? A part of your brain called the *reticular formation* serves the important function of helping you focus on certain stimuli while ignoring others.[9] It is the primary reason why, when having a conversation with a colleague in a noisy coffee shop, you can focus on what your colleague is saying and tune out the other sights and sounds bombarding your senses at the time.

Organization is the second stage. Once you have noticed a particular stimulus, the next step in the perception process is **organization**, the classification of information according to its similarities to and differences from other things you know about. To classify a stimulus, your mind applies a *perceptual schema* to it, a mental framework for organizing information into categories we call *constructs*.

According to communication researcher Peter Andersen, we use four types of schema to classify information we notice about other people:[10]

1. *Physical constructs* emphasize people's appearance, causing us to notice objective characteristics such as height, age, ethnicity, and body shape, as well as subjective characteristics such as physical attractiveness.
2. *Role constructs* emphasize people's social or professional position, so we notice that a person is a sales rep, an accountant, a stepmother, and so on.[11]
3. *Interaction constructs* emphasize people's behavior, so we notice that a person is outgoing, aggressive, shy, or considerate.
4. *Psychological constructs* emphasize people's thoughts and feelings, such as anger, self-assurances, insecurity, or lightheartedness.

Whichever constructs we notice about people—and we may notice more than one at a time—the process of organization helps us identify how the items we select for attention are related to one another.[12] If you notice that your human resources director is a Little League softball coach and the father of three children, for example, those two pieces of information go together because they both relate to the roles he plays. If you notice that he seems irritated or angry, those pieces of information go together as examples of his psychological state.

Interpretation is the final stage. After noticing and classifying a stimulus, you have to assign it an **interpretation** to figure out its meaning for you. Let's say one of your co-workers has been especially friendly toward you since last week. She asks you how your current project is going, and she offers to run errands for you over her lunch break. Her behavior is definitely noticeable, and you've probably classified it as a psychological construct because it relates to her thoughts and feelings about you.

What is her behavior communicating? How should you interpret it? Is she being nice because she's getting ready to ask you for a big favor? Or, is she simply trying to look good in front of her manager because she is hoping for a promotion?

To address those questions, you likely will pay attention to three factors: your *personal experience,* your *knowledge* of this co-worker, and the *closeness of your relationship* with her. First, your personal experience helps you assign meaning to behavior. If some co-workers have been nice to you in the past just to get favors from you later, you might be suspicious of this person's behavior.[13] Second, your knowledge of the person helps you interpret her actions. If you know she's friendly and nice to everyone, you might interpret her behavior differently than if you notice she's being nice only to you.[14] Finally, the closeness of your relationship influences the way you interpret a person's behavior. When your best friend does you an unexpected favor, you probably interpret it as a sincere sign of friendship. With a co-worker, you may be more likely to wonder about an ulterior motive.[15]

THE CIRCULAR NATURE OF PERCEPTION

Although perception occurs in stages—selecting, organizing, and interpreting information—the stages all overlap.[16] Thus, for example, the way we interpret a communication behavior depends on what we notice about it, but what we notice can also depend on the way we interpret it.

Suppose you are listening to a speech by the regional vice president of your company. If you like her ideas and proposals, you might interpret her demeanor and speaking style as examples of her intelligence and confidence. If you oppose her ideas, however, you might believe her demeanor and speaking style reflect arrogance or incompetence. Either interpretation, in turn, might lead you to select for attention only those behaviors or characteristics that support your interpretation and to ignore those that do not. So, even though perception happens in stages, the stages don't always take place in the same order. We're constantly noticing, organizing, and interpreting things around us, including other people's behaviors.

WE COMMONLY MISPERCEIVE OTHERS' COMMUNICATION BEHAVIORS

LO5.2

Explain the reasons why people commit perceptual errors.

Although we get a lot of opportunities to practice perception, mistakes are easy to make. Imagine that during an overseas sales trip, you perceive that two adults you see in a restaurant are having a heated argument. As it turns out, you later discover they are not arguing but engaging in behaviors that, in their culture, communicate interest and involvement.

Why do we commit such a perceptual error despite our accumulated experience? The reason is that each of us has multiple lenses through which we perceive the world. As we'll see below, those lenses include our cultural and co-cultural backgrounds, stereotypes, primacy and recency effects, and our perceptual sets. In each case, those lenses have the potential to influence not only our own communication behaviors but also our perceptions of the communication of others.

Cultures and co-cultures influence perceptions. One powerful influence on the accuracy of our perceptions is the culture and co-cultures with which we iden-

Culture is one of many influences on our perceptions of others.
©sjenner13/123RF

tify. Recall from Chapter 2 that culture is the learned, shared symbols, language, values, and norms that distinguish one group of people—such as Russians, South Africans, or Thais—from another. Co-cultures are smaller groups of people—such as single parents, bloggers, and history enthusiasts—who share values, customs, and norms related to mutual interests or characteristics besides their national citizenship.

Many characteristics of cultures can influence our perceptions and interpretations of other people's behaviors.[17] For instance, people from individualistic cultures frequently engage in more direct, overt forms of conflict communication than do people from collectivistic cultures. In a conflict, then, an individualist might perceive a collectivist's communication behaviors as conveying weakness, passivity, or a lack of interest. Likewise, the collectivist may perceive the individualist's communication patterns as overly aggressive or self-centered, even though each person is communicating in a way that is normal in his or her culture.

Co-cultural differences can also influence perceptions of communication. Younger workers might perceive their older supervisors' advice as outdated or irrelevant, whereas the supervisors may perceive their younger workers' indifference to their advice as naive.[18] Likewise, liberals and conservatives may each see the other's communication messages as rooted in ignorance.

Stereotypes influence perceptions.   A **stereotype** is a generalization about a group or category of people that can have a powerful influence on the way we perceive others and their communication behavior.[19] Stereotyping is a three-part process:

- First, we identify a group to which we believe another person belongs ("you are an accountant").
- Second, we recall a generalization others often make about the people in that group ("accountants have no sense of humor").
- Finally, we apply that generalization to the person ("therefore, you must have no sense of humor").

You can probably think of stereotypes for many groups. What stereotypes come to mind for people with physical or mental disabilities? Wealthy people? Science fiction fans? Immigrants? What stereotypes come to mind when you think about yourself?

Many people find stereotyping distasteful or unethical, particularly when stereotypes have to do with characteristics such as sex, race, and sexual orientation.[20] Unquestionably, because it underestimates the differences among individuals in a group, stereotyping can lead to inaccurate, even offensive, perceptions of other people. It may be true, for instance, that women are more emotionally sensitive than men, but that doesn't mean *every* woman is emotionally sensitive. Similarly, people of Asian descent may often be more studious than those from other ethnic groups, but not every Asian is a good student, and not all Asians do equally well in school.[21]

Although perceptions based on stereotypes are often inaccurate, they aren't necessarily so.[22] For example, consider the stereotype that women love taking care of children. Not every woman enjoys taking care of children, but some do. Before assuming your perceptions of others are correct, get to know those people, and let your perceptions be guided by what you learn about them as individuals rather than as members of a group. That advice is especially useful when you find yourself in conflict with someone you disagree with, as the "People First" box explains.

Primacy and recency effects influence perceptions.   As the saying goes, you get only one chance to make a good first impression. According to a principle called the **primacy effect**, first impressions are critical because they set the tone for all future interactions.[23] Our first impressions of someone's communication behaviors seem to stick in our mind more than our second, third, or fourth impressions do. In an early study of the primacy effect, psychologist Solomon Asch found that a person described as "intelligent, industrious, impulsive, critical, stubborn, and envious" was evaluated more favorably than one described as "envious, stubborn, critical, impulsive, industrious, and intelligent."[24] Notice that most of those adjectives are negative, but when the description begins with a positive adjective (*intelligent*), the effects of the more negative ones that follow it are diminished.

Asch's study illustrates that the first information we learn about someone tends to have a stronger effect on how we perceive that person than information we receive later.[25] That finding explains why we work so hard to communicate competently during a job interview, on a date, or in other important situations. When people

PEOPLE **FIRST**

Being Aware of Stereotypes

IMAGINE THIS: While on your break at work, you and your colleague Karina are discussing your company president's recent public statement about immigration. Karina's comments lead you to realize that you have strongly opposing opinions. One of you feels undocumented workers waste taxpayers' money by using social services without defraying their cost. The other believes everyone deserves to share in the "American dream," and that some U.S. industries, such as agriculture and construction, employ large numbers of undocumented workers.

You find Karina's opinions infuriating and wonder aloud how she can possibly think the way she does. She wonders the same about you, and soon your conversation has turned into an argument, with each of you calling the other's beliefs ignorant and dangerous. You both go back to work angry and frustrated.

Now, consider this: Your conflict with Karina was based partly on your differing opinions about immigration. However, it likely was also influenced by your perceptions of each other. In particular, once you realized the difference in your positions, you may have stereotyped each other as "conservative" or "liberal." Doing so may have led you to make inaccurate assumptions about the other and to consider yourself open-minded while dismissing the other person's arguments as uninformed.

- The first step in keeping stereotypes from influencing your perceptions is awareness. Because Karina's position differs from yours, do you assume she is narrow-minded or naive? Do you presuppose anything about her background or experiences?

- If you do recognize assumptions you are making about Karina, remind yourself that stereotypes are often inaccurate when applied to individuals. It may be true that people with liberal and conservative viewpoints have different backgrounds and life experiences, but that doesn't necessarily mean every conservative person is the same, nor every liberal person.

- Instead of dismissing Karina's arguments as wrong, ask her why she feels as she does, and listen to her answer with an open mind. You may find her positions well informed and logical, even if you disagree with them.

Stereotypes can easily influence our perceptions of others, even without our being aware. It leads us to think superficially about others and their ideas, which can make it difficult for us to prioritize people above the disagreements we may have with them.

THINK ABOUT THIS:

Why do you think stereotyping is so easy to do, and so challenging to combat? When have your stereotypes about other individuals turned out to be inaccurate in the past?

evaluate us favorably at first, they are more likely to perceive us in a positive light from then on.[26]

Stand-up comedians will tell you, however, that the two most important jokes in a show are the first *and* the last. That advice follows a principle known as the **recency effect**, which says that the most recent impression we have of a person's communication is more powerful than our earlier impressions.[27]

Which is more important, the first or the most recent impression? The answer is that *both* appear to be more important than any impressions we form in between.[28] To grasp this key point, consider the last significant conversation you had with someone. You probably have a better recollection of how the conversation started and ended than you do of what was communicated in between. Figure 5.2 illustrates the relationship between the primacy effect and the recency effect by showing how our first and most recent impressions of people overshadow our other perceptions of them.

Perceptual sets influence perceptions. "I'll believe it when I see it," people often say. However, our perception of reality is influenced by more than what we see.

Stereotyping can be easy to do, but perceptions formed on the basis of stereotypes are often inaccurate. What stereotypes come to mind when you see the people in these photos?

Top: ©Andrea De Martin/123RF; **bottom left:** ©tixti/123RF; **bottom right:** ©jenjen42/Getty Images

Our biases, expectations, and desires can create what psychologists call a **perceptual set**, or a predisposition to perceive only what we want or expect to perceive.[29] An equally valid motto might therefore be "I'll see it when I believe it."

For example, our perceptual set regarding gender guides the way we perceive and interact with newborns. Without the help of a contextual cue such as blue or pink baby clothes, we sometimes have a hard time telling whether a dressed infant is male or female. However, research shows that if we're told an infant's name is David, we perceive that child to be stronger and bigger than if the same infant is called, say, Diana.[30] Our perceptual set tells us that male infants are usually bigger and stronger than female ones, so we "see" a bigger, stronger baby when we're told it's a boy. Our perceptions can then affect our communication behavior: we may also hold and talk to the "female" baby in softer, quieter ways than we do with the "male" baby.

Our perceptual set also influences how we make sense of people, circumstances, and events. Deeply religious individuals may talk about healings as miracles or answers to prayer, whereas others may describe them as natural responses to medication.[31] Highly homophobic people are more likely than others to perceive affectionate communication between men as sexual in nature.[32]

CAREER TIP

Many people recognize Andre Iguodala as a star professional basketball player who has contributed to multiple NBA championships. Fewer people may know of his other professional accomplishments as a successful tech venture capitalist and sought-after speaker about leadership and technology.

Iguodala has overcome many stereotypes and misperceptions about athletes and their aptitude for business ventures. As he explained, "I try to let the people I do business with off the court know that I'm serious about my business off the court. So, I try not to mix the two. . . . I want them to know that I'm serious about what I'm doing and it's a priority to me."[33]

Iguodala has overcome the primacy effect (most people's first impressions of him are as a basketball player) to demonstrate his talent for business. He networks among insiders in the tech industry. He spends hours each day learning about the latest trends in business and technology. He grills potential business partners and demonstrates his thorough background in the tech industry. He actively seeks out speaking opportunities at technology events and has gained a reputation as an innovative thinker and leader.[34]

Iguodala's awareness of the way he may be perceived has helped him intentionally develop his skills and communicate in ways that make a lasting impression based on

Andre Iguodala
©Drew Altizer/Sipa Press/San Francisco/CA/United States

his most recent encounters in business (recency effect). Identify the misperceptions others may have of you and then look for opportunities to challenge those misperceptions. If you believe others see you as lacking initiative, for instance, volunteer to lead a work team or organize an after-work social event. If others perceive that you're not a team player, make a point to ask co-workers for their input on a project or invite them to brainstorm with you on a problem. Like Iguodala, you can then find ways to reinvent yourself as your career interests change or expand.

Perception is a complex process. As we will discover in the next section, we are vulnerable to mistakes not only when we form perceptions but also when we try to explain what we perceive.

Communicating and Explaining Our Perceptions

Suppose you're meeting with a committee at work that is focused on restructuring the employee evaluation process. In the middle of your discussion, your supervisor enters the room, walks over to your co-worker Erika, and whispers something to her. Erika's eyes start to water immediately, and then she gets up from the table and follows your supervisor out of the room. The rest of you stare at each other, wondering what just happened. Did Erika just receive some upsetting news? Was she tearing up because she was happy about what your supervisor told her?

Figure 5.2

Primacy and Recency Effects

Our first impressions and our most recent impressions are more important than those that come in between.

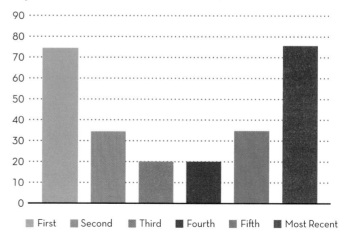

When we perceive social behavior, especially behavior we find surprising, our nearly automatic reaction is to try to make sense of it.[35] We need to understand what is happening to know how to react. After all, if you perceive that someone is communicating out of anger or jealousy, you will react differently than if you perceive the motivation is humor or sarcasm. Our ability to explain social behavior—including our own—helps us perceive our social world. In this section, we will see that we explain behaviors by forming attributions for them, and we will discover how to avoid two of the most common errors people make when doing so.

WE EXPLAIN BEHAVIOR THROUGH ATTRIBUTIONS

An **attribution** is an explanation of an observed behavior, the answer to the question "Why did this occur?"[36] Attributions tend to vary along three important dimensions: locus, stability, and controllability.[37]

Attributions vary in locus.   Locus describes the place where the cause of a behavior is "located," whether within or outside ourselves.[38] Some of our behaviors have *internal* loci (the plural of *locus*), meaning they're caused by a particular characteristic of ourselves. Other behaviors have *external* loci, meaning they are caused by something outside ourselves. If your boss is late for your 9 a.m. performance review, an internal attribution you might make about her is that she has lost track of time or she's making you wait on purpose. In other words, it is something about *her* that is making her late. An external attribution is that the traffic is heavy or an earlier meeting she is attending has run long.

Attributions vary in stability.   A second dimension of attributions is whether the cause of a behavior is stable or unstable.[39] A *stable* cause is one that is permanent, semipermanent, or at least not easily changed. Why was your boss late? Rush hour traffic is a stable cause for lateness because it's a permanent feature of many people's morning commute. The attribution that she is rarely punctual would likewise be stable because it identifies an enduring aspect of her behavior. In contrast, a traffic accident or an overly long morning meeting would be an *unstable* cause of your boss's lateness because those events occur only from time to time and are largely unpredictable.

Attributions vary in controllability. Finally, causes for behavior vary in how controllable they are.[40] You make a *controllable* attribution for someone's behavior when you believe the cause was under that person's control. In contrast, an *uncontrollable* attribution identifies a cause beyond the person's control. If you perceive that your boss is late for your appointment because she has spent too much time socializing with other co-workers beforehand, that is a controllable attribution because socializing is under her control.

Alternatively, if you perceive she's late because she was in a car accident on the way to work, that is an uncontrollable attribution because she couldn't help but be late if she wrecked her car.

AVOIDING TWO COMMON ATTRIBUTION ERRORS

Although most of us probably try to generate accurate attributions for other people's behaviors, we are still vulnerable to making attribution mistakes.[41] Suppose you have

---

SHARPEN YOUR SKILLS

Attribution Making

Working with a partner or in a small group, consider Erika's reaction to what your manager told her, and generate an attribution for her reaction that is internal and stable. Then, generate an attribution that is external and unstable. Finally, generate an attribution that is internal and unstable. Take note of which attributions are easier to generate than others.

LO5.3

Differentiate self-serving bias and fundamental attribution error.

worked at a restaurant for many years. You started out bussing tables, then became a server, and you're now the weekend manager. You have been a loyal employee to the restaurant's owner, Olivia, even accepting reduced hours when business has been slow. Thus, you are shocked to learn that Olivia is selling the restaurant and moving out of state. After many years of loyalty, you feel betrayed at her decision and uncertain about the future of your own job. You conclude that Olivia is being greedy and thinking only of herself. You learn later, however, that she decided to sell her business and move in order to provide care for her elderly father after his diagnosis of dementia.

We're all prone to taking mental shortcuts when generating attributions. As a result, our attributions are often less accurate than they should be. Two of the most common attribution errors—which we can better avoid if we understand them—are the self-serving bias and the fundamental attribution error.

Be aware of the self-serving bias.   The **self-serving bias** is our tendency to attribute our successes to stable, internal causes and our failures to unstable, external causes.[42] For instance, if you gave a successful sales presentation to a potential client, you may say it was great because you were well prepared, but if it went poorly, you might say the noise in the room was distracting you. Such attributions are self-serving because they suggest that our successes are deserved but our failures are not our fault.

Although the self-serving bias deals primarily with attributions we make for our own behaviors, research shows that we often extend this tendency to important people in our lives.[43] In a satisfying relationship, for instance, people tend to attribute their partner's positive behaviors to internal causes ("She remembered my birthday because she's thoughtful") and negative behaviors to external causes ("He forgot my birthday because he's been very preoccupied at work"). In a distressed relationship, the reverse is often true: people attribute negative behaviors to internal causes ("She forgot my birthday because she's completely self-absorbed") and positive behaviors to external causes ("He remembered my birthday only because I reminded him five times").

Avoid the fundamental attribution error.   How did you react the last time someone cut you off in traffic? Did you think, "He must be late for something important" or "What a jerk"?

It is a human tendency to commit the **fundamental attribution error**, in which we attribute other people's behaviors to internal rather than external causes.[44] But bear in mind that people's behaviors—including your own—are often responses to external forces. For instance, when a new doctor spends only three minutes with you before moving on to the next patient, you might perceive that she's not very caring. That would be an internal attribution for her communication behavior, which the fundamental attribution error makes more likely. To judge the merits of that attribution, however, ask yourself what external forces might have motivated the doctor's behavior. Maybe another doctor's absence that day left her with twice as many patients as usual. Good communicators recognize the tendency to form internal attributions for people's behaviors, and they force themselves to consider external causes that might also be influential.

We do make accurate attributions for people's behaviors (including our own). But the self-serving bias and the fundamental attribution error are easy mistakes to commit. The more we know about them, the more often we can base our communication behaviors on accurate perceptions of ourselves and others.

The self-serving bias leads many of us to believe our successes are deserved but our failures are not our fault.

©Dean Drobot/123RF

LO5.4

Explain how the nature of self-concept is partially subjective.

How We Perceive Ourselves

As much as your communication's effectiveness depends on your ability to perceive others, it also depends on your ability to perceive yourself. In this section, we will discover that each of us perceives our self through our self-concept, and we will examine the characteristics of a self-concept. We will also learn how self-concept influences communication behavior and relates to self-esteem.

SELF-CONCEPT DEFINED

Let's say you are asked to come up with ten ways to answer the question "Who am I?" What words will you pick? Which answers are most important? Each of us has a set of ideas about who we are that isn't influenced by moment-to-moment events (such as "I'm happy right now") but is fairly stable over the course of our lives (such as "I'm a happy person"). Your **self-concept**, also called your **identity**, is composed of your own stable perceptions about who you are. As we'll see in this section, self-concepts are multifaceted and partly subjective.

Self-concept is multifaceted.   We define ourselves in many different ways. Some of these ways rely on our name: "I'm Sunita" or "I'm Darren." Some rely on physical or social categories: "I am a vegan" or "I am Australian." Others make use of our skills or interests: "I'm artistic" or "I'm good with numbers." Still others are based on our relationships to other people: "I am an uncle" or "I do volunteer work with homeless children." Finally, some rely on our evaluations of ourselves: "I am honest" or "I am impatient." You can probably think of several other ways to describe who you are.

Which of those descriptions is the *real* you?

The answer is that your self-concept has several different parts, and each of your descriptions taps into one or more of those parts. What we call *the self* is a collection of smaller *selves*. If you're female, that's a part of who you are, but it isn't everything you are. Asian, athletic, agnostic, or asthmatic may all be parts of your self-concept, but none of those terms defines you completely. All the different ways you would describe yourself are pieces of your overall self-concept.

One way to think about your self-concept is to distinguish between aspects of yourself that are known to others and aspects that are known only to you. In 1955, U.S. psychologists Joseph Luft and Harry Ingham created the **Johari window**, a visual representation of the self as composed of four separate parts.[45] According to this model, which is illustrated in Figure 5.3:

- The *open area* consists of characteristics known both to the self and to others. Those probably include your name, sex, hobbies, academic major, and other aspects of your self-concept that you are aware of and freely share with others.
- The *hidden area* consists of characteristics that you know about yourself but choose not to reveal to others, such as emotional insecurities or traumas from your past that you elect to keep hidden.
- The *blind area* refers to aspects of ourselves that others see in us, but of which we are unaware. For instance, others might see us as impatient or moody even if we don't recognize these traits in ourselves.

Figure 5.3

Johari Window

The Johari window consists of open, blind, hidden, and unknown quadrants, each representing a different combination of what is known to us and what is known to others about us.

	Known to Self	Unknown to Self
Known to Others	**OPEN** What you know, and choose to reveal to others, about yourself.	**BLIND** What others know about you, but you don't recognize in yourself.
Unknown to Others	**HIDDEN** What you know about yourself, but choose not to reveal.	**UNKNOWN** The dimensions of yourself that no one knows.

- Finally, the *unknown area* comprises aspects of our self-concept that are not known either to us or to others. For example, no one—including you—knows what kind of parent you will be until you actually become one.

If you think about people who are important to you professionally or personally, you can construct a different Johari window that reflects your self-concept with each of those people. Perhaps you share more about yourself with some people than with others, making your *open* pane larger and your *hidden* pane smaller in those relationships. Some people may know certain details about you that you don't recognize in yourself (your *blind* pane), whereas others do not. The point is that our self-concept can differ with different people in our lives.

Self-concept is partly subjective.   Some of what we know about ourselves is based on objective facts. Suppose, for instance, that you are 5'8" tall, have brown hair, and were born in San Francisco but now live in Dallas. Those aspects of your self-concept are objective—they are based on fact and not on someone's opinion. That doesn't mean you have no choice about them. You might have chosen to move to Dallas to attend school or take a great job, and although you were born with brown hair, you could change your hair color if you wanted to. Referring to those personal characteristics as "objective" simply means that they are factually true. Many aspects of our self-concept are subjective rather than objective, however. "Subjective" means that they are based on the impressions we have of ourselves rather than on objective facts.

It is often difficult for people to judge themselves accurately or objectively. Sometimes our self-assessments are unreasonably positive. For instance, you might know individuals who have unrealistic ideas about their intelligence, their talents, or their understanding of the world. In one study, the College Board (the company that administers the SAT college entrance examination) asked almost a million U.S. high school seniors to rate their ability to get along with others. *Every single student* in the study responded that he or she was "above average"—a result that is mathematically impossible! Moreover, 60 percent claimed their ability to get along with others was in the top 10 percent, and a whopping 25 percent rated themselves in the top 1 percent.[46]

In contrast, sometimes our judgments of ourselves are unreasonably negative. That is especially true for people with low self-esteem. Several studies have shown that such individuals tend to magnify the importance of their failures.[47] They often underestimate their abilities, and when they get negative feedback, such as a poor evaluation at work or a disrespectful remark from someone they know, they are likely to believe it accurately reflects their worth as individuals.

Several studies have also suggested that people with low self-esteem have a higher-than-average risk of clinical depression, a condition that impairs not only mental and emotional well-being but also physical health and the ways people communicate in their social relationships.[48] We return to self-esteem a little later in this chapter.

AWARENESS OF THE SELF-CONCEPT

Part of being a competent, skilled communicator is being aware of your self-concept and its influences on your communication with others. Three pathways by which self-concept can shape communicative behavior are self-monitoring, the self-fulfilling prophecy, and self-esteem.

Self-monitoring is being self-aware.   Recall from Chapter 1 that *self-monitoring* is an awareness of how you look and sound and how your behavior is affecting those around you. The tendency toward self-monitoring ranges along a continuum from high to low. People on the high end of the scale pay attention to how others are reacting to their own behaviors, and they have the ability to adjust their communication as needed. People on the low end express whatever they are thinking or feeling without paying attention to the impression they're creating.

LO5.5

Describe three pathways through which self-concept can shape communicative behavior.

THE COMPETENT COMMUNICATOR

Googling Yourself: Managing Your Online Image

Employers, creditors, and even prospective romantic partners use the Internet to learn about you. According to one study, 70 percent of employers use social media to screen prospective job candidates, and 54 percent have decided not to hire someone based on the person's social media profile. When people search online for information about you, will you like what they find? To assess your online image, type your name into google.com or a similar search engine and explore the first dozen websites your search identifies that are relevant to you (rather than to someone else with your name). Read each of the following statements, and indicate whether you think it is true or false with respect to yourself by placing a checkmark in the appropriate column.

	True	False
1. I would be fine knowing that a prospective employer was looking at these websites.	_____	_____
2. I found pictures of myself that I wouldn't be comfortable letting my employer see.	_____	_____
3. Most people would have a positive impression of me after seeing the websites I found.	_____	_____
4. Some of the information I found might make me look irresponsible.	_____	_____
5. I'd feel comfortable letting my parents read the websites I came across.	_____	_____
6. At least some of what I found online about myself was inaccurate.	_____	_____

It's best if you answered "true" to the odd-numbered statements and "false" to the even-numbered statements. If any of your answers are otherwise, consider taking steps to alter the online content. If the information or photos that concern you appear on websites over which you have some control—such as your Facebook page or a friend's personal web page—remove the material or make it viewable only by close acquaintances. This may be a particularly important consideration before you go on a job interview or set up a date.

SOURCE: CareerBuilder. (2017, June 15). Number of employers using social media to screen candidates at all-time high, finds latest CareerBuilder study. Retrieved from http://press.careerbuilder.com/2017-06-15-Number-of-Employers-Using-Social-Media-to-Screen-Candidates-at-All-Time-High-Finds-Latest-Career Builder-Study.

High self-monitors pay close attention to how they look, how they sound, and how others react to their behavior.

©Sven Hagolani/Getty Images

Suppose you've arranged for your supervisor Caleb to interview your friend Keith for an internship position. As a high self-monitor, Caleb pays attention to his clothes and grooming to make sure he looks good and presents himself positively. In contrast, as a low self-monitor, Keith doesn't spend much time thinking about those things. During their interview, Caleb is aware of what he's saying, so he comes across as thoughtful and capable. Keith, however, says whatever is on his mind, without considering what Caleb might think. Caleb notices if his behavior seems to make Keith uncomfortable, and he adjusts his actions accordingly. In contrast, Keith doesn't tune in to what he's saying or how his behavior affects Caleb—and unsurprisingly, he is not offered the internship.

From that example, you might get the impression that it's best to be a high self-monitor. Self-monitoring certainly has advantages. High self-monitors tend to be better at making whatever kind of impression they want to make. They often find it easier than low self-monitors to put other people at ease in social situations and tend to be good at figuring out what others are thinking and feeling, a skill that gives them a clear advantage in many social settings.

High self-monitors also pay attention to the way they are portrayed online. What would people learn about you if they Googled your name? Check out "The Competent Communicator" box to find out.

Being a low self-monitor also has advantages, however. Low self-monitors spend less time and energy thinking about their appearance and behavior, so they are probably more relaxed than high self-monitors in many situations. In addition, because they are less aware of, or less concerned about, the impressions they make, they are often more straightforward communicators. They may even be seen as more genuine and trustworthy than high self-monitors.

Self-fulfilling prophecies make predictions come true.   Imagine meeting a new co-worker whom you've heard other people describe as painfully shy. Because you don't want to make her uncomfortable, you spend little time talking to her when you meet her, and you don't invite her to join you and your friends for lunch. Consequently, she says little to you all day and eats lunch alone at her desk. You think to yourself, "I guess everyone was right about her; she really *is* shy." Why did your expectation about a shy co-worker come true? Most likely, the cause is a phenomenon called a **self-fulfilling prophecy**—a situation in which a prediction causes people to act and communicate in ways that make it come about.

How do self-fulfilling prophecies affect the way we communicate? Sometimes our expectations influence our communication behavior—as when we treat someone we think is shy as if she were. Similarly, when we expect our relationships to succeed, we behave in ways that strengthen them, and when we expect to be socially rejected, we perceive and react to rejection even when it isn't really there.[49]

There is one very important clarification here. For a prophecy to be self-fulfilling, it's not enough that you expect something to happen and then it does. Rather, it has to be the case that your expectation *causes* it to happen. Let's say that yesterday morning you expected it to rain, and later it did rain. That isn't a self-fulfilling prophecy, because your expectation didn't cause the rain: it would have rained regardless of what you thought. In other words, your expectation was fulfilled, but it was not *self*-fulfilled. A self-fulfilling prophecy is one in which the expectation itself causes the behaviors that make it come true. That is the case when your expectation about someone leads you to communicate in a manner that produces the expected outcome.

Self-esteem is our assessment of self-worth.   *Knowing* your self-concept and *being happy with* it are two different things. How do you feel about yourself? Your accomplishments? Your relationships? Do you feel confident about and proud of who you are? Such questions concern your **self-esteem**, your subjective evaluation of your value and worth as a person.

Like self-monitoring, your level of self-esteem ranges along a continuum from high to low. If you evaluate yourself positively and feel happy about who you are, you probably have high self-esteem. In contrast, if you are pessimistic about your abilities and dissatisfied with your self-concept, you probably have low self-esteem.

Maintaining a positive image of ourselves does appear to have its advantages when it comes to communication behavior. Individuals with higher self-esteem are generally more outgoing and more willing to communicate and build relationships with others.[50] They are more comfortable initiating relationships, and they are more likely to believe that other people's expressions of support are genuine.[51]

However, although several researchers have speculated that having low self-esteem promotes aggressive and antisocial behavior, the reverse is actually true: aggressive people have higher self-esteem, not lower.[52] Moreover, when they encounter problems in their relationships with others, people with high self-esteem are more likely to end those relationships and seek out new ones instead of working to fix what's wrong.[53]

In this section, we have considered that we perceive ourselves through our self-concepts. Next we discover how people use a variety of communication behaviors to express their desired self-perceptions to others.

Managing Our Image

LO5.6

Identify the ways in which image management is collaborative, involves the management of multiple identities, and is complex.

Our self-concept is related to the way we see ourselves. When we communicate with other people, we are also interested in the way we want them to see us. Our concern is with the *image* we want to project—that is, the personal "face" we want others to see. Is it friendly, outgoing, fun? Or perhaps it is reliable, competent, and serious, depending on the occasion. In this section, we examine what scholars call *image management,* and research that has shed light on that process.

COMMUNICATION AND IMAGE MANAGEMENT

Few methods of communicating our image to others are more popular, even among professionals, than the selfie. Millennials (those born between 1980 and 2000) are expected to take over 25,000 selfies each over the course of their lives.[54] The selfie allows you to exert a high degree of control over the way you present your image. You can give others the impression that you lead a more glamorous, enviable life than you might in reality. You can digitally alter your image to make yourself appear more attractive or socially desirable to others. Between a third and a fifth of social media users admit to altering their selfies before posting them, according to research.[55]

The process of behavioral adjustment to project a desired image is known as **image management**. In the following discussion, we consider that image management is collaborative, that we manage multiple identities, and that managing an image is complex.

Image management is collaborative. To some extent, managing your image is an individual process. After all, your image is yours. Yet you also get a lot of help managing your image from the people around you. As psychologist Dan McAdams has suggested, each of us develops a **life story**, a way of presenting ourselves to others that is based on our self-concept but is also influenced by other people.[56] In this sense, image management is collaborative.

In many situations, we carefully consider how we want others to perceive us. That is the process of image management.

©swissmediavision/Getty Images

If others accept the image you portray, they will tend to behave in ways that encourage that image. Let's say you see and project yourself as a confident person. If other people see you as confident, they will treat you as though you are—and their behavior will strengthen that part of your identity in your own mind. If others don't accept that image of you, however, they may treat you as less credible or as untrustworthy.

Perhaps you have encountered people who seem as though they are trying to be someone they aren't, or who are portraying an image that you don't accept as genuine. In June 2015, for instance, civil rights activist Rachel Dolezal resigned as a chapter president of the National Association for the Advancement of Colored People (NAACP) amid controversy about her racial identity. After Dolezal reported to police and local news media that she had been a victim of several hate crimes, her parents—who are both Caucasian—said publicly that she is a white woman pretending to be African American. Investigations of that claim revealed that Dolezal had made public statements claiming to be black and had listed herself as black on at least one job application, even though she had sued Howard University (a predominantly African American school) in 2002 for discriminating against her for being white. These and other discrepancies ignited a controversy about whether Dolezal had misrepresented who she was. Although the NAACP stated that racial identity is not a criterion for holding leadership positions in the organization, the credibility of Dolezal's self-identification, when it was challenged by others, may have harmed her ability to lead effectively.

Rachel Dolezal
©Splash News/Alamy Stock Photo

We manage multiple identities.   Most people know you only in certain contexts. Your professional contacts know you as an employee, a supervisor, or a co-worker. Your family members know you as a mother, a son, an aunt, a brother, a cousin, or a grandchild. People in your social circle know you as a neighbor or friend.

FOCUS ON ETHICS
Communicating under Multiple Identities

As the new manager of a local hotel, Jerome is aware that many potential customers check out reviews on Yelp before deciding where to stay. To make his competitors look bad, therefore, he creates several fake Yelp accounts and posts highly negative reviews of other hotels, hoping to make his hotel look better by comparison. When a friend questions the ethics of his behavior, Jerome notes that he is simply expressing his honest opinions about his competitors' hotels. His friend then questions why he's hiding behind made-up accounts to express his opinions, and wonders aloud how Jerome would react if other hotel owners did the same to him.

CONSIDER THIS: Even if the opinions Jerome is expressing on Yelp are honest, how ethical is it for him to use multiple fake identities to communicate them? Besides embarrassment if exposed, what risks is he incurring by doing so?

TECH TIP
Image Management on LinkedIn

Nearly all professionals create profiles and post content on professional networking websites such as LinkedIn to use for job seeking and networking. Consider these tips as you develop your LinkedIn profile:

- *Upload a professional, high-resolution photo.* The first impression most people form is based on your photo, which they nearly always see first. Do you want to display yourself in a suit or in business casual attire? Do you want to smile (perhaps to project friendliness or optimism) or not (perhaps to project seriousness or purpose)? What do you want in the background, and what message does that send?

- *Develop a narrative you want to tell with your profile.* Do you want to project yourself as a problem solver, a team player, a creative thinker, or an expert at helping customers? The basic professional story you want to tell

about yourself should dictate the content you add to your profile.

- *Create a concise, compelling summary statement.* Many professionals do not complete the summary statement in their profile. This is a major missed opportunity. In three to ten sentences, share who you are as a professional.

- *Focus on quality rather than quantity.* LinkedIn allows you to add dozens of sections and gives you nearly unlimited space to post content. Add only content that supports your professional narrative and avoid adding clutter that detracts from your overall story.

- *Ask some trusted colleagues and friends about the image you project with your profile.* Make sure to get feedback and advice from five to ten people about the image they think you project from your profile. This will help you refine it to best project your intended image.

Each of those contexts carries its own distinctive role expectations, so you probably enact a somewhat different identity in each one. In fact, we all manage multiple identities. That is, we show different parts of ourselves to different people in our lives.

In the virtual world of the Internet, a person can create and maintain as many different identities as he or she chooses, simply by generating multiple email addresses or web pages or participating in various virtual communities.[57] For instance, you might have one email address associated with your college or university that identifies your name and school. You might have another from a free email server, such as iCloud or Gmail, containing no identifying information about yourself (for example, mybro4816@gmail.com). Perhaps you use such an anonymous address when you want to communicate online without revealing your identity. In virtual communities, such as chat rooms and Second Life, you can manipulate your identity to appear as though you are of a different sex, a different ethnicity, or even a different species.[58] Some people may create multiple online identities to protect themselves when interacting with strangers; others may do so for amusement or to explore various aspects of their personalities.

Image management is complex. Image management is often complicated and may generate competing goals for our interactions with others. Let's say you encounter some unexpected expenses and decide to ask your supervisor for an advance on your salary. You want your supervisor to think of you as a responsible employee, so you have to present your request in a way that projects your image as a mature person who makes good decisions. At the same time, though, you want to persuade your supervisor that you really need the advance. Thus, you may find your image needs in conflict: you want to appear responsible but also in need of assistance. Managing those competing image needs—while still persuading your employer to advance you the money you need—can be complex.

Communication researcher Myra Goldschmidt found that when people ask others for favors, they often create narratives—ways of telling their stories—that help them to maintain their image while still being persuasive.[59] To your employer, you might make such statements as "I wouldn't ask for this advance if I weren't in a bind" and "I'll even work extra hours if you need me to." Such strategies can help preserve your image as a responsible individual even in a situation where that image might be threatened.

COMMUNICATION AND FACE NEEDS

The reason most of us hate being embarrassed is that it threatens the image of ourselves we are trying to project. Helping someone "save face" means helping that person avoid embarrassment and preserve dignity in a situation where that dignity is threatened. Sometimes we associate this concept with collectivistic cultures such as Korea and Japan. In reality, saving face is important in many cultures.[60] Let's consider what happens when our desired public image is threatened.

Face and face needs constitute our desired public image.   Each of us works to maintain our desired public image through the ways we communicate. If you want others to see you as intelligent and competent, you will likely communicate in ways that nurture that impression and try to avoid situations that would make you look uninformed or incompetent. Sociologist Erving Goffman coined the term **face** to describe our desired public image and the term **facework** to describe the behaviors we use to project that image to others.[61]

Researchers believe our face is made up of three different **face needs**, or important components of our desired public image.[62] Helpfully, the first letter of each of their names—fellowship, autonomy, and competence—are also the first three letters in the word *face.*

Fellowship face refers to the need to have others like and accept us. This is the part of our identity that motivates us to make friends, join clubs and social groups, and communicate pleasantly with others. **Autonomy face** refers to our need to avoid being imposed on by others. It's our autonomy face that motivates us to be in control of our time and resources and to dislike having other people make decisions for us. Finally, **competence face** is our need to be respected—to have others acknowledge our abilities and intelligence. That need drives us to seek careers and hobbies in which we can excel and to avoid situations that will embarrass us.

Some people have a very strong fellowship face need, meaning it is extremely important that others like them. Other people may have a very high need for autonomy, whereas others don't mind having decisions made for them. Those differences are part of what makes everyone's identity unique.

Competence face is our need to be respected for our abilities and our intelligence.

©Dean Drobot/Shutterstock

We are confronted with face threats. We often become consciously aware of our face needs only when they are threatened. Let's say you apply for an internship in a prestigious public relations firm but are not chosen. That news could threaten your fellowship face. It could also threaten your competence face by making you feel you aren't smart enough to work for that company. The rejection of your application, therefore, is a **face-threatening act** because it hinders the fulfillment of one or more of your face needs.

Face-threatening acts often lead people to behave in ways that help them restore their face. In the case of the internship, you might say to others, "I didn't really want to

Minimizing Face Threats

With others in your class, role-play a conversation in which you are a supervisor having to criticize an employee's work. Practice delivering your critiques to each other in ways that minimize face threats for the recipients.

work for that firm anyway."[63] In truth, you probably *did* want to work for that firm, or you wouldn't have applied. So, you would likely make such a statement as a way of managing your image with others—that is, you want it to *appear* that your face needs have not been threatened. Your statement is thus a type of *defense mechanism*—a response that minimizes the effects of a face-threatening act.

CHAPTER WRAP-UP

By understanding perspective taking, we equip ourselves to communicate with one another more effectively inside and outside the workplace. Here's a quick review of the chapter.

LO5.1 Illustrate how selection, organization, and interpretation occur during perception.

- Selection is the process by which your mind and body help you isolate certain stimuli to pay attention to. Your perceptions are influenced partly by the stimuli you select for attention.
- Organization is the process of classifying the information you notice. We can organize information into categories of physical constructs, role constructs, interaction constructs, and psychological constructs.
- Interpretation means assigning meaning to a stimulus you have selected for attention and organized. How we interpret a stimulus, such as a behavior, affects our perception of the person enacting that behavior.

LO5.2 Explain the reasons why people commit perceptual errors.

- Cultures and co-cultures influence perceptions and can cause perceptual errors.
- Stereotypes influence perceptions and can cause perceptual errors.
- Primacy and recency effects influence perceptions and can cause perceptual errors.
- Perceptual sets influence perceptions and can cause perceptual errors.

LO5.3 Differentiate self-serving bias and fundamental attribution error.

- The self-serving bias is our tendency to attribute our successes to stable, internal causes

while attributing our failures to unstable, external causes.
- The fundamental attribution error is the tendency to attribute other people's behaviors to internal rather than external causes.

LO5.4 Explain how the nature of self-concept is partially subjective.

- Our self-concept is composed of our stable perceptions about who we are. It is also called our identity.
- The self-concept has many possible facets.
- Some facets of the self-concept are objective, meaning they are based on fact and not on someone's opinion. Many other facets, however, are subjective, meaning they are based on the impression we have of ourselves rather than on objective facts.

LO5.5 Describe three pathways through which self-concept can shape communicative behavior.

- Self-monitoring is an awareness of how you look and sound and how your behavior is affecting those around you.
- A self-fulfilling prophecy occurs when a prediction causes people to act and communicate in ways that make that prediction come true.
- Self-esteem is your subjective evaluation of your value and worth as a person.

LO5.6 Identify the ways in which image management is collaborative, involves the management of multiple identities, and is complex.

- How you manage your image is affected by the people around you, and whether they accept or question the image you are portraying of yourself, making image management collaborative.

- Most people manage multiple identities, meaning they show different parts of themselves to different people in their lives.

- Image management can be complex because we often have multiple competing goals for our interactions with others.

A LOOK BACK

Let's go back to the opening scenario to see some of the ways perception may influence our interactions. Liz complains to Caleb about Aisha, one of the graphics designers, in a way that shows they may be misperceiving Aisha because of self-serving bias, the fundamental attribution error, and stereotypes. Even though Liz did get the graphics a day before a deadline with the client, she attributes her own inability to finish the website updates by the deadline to external causes (scheduled meetings). Caleb reinforces this self-serving explanation by telling Liz she wasn't at fault. Liz may make the fundamental attribution error by thinking the cause of Aisha's delay is internal (Aisha doesn't care about meeting deadlines). Finally, Caleb uses a stereotype (graphics designers don't worry about clients' wants) to reinforce and justify Liz's and his perceptions of Aisha.

KEY TERMS

attribution 110
autonomy face 119
competence face 119
face 119
face needs 119
face-threatening act 119
facework 119
fellowship face 119

fundamental attribution error 111
identity 112
image management 116
interpretation 104
Johari window 112
life story 116
organization 104
perception 102

perceptual set 108
primacy effect 106
recency effect 107
selection 103
self-concept 112
self-esteem 115
self-fulfilling prophecy 115
self-serving bias 111
stereotype 106

CHAPTER REVIEW QUESTIONS

1. What is perception, and how is it distinct from interpersonal perception? LO5.1

2. Define and give examples of selection, organization, and interpretation as they relate to the perception-making process. LO5.1

3. What are three characteristics that make a given stimulus more likely to be selected for attention? LO5.1

4. Define and give workplace examples of physical, role, interaction, and psychological constructs. LO5.1

5. How do personal experience, knowledge, and relationship closeness affect the interpretations you make of someone's behavior? LO5.1

6. In what ways might people from individualistic and collectivistic cultures differ in their perceptions of the same behavior? LO5.2

7. What are the three parts of the stereotyping process? Using the three parts, give an example of a stereotype that is common in your personal or professional life. LO5.2

8. Compare and contrast the primacy and recency effects and explain their relevance to the perception-making process. LO5.2

9. What is a perceptual set? How does it embody the idea that "I'll see it when I believe it"? LO5.2

10. What question does an attribution answer? LO5.3

11. What do we mean when we say that attributions vary in locus, stability, and controllability? **LO5.3**

12. When making attributions, why do you suppose people are susceptible to the self-serving bias? **LO5.3**

13. How does the fundamental attribution error influence people's attributions? **LO5.3**

14. What constitutes a self-concept? **LO5.4**

15. Define and give examples of the open, hidden, blind, and unknown areas of the Johari window. **LO5.4**

16. What does it mean to say that the self-concept is partly subjective? **LO5.4**

17. In the working world, how might it be an advantage to be a high self-monitor? How might it be a disadvantage? **LO5.5**

18. When does a self-fulfilling prophecy occur? **LO5.5**

19. What are some advantages of having high self-esteem? What are some drawbacks? **LO5.5**

20. What is image management, and how is it related to one's life story? **LO5.6**

21. In what way(s) do you manage multiple identities in your own life? **LO5.6**

22. According to Goffman, what is "face," and what is "facework"? **LO5.6**

23. Define and give examples of fellowship, autonomy, and competence face. **LO5.6**

24. What are people usually motivated to do when they experience a face-threatening act? **LO5.6**

SKILL-BUILDING EXERCISES

Differentiating Attribution Errors (LO5.3)

Divide students into groups to share examples of a time when they have committed the self-serving bias or fundamental attribution error in either their professional or personal life. As a class, discuss an example from each group and brainstorm ideas for avoiding biases in the future.

Engaging with Face Needs (LO5.6)

Divide students into three teams and assign a fundamental face need to each group. Have the teams create dramatic skits that illustrate a workplace interaction in which participants needed to save fellowship, autonomy, or competence face.

Understand the Limitations of Stereotypes (LO5.1, LO5.2)

Watch the TED talk *The Danger of a Single Story* by Nigerian novelist Chimamanda Adichie. Then hold a class discussion by posing these questions:

- How was Adichie influenced by the stories she read as a child?
- What is the "single story" that Adichie discusses?
- What does Adichie mean by suggesting that the way to reduce a people to a single story is to start that story by saying "secondly"?
- In what way are stereotypes an incomplete story? Are they also untrue?
- How do stereotypes make it difficult to see the truth about other people?

Aspects of Self-Awareness (LO5.4, LO5.5)

Assign students to watch YouTube clips of business leaders being interviewed or describing their work. Ask students to analyze the business leaders' statements with respect to which pane(s) of the Johari window those statements reflect. When do they reveal information known to the self but unknown to others, for instance? When do they allude to information known to others but not to the self?

Online Image Collage (LO5.4, LO5.6)

To underscore the importance of managing their online image professionally, pair students with a classmate they do not know well and ask each person in the pair to Google the other. Each student should prepare a report or collage of some sort reflecting the information learned online about his or her classmate. Then, ask each student to imagine being a prospective employer and to reflect on whether his or her classmate's online profile would help or hinder the classmate's chances of being hired.

Personal Ad for a Job (LO5.5, LO5.6)

As an in-class or out-of-class writing assignment, challenge students to write their own personal ad seeking a new job. Have students swap their ads with a classmate. Classmates should identify the characteristics and attributes that students used to describe themselves and the type of job they are seeking, and comment on how these reflect the students' self-concepts and aspirations.

ENDNOTES

1. Frieder, R. E., Van Iddekinge, C. H., & Raymark, P. H. (2016). How quickly do interviewers reach decisions? An examination of interviewers' decision-making time across applicants. *Journal of Occupational and Organizational Psychology, 89,* 223–248.

2. Gosling, S. D., Ko, S. J., Mannarelli, T., & Morris, M. E. (2002). A room with a cue: Personality judgments based on offices and bedrooms. *Journal of Personality and Social Psychology, 82,* 379–398.

3. Vazire, S., & Solomon, B. C. (2015). Self- and other-knowledge of personality. In M. Mikulincer, P. R. Shaver, M. L. Cooper, & R. J. Larsen (Eds.), *APA handbook of personality and social psychology. Vol. 4: Personality processes and individual differences* (pp. 261–281). Washington, DC: American Psychological Association.

4. Uhl-Bein, M., Schermerhorn, J. R., & Osborn, R. N. (2015). *Organizational behavior* (13th ed.). New York, NY: Wiley.

5. Goldstein, E. B. (2009). *Sensation and perception* (8th ed.). Pacific Grove, CA: Wadsworth.

6. Floyd, K., Ramirez, A., & Burgoon, J. K. (2008). Expectancy violations theory. In L. K. Guerrero, J. A. DeVito, & M. L. Hecht (Eds.), *The nonverbal communication reader: Classic and contemporary readings* (3rd ed., pp. 503–510). Prospect Heights, IL: Waveland.

7. Zajonc, R. B. (2001). Mere exposure: A gateway to the subliminal. *Current Directions in Psychological Science, 10,* 224–228.

8. Goldstein, E. B. (2009). *Sensation and perception* (8th ed.). Pacific Grove, CA: Wadsworth.

9. Floyd, K., Mikkelson, A. C., & Hesse, C. (2007). *The biology of human communication* (2nd ed.). Florence, KY: Thomson/Cengage.

10. Andersen, P. A. (2007). *Nonverbal communication: Forms and functions* (2nd ed.). Long Grove, IL: Waveland Press.

11. Sowa, J. F. (2000). *Knowledge representation: Logical, philosophical, and computational foundations.* Pacific Grove, CA: Brooks/Cole.

12. Krueger, J. (2014). The phenomenology of person perception. In M. J. Bruhn & D. R. Wehrs (Eds.), *Cognition, literature, and history* (pp. 153–173). New York, NY: Routledge.

13. Coombs, W. T. (2012). Attribution theory in communication research. In N. M. Seel (Ed.), *Encyclopedia of the sciences of learning* (pp. 375–379). New York, NY: Springer.

14. Spitzberg, B. H., & Manusov, V. (2015). Attribution theory: Finding good cause in the search for theory. In D. O. Braithwaite & P. Schrodt (Eds.), *Engaging theories in interpersonal communication: Multiple perspectives* (2nd ed., pp. 37–50). Thousand Oaks, CA: Sage.

15. See, e.g., Manusov, V. (1993). It depends on your perspective: Effects of stance and beliefs about intent on person perception. *Western Journal of Communication, 57,* 27–41.

16. Andersen, P. A. (2007). *Nonverbal communication: Forms and functions* (2nd ed.). Long Grove, IL: Waveland Press.

17. Kastanakis, M. N., & Voyer, B. G. (2014). The effect of culture on perception and cognition: A conceptual framework. *Journal of Business Research, 67,* 425–433.

18. Gaggioli, A., Morganti, L., Bonfiglio, S., Scaratti, C., Cipresso, P., Serino, S., & Riva, G. (2014). Intergenerational group reminiscence: A potentially effective intervention to enhance elderly psychosocial well-being and to improve children's perception of aging. *Educational Gerontology, 40,* 486–498.

19. Bigler, R. S., & Clark, C. (2014). The inherence heuristic: A key theoretical addition to understanding social stereotyping and prejudice. *Behavioral and Brain Sciences, 37,* 483–484.

20. See, e.g., Johnson, K. L., Freeman, J. B., & Pauker, R. (2012). Race is gendered: How covarying phenotypes and stereotypes bias sex categorization. *Journal of Personality and Social Psychology, 102,* 116–131.

21. Spencer, S. J., Logel, C., & Davies, P. G. (2016). Stereotype threat. *Annual Review of Psychology, 67,* 415–437.

22. Hrebickova, M., & Graf, S. (2014). Method for self-report and age of stereotype rater can influence accuracy of national stereotype. *Personality and Individual Differences, 60*(Suppl.), S61.

23. Li, C. (2014). Primacy effect or recency effect? A long-term memory test of the 2006 Super Bowl commercials. *Proceedings of the 2007 Academy of Marketing Science (AMS) Annual Conference, 4.*

24. Asch, S. (1946). Forming impressions of personality. *Journal of Abnormal and Social Psychology, 41,* 258–290.

25. Parsons, C. K., Liden, R. C., & Bauer, T. N. (2001). Personal perception in employment interviews. In M. London (Ed.), *How people evaluate others in organizations* (pp. 67–90). Mahwah, NJ: Lawrence Erlbaum Associates.

26. Vallejo, C. G., Cheng, J., Phillips, N., Chimeli, J., Bellezza, F., Harman, J., . . . Lindberg, M. J. (2014). Early positive information impacts final evaluations: No deliberation-without-attention effect and a test of a dynamic judgment model. *Journal of Behavioral Decision Making, 27,* 209–225.

27. Forgas, J. P. (2011). Can negative affect eliminate the power of first impressions? Affective influences on primacy and recency effects in impression formation. *Journal of Experimental Social Psychology, 47,* 425–429.

28. See, e.g., Garnefeld, I., & Steinhoff, L. (2013). Primacy versus recency effects in extended service encounters. *Journal of Service Management, 24,* 64–81.

29. Schyns, P. G., & Oliva, A. (1999). Dr. Angry and Mr. Smile: When categorization flexibly modifies the perception of faces in rapid visual presentations. *Cognition, 69,* 243–265.

30. Stern, M., & Karraker, K. H. (1989). Sex stereotyping of infants: A review of gender labeling studies. *Sex Roles, 20,* 501–522.

31. Luhrmann, T. M. (2013). Making God real and making God good: Some mechanisms through which prayer may contribute to healing. *Transcultural Psychiatry, 50,* 707–725.

32. Floyd, K. (2000). Affectionate same-sex touch: Understanding the influence of homophobia on observers' perceptions. *Journal of Social Psychology, 140,* 774–788.

33. Strauss, E. S. (2016, January 14). Andre Iguodala Q&A: Aspirations bigger than basketball. *ESPN.* Retrieved

from http://www.espn.com/nba/story/_/id/14565088/qa-golden-state-warriors-andre-iguodala.

34. Boudway, I. (2017, August 24). The new off-court play for NBA stars is startup equity. *Bloomberg Businessweek.* Retrieved from http://www.bloomberg.com/news/features/2017-08-24/the-new-off-court-play-for-nba-stars-is-startup-equity; Terdiman, D. (2017, February 28). How Golden State Warrior Andre Iguodala became the NBA's ambassador to Silicon Valley. *Fast Company.* Retrieved from http://www.fastcompany.com/3064934/how-golden-state-warrior-andre-iguodala-became-the-nbas-ambassador-to-silicon-valley.

35. Floyd, K., & Yoshimura, C. G. (2002). The extended self-serving bias in attribution making about communication behavior. In A. V. Stavros (Ed.), *Advances in communications and media research* (vol. 1, pp. 129–138). Hauppauge, NY: Nova Science.

36. Rittenour, C. E., & Koenig Kellas, J. (2015). Making sense of hurtful mother-in-law messages: Applying attribution theory to the in-law triad. *Communication Quarterly, 63,* 62–80.

37. Weiner, B. (2000). Intrapersonal and interpersonal theories of motivation from the attributional perspective. *Educational Psychology Review, 12,* 1–14.

38. Perrin, S., & Testé, B. (2010). Impact of the locus of causality and internal control on the social utility of causal explanations. *Swiss Journal of Psychology, 69,* 173–179.

39. Gonzalez, A. S. (2016). Attribution theory: Dimensions of causality, stability and controllability according to learners. In C. Gkonou, D. Tatzl, & S. Mercer (Eds.), *New directions in language learning psychology* (pp. 209–232). Cham, Switzerland: Springer; Weiner, B. (2012). An attribution theory of motivation. In P. A. M. Van Lange, A. W. Kruglanski, & E. T. Higgins (Eds.), *Handbook of theories of social psychology* (pp. 135–155). London, England: Sage.

40. Hooley, J. M., & Campbell, C. (2002). Control and controllability: Beliefs and behaviour in high and low expressed emotion relatives. *Psychological Medicine, 32,* 1091–1099.

41. Uher, J., Werner, C. S., & Gosselt, K. (2013). From observations of individual behaviour to social representations of personality: Developmental pathways, attribution biases, and limitations of questionnaire methods. *Journal of Research in Personality, 47,* 647–667.

42. Wiggin, K. L., & Yalch, R. F. (2015). Whose fault is it? Effects of relational self-views and outcome counterfactuals on self-serving attribution biases following brand policy changes. *Journal of Consumer Psychology, 25,* 459–472.

43. Durtschi, J. A., Fincham, F. D., Cui, M., Lorenz, F. O., & Conger, R. D. (2011). Dyadic processes in early marriage: Attributions, behavior, and marital quality. *Family Relations, 60,* 421–434.

44. Berry, Z., & Fredrickson, J. (2015). Explanations and implications of the fundamental attribution error: A review and proposal. *Journal of Integrated Social Sciences, 5,* 44–57.

45. Luft, J., & Ingham, H. (1955). The Johari window: A graphic model of interpersonal awareness. *Proceedings of the Western Training Laboratory in Group Development.* Los Angeles: UCLA.

46. Reported in Myers, D. G. (1980). *The inflated self.* New York, NY: Seabury.

47. Brown, J. D., Dutton, K. A., & Cook, K. E. (2001). From the top down: Self-esteem and self-evaluation. *Cognition & Emotion, 15,* 615–631.

48. Sowislo, J. F., & Orth, U. (2013). Does low self-esteem predict depression and anxiety? A meta-analysis of longitudinal studies. *Psychological Bulletin, 139,* 213–240.

49. Zimmer-Gembeck, M. J., Trevaskis, S., Nesdale, D., & Downey, G. A. (2014). Relational victimization, loneliness and depressive symptoms: Indirect associations via self and peer reports of rejection sensitivity. *Journal of Youth and Adolescence, 43,* 568–582.

50. MacDonald, G., & Leary, M. R. (2012). Individual differences in self-esteem. In M. R. Leary & J. P. Tangney (Eds.), *Handbook of self and identity* (2nd ed., pp. 354–377). New York, NY: Guilford.

51. Buhrmester, D., Furman, W., Wittenberg, M. T., & Reis, H. T. (1988). Five domains of interpersonal competence in peer relations. *Journal of Personality and Social Psychology, 55,* 991–1008; Murray, S. L., Rose, P., Bellavia, G., Holmes, J. G., & Kusche, A. (2002). When rejection stings: How self-esteem constrains relationship-enhancement processes. *Journal of Personality and Social Psychology, 83,* 556–573.

52. Bushman, B. J., Baumeister, R. F., Thomaes, S., Ryu, E., Begeer, S., & West, S. G. (2009). Looking again, and harder, for a link between low self-esteem and aggression. *Journal of Personality, 77,* 427–446.

53. Bishop, J., & Inderbitzen-Nolan, H. M. (1995). Peer acceptance and friendship: An investigation of their relation to self-esteem. *Journal of Early Adolescence, 15,* 476–489; Rusbult, C. E., Morrow, G. D., & Johnson, D. J. (1987). Self-esteem and problem solving behaviour in close relationships. *British Journal of Social Psychology, 26,* 293–303.

54. Galuppo, M. M. (2017, May 19). Millennials expected to take over 25,000 selfies in their lifetime. Retrieved from https://www.aol.com/article/news/2017/05/19/millennials-expected-to-take-over-25-000-selfies-in-their-lifeti/22099995.

55. DailyMail.com. (2017, July 18). Fifth of young people "alter" selfies before posting them. Retrieved from http://www.dailymail.co.uk/wires/pa/article-4706164/Fifth-young-people-alter-selfies-posting-them.html; Tobin, A. (2014, October 26). Millennial think tank: Self-expression, selfies, and personal branding. Retrieved from http://arcompany.co/millennial-think-tank-self-expression-selfies-and-personal-branding.

56. McAdams, D. P., & Manczak, E. (2015). Personality and the life story. In M. Mikulincer, P. R. Shaver, M. L. Cooper, & R. J. Larsen (Eds.), *APA handbook of personality and social psychology. Vol. 4: Personality processes and individual differences* (pp. 425–446). Washington, DC: American Psychological Association.

57. Bertino, E., Caverlee, J., & Ferrari, E. (2014). Identity, privacy, and deception in social networks. *Internet Computing, IEEE, 18,* 7–9.

58. Martey, R. M., Stromer-Galley, J., Banks, J., Wu, J., & Consalvo, M. (2014). The strategic female: Gender-switching and player behavior in online games. *Information, Communication & Society, 17,* 286–300.

59. Goldschmidt, M. M. (2004). Good person stories: The favor narrative as a self-presentation strategy. *Qualitative Research Reports in Communication, 5,* 28–33.

60. Kim, W., Guan, X., & Park, H. S. (2012). Face and facework: A cross-cultural comparison of managing politeness norms in the United States and Korea. *International Journal of Communication, 6,* 1100–1118.

61. Goffman, E. (1959). *The presentation of the self in everyday life.* New York, NY: Doubleday; see also Brown, P., &

Levinson, S. C. (1987). *Politeness: Some universals in language use.* Cambridge, England: Cambridge University Press.

62. Lim, T. S., & Bowers, J. W. (1991). Facework: Solidarity, approbation, and tact. *Human Communication Research, 17,* 415–449.

63. Cupach, W. R., & Metts, S. (1994). *Facework.* Thousand Oaks, CA: Sage.

Learning Objectives

After reading this chapter, you should be able to do the following:

LO6.1 Explain the stages of development for high-performing teams.

LO6.2 Describe the behaviors of effective teams.

LO6.3 Explain distinct styles of leadership.

LO6.4 Analyze functional and dysfunctional approaches to making team decisions.

LO6.5 Recognize when and how to communicate virtually in teams.

CHAPTER 6

Effective Team Communication

Simi, Chang, Geoff, and Casey sat in stunned silence. They had just heard the news that their pitch to a prospective client had failed. It was a big loss. They had competed against two rival firms, each of which emphasized its lower pricing. Their team, in contrast, had emphasized the many superior services and support they offered.

Simi, the team lead, wondered what she may have done wrong. She had assigned each person a different part of the proposal based on his or her strengths, then tied the pieces of the proposal together and shared the final proposal and related pitch at the team meeting last week. Every member of the team said the proposal was strong.

Chang thought about his lingering concerns that they were adding too many technical services to their pitch, which raised the price to the client. He had thought about saying something to the team in the launch meeting, but it never felt like the right time. Afterward, it was too late.

Geoff thought about their launch meeting too. He had suggested they meet at least weekly. In response, Casey suggested instead that she could work out the pricing as long as everyone shared updates in their WhatsApp group. Simi agreed with Casey. She said, "All of you are great at what you do. Let's each do our parts and not make this too complicated."

Casey recalled a moment at the final meeting when she had thought about mentioning that the proposal was simply too costly for the client, but everyone else said they supported it.

All of them wondered, "What should we do differently next time?" As you read this chapter, you'll learn some of the principles that explain some of the team miscommunication that occurred between Simi, Chang, Geoff, and Casey.

Archeologists tell us that thousands of years ago our prehistoric ancestors lived in small collections of hunters and gatherers and may have interacted with only a couple of dozen people over their entire lives.[1] Although the world is considerably different today, our tendency to work in small groups of people—such as teams—endures.

Communicating and making decisions in teams can be difficult, however. People often have strikingly different ideas about what decisions a team should make and how they should be implemented. Coming together over ideas can therefore be a challenging process. For that reason, it's beneficial to know how team communication operates and how we can excel at it so we reach our goals and enjoy our relationships with team members. We can apply that knowledge to almost any team to which we belong.

Developing Effective Teams

You will likely belong to many types of team over the course of your career and your life. As you will discover in this section, much of a team's success depends on having a clear understanding of its purpose, composition, and permanence, and on making deliberate decisions about its development and its culture.

TEAMS VARY IN SEVERAL DIMENSIONS

Teams come in many forms, and we can appreciate their diversity by examining how they vary in their purpose, their composition, and their permanence.

Teams vary in their purpose.   Teams come together to serve a variety of functions. In business the most common are handling special projects, completing the work of particular departments, developing internal systems innovations,

You will have opportunities to work on dozens, if not hundreds, of teams during your career.

©ammentorp/123RF

creating customer service innovations, developing product innovations, engaging in employee development, and reducing time to market for products and services.[2] Some teams—often called task forces or committees—primarily serve in advisory roles. Yet other teams, primarily at management levels (like executive teams and boards), function to set strategy and goals, approve major decisions, and oversee financial performance.

Teams vary in their composition.   Some teams include members of a single department (a customer service team) or a single function (a marketing team). Others are **cross-functional** (including members from various functional backgrounds, such as finance, marketing, and operations) or cross-departmental to ensure they diagnose problems and generate solutions using a diverse set of perspectives. With the many communication technologies available, companies increasingly depend on virtual teams. **Virtual teams** are composed of employees who rarely see one another in person and are usually geographically dispersed. The value of virtual teams is their ability to let employees with many areas of expertise and often in different business units work together.

Teams vary in their permanence.   Finally, teams vary in how permanent they are. Some are formally and permanently organized and titled (such as the *marketing team*). Others are formed temporarily to complete a project or activity (project team, committee). Traditionally, teams worked together for many years. Now, companies increasingly rely on teams that are formed and disbanded in as short a time as one to six months. Many companies also frequently rotate members in and out of teams. These short-term teams help organizations remain nimble and responsive to rapidly changing business environments. They also face unique challenges in achieving optimal performance and trust.

TEAMS GO THROUGH FOUR NATURAL STAGES TO REACH HIGH PERFORMANCE

LO6.1

Explain the stages of development for high-performing teams.

Nearly all high-performing teams go through four stages before they maximize their performance.[3] In best-case scenarios, they take roughly six to seven months to reach this level (see Figure 6.1).[4] Typically, leaders become less directive and more consultative as the team progresses through the stages:

1. In the **forming stage** (months 1 and 2), team members focus on gaining acceptance and avoiding conflict. In some ways, this stage is a honeymoon period in which team members get to know one another.

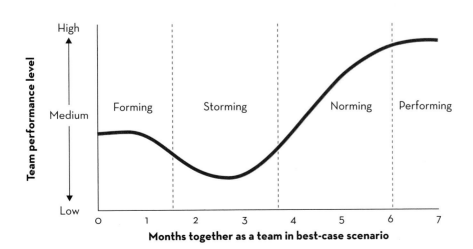

Figure 6.1

Stages of Development in High-Performance Teams

High-performing teams go through various development stages.

Source: Adapted from Wheelan, S. A. (2014). *Creating effective teams: A guide for members and leaders* (5th ed.). Thousand Oaks, CA: Sage. This text examines hundreds of scholarly studies on teamwork.

2. In the **storming stage** (months 2 and 3), team members open up with their competing ideas about how the team should approach work. This stage is typically the least productive, since members are attempting to make sense of uncertain roles, goals, and accountabilities.

3. In the **norming stage** (months 4 and 5), the team arrives at a work plan, including the roles, goals, and accountabilities.

4. In the **performing stage** (months 6 and 7), teams operate efficiently toward accomplishing their goals. They have evolved to a level at which they can transform disagreement and conflict into consensus for future action.

EFFECTIVE TEAMS BUILD A WORK CULTURE AROUND VALUES, NORMS, AND GOALS

Organizations and teams constantly attempt to foster unity and high performance. **Team culture** refers to a team's set of shared perceptions and commitment to collective values, norms, roles, responsibilities, and goals.[5] Typically, teams rapidly develop such shared perceptions and commitment during the norming stage. Only at the performing stage, however, does team culture lead to peak performance.

High-performing teams avoid simply going with the flow. Rather, they frequently discuss the set of values, norms, and goals they share. This process is critical, since team members often attach different meanings to the same goals. Open discussion helps them avoid misinterpreting each other's motivations and actions.

Discussing shared values can be time-consuming, but it provides long-lasting impact for organizations and teams. Drew Houston, chief executive at Dropbox, and his senior teams spent months identifying their shared values. Ultimately, they chose five: "be worthy of trust; sweat the details; aim higher; 'we,' not 'I'; and the fifth is an image of a smiling cupcake, because we don't want to take ourselves too seriously." These values now guide teams in all the work they do.[6]

One way high-performing teams ensure they live up to their shared values, norms, and goals is to create a team charter. This document provides direction for the way the team functions to meet its objectives. Common elements of team charters include purpose or mission statements, values, goals, team member roles (including leadership), tasks, ground rules, communication and meeting protocols, decision-making rules, and conflict resolution and feedback mechanisms. For short-term teams and groups, such as those that operate for school projects, the charter should also include contact information for each team member and deadlines for task completion.[7] Figure 6.2 shows an abbreviated but typical team charter created by a marketing team. From time to time, your team should evaluate its charter and modify it to better meet the team's needs.

LO6.2

Describe the behaviors of effective teams.

Evaluating Team Performance

In a recent survey of business professionals, 66 percent of respondents cited ineffective communication as the biggest barrier to team effectiveness. Other major barriers included lack of effective chartering and goal setting (56 percent), lack of clarity and understanding of roles (47 percent), low morale (44 percent), low productivity (42 percent), and lack of trust (36 percent). When they ranked the most frustrating aspects of being part of a team, business professionals cited the following: ineffective use of meeting time (54 percent), ineffective communication among team members (50 percent), lack of accountability (47 percent), individuals who don't complete assignments (44 percent), and lack of preparation in meetings (41 percent).[8] All these factors in turn relate to communication competencies.

Your teams will perform far better if they follow the basic principles of team communication, all of which depend on a strong listening-centered approach. Work in

Prestigio Marketing Team Charter

Mission Statement: We provide marketing for Prestigio that matches its mission of outstanding guest service, superior financial results, and sustainability.

Values: Excellence in all work, creativity, honesty, sharing and collaboration, professional growth.

Goals: (a) To become the premier resort destination for sustainable conferences in this region; (b) to increase revenue annually by 12 percent; and (c) to maintain 95 percent guest satisfaction among business travelers and reach 85 percent guest satisfaction among conference attendees.

Team Member Roles/Responsibilities

Team Member	Position	Responsibilities
Andrea Garcia	General manager	Oversee all marketing initiatives.
Nancy Jeffreys	Director of marketing	Lead marketing efforts for non-convention guests.
Barbara Brookshire	Director of conventions	Lead marketing efforts for convention guests.
Kip Yamada	Marketing associate	Develop campaigns for business travelers.
Jeff Anderton	Marketing assistant	Conduct market research and analytics.
Kailey Chang	Marketing assistant	Create concepts and graphics for campaigns.

Communication Protocol

- We will post project updates, recommendations, and relevant experiences to our team blog. Team members should post roughly twice per week.
- We will respond to direct messages from each other (emails, phone calls) within four hours.
- We recognize the value of each team member's ideas. We will discuss differences of opinion with one another immediately, directly, and respectfully.

Meetings

- We will hold meetings on the 1st and 3rd Wednesdays of each month at 10:00 a.m.
- We will rotate facilitators for each meeting. The facilitator will ensure agenda items are covered with the input of all team members.
- The facilitator should create the agenda. By the Monday preceding each meeting, the facilitator should make a call for agenda items. The facilitator should distribute the final agenda as a blog post by Tuesday at noon on the day before each meeting.
- We will rotate note-takers for each meeting.
- The note-taker should post minutes to the team blog by the end of the day on Tuesday. The note-taker will create calendar entries for all action items.

Decision Making

We aim for consensus. If we do not achieve consensus, decisions will be based on a majority vote of the general manager, the director of marketing, and the director of conventions.

Feedback

- After each major marketing initiative, we will evaluate each team member's performance.
- In June and December each year, we will evaluate team performance and communication.
- We are dedicated to professional growth. We will constantly help one another reach our professional goals.

Figure 6.2

Team Charter for a Marketing Team

Team charters help teams develop purpose and common approaches to accomplishing work.

teams is among the most researched aspects of work performance. In this section, we will discover that effective teams:

- Focus first and foremost on performance.
- Meet often.
- Embrace differing viewpoints and conflict.
- Learn the communication styles and preferences of their members.
- Provide positive feedback and evaluate their performance.

FOCUS ON ETHICS
Social Loafing

Suppose you're serving on a student government committee charged with organizing the annual campus safety fair. Although the committee has 12 members, only 10 of you are doing any work. The other 2 are engaged in *social loafing*, meaning they contribute significantly less than the average group member. The rest of you are accomplishing all the tasks, yet you realize that all members will receive the same level of recognition when you finish.

CONSIDER THIS: Do you have an ethical obligation to report the social loafers to the student government's leadership? Why or why not? What factors would influence your decision in this situation?

SOURCE: Based on Simms, A., & Nichols, T. (2014). Social loafing: A review of the literature. *Journal of Management Policy and Practice, 15,* 58–67.

TEAMS SHOULD FOCUS FIRST AND FOREMOST ON PERFORMANCE

The most basic ingredient of excellent teams is a focus on high performance. Make sure your team has a sense of urgency and direction to achieve excellence.[9] One signal that teams are sufficiently focused on performance is how often they talk directly about work priorities. Of every 100 comments team members in high-performing groups make, 60 to 70 directly relate to work—goals, coordination, roles, task clarification, and other project-related issues. Another 15 to 20 statements are supportive, intended to show goodwill and encouragement, and 10 to 15 are primarily social.[10] In contrast, team members in lower-performing groups make far fewer work-related and supportive statements. They typically replace these with social statements that may help team members bond, but not around work issues.

EFFECTIVE TEAMS MEET OFTEN

Marissa Mayer, recently CEO and president of Yahoo!, became well known in the technology world during her transformational successes while working at Google. Hired during its start-up days as Google's twentieth employee, Mayer built and led most of the teams responsible for the company's major products. She was committed to their generating excellent ideas and producing outstanding results. To help her teams at Google, she attended up to 70 meetings per week![11]

Most groups underperform because they do not meet often enough. Fundamentally, spending time together establishes and reinforces the social bonding and loyalty a team needs to work well together. Frequent meetings are necessary to establish shared perceptions of roles, goals, and accountabilities. (See Chapter 7 on managing meetings.) Meetings also force team members to meet deadlines. Teams that do not meet often may never reach the performing stage. Or they regress from the performing stage to an even less productive stage. Effective teams, on the other hand, prioritize first meetings and actions. They recognize that the initial series of meetings often set the tone and build a foundation for high performance for an entire project.

EFFECTIVE TEAMS EMBRACE
DIFFERING VIEWPOINTS AND CONFLICT

High-performing teams embrace conflict. They see differences of opinion as natural and as a path to creativity and innovation. So members encourage one another to share their ideas, even when those ideas differ from their own.

One way teams can welcome new ideas is to embrace diversity. Increasingly, research shows that diversity brings better business returns. Diversity comes in two forms: inherent and acquired. **Inherent diversity** describes differences in traits such as age, gender, ethnicity, and sexual orientation. **Acquired diversity** describes differences you gain through experience, such as customer service experience, retail experience, or engineering experience. **2-D diversity** is the presence of both types. Companies with 2-D diversity are about 45 percent more likely to report growth in market share during the past year, and about 70 percent more likely to have captured a new market.[12]

The following behaviors help drive acquired diversity: (1) making sure everyone is heard, (2) making it safe to let team members express novel ideas, (3) giving team members decision-making authority, (4) sharing credit, (5) giving useful feedback, and (6) putting feedback into action. In short, these behaviors drive an innovative, "speak-up culture."[13] Because diversity provides such financial returns and social value, leading organizations focus extensively on cultivating it throughout their organizations and in their teams. For example, General Electric (GE) believes that "in order to fulfill that promise around big issues like clean energy and affordable healthcare, we rely on a culture of leadership and diversity to drive innovation and productivity." GE invests extensive resources to increase its diversity in teams.[14]

Ensuring that teams are innovative requires discipline, because team cultures can easily fall into groupthink. In the past decade, businesses have increasingly encouraged teamwork and developed open-space environments in which team members stay together for longer periods. However, for teams to function well, most members need time to work independently and without interruption. The most innovative teams balance time in teams with time for independent work to capture a diversity of strong ideas.[15]

Later in this chapter, we will discuss principles for handling differences of opinion and even conflict. Here, we present two principles that team members use to embrace differing viewpoints: disassociation and association. **Disassociation** is a process by which professionals accept critiques of their ideas without taking them personally or becoming defensive. **Association** is the psychological bonding that occurs between people and their ideas. Because the purpose of most meetings and team communications is to increase agreement and strengthen the group's sense of purpose, members should seek association by the end of these interactions. Generally, high-performing teams go through repeated cycles of disassociation and association. That is, they suspend attachment to ideas in the initial discussion phase and then attach themselves to ideas as they commit to mutually developed goals and related action items (see Figure 6.3).[16]

You probably noticed that the sample team charter in Figure 6.2 lists several ways of providing feedback. One way is to complete a team assessment several times per year. In Figure 6.4, you can see an abbreviated example of this team assessment. Common topics are results, communication climate (including conflict resolution), accountability, commitment, and trust.

Figure 6.3

The Cycle of Disassociation and Association in Team Communication

Effective teams repeatedly go through cycles of disassociation and association.

Figure 6.4   **Sample Team Assessment for the Prestigio Marketing Team**

Effective teams assess their own performance.

Our Team...	1 (Never)	2 (Rarely)	3 (Sometimes)	4 (Usually)	5 (Always)
Focuses on high performance.	1	2	3	4	5
Sets high goals and standards.					
Follows the team charter.					
Gives each team member a chance to participate.					
Engages in open and candid conversation.					
Holds high-value meetings.					
Handles differences of opinion constructively.					
Develops creative solutions together.					
Helps team members grow professionally.					
Trusts one another.					

EFFECTIVE TEAMS LEARN THE COMMUNICATION STYLES AND PREFERENCES OF THEIR MEMBERS

One particularly effective approach to developing excellent team communication is for all members to complete assessments of personality and communication styles and share their results with one another. The major benefit is to spark informative conversations about people's styles and preferences.

For example, several studies have indicated that effective team leaders are more likely to be outgoing and expressive than shy and withdrawn. One project examined the findings of 73 different studies and found that people are more apt to become leaders—and more apt to be *effective* leaders—if they are extraverted rather than introverted.[17] **Extraversion** is a personality trait shared by people who are friendly, assertive, and outgoing with others. In teams, leadership is inherently social, so extraverts tend to excel at leadership because they are comfortable interacting socially with others. How extraverted are you? Take the quiz in "The Competent Communicator" box to find out. Also, in the "Career Tip," read the experience of a highly accomplished executive who is introverted and who has learned to thrive in teams.

In contrast, **introversion** characterizes people who are shy, reserved, and aloof. Because of their more reserved nature, introverts often experience **communication apprehension**, anxiety, or fear about communicating with others. Apprehensive communicators often have difficulty leading. One study found that people who scored high on a test of communication apprehension perceived themselves—and were perceived by others—as less likely to be good leaders than were people who scored low on communication apprehension.[18] The difference between extraversion and introversion is just one example of the way evaluating and sharing their communication styles and preferences can help team members adapt to each other more effectively.

Your Degree of Extraversion—High, Low, or No?

Extraversion is a personality trait reflecting how assertive, friendly, and outgoing you are. How extraverted are you? Read each of the following statements, and indicate whether you think it is true or false with respect to yourself by placing a checkmark in the appropriate column. There are no right or wrong answers. Simply respond to each statement in the way that seems to best represent you.

	True	False
1. I see myself as someone who is talkative.	_____	_____
2. I see myself as someone who is unreserved.	_____	_____
3. I see myself as someone who is full of energy.	_____	_____
4. I see myself as someone who generates a lot of enthusiasm.	_____	_____
5. I see myself as someone who doesn't tend to be quiet.	_____	_____
6. I see myself as someone with an assertive personality.	_____	_____
7. I see myself as someone who is rarely shy or inhibited.	_____	_____
8. I see myself as someone who is outgoing and sociable.	_____	_____

When you're finished, add up the number of statements you marked as true. If your total was 7 or above, you are highly extraverted. You are generally outgoing and sociable, and rarely inhibited or shy. If your total was between 4 and 6, you are moderately extraverted. You're outgoing and assertive, but not to a substantial degree. If your total was 3 or lower, you are not particularly extraverted. You tend to be more reserved and shy in social interaction.

SOURCE: Items adapted from John, O. P., & Srivastava, S. (1999). *The Big-Five trait taxonomy: History, measurement, and theoretical perspectives.* In L. A. Pervin & O. P. John (Eds.), *Handbook of personality: Theory and research* (Vol. 2, pp. 102–138). New York, NY: Guilford.

In teams, introverts can do a number of things to bring out the best in extraverted teammates: they can give their extraverted colleagues enough time to interact with all team members; engage in small talk and light topics during conversations; speak up more quickly than feels natural so their colleagues know they want to share their thoughts; offer personal information more often; and express their preference to respond to questions after they've had time to gather their thoughts. Extraverts can take a number of actions to help their introverted teammates: make sure their introverted colleagues have enough time to prepare for presentations or meetings; allow conversations to have fewer and more in-depth topics; pause more often and allow longer periods of silence; spend less time talking about personal interests; express their preference to discuss things immediately; and give their introverted teammates more opportunities to be alone and recharge.

SHARPEN YOUR SKILLS

Positive Feedback

After your next class assignment, pair up with another student and share your performance on your assignment, indicating what you did well and what you did poorly. Next, offer each other positive feedback on your assignment that provides encouragement and clearly suggests what the other student should work to improve before the next assignment. After each of you has received your feedback, say whether you perceived it as helpful and encouraging, and offer recommendations for improving its quality.

CAREER TIP

Beth Comstock, vice chairperson at General Electric, is credited with supporting a culture of innovation and creativity thorough excellent teamwork. Yet working in teams and groups hasn't always been easy for her. As Comstock explained, "I identify more as an introverted person, and I've had to really work through my career to not let that hold me back." Early in her career, she says, "I'd leave a meeting, and I'd be thinking, ugh, I didn't speak up.... Early on, I wasn't confident, and I'm sure it showed." Her experience is quite normal for introverted professionals.

Comstock had to overcome her tendency to not speak up in teams in the early years of her career. She often felt uncomfortable sharing an idea until she'd thought it through carefully. Later, as she became more adept at speaking up sooner, she saw how teams can innovate better when everyone is engaged. As she stated, "When you get the teamwork right, it's like magic because everybody has a role."

Beth Comstock, vice chairperson at General Electric

©Bloomberg/Getty Images

SOURCES: Bryant, A. (2016, June 17). Beth Comstock of General Electric: Granting permission to innovate. *The New York Times*. Retrieved from https://www.nytimes.com/2016/06/19/business/granting-permission-to-try-something-new.html; Moorman, C., Chavis, A., & Moreno, J. (n.d.). Marketing in a technology company: GE's organizational platform for innovation. *CMO Insights* blog. Retrieved from https://cmosurvey.org/about/cmo-insights/beth-comstock-chief-marketing-officer-ge/marketing-tech-company-interview-beth-comstock.

EFFECTIVE TEAMS PROVIDE POSITIVE FEEDBACK AND EVALUATE THEIR PERFORMANCE OFTEN

High-performing teams consistently provide their members with feedback—most of which should be positive. They may measure aspects of individual and team performance. They may evaluate performance for projects or initiatives or for certain periods of time. Many teams take time at each meeting to briefly evaluate their performance. Three keys to effective evaluation are: (a) the process should be primarily positive and goal-driven and rarely punitive; (b) the process should include clear expectations; and (c) all team members should participate.[19]

Leadership and Decision-Making Styles

Successful team communication relies on many factors, among them the leader's ability to manage team decision making. Effective leadership and decision making are not always easy to achieve. But the more we understand about the needed skills, the better equipped we are to contribute positively to the groups we lead and belong to. As we'll see in this section,

- Leaders enact distinct styles.
- Leaders manage conflict constructively.
- Leaders avoid groupthink.
- Leaders listen carefully.

LEADERS ENACT DISTINCT STYLES

Think about the leaders of groups to which you've belonged. How would you describe their leadership styles? Chances are each leader had a specific way of fulfilling leadership responsibilities. Many years ago, a team of social psychologists found that most leaders enact one of three distinct styles—democratic, autocratic, and laissez-faire. Let's take a quick look at each.

LO6.3

Explain distinct styles of leadership.

Some leaders are democratic.   One of the underlying principles of a democracy is that every citizen has the right to participate in decision making. Group leaders who enact a **democratic style** reflect that principle in their leadership by engaging as many people as possible in decision making.[20] Indra Nooyi, former CEO of PepsiCo, is known for her democratic style of leadership. Nooyi relies heavily on the input of executives and managers throughout the company to identify solutions that can help the company innovate and meet its goals. In fact, she feels so grateful for the input of executives and other employees at PepsiCo that she writes over 400 letters each year to their parents![21]

Some leaders are autocratic.   Some leaders view themselves as having both the authority and the responsibility to take action on behalf of their groups. When decisions need to be made, they make them, usually without asking others in the group what they want.[22] Jeff Bezos, CEO of Amazon, has been described by many employees as employing an **autocratic style**. With an intense focus on raising customer satisfaction, he issues mandates to managers and employees to meet challenging standards. He also has specific requests for managers who report to him. For example, he is known to ask them to prepare six-page documents—not PowerPoint decks—for each meeting with him.[23]

Some leaders are laissez-faire.   Some leaders believe employees and group members should work independently, with little direction or personal involvement from the leader. Leaders with this **laissez-faire style** rarely interact with employees, give them little feedback on job performance, and generally trust others to make the right decisions. When they are forced to oversee decisions or mediate conflicts, they step in for only as long as is necessary. This approach doesn't mean these leaders don't care about their employees; rather, they simply think others function best with minimal supervision.[24] Mark Zuckerberg, CEO of Facebook, has been described as laissez-faire in most cases. Many people recognize that he has hired strong executives and managers and relies on these excellent leaders to operate with a lot of freedom and authority. However, like most people, Zuckerberg also employs other styles in some situations. For example, he applies a democratic style by overseeing a "growth team" made up of hundreds of employees and regularly provides everyone with input about the performance and direction of the company.[25]

Each leadership style has its strengths. For which type of leader—democratic, autocratic, or laissez-faire—would you prefer to work? If you were raised in a country with a democratic style of government, such as the United States, you might be inclined to say democratic leaders are best because they value everyone's input equally. You might also like laissez-faire leaders because they

Many leaders such as Indra Nooyi exhibit a democratic style of leadership.

©Paul Morigi/Getty Images

SHARPEN YOUR SKILLS

Leadership Styles

In a small group, discuss and identify the primary leadership styles of several leaders with whom you're familiar, such as the U.S. president, the governor of your state, the mayor of your city, the president of your college, and your student body president. Identify the behaviors and characteristics that lead you to make each assessment. Afterward, compare your assessments with those of other groups in your class.

allow you to work autonomously. If you value equality and autonomy, you might say that autocratic leaders are least preferable because they give you neither equality nor autonomy. The examples of Indra Nooyi, Jeff Bezos, and Mark Zuckerberg illustrate that leaders with each style can be extremely successful.

Preferences aside, each style of leadership is best under certain circumstances. When it's important that everyone in a group believe he or she has an equal voice in decision making, the democratic style of leadership is the most likely to accomplish that goal.[26] Even if everyone doesn't agree with the group's decision, the democratic style helps ensure that no one feels neglected or unimportant.

If the group's priority is to accomplish its tasks quickly, however, the autocratic style is best because only one person needs to make the decisions. The autocratic style is also the most effective when the leader has knowledge or expertise that the group members at large lack. If a senior physician is leading a group of interns in a complicated surgery, for instance, it's best for everyone if the physician takes charge and gives orders rather than taking a vote about how to proceed with the surgery, because the surgeon's experience confers knowledge the interns don't yet have.

In groups of people who are proficient at working on their own, the laissez-faire style can be best because it gives them the greatest autonomy to do their work. Although most leaders need to provide some level of oversight, a laissez-faire leader lets his or her group members work independently, giving direction only when absolutely necessary. That approach backfires when group members lack the skills or training to work autonomously, but it can be very effective when group members are proficient at working on their own.

The relative mix of democratic, autocratic, and laissez-faire styles is often a reflection of an organization's culture. Increasingly, organizations are seeking to become flatter with fewer layers of management, a more participative approach intended to improve communication and collaboration. An extreme version of this idea is a *holacracy,* in which organizations seek to allow employees total freedom to self-organize around projects that interest them the most.[27]

In practice, it's difficult to maintain effective performance by relying on just one leadership style. Most companies contain a mix of leaders and managers with democratic, autocratic, and laissez-faire styles to help encourage contributions from all employees while maintaining structure and efficiency.

LO6.4

Analyze functional and dysfunctional approaches to making team decisions.

LEADERS MANAGE CONFLICT CONSTRUCTIVELY

Because the members of a group are interdependent, they are bound to experience conflict from time to time. Recall that conflict occurs when two or more interdependent parties enact a struggle over goals they perceive to be incompatible. Especially when groups are faced with decisions, conflict can arise because of perceived differences among members' goals. Conflict is not necessarily problematic. In fact, it can motivate groups to make more creative decisions than they otherwise might. What matters is the way groups *manage* conflict when it arises.

According to researchers Robert Blake and Jane Mouton, our options for dealing with conflict are based on two underlying dimensions: our concern for our own needs and desires, and our concern for the other party's needs and desires.[28] When plotted on a graph (see Figure 6.5), these dimensions give rise to five major strategies for engaging in conflict: competing, avoiding, accommodating, compromising, and collaborating. These strategies are behaviors rather than personality types, so we can learn to use any of them. Some may seem more appropriate or more desirable than others. As we examine them, however, consider that each may be best under certain circumstances.

Managing conflict through competing. The **competing style** represents a high concern for our own needs and desires and a low concern for those of the other party. The goal is to win the conflict while the other party loses. Engaging in conflict in this style is much like playing football. There are no tied games—rather, one team's win is the other team's loss.

Competing might be appropriate when there is a concrete outcome that cannot be shared, such as when two people are vying to become a committee chair. People may also see ongoing competition as a positive aspect of their relationship if it motivates each to perform at his or her best. The competing style of managing conflict becomes problematic, however, when it leads to resentment or a desire to get even with people who win.[29]

Managing conflict through avoiding. A very different approach to conflict is the **avoiding style**, which demonstrates low concern for both the self and the other party. Adopting this style means ignoring the conflict and hoping it will go away on its own. Some people choose avoidance because they are uncomfortable engaging in conflict. Others choose it because they don't care enough about the outcome of the conflict to bother. Avoiding conflict isn't always the wrong choice; many people in groups opt to ignore or avoid certain points of contention among themselves to maintain harmony.[30] When avoidance becomes a group's primary way of managing conflict, however, it often leaves important matters unresolved. The result can be dissatisfying relationships within the group.

Managing conflict through accommodating. The **accommodating style** is the opposite of competing and reflects a high concern for the other party but a low concern for the self. The goal of accommodating is to sacrifice so the other party wins. People in a group sometimes accommodate to keep the peace, which may work well in the short term. In the long run, however, continually accommodating the other party can lead to resentment.

Cultural ideas play an important role in the use of accommodation. In collectivistic societies, accommodating in response to conflict is often expected and is viewed as respectful or noble. In contrast, in individualistic societies, people may be seen as weak or spineless if they consistently accommodate others.[31]

Managing conflict through compromising. The **compromising style** reflects a moderate concern for everyone's needs and desires. In this strategy, both parties in the conflict give up something in order to gain something. No one gets exactly what he or she wants, but everyone leaves the conflict having gained something valuable.[32]

Let's say you're negotiating a job offer with a new work group, and you want a higher salary than the group leader wants to pay. Through your negotiation, you agree to accept a lower salary than you originally wanted, and the group leader agrees to give you an extra week of vacation in return. Neither of you got exactly what you

Figure 6.5

Five Styles of Conflict

Our options for dealing with conflict rest on two underlying factors: concern for our own needs and desires, and concern for the other party's needs and desires. These factors give rise to five main strategies for engaging in conflict: competing, avoiding, accommodating, compromising, and collaborating.

Source: Adapted from Blake, R. R., & Mouton, J. S. (1984). *The managerial grid III* (3rd ed.). Houston, TX: Gulf.

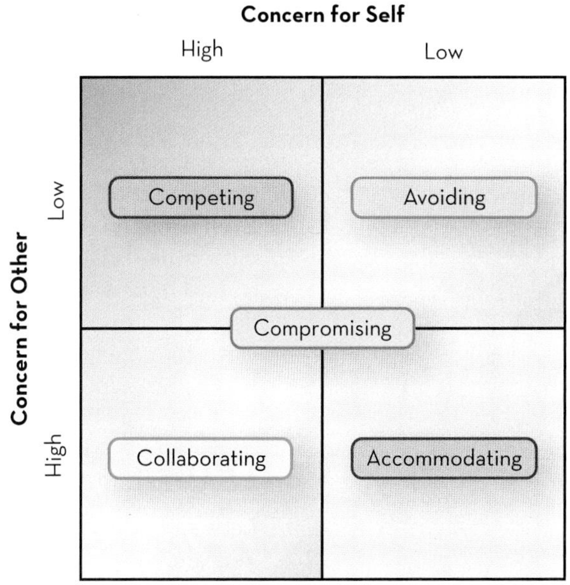

wanted, but you each got something you valued in return for giving up something else. Compromising takes time and patience, but it often leads to more satisfying outcomes than does competing, avoiding, or accommodating.

Managing conflict through collaborating. The **collaborating style** represents a high concern for the needs of both sides in a conflict. The goal is to arrive at a win–win situation that maximizes both parties' gains.[33]

Let's take two colleagues, Sandee and Jakob, for example. Their work requires them to travel several times per month and meet clients. Sandee loves the travel—she likes meeting new people, and she likes going to new places. In fact, she always volunteers for clients who are farther away and require several nights away from home. When Jakob admits to Sandee he doesn't like spending so much time away from home, Sandee adopts a collaborative style by seeking a solution that works for them both. After candidly sharing their preferences, Sandee and Jakob work out an arrangement in which they take fewer long-distance trips and in which Jakob can meet with the client online rather than travel on some of Sandee's trips.

Because it can allow everyone to win, collaborating is often the best way for groups to handle conflict. Yet it can require a great deal of energy, patience, and imagination. Even when it is the ideal approach to managing conflict, it can therefore also be the most time-consuming and laborious solution.

Few of us enjoy conflict, yet it is virtually inevitable whenever we work with and depend on others. The key to dealing with conflict is usually not to avoid it, but to learn to manage it effectively, which means negotiating the points of disagreement while preserving your relationship with the other party. For tips on doing so successfully, see the "People First" box.

LEADERS AVOID GROUPTHINK

Let's suppose you are part of a team of engineers designing a new toy for children. You are concerned that the paint on its exterior could be unsafe for children, but when the team meets to consider approving the design, you feel pressured to keep your concerns to yourself. You sense that some other engineers are also concerned, but most don't speak up. When someone asks about the paint, the team leader says, "Yes, it's safe; now let's move on." You feel pressured to ignore your misgivings—and, along with everyone else on the team, you vote to approve the design.

That example illustrates the problem of **groupthink**, which occurs when team members seek unanimous agreement despite their individual doubts.[34] According to psychologist Irving Janis, a pioneer of groupthink research, there are eight major warning signs that a team has fallen victim to groupthink:[35]

- *Illusion of invulnerability:* Team members are overly confident in their position, ignoring obvious problems.
- *Collective rationalization:* Members "explain away" any ideas that are contrary to the team's position.
- *Illusion of morality:* Members believe the decisions they make are morally correct, ignoring any arguments to the contrary.
- *Excessive stereotyping:* Members construct negative stereotypes of anyone who disagrees with them.
- *Pressure for conformity:* Members feel pressure to conform to the team's decision and are branded as disloyal if they do not.
- *Self-censorship:* Members don't speak up if they have dissenting viewpoints.
- *Illusion of unanimity:* Members falsely perceive that everyone agrees with the team's decision, because they don't hear anyone offering counterarguments.
- *Mindguards:* Some members actively prevent the team from hearing about arguments or evidence against the team's position.

PEOPLE **FIRST**

Handling Conflict Constructively

IMAGINE THIS: Your co-worker Shaun and you are both on the public outreach team at the nonprofit organization where you work. One evening, while thinking about your team's mission, you come up with a catchy slogan to use in an upcoming media campaign, and you casually mention it to Shaun the next morning when you both arrive at the office. That afternoon, you discover that Shaun has taken your idea to the CEO and claimed it as his own, and you plan to confront him about this tomorrow.

Now, consider this: Even though you're angry—and feel you have a right to be—you also want your conflict to be constructive, not destructive. After all, Shaun is your co-worker and you want to preserve a positive working relationship with him. Consider the following suggestions for handling your conflict constructively:

- Try to think of conflict as an opportunity rather than as a problem. Conflict doesn't often feel good, but that doesn't mean it can't produce positive results. Use your conflict conversation as a chance to understand Shaun's feelings and expectations better and to identify solutions you may not have considered before.

- If you're feeling particularly angry when it comes time to talk to Shaun, consider rescheduling your conversation. Giving yourself time to cool off before your conversation can help you stay focused.

- Hold both yourself and Shaun accountable for staying calm and respectful during your conversation. If he interrupts you while you're speaking, say "Please let me finish . . ." and then make sure you don't interrupt him, either.

- Clearly describe the source of your dissatisfaction—Shaun's having taken credit for your idea. Then try to keep your conversation focused on that particular problem until you come to a resolution. Avoid bringing up past disagreements that are unrelated to the present problem.

- Pick your battles. Remember that not every problem is worth arguing about. Even if you're angry about someone else's behavior, it may be best to let little problems go and save conflict conversations for issues that are more consequential.

> **THINK ABOUT THIS:**
>
> In what ways, if any, can conflict be beneficial for a relationship? Why should you avoid engaging in conflict during a state of heightened anger? How can you tell whether a conflict is worth engaging in?

Groupthink is particularly likely to occur when a team has a strong, authoritarian leader, is composed of members with similar backgrounds, and is isolated from outside influence.[36] Under those conditions, teams can produce decisions that appear both unanimous and well informed but are actually neither. Indeed, decisions produced by groupthink tend to be problematic because they have not been subjected to critical thought. In fact, team members are nearly 200 percent more likely to voice disagreement if groupthink is not occurring than if it is.[37] Groupthink discourages all attempts to consider a decision critically, because critical analysis might prevent members from reaching consensus.

Decisions reached by groupthink can have disastrous effects, such as exposing thousands of children to potentially unsafe paint on a new toy. In fact, groupthink has been identified as a contributing factor in several national disasters, including the attack on Pearl Harbor, the Cuban Missile Crisis, the Watergate scandal, the 1986 explosion of the space shuttle *Challenger,* and more recently defective ignition switches in GM cars that led to at least 12 deaths.[38] What is most troubling about these examples is that some of them might have been avoided if the teams in charge had thought critically about their decisions instead of falling victim to groupthink.

Groupthink is believed to have played a role in the fatal explosion of the space shuttle *Challenger.*

©*Everett Historical/Shutterstock*

Avoiding groupthink is therefore an important aspect of communicating competently on teams.[39] Team members can take several specific steps to prevent groupthink from occurring:

- *Be aware of the potential for groupthink.* Teach others on the team about what groupthink is, why it is so problematic, and what its warning signs are. If you detect any of the warning signs, speak up and remind others how important it is to avoid groupthink.

- *Make sure the group has sufficient time to make decisions.* Groupthink can occur when members feel pressured to arrive at a decision quickly. If your team is making an important decision, remind members to allow sufficient time for discussion. If the process feels rushed, say "It might be better to put off making this decision until we have more time."

- *Encourage dissenting viewpoints.* When it appears that most members have the same position on an issue, ask, "What are some alternative ideas?" Encourage members to play devil's advocate by questioning the merits of one another's positions. Remind the team to examine each idea critically and not accept any at face value.

- *Seek input from outside the team.* Suggest that team members consult with people outside the team who might offer useful input on the team's decision. Look up relevant research and bring it to the team's attention.

- *Give important decisions a second chance.* Even after the team has made its decision, recommend that members meet once more to reconsider it. Encourage members to express any doubts or second thoughts they have about the decision. Listen to all arguments, whether they are for the decision or against it. Then ask the team to vote on its decision again.

It might seem that these recommendations will discourage a team from reaching any decision at all. Their purpose, however, is to help the team make a *good* decision by avoiding the problems of groupthink.

LEADERS LISTEN CAREFULLY

When we interact with others, our ability to communicate effectively relies heavily on how well we listen. That observation is especially true when we interact on teams, a setting in which multiple ideas or positions are often discussed at the same time. One way to become a better team communicator is to build listening competence. Particularly useful strategies are knowing how to recognize barriers to effective listening and practicing listening skills.

Recognize barriers to effective listening on teams. A starting point for honing your listening skills is to acknowledge factors that might be inhibiting your ability to listen attentively. Barriers to effective listening that are common in many teams include these:

- *Noise:* Noise is anything in the physical environment (such as sound) or in your individual experience (such as hunger) that distracts you from listening effectively. Try to identify what is causing the noise and do what you can to reduce its effect.

- *Boredom:* If you find that boredom is preventing you from listening effectively, suggest to the team that members take a break and come back to the discussion later. If a break isn't possible, try to identify some aspect of what's being said that you find interesting, and focus on that so you can listen more actively.

- *Information overload:* If a member of your team is overloading you with information, making it difficult to listen effectively, politely suggest that he or she identify the most critical pieces of information and focus specifically on those.

- *Rebuttal tendency:* We saw in the chapter on listening that the rebuttal tendency is the propensity to debate a speaker's point and formulate your reply while the person is still speaking. It can be a particularly common barrier to effective listening on teams that evaluate or analyze—such as juries and advisory boards—because members of such teams may disagree on the merits of the various ideas they're discussing. Remember to listen to everything a speaker says *before* you formulate your response.

Practice listening.   Listening is a skill, not an innate ability. Thus, you can hone your ability to listen through practice. Perhaps you're unsure about how you can *practice* listening. As we considered in the listening chapter, people sometimes engage in informational listening, which is listening to learn. At other times, they engage in critical listening, which is listening to evaluate and analyze what they hear. Individuals also engage in empathic listening, when the goal is to experience what another person is thinking or feeling. These goals are quite different from one another. You can therefore practice your listening skills by paying attention to the specific listening goals that are most useful to you in a given situation.

Informational listening skills are particularly important when you need to understand and retain what you're hearing, such as when you take part in a study group. To ensure you have understood what you've heard, try paraphrasing the speaker's message. Paraphrasing is restating the speaker's message in your own words to clarify its meaning. If you paraphrase a statement in a way that accurately reflects its meaning, the speaker will usually reply by confirming your understanding. If you paraphrase in a way that changes the meaning of a statement, however, the speaker will generally correct your misunderstanding. Paraphrasing can therefore help you understand a speaker's message more accurately.

Critical listening skills are especially important on teams that must make important decisions, such as a corporate board of directors. To improve your critical listening skills, remind yourself not to accept what you hear at face value. Instead, question it. Start by considering the credibility of the speakers. Are they experts on the topic about which they're speaking? Are they biased toward one point of view? If you find the speakers to be credible, ask yourself whether their statements have merit. Are their assertions logical and well thought out, or do they seem inconsistent? Do the speakers make claims that are improbable? Keep in mind, too, that it's relatively easy to listen critically when you are hearing ideas or claims you don't like, because you may already be inclined to discredit such information. If you *approve* of the speakers or their message, that is the most important time to listen critically to be sure you accept ideas on their merits rather than at face value.

Finally, empathic listening skills are most important in groups that provide comfort, such as support groups. In such groups, people often listen to understand how others are thinking or feeling. If that's your goal, practice listening without interrupting. Being interrupted is frustrating. Also, practice listening without offering advice. Unless they specifically ask for your advice, many people would prefer that you simply listen to what they have to say.

TECH TIP

We live in a fantastic time to collaborate in teams—so many communication tools exist to improve team communication! Make sure you and your teams choose technologies that support your goals. Asking these five questions will help:

Do we have a single platform that supports our work and communication? Ensuring you have a single, go-to platform where you can communication and collaborate helps your team accomplish your tasks more efficiently and produce better work. Otherwise, your team's communication may become fragmented.

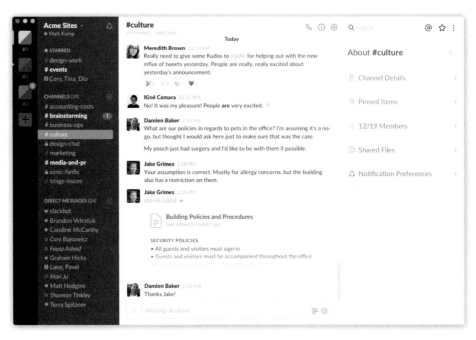

Slack is an example of a popular team messaging platform.

Source: Slack, Inc.

Do we use synchronous and asynchronous communication tools in the right balance? The best-performing teams gain a rhythm of working together and independently. They both communicate in real time (for example, meeting in online conferences or communicating via messaging apps) and work separately and at different times (for example, independently drafting sections of a report).

Do we track and recognize individual and team performance? The most productive teams use project management tools to ensure individual and team accountability. With action items, checklists, and other assessment features, teams document their progress.

Does our use of communication technologies support and include all team members in our decision making? Teams should often discuss whether the technologies they use ensure that all team members feel they have an equal voice in decision making.

Do we experiment with new tools? The best-performing teams are experimental. This applies to everything they do, including trying out new communication tools to identify new ways of working together.

Your team charter is an agreement among your team members about how you'll perform well together. As part of your charter, state how your team will use technology to support your team goals.

LO6.5

Recognize when and how to communicate virtually in teams.

Principles for Virtual Team Communication

Organizations increasingly rely on virtual teams to complete a variety of tasks. These virtual teams generally consist of team members at various offices (including home offices) who rely almost entirely on virtual technologies to work with one another. One recent survey showed that about 85 percent of professionals in multinational companies report working on a team with members in different locations. Of those in virtual teams, roughly 41 percent have never met their teammates in person, and another 28 percent meet in person about once per year.[40] Nearly all teams, including teams located in the same office, rely on virtual technologies for a substantial amount of their communication.

Virtual teams are often created because they cost less, are more convenient, and help assemble experts who are not located in the same office. Many times, they can be more productive and effective than co-located, in-person teams (we'll call these *traditional teams*). However, virtual teams present unique challenges. Members are more likely than those in traditional teams to feel isolated and disconnected from colleagues, be unable to read nonverbal cues, and struggle to manage conflict, make decisions, and express opinions (introverts generally feel more comfortable expressing opinions in virtual teams; extraverts generally feel more comfortable expressing opinions in traditional teams). Virtual teamwork is further complicated by issues such as time zone differences, language differences, and choice of communication technologies.[41] In addition to the principles for working effectively in traditional teams, consider the following tips when working in virtual teams.[42]

FOCUS ON BUILDING TRUST AT EACH STAGE OF YOUR VIRTUAL TEAM

Compared to traditional teams, virtual teams typically find it more challenging to maintain trust over the duration of their work together. One way to ensure trust within the team is to live up to the characteristics you most desire in your virtual teammates. Professionals in virtual teams rank the following characteristics as most important: willingly sharing information, being proactively engaged, and collaborating.[43] Typically, you can take actions across the entire life cycle of a virtual team that bolster your credibility and help establish trust (compared to traditional teams, virtual teams go through the storming stage far less often).[44] In Table 6.1, you can see various strategies for developing trust at each stage of virtual teamwork.[45]

MEET IN PERSON AT THE LAUNCH OF THE VIRTUAL TEAM

The most effective long-term virtual teams meet in person at the beginning of projects to help the team members build rapport. These kickoffs help team members do the tricky work of forming and norming. Not only are these stages of teamwork more

Table 6.1 Maintaining Trust over the Life of a Virtual Team Project

Stage of Project	Key Actions to Foster Trust
Forming	• Asking and responding to questions about one another's professional accomplishments, strengths, and weaknesses • Showing interest in teammates • Expressing a desire to work with teammates • Making commitments to high team performance • Discussing shared values for a team charter
Norming	• Demonstrating strong performance in early deliverables • Preparing well for initial meetings • Sharing information, offering to help teammates, and staying accessible to teammates • Responding promptly to the requests of teammates • Living up to commitments in the team charter
Performing	• Completing all tasks with excellence • Encouraging and supporting teammates to complete tasks near final deadlines when the pressure is highest • Ensuring all team outcomes are fair to team members and stakeholders

natural for most professionals to accomplish in person, but meetings also generally force team members to take enough time together to clearly articulate goals and objectives, values, responsibilities, communication protocol, and other elements of a team charter.

GET TO KNOW ONE ANOTHER

Getting to know one another is important for all team members, and even more for virtual team members. Especially in the early stages, forming and norming, virtual team members should schedule plenty of time to bond with one another. This social cement pays off later with stronger teamwork. Colleagues who work in the same location often rely on informal, *water cooler* conversations to get to know each other better and discuss emerging opportunities in a relaxed environment. Effective virtual teams find ways to establish *virtual water coolers,* where teammates regularly and spontaneously interact. Many tools exist to help virtual teams do this.

USE COLLABORATIVE TECHNOLOGIES

This chapter's "Tech Tip" box focuses on using up-to-date collaborative technologies. Those tips are particularly helpful for virtual teams. Make sure you and your team members consistently discuss which tools work best for you.

CHOOSE AN ACTIVE TEAM LEADER

The primary obstacle to virtual team performance is the lack of regular communication. Team leaders should ensure frequent contact and communication to keep the team moving toward its goals. One strategy many virtual teams use is to periodically rotate team leaders. This helps energize the team and keeps team leaders from burning out. This strategy also helps develop leadership skills of team members.

RUN EFFECTIVE VIRTUAL MEETINGS

Professionals in virtual teams report that their primary challenge in meetings is not enough time to build relationships (90 percent). They also cite the need to make decisions too quickly (80 percent), differing leadership styles (77 percent), unclear decision-making rules (76 percent), and lack of participation (75 percent).[46] Consider the following tips to make your virtual meetings more productive:

- *Start the meeting with social chat.* One long-time expert and observer of virtual teams, Keith Ferrazzi, recommends the "Take 5" strategy—for the first five minutes of the meeting, each person takes a turn to briefly share how he or she is doing.
- *Start with a contentious question.* Opening meetings with energetic and lively conversation causes virtual team members to embrace the meeting.
- *Ask "what do you think about" questions.* Virtual teams—perhaps more than traditional teams—can profit from diversity. Make sure your team is capturing the perspectives of all team members.
- *Make sure each team member is involved.* Some team members are more comfortable and outspoken than others using virtual technologies. Make sure all team members get opportunities to share their views. You might even consider protocols for taking turns in your discussions.
- *Articulate views precisely.* Most virtual teams focus on efficiency in meetings. This forces you to prepare carefully ahead of time and state your views precisely when you have the chance.
- *Take minutes in real time.* In real-time virtual meetings, you can take minutes—particularly those related to decisions—in real time so meeting participants can comment on and correct information during the meeting. This practice often leads to more accurate recollections of the meeting, more buy-in from team members, and a higher likelihood that action items get accomplished.

Using video communication dramatically improves virtual team communication.

©vectorfusionart/Shutterstock

- *Focus on your teammates and avoid multitasking.* Up to 90 percent of virtual team members admit they multitask during meetings.[47] Many new collaboration tools allow teammates to participate in several conversations at a time during an online meeting, as does texting. However, multitasking can take your focus away from the larger meeting, and it can allow cliquish subgroups to form. Make sure you focus sufficiently on your teammates.

- *Use video when possible.* Using video allows virtual team members to better interpret one another's verbal and nonverbal cues. It also generally leads to faster decision making and makes it more difficult for participants to multitask during the meeting. In one recent survey of professionals in virtual teams, 72 percent believed video would make team communication more effective, yet only 34 percent used video to communicate with one another.[48] While video communication improves team communication, it requires effective scheduling and coordination.

CHAPTER WRAP-UP

You will spend much of your career working in teams. Learning the principles of team communication will make your work in teams much more effective and enjoyable. Here's a quick review of the chapter.

LO6.1 **Explain the stages of development for high-performing teams.**

- High-performing teams generally go through four stages: forming, storming, norming, and performing.

LO6.2 **Describe the behaviors of effective teams.**

- Effective teams build a work culture around values, norms, and goals.
- Effective teams focus first and foremost on performance.
- Effective teams meet often.
- Effective teams embrace differing viewpoints and conflict.

- Effective teams learn the communication styles and preferences of their members.
- Effective teams provide positive feedback and evaluate their performance often.

LO6.3 **Explain distinct styles of leadership.**

- Leaders enact distinct styles, including democratic, autocratic, and laissez-faire.

LO6.4 **Analyze functional and dysfunctional approaches to making team decisions.**

- Leaders manage conflict constructively and understand the strengths and limitations of the following conflict management styles: competing, avoiding, compromising, collaborating, and accommodating.

- Leaders avoid groupthink.
- Leaders listen carefully.

LO6.5 **Recognize when and how to communicate virtually in teams.**

- Focus on building trust at each stage of the virtual team.
- Meet in person at the launch of the virtual team.
- Get to know one another.
- Use collaborative technologies.
- Choose an active team leader.
- Run effective virtual meetings.

A LOOK BACK

We have now explored how teams come together, how they evaluate their performance, how they encourage leadership and effective decision making, and how they communicate virtually. So, what exactly went wrong for Simi, Chang, Geoff, and Casey? What can they do differently next time they work as a team to develop a pitch?

There are two signs the team clearly suffered from *groupthink*. Chang was concerned that their proposal was too expensive, but he never said anything to the team. He wanted to make sure his reasoning was tight before expressing his concern, a sign of an *introverted* personality. His behavior is best labeled as *self-censorship*. Casey was also concerned the proposal was too expensive. At the final meeting, she thought everyone already agreed with their existing proposal, so she didn't say anything. Her behavior is best labeled as an *illusion of unanimity*.

Simi's leadership style is most likely *laissez-faire*. She believes in her team members and doesn't want to intrude on their work. This style works in many cases but seems not to have worked in this case, especially because each person worked primarily independently and never integrated the ideas of other team members into the proposal.

The most fundamental problem for the team is that it has never advanced beyond the *forming* stage. The team members do not seem to have written a *charter* and established the norms, values, goals, and preferences that will support real teamwork. Because the team rarely meets in person, many of the problems are exacerbated and the team is unlikely to avoid groupthink. The team should immediately evaluate its performance, discuss how to ensure all ideas are heard before generating solutions, and create a charter that supports high performance in the future.

KEY TERMS

CHAPTER REVIEW QUESTIONS

1. What are the four stages that high-performing teams go through? What characterizes each stage of development? **LO6.1**

2. What are some common elements of a high-performing team's culture? **LO6.2**

3. Why should a team develop a charter? **LO6.2**

4. How can teams focus first and foremost on performance? What are the obstacles to focusing on team performance? **LO6.2**

5. In what ways can teams embrace diversity? **LO6.2**

6. How are introversion and extraversion relevant for effective team performance? **LO6.2**

7. What are the strengths and limitations of democratic, autocratic, and laissez-faire styles of leadership? **LO6.3**

8. How are Blake and Mouton's five styles of conflict similar? How are they different? **LO6.4**

9. What are the signs of groupthink? How can groupthink be avoided? **LO6.4**

10. What are the barriers to listening effectively in teams? **LO6.4**

11. In what ways can you practice listening? **LO6.4**

12. Which actions can teams take to foster trust when communicating virtually? **LO6.5**

13. Why is it important to launch a virtual team with an in-person meeting? **LO6.5**

14. How can a team leader enhance productivity in a virtual team meeting? **LO6.5**

SKILL-BUILDING EXERCISES

Compare a Good Team and a Poor Team (LO6.1)

Think about a good team and a poor team you've participated on. These could be school, work, volunteer, or other teams. Explain the ways each team performed well or poorly. Specifically, trace the teams' development in terms of forming, norming, storming, and performing.

Evaluate Your Leadership Style (LO6.3)

Describe your leadership style in terms of autocratic, laissez-faire, and/or democratic. Provide several examples to show how you use this style. Explain two strengths and one weakness of your leadership style.

Evaluate Your Conflict Style (LO6.4)

In school team situations, explain what your natural tendencies are when you address conflict (choose from competing, avoiding, collaborating, accommodating, and compromising). Provide a concrete example of when you used this conflict style in a school group setting. What are the strengths and weaknesses of this style?

Evaluate Groupthink (LO6.4)

Think about a time when you believe you were part of a team that engaged in groupthink. Be specific about the ways in which your group failed to carefully evaluate your options and make sound decisions. If you could go back in time, what three specific strategies could you have taken to help your team avoid groupthink?

Create a Team Charter (LO6.2, LO6.4)

For a team project you're currently working on, create a team charter. Consider using categories such as the following: purpose or mission statements, values,

goals, team member roles (including leadership), tasks, ground rules, communication protocol, meeting protocol, decision-making rules, conflict resolution, and feedback mechanisms. Feel free to add your own categories as you and your team deem appropriate.

Create a Team Assessment (LO6.2, LO6.4)

For a team project you're currently working on, create a team assessment. You can use ratings and/or open-ended questions. Consider including items such as the following: focus on results, communication climate (including conflict resolution), accountability, commitment, and trust. Feel free to add other categories as you and your team deem appropriate.

Evaluating a Recent Group Project (LO6.2, LO6.4)

Think about a recent team or group project you were part of. Evaluate your team's performance in the following ways:

- How well did your team set goals and purposes for your project up front?

- How did your team establish roles for the project? Was the rationale for these roles appropriate?

- Did your team ever change direction during the project? Did you not change direction but wanted to? Explain how flexible your team was over the course of the project.

- How effective were your meetings? Explain.

- How well did all team members participate? Explain reasons for participation and nonparticipation.

- How well did your team handle differences of opinion?

If you were to start the project over again, what three pieces of advice would you give to your team to create a better final project?

ENDNOTES

1. Relethford, J. H. (2003). *Reflections of our past: How human history is revealed in our genes.* New York, NY: Basic Books.

2. The Ken Blanchard Companies. (2006). *The critical role of teams.* Escondido, CA: Author.

3. Wheelan, S. A. (2014). *Creating effective teams: A guide for members and leaders* (5th ed.). Thousand Oaks, CA: Sage. The terms *forming, storming, norming,* and *performing* are among the most commonly used terms for stages in team development. They are used in close approximation to Wheeler's stages of dependency and inclusion, counterdependency and fight, trust and structure, and work.

4. Wheelan, S. A. (2014). *Creating effective teams: A guide for members and leaders* (5th ed.). Thousand Oaks, CA: Sage.

5. Wheelan, S. A. (2014). *Creating effective teams: A guide for members and leaders* (5th ed.). Thousand Oaks, CA: Sage.

6. Bryant, A. (2016, June 3). Drew Houston of Dropbox: Figure out the things you don't know. *The New York Times.* Retrieved from https://www.nytimes.com/2016/06/05/business/drew-houston-of-dropbox-figure-out-the-things-you-dont-know.html.

7. Byrd, J. T., & Luthy, M. R. (2010). Improving group dynamics: Creating a team charter. *Academy of Educational Leadership Journal, 14,* 13–26; Hillier, J., & Dunn-Jensen, L. M. (2012). Groups meet . . . teams improve: Building teams that learn. *Journal of Management Education, 37,* 704–733.

8. The Ken Blanchard Companies. (2006). *The critical role of teams.* Escondido, CA: Author.

9. Katzenbach, J. R., & Smith, D. K. (2003). *The wisdom of teams: Creating the high-performance organization.* New York, NY: HarperCollins; Katzenbach, J. R., & Smith, D. K. (2005, July/August). The discipline of teams. *Harvard Business Review,* 162–171.

10. Wheelan, S. A. (2014). *Creating effective teams: A guide for members and leaders* (5th ed.). Thousand Oaks, CA: Sage.

11. Halliday, J., & Arthur, C. (2012, July 17). Google's Marissa Mayer: A savvy boss with skills to turn Yahoo around. *The Guardian.* Retrieved from https://www.theguardian.com/technology/2012/jul/17/google-marissa-mayer-yahoo-profile.

12. Hewlett, S. A., Marshall, M., & Sherbin, L. (2013, December 30). How diversity can drive innovation. *Harvard Business Review.*

13. Hewlett, S. A., Marshall, M., & Sherbin, L. (2013, December 30). How diversity can drive innovation. *Harvard Business Review.*

14. General Electric. (2017). Diversity. Retrieved from https://www.ge.com/careers/culture/diversity.

15. Cain, S. (2012). *Quiet: The power of introverts in a world that can't stop talking.* New York, NY: Crown Publishers; Cain, S. (2012, January 13). The rise of the new groupthink. *The New York Times.* Retrieved from http://www.nytimes.com/2012/01/15/opinion/sunday/the-rise-of-the-new-groupthink.html.

16. Watson, R. T., & Saunders, C. (2005). Managing insight velocity: The design of problem solving meetings. *Business Horizons, 48,* 285–295.

17. Judge, T. A., Bono, J. E., Ilies, R., & Gerhardt. M. W. (2002). Personality and leadership: A qualitative and quantitative review. *Journal of Applied Psychology, 87,* 765–780; see also Zopiatis, A., & Constanti, P. (2012). Extraversion, openness and conscientiousness: The route to transformational leadership in the hotel industry. *Leadership & Organizational Development Journal, 33,* 86–104.

18. Hawkins, K., & Stewart, R. A. (1991). Effects of communication apprehension on perceptions of leadership and intragroup attraction in small task-oriented groups. *Southern Communication Journal, 57,* 1–10; Blume, B. D., Baldwin, T. T., & Ryan, K. C. (2013). Communication apprehension: A barrier to students' leadership ability, adaptability, and multicultural appreciation. *Academy of Management: Learning & Education, 12,* 158–172.

19. Hillier, J., & Dunn-Jensen, L. M. (2012). Groups meet . . . teams improve: Building teams that learn. *Journal of Management Education, 37,* 704–733.

20. Adams, K. L., & Galanes, G. J. (2014). *Communicating in groups: Applications and skills* (9th ed.). New York, NY: McGraw-Hill.

21. Safian, R. (2017, January 17). How PepsiCo CEO Indra Nooyi is steering the company toward a purpose-driven future. *Fast Company.* Retrieved from https://www.fastcompany.com/3066378/how-pepsico-ceo-indra-nooyi-is-steering-the-company-tow; Useem, M. (2008, November 19). America's best leaders: Indra Nooyi, PepsiCo CEO. *U.S. News & World Report.* Retrieved from https://www.usnews.com/news/best-leaders/articles/2008/11/19/americas-best-leaders-indra-nooyi-pepsico-ceo; Ward, M. (2017, February 1). Why PepsiCo CEO Indra Nooyi writes letters to her employees' parents. *CNBC.* Retrieved from http://www.cnbc.com/2017/02/01/why-pepsico-ceo-indra-nooyi-writes-letters-to-her-employees-parents.html.

22. Bhatti, N., Maitlo, G. M., Shaikh, N., Hashmi, M. A., & Swaikh, F. M. (2012). The impact of autocratic and democratic leadership on job satisfaction. *International Business Research, 5,* 192–201.

23. Anders, G. (2012, April 4). Jeff Bezos reveals his no. 1 leadership secret. *Forbes.* Retrieved from https://www.forbes.com/forbes/2012/0423/ceo-compensation-12-amazon-technology-jeff-bezos-gets-it.html; Fortune Video. (2016, March 24). How Jeff Bezos' unconventional leadership style brought him to success. *Fortune.* Retrieved from http://fortune.com/video/2016/03/24/worlds-greatest-leaders-jeff-bezos.

24. Hackman, M. Z., & Johnson, C. E. (2013). *Leadership: A communication perspective* (6th ed.). Long Grove, IL: Waveland.

25. Lashinsky, A. (2016, November 10). The unexpected management genius of Facebook's Mark Zuckerberg. *Fortune.* Retrieved from http://fortune.com/facebook-mark-zuckerberg-business.

26. Foels, R., Driskell, J. E., Mullen, B., & Salas, E. (2000). The effects of democratic leadership on group member satisfaction: An integration. *Small Group Research, 31,* 676–701.

27. Roelofsen, E., & Yue, T. (2017, March/April). Case study: Is holacracy for us? *Harvard Business Review.*

28. Blake, R. R., & Mouton, J. S. (1984). *The managerial grid III* (3rd ed.). Houston, TX: Gulf.

29. Messman, S. J., & Mikesell, R. J. (2000). Competition and interpersonal conflict in dating relationships. *Communication Reports, 13,* 21–34.

30. Olson, L. N., & Braithwaite, D. O. (2004). "If you hit me, I'll hit you back": Conflict management strategies of individuals experiencing aggression during conflicts. *Communication Studies, 55,* 271–285.

31. Hocker, J. L., & Wilmot, W. W. (2013). *Interpersonal conflict* (9th ed.). New York, NY: McGraw-Hill.

32. Lin, W.-F., Lin, Y.-Ch., Huang, C.-L., & Chen, L. H. (2016). We can make it better: "We" moderates the relationship between a compromising style in interpersonal conflict and well-being. *Journal of Happiness Studies, 17,* 41–57.

33. Way, K. A., Jimmieson, N. L., & Bordia, P. (2016). Shared perceptions of supervisor conflict management style: A cross-level moderator of relationship conflict and employee outcomes. *International Journal of Conflict Management, 27,* 25–49.

34. Packer, D. J. (2009). Avoiding groupthink: Whereas weakly identified members remain silent, strongly identified members dissent about collective problems. *Psychological Science, 20,* 546–548.

35. Janis, I. L. (1972). *Victims of groupthink.* Boston, MA: Houghton Mifflin.

36. Solomin, M. (2006). Groupthink versus The Wisdom of Crowds: The social epistemology of deliberation and dissent. *Southern Journal of Philosophy, 44,* 28–42.

37. McCauley, C. (1998). Group dynamics in Janis's theory of groupthink: Backward and forward. *Organizational Behavior and Human Decision Processes, 73,* 142–162.

38. Schafer, M., & Crichlow, S. (1996). Antecedents of groupthink: A quantitative study. *Journal of Conflict Resolution, 40,* 415–435; Vaughan, D. (1996). *The* Challenger *launch decision: Risky technology, culture, and deviance at NASA.* Chicago, IL: University of Chicago Press; Edmonson, A. C. (2014, March 20). Fixing a weak safety culture at General Motors. *Harvard Business Review.* Retrieved from https://hbr.org/2014/03/fixing-a-weak-safety-culture-at-general-motors.

39. Courtright, J. A. (1978). A laboratory investigation of groupthink. *Communication Monographs, 45,* 229–246.

40. CultureWizard. (2010). *Virtual teams survey report 2010—The challenges of working in virtual teams.* New York, NY: Author.

41. Majchrzak, A., Malhotra, A., Stamps, J., & Lipnack, J. (2004). Can absence make a team grow stronger? *Harvard Business Review, 82,* 131–137; Greenberg, S., Greenberg, R. H., & Lederer Antonucci, Y. (2007). Creating and sustaining trust in virtual teams. *Business Horizons, 50,* 325–333.

42. Ferrazzi, K. (2012, May 3). Five ways to run better virtual meetings. *HBR Blog Network.* Retrieved February 25, 2017, from https://hbr.org/2012/05/the-right-way-to-run-a-virtual.

43. CultureWizard. (2010). *Virtual teams survey report 2010—The challenges of working in virtual teams.* New York, NY: Author.

44. Berry, G. R. (2011). Enhancing effectiveness on virtual teams: Understanding why traditional skills are insufficient. *Journal of Business Communication, 48,* 186–206.

45. This table is inspired by the work of Greenberg, S., Greenberg, R. H., & Lederer Antonucci, Y. (2007). Creating and sustaining trust in virtual teams. *Business Horizons, 50,* 325–333.

46. CultureWizard. (2010). *Virtual teams survey report 2010—The challenges of working in virtual teams.* New York, NY: Author.

47. Majchrzak, A., Malhotra, A., Stamps, J., & Lipnack, J. (2004). Can absence make a team grow stronger? *Harvard Business Review, 82,* 131–137.

48. Ferrazzi, K. (2012, May 3). Five ways to run better virtual meetings. *HBR Blog Network.* Retrieved February 25, 2017, from https://hbr.org/2012/05/the-right-way-to-run-a-virtual.

Learning Objectives

After reading this chapter, you should be able to do the following:

LO7.1 Describe approaches to planning meetings.

LO7.2 Apply principles for effectively running in-person meetings.

LO7.3 Apply techniques for effectively conducting online meetings.

LO7.4 Recognize strategies for managing difficult conversations constructively.

CHAPTER 7

Effective Meetings

Al sat down and opened the meeting. "So, thanks for coming, everyone. Before I share some items I want to cover, does anyone have anything you want to discuss for today's meeting?"

No one said anything. Nidhi thought, "Oh no, another meeting that's a waste of my time." Frederick thought, "I could be preparing my sales presentation right now, but I'm stuck here."

After a silence, Al continued, "Okay, well, I guess we can just move forward then. I thought we'd start by going over assignments for the new housing project. . . ." Annie sighed and thought, "We've gone over assignments for this project at the last few meetings but no one ever follows up."

What are some of the signs that this meeting will be ineffective?

LO7.1

Describe approaches to planning meetings.

Planning for Meetings

Meetings are one of the primary forums for team members to share and listen to one another's ideas. Done well, meetings can be invigorating, increase productivity, and produce new insights.

Yet, there are some trade-offs. The biggest drawback is that meetings take a lot of time. A study of one large company found that employees collectively spent 300,000 hours per year attending meetings. In fact, a single weekly committee meeting consumed 7,000 hours every year.[1]

Ineffective meetings are more than just a waste of time. They can create division, lower morale, and decrease productivity.[2] Thus, managers who run effective meetings help their teams work more productively and have better career opportunities.[3]

Like other communication responsibilities, running effective meetings starts with planning. For routine meetings, it is not unreasonable to spend between 30 and 60 minutes preparing.[4] Especially important meetings, however, may require several hours or even days to plan. Planning for an effective meeting requires asking yourself some essential questions about the meeting's purpose and characteristics and then creating and distributing an agenda.

ASK ESSENTIAL QUESTIONS

Planning for meetings requires strategy, scheduling, and coordination. As you prepare, ask yourself the following questions:[5]

- What is the purpose of the meeting? What outcomes do I expect?
- Who should attend?
- When should the meeting be scheduled?
- What roles and responsibilities should people at the meeting have?
- What will be on the agenda?
- What materials should I distribute prior to the meeting?
- When and how should I invite others?
- What logistical issues do I need to take care of (reserving rooms, getting equipment, printing materials)?

Poorly organized meetings are a waste of time and productivity.

©Prasit Rodphan/Shutterstock

As you consider these questions, keep in mind your purpose and ensure that your plans focus on productive outcomes. Also, think about how scheduling will affect the productivity of the people who are invited. If at all possible, put people's needs first and avoid holding meetings—especially brainstorming meetings—during the least productive time of the day (usually the afternoon); most employees perform best in the morning (see Figure 7.1).[6] As far as day of the week goes, Tuesdays are overwhelmingly considered the most productive days (57 percent of employees think so). In contrast, Fridays are the least productive days (only 3 percent of employees think they are the most productive).[7]

In addition, think about the materials you should send attendees ahead of time. Plan to send these materials far enough in advance for people to do the required preparation, such as reading a report you plan to discuss.

Consider the type of meeting you want. **Coordination meetings** primarily focus on discussing tasks, roles, goals, and accountabilities. **Problem-solving meetings** usually include brainstorming about how to address and solve a particular work problem. In truth, nearly all meetings consist of both coordination and problem-solving tasks. But coordination meetings typically include many agenda items with a reasonable expectation of accomplishing each one in the allocated time. Problem-solving meetings, in contrast, cover more fluid issues that are less easy to classify or to fit into predetermined time slots. For especially difficult issues (such as handling the transition period during a merger), some teams commit to meeting at the same time each day and without a preset agenda until they clearly define the issues at hand.[8]

CREATE AND DISTRIBUTE AN AGENDA

An **agenda** is a list of items to be discussed at a meeting. A good agenda provides the meeting with structure, and distributing it ahead of time (typically, at least a day in advance) allows each participant to form expectations about the meeting and prepare.[9]

Most agendas should include items to be covered, time frames, goals and/or expected outcomes, roles, and materials needed. You can foster more effective participation by engaging others in the agenda-creation process. For example, at least several days in advance, ask meeting participants for agenda items they want included. You can also consider assigning roles. For example, you might assign different people to be a facilitator, a note-taker (to take the meeting's "minutes"), a timer, and so on.[10]

As you develop the agenda, pay attention to the ordering of items so that it flows logically, much as you would expect other written communications to flow from point to point. It's a good idea to place the most important agenda items near the top. That way, if some issues take longer than expected and you are forced to ignore others, you still have addressed the highest-priority items. See Figure 7.2 for a sample agenda.

In some situations, leaders may not want a meeting's participants to know the true purpose of the meeting beforehand. Perhaps a sensitive or uncomfortable topic is planned for discussion, and the leader is concerned that some people may not show up if they know what's planned. Consequently, a leader may give participants only vague or incomplete information about the purpose of a meeting until it actually convenes. Check out the "Focus on Ethics" box for a discussion about the ethical implications of this action.

Figure 7.1

Least Productive Parts of the Workday

Research shows that late mornings are the most productive time of the workday for most people.

Source: Accountemps. (2010, August 17). *Accountemps survey: Employee output is weakest late in the day.* Retrieved May 18, 2018, from https://www.newswire.ca/news-releases/accountemps-survey-employee-output-is-weakest-late-in-the-day-545226522.html.

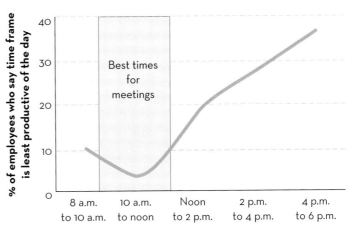

Figure 7.2

Sample Meeting Agenda
A well-planned agenda can help meetings run in an organized and efficient manner.

Prestigio Marketing Team
Meeting Agenda

Date: November 9   **Start Time:** 10 a.m.   **End Time:** 11 a.m.

Purposes:
1. Discuss plans to conduct market research about (a) Internet pricing for groups and (b) customer satisfaction levels relative to our local competitors.
2. Discuss progress on our Staff & Service Initiative started in January.
3. Examine ways to improve participation on our marketing team blogs and wikis.
4. Finalize plans for the Valentine's Day marketing campaign.

Desired Outcome:
Create action items to complete within the next month (by December 15). At our December 15 meeting, we will develop our annual marketing plan, which will include priorities for improving guest satisfaction and pricing.

Agenda Item 1: Internet Pricing for Groups (20 minutes)
- Summary of findings from Internet pricing survey for groups (Jeff)   5 min.
- Industry standards for Internet pricing for conference groups (Barbara)   5 min.
- Group discussion of findings and options   10 min.
- Develop action items   5 min.

Agenda Item 2: Improving Customer Satisfaction (20 minutes)
- Summary of findings from customer satisfaction research on external websites (Jeff)   5 min.
- Group discussion of findings and options   10 min.
- Develop action items   5 min.

Agenda Item 3: Enterprise Social Software
- Discuss goals for increased use of wikis and discussion forums (Andrea)   5 min.

Agenda Item 4: New Promotions
- Valentine's Day hotel promotions (Nancy)   5 min.

Summarize Action Items   3 min.

Participants: Andrea Garcia, Nancy Jeffreys, Barbara Brookshire, **Kip Yamada (note-taker)**, Jeff Anderton

---

FOCUS ON ETHICS
Misleading about the Purpose of a Meeting

Terrance oversees the governmental relations section of a nonprofit organization, with a staff of 12 employees. Because donations to the organization have dropped sharply in the last year, he has been told to restructure his section by terminating three employees and transferring another three to a separate division. He wants to call a meeting of his entire staff, but he fears that some may not show up if they know the meeting's true purpose. His inclination is to send out an agenda listing only vague, ambiguous agenda items, such as "organizational priorities" and "staffing," and then to reveal the meeting's purpose only after everyone has arrived. If his employees feel misled or tricked, Terrance feels that is an acceptable price to pay to ensure that everyone is in attendance.

CONSIDER THIS: Is Terrance deceiving his employees, or simply being strategically ambiguous? What is the ethical difference between strategic ambiguity and deception? Can you think of a more ethical way in which Terrance could have handled this situation?

Running Effective Meetings

If you've planned and prepared well for the meeting, you are in a great position to carry out your meeting objectives. Ideally, you've provided clear expectations for meeting participants—what they should have done before the meeting and what they can expect in terms of content and length of the meeting. Once the meeting begins, you have several options for achieving productive outcomes.

LO7.2

Apply principles for effectively running in-person meetings.

BEGIN ON TIME

Too many leaders waste time by starting meetings late, waiting "just a couple more minutes" for additional people to arrive and then reexplaining material to latecomers two or even three times. That behavior pattern punishes those who are punctual and cultivates the mindset that lateness is acceptable. Time management experts stress that effective leaders begin meetings on time, even if only two people are there.[11] If the meeting is scheduled to start at 10 a.m., an effective leader starts at 10 a.m., not 10:05 or 10:10. That advice applies unless you are leading a meeting with guests from a polychronic culture, who do not necessarily expect events to start at a specified time.

> **SHARPEN YOUR SKILLS**
>
> ### Starting Meetings on Time
>
> Beginning meetings on time can be difficult, especially if only you and one other person are present. Remember, however, that meetings that start on time are more likely to finish on time and are often more productive. When you are in charge of a meeting, make certain you are in the room and prepared to begin at the appointed time, and then begin your meeting at that time, even if some haven't yet arrived. Doing so will send a message that time is valuable and set an expectation that people need to be punctual if they want to participate in discussion and decision making.

CREATE TRADITION, CULTURE, AND VARIETY

Most meetings at Starbucks Coffee start with a customer story,[12] and many manufacturing companies start meetings with safety stories. You can create your own traditions that take only moments but reinforce the culture and core values of your organization, such as having participants share news of each other's successes. These actions create a common sense of purpose (one of the key ingredients of effective teamwork) and are a light and fun way to engage people at the start of meetings.

Effective leaders begin meetings on time, regardless of how many participants are present.

©Roman Samborskyi/Shutterstock

A skilled facilitator encourages participation from all participants.

©*El Nariz/Shutterstock*

SET EXPECTATIONS AND FOLLOW THE AGENDA

Take a few moments to explain the purpose of the meeting and what you hope to accomplish. You may also want to set some ground rules, such as your expectations for others to participate (with cell phones off), the amount of time available for comments, or the way you will deal with differences of opinion. If you haven't already done so, you can now assign the roles of timer and note-taker. You may also point out whether certain issues are considered confidential and shouldn't be discussed outside the meeting.

For most meetings, keep the discussion focused on agenda items and stick to allotted times. Some meeting participants may become uninterested or annoyed if they perceive the meeting as unstructured or off schedule.

ENCOURAGE PARTICIPATION AND EXPRESSION OF IDEAS

Each meeting should have a facilitator. The **facilitator** acts from a neutral position to get each person to participate in the conversation and ensure that each agenda item is properly discussed. Facilitators should acknowledge each person's comments, check for understanding, paraphrase and summarize, not judge, ask for elaboration, and get everyone engaged. Sometimes, this may require using explicit phrases such as "I'd like each person to take two minutes to discuss. . . ." For routine meetings, the facilitator is often the person who called the meeting.[13]

Neutrality is critical in facilitating. If others view the facilitator as predisposed toward certain positions or perspectives, they are less likely to express their real thoughts. This is especially the case when the facilitator is a person of higher authority. Maintaining neutrality isn't always easy, however, especially when the facilitator has a personal stake in the issue being discussed. See the "People First" box for a discussion on how to create an inclusive environment where all voices can be heard.

Making your meetings "safe" for each team member requires conscious effort. After all, in surveys of nearly 2.5 million employees, just 15 percent of respondents agreed that *work teams function in a safe, "win–win" work environment,* and only 17 percent agreed that *work teams have mutual understanding and creative dialogue.*[14] As a meeting leader, encourage debate but defuse any comments that are perceived as noncollegial. The art of encouraging discussion but avoiding arguments takes time to develop. Research has shown that teams that have more dissent during meetings reach higher-quality decisions. By opening discussion to all available information and options, you can help your team adopt the best options more often and become more committed to them.[15]

In problem-solving meetings, the leader must establish a pattern for discussion and debate. Generally, the first focus is getting agreement on the definition of the problem. Then, the focus switches to the history of the problem and its current impacts. Third, participants consider the causes and future consequences if the problem is not solved. Finally, the group is ready to brainstorm options for addressing the problem.[16]

BUILD CONSENSUS AND A PLAN OF ACTION

The primary purpose of meetings is usually to evaluate alternatives and create a plan of action. For important decisions, the group should build consensus around specific tasks, assignments, and timelines. A group has **consensus** when it has identified an

PEOPLE **FIRST**

Including All Voices in a Discussion

IMAGINE THIS: Your production team has interviewed candidates for a new employee position and has narrowed the finalists down to two. Candidate A has the stronger résumé by far but is very similar demographically to the rest of your team members. Candidate B has less impressive credentials but would bring much-needed diversity to your group. Both have support among team members, so as team leader, you have called a meeting to discuss the candidates and choose one to hire.

Now, consider this: You feel strongly that the value of Candidate A's qualifications is outweighed by the value of increasing diversity on your team, so you are strongly in favor of hiring Candidate B. Your job is to facilitate the meeting, however, to make sure that all perspectives get equal consideration, and help your team come to an informed decision. How do you do this when you prefer one candidate? These suggestions can help:

- Acknowledge at the beginning that each candidate has support. This communicates to your team members that you recognize their positions, regardless of what they are.

- If feasible, alternate calling on those who support Candidate A and those who support Candidate B. To ensure no one feels marginalized, allow everyone to speak once before calling on anyone a second time.

- Stress that both candidates bring value, and that your goal is to make the best hire for the team. Hiring one person does not imply that the other has no value.

- If the decision is not going your way, accept the will of the majority. Even if you are casting a vote, as facilitator your goal is to facilitate, not dictate—so focus your attention on enabling a respectful and informed discussion rather than trying to steer the decision your way.

THINK ABOUT THIS:

Why is it hard to listen to arguments with which you disagree? In the situation described here, what would you do as a facilitator to make Candidate A's supporters feel respected and heard, even though your preference is for Candidate B?

acceptable plan of action that all or most group members can support, even if that specific plan isn't everyone's preference. Consensus can be challenging to achieve on high-priority issues, so it is often helpful to start by building consensus on smaller, lower-priority ones.

CLOSE THE MEETING

A key priority should be to end the meeting on time. First, briefly summarize what you have accomplished and recap action items the team has agreed on. Make sure roles and assignments are clear for each of these, to establish accountability for follow-up.

After a meeting ends (even a meeting you do not lead), you should mentally evaluate your performance. Consider these questions:[17]

- How much information, analysis, and interpretation did I provide?
- Did I communicate my ideas even if they conflicted with someone else's?
- Did I participate in the implementation of the timeline?
- Did I facilitate the decision-making process? Or did I just "go with the flow"?

Follow up as quickly as possible by distributing the minutes of the meeting (as a memo, in an email, in a meetings folder on the corporate intranet, or as part of

Figure 7.3

Meeting Follow-Up/ Minutes Components

Follow up after the meeting with these essential points.

- Date and time
- Team members present
- Meeting roles
- Key decisions
- Key discussion points (optional)
- Open issues (optional)
- Action items and deadlines

a team blog or wiki). **Minutes** should include the date and time, team members present, decisions, key discussion points, open issues, and any action items, the people undertaking them, and related deadlines (see Figure 7.3). You can also include assigned roles (such as the note-taker), the names of people who were invited but absent, and information about future meetings (if any). The minutes serve as a record of what your team accomplished and a checklist of follow-up items to be done. Figure 7.4 provides an example of meeting minutes.

Figure 7.4

Sample Meeting Minutes

Minutes should provide detail on what participants discussed and decided at a meeting.

Prestigio Marketing Team
November 9 Meeting Minutes

Date: November 9   **Start Time:** 10 a.m.   **End Time:** 11 a.m.

Agenda Item 1: Internet Pricing for Groups
Discussion: Jeff presented survey findings about conference attendees' purchases of Internet service while here. The group agreed that Internet-service purchases are far too low and that less use for lower-income groups suggests high price sensitivity.

Action Items	Responsibility	Completion Time
• Develop and conduct survey that identifies price points at which conference guests are willing to purchase Internet service.	Barbara, Jeff	December 15
• Develop price sensitivity estimates and related revenue impacts.	Barbara	December 15

Agenda Item 2: Improving Customer Satisfaction
Discussion: Jeff presented customer satisfaction ratings of Prestigio and three local competitors. The group agreed that our customer satisfaction ratings have improved, particularly in relation to competitors. We are most concerned about the areas of cleanliness, business center, and meeting rooms.

Action Items	Responsibility	Completion Time
• Develop plans to improve the equipment and furnishings of the business center.	Andrea	December 15
• Develop plans for improving cleanliness and meeting rooms.	Nancy, Andrea	January 15

Agenda Item 3: Enterprise Social Software
Discussion: Andrea encouraged the group to log on to the new enterprise social platform throughout the day, share documents, use wikis, and stay aware of progress on shared projects.

Action Item	Responsibility	Completion Time
• Use a wiki to collaborate on a joint project with another member of the marketing team.	All members of marketing team	December 15

Agenda Item 4: New Promotions
Discussion: Nancy introduced her plans for Valentine's promotions, including a price special and advertising campaign designed to cater to local-area couples.

Action Item	Responsibility	Completion Time
• Negotiate TV and print ad campaign details with ad agency.	Nancy, Kip	December 1

Participants: Andrea Garcia, Nancy Jeffreys, Barbara Brookshire, **Kip Yamada (note-taker)**, Jeff Anderton

TECH TIP
Using Chat and Online Polls during Meetings

As the number of people in meetings increases, getting input from everyone becomes much more challenging. For meetings of ten or more people (whether in person or online), you should consider ways to ensure everyone's voice is heard. Many professionals now use chat and online polls during meetings to include everyone and keep them engaged. Here are a few tips for using online polls:

Use an icebreaker question. Taking two or three minutes at the start of the meeting to get everyone engaged increases the likelihood you'll get participation throughout the meeting. Ask a light, trivial question that everyone can respond to within seconds.

Create an avenue for questions. Chat and online polling features allow participants to ask questions throughout a meeting. For particularly large meetings (say, more than 20 participants), meeting leaders can respond to issues of most interest to meeting participants.

Ask for input on decisions and future agenda items. Throughout a meeting, you can request input with open-ended questions (for example, *Whom should we place on the new task force?*) and closed-ended questions (*Which topic should we prioritize at our next meeting: customer service goals, sales goals, or new employee satisfaction?*).

There are many ways to encourage interaction and engagement in meetings.

©Andrey_Popov/Shutterstock

Use chat and polling with purpose and moderation. Excessive use of chat and polling can make a meeting feel directionless, distracting, or even gimmicky. Never lose sight of the overall goals for your meeting and stick to your agenda as much as possible.

If you are the team leader, make sure your team members follow through on their action items, and as soon as possible pursue those issues you were not able to resolve during the meeting. If you do not, team members are more likely to view the meeting as a waste of time.

Conducting Effective Online Meetings

LO7.3

Apply techniques for effectively conducting online meetings.

Business professionals increasingly use online meetings for many purposes: to bring together teams whose members work in different locations, to allow marketers and account representatives to show their products and services to distant customers and clients, to provide employee training and development, and to give manufacturers and suppliers a forum to work out quality issues from a distance, among other uses.

Online meetings allow you to conduct a meeting in a true, multimedia format. Typically, they are appropriate when people are far away, when the group is large (25 or more), when you feel too emotional or nervous for a face-to-face meeting, when you've already established trust with meeting participants, or when the agenda is fairly routine. Consider face-to-face meetings if possible when trust has not yet been established or when you're discussing sensitive topics such as bad news or big changes.

Professionals in one survey reported that the primary challenge of online meetings is lack of time to build relationships (90 percent). They also cited the need to make decisions too quickly (80 percent), differing leadership styles (77 percent), unclear decision-making rules (76 percent), and lack of participation (75 percent).[18] Consider the following tips to make your online meetings more productive.

LEARN THE FUNCTIONS AND LIMITATIONS OF MEETING SOFTWARE

Software platforms for online meetings such as Zoom, Google Hangouts, Skype, WebEx, and GoToMeeting offer many functions. They include video calling, picture and drawing windows, screen sharing capability, virtual breakout rooms, instant polls, email, chats, slide shows, electronic whiteboards, discussion boards, shared folders, and a variety of online resources. Learn about each of these tools, experiment with them, and make sure you use them to accomplish the key objectives of your meetings.

Keep in mind that despite their advantages, with some online platforms you may lack the visual cues that help develop trust and rapport. Participants can also easily detach from the meeting and focus on other things going on in their own offices. And technology failure is always a possibility. Your job is to know the platforms well enough to overcome most of these limitations and orchestrate an effective meeting.

HELP PARTICIPANTS USE THE MEETING SOFTWARE

Even if you're strong at using the online meeting software, remember that not all meeting participants may be familiar with it and adept at using it. Make sure to send them some tips ahead of time for using the software effectively. Encourage people to log on a few minutes early if they're not familiar with the software (and be there early yourself to help) so you don't spend the precious opening minutes of your meeting resolving technical issues.

DECIDE HOW TO DOCUMENT AND DISTRIBUTE THE DISCUSSION

Face-to-face meetings are fairly straightforward to document with minutes distributed to everyone later as a reminder of decisions and follow-up assignments. In contrast, online meetings generally utilize many types of media. Plan how you will document the meeting and make it available to meeting participants later. For example, you can share the minutes in real time so participants can comment on and correct information during the meeting. This practice often leads to more accurate recollections of the meeting, more buy-in from team members, and a higher likelihood that action items get accomplished.

START THE MEETING WITH SOCIAL CHAT OR A LIVELY QUESTION

One long-time expert and observer of virtual teams, Keith Ferrazzi, recommends the "Take 5" strategy: For the first five minutes of the meeting, each person takes a turn to share how he or she is doing. As long as you do this rapidly, you help build the social foundation you need to accomplish your work objectives together.

Many professionals worry that online meetings will consist of their simply being "talked to" and assume their participation is not particularly important. Posing a lively or contentious question at the start of the meeting is another way to engage attendees and encourage their participation.

AVOID MULTITASKING

Up to 90 percent of virtual team members admit they multitask during virtual team meetings.[19] Many new collaboration tools allow teammates to participate in several

CAREER TIP

Tony Hsieh (pronounced *shay*) is the CEO of the popular online retailer Zappos, which he sold to Amazon in 2009 for $1.2 billion but continues to operate independently. Although he's a multimillionaire, he lives in an Airstream in a trailer park to stay grounded and creative. "I just love it," he says, "because there's so many random, amazing things that happen around the campfire at night."[20]

Hsieh is recognized for creating a unique culture with a focus on delighting customers and making work enjoyable. Zappos has promoted concepts such as *self-organized teams* of *radical transparency*. The core values for the company were crowdsourced from employees and include "deliver WOW through service," "create fun and a little weirdness," "build a positive team," and "build open and honest relationships with communication."[21] To make sure employees literally run into each other, enabling candid and creative conversations, Zappos offices have about 100 square feet per employee compared to an average of 300 in most workplaces.[22]

Meetings at Zappos are candid; a trained facilitator ensures that everyone is open and honest. Hsieh maintains, "The main thing is that everyone's voice is heard." In fact, anyone can set the agenda for meetings.[23] Throughout your career—whether it's in an entry-level role or in a senior

Tony Hsieh, CEO of Zappos
©Tannen Maury/EPA/REX/Shutterstock

leader's role—you'll open many opportunities for yourself and others as you contribute to candid conversations and make meetings fun, open, and inclusive.

conversations at a time during an online meeting. Participants may also send text messages or use messaging apps during online meetings. Sometimes side conversations help the meeting run more efficiently. However, there are some risks. First, multitasking may distract people from the larger meeting. Second, it can lead to cliquish subgroups. Make sure you focus sufficiently on your teammates.

USE VIDEO WHEN POSSIBLE

Using video has many benefits. First and foremost, it allows team members to better interpret one another's verbal and nonverbal cues. With this added layer of understanding, it can lead to faster decision making, and—an important but often unintended consequence—team members are less likely to multitask on camera. Many professionals on virtual teams think video communication makes the most sense but rarely actually use it.[24] You can set a ground rule that all team members have their webcam on.

Multitasking during a meeting can be distracting and reduce productivity if not managed properly.
©antoniodiaz/Shutterstock

Managing Difficult Conversations

Business professionals routinely—often daily—hold difficult conversations, especially when working in teams and collaborating with others. Douglas Stone, Bruce Patton, and Sheila Heen of the Harvard Negotiation Project have spent three decades training business professionals to confront difficult conversations, which they define this way:

> Any time we feel vulnerable or our self-esteem is implicated, when the issues at stake are important and the outcome is uncertain, when we care deeply about what is being discussed or about the people with whom we are discussing it, there is potential for us to experience the conversation as difficult.[25]

Difficult conversations often center on disagreements, conflict, and bad news. Sometimes they reveal unresolved problems. Entry-level professionals can feel some apprehension, nervousness, or even fear when receiving a bad performance review, having their ideas rejected, critiquing a colleague, giving feedback to a boss, correcting someone, approaching rule breakers about their behavior, talking to a slacker on a group project, and dealing with office politics.[26]

Many people prefer to sidestep difficult conversations because they want to prevent conflict or avoid hurting the feelings of others. However, conflict is not necessarily harmful. Managers and executives who approach difficult conversations in a timely, honest, and caring manner typically accomplish much more in their careers.

After working with corporate clients for nearly three decades, one research team concluded that the most influential people are those who can effectively handle difficult conversations:[27]

> As it turns out, you don't have to choose between being honest and being effective. You don't have to choose between candor and your career. People who routinely hold crucial conversations and hold them well are able to express controversial and even risky opinions in a way that gets heard. Their bosses, peers, and direct reports listen without becoming defensive or angry.[28]

In this section, we briefly present tried-and-true principles for handling difficult conversations in the workplace (see Figure 7.5).

Difficult conversations aren't always fun, but they can be productive if viewed as an opportunity.

©NicolasMcComber/Getty Images

CASE STUDY:
Nancy and Kip Hold Grudges from a Prior Disagreement

Nancy and Kip have ignored each other as much as possible in recent months. Problems started when Kip authorized refunds totaling nearly $4,000 to ten business travelers because they were frequent guests who, he felt, deserved special considerations. Nancy, Kip's boss, was furious when she found Kip had acted without checking with her, especially because the travelers were at fault, not the hotel. When she called Kip into her office and scolded him, he abruptly said, "So much for our famous customer service," and left the room. Since then, Nancy has complained to co-workers that Kip doesn't understand the business side of running a hotel. Kip complains that Nancy doesn't relate to guests and that the hotel is losing business because of it.

These principles rely on active listening and a real desire to learn. First read the nearby short case study. Then, as you read about the principles, notice how they apply to the short case in Table 7.1.

EMBRACE DIFFICULT CONVERSATIONS

It's tempting to back away from uncomfortable or unpleasant conversations, especially when we feel we have a lot to lose if the conversation doesn't go right. This in turn often adds an emotional challenge to the situation. Successful professionals do not evade difficult conversations, however. In fact, those who regularly tackle them with skill and tact improve their own and others' work performance.

One way to embrace difficult conversations is to view conflict as an opportunity.[29] That is, the exchange of perspectives and competing ideas offers an open and honest communication. If there is no conflict, employees are likely not voicing their true perspectives. Generally, colleagues tend to respect one another more when they know they can safely disagree.

ASSUME THE BEST IN OTHERS

To make a difficult conversation safe, follow the advice of Jacqueline Kosecoff, CEO of Prescription Solutions:

> Assume positive intent. It's one of the ways to . . . keep communication on the high road. Perhaps somebody was misunderstood, or they misheard something. You have to go back and ask for the context, and it's very likely to be simply a misunderstanding. And if you listen, it can be resolved. And it tends to, I think, breed a lot more trust and respect among us.[30]

ADOPT A LEARNING STANCE

In emotionally charged, high-stakes conversations, assuming a learning mindset will often lead to productive outcomes. You can do this, first, by avoiding the message-delivery stance.[31] The message-delivery stance implies that you have nothing to learn from the other person in the conversation. In sensitive situations, others will resist your attempts to impose solutions. Each person should instead participate in a joint process of understanding the problems and creating solutions. Another element of the learning stance is making a commitment to understand others' **stories**— their versions of past interactions or explanations of business successes and failures. In difficult conversations, invite others to describe, uninterrupted, their views of and feelings about disputed events. Sharing stories with one another can lead to shared interpretations of events, empathy, and new ways of viewing workplace relationships and business possibilities.[32]

One major benefit of allowing all participants in a difficult conversation to share their views is that this creates buy-in to a solution. Research has shown that when everyone involved shares their ideas, they tend to be more committed to the ultimate decision of the group, even when their ideas are not adopted. When they remain silent, they tend not to commit to the decision of the group.[33]

STAY CALM AND OVERCOME NOISE

Few business professionals prepare for difficult conversations. And because emotions run high during such conversations, they often do not go well. Participants are nervous about the outcome for themselves and others, and this internal noise often makes them feel incapable of constructively expressing all their thoughts and emotions.

Figure 7.5

Principles of Difficult Conversations

Follow these principles when conducting a difficult conversation.

- Embrace difficult conversations
- Assume the best in others
- Adopt a learning stance
- Stay calm/overcome noise
- Find common ground
- Disagree diplomatically
- Avoid exaggeration and either/or approaches

High emotional intelligence and self-awareness are crucial. When you feel angry or defensive, ask yourself, "What do I really want?" and "How are my feelings affecting my actions?" These questions redirect activity to the rational part of your brain, de-escalating the perception of threat in your mind and allowing you to respond more rationally.

Although you should pay a lot of attention to your own emotions, intentions, and goals, you must also focus on the people with whom you are speaking. They are likely experiencing similar emotions. Apply your active listening skills to feel and show empathy. If someone gets angry, instead of returning the anger, help him or her channel it appropriately and rationally. Consider asking your conversational partner to sit down or offer him or her a refreshment. As you summarize his or her thoughts and feelings, you defuse strong emotions and make the conversation constructive and rational.[34]

SHARPEN YOUR SKILLS

Finding Common Ground

When we disagree with someone on an issue that matters to us, it is easy to assume we have absolutely nothing in common with that person. This is hardly ever true, however. Think of someone you know (or know of) who has a different position from yours on an issue you care deeply about. Imagine you're in a discussion with that person. In a short journal entry or blog post, identify five separate things you have in common with this person—such as experiences or values you share or issues on which you agree—and describe how you might appeal to these commonalities when discussing the point on which you disagree strongly.

FIND COMMON GROUND

Finding common ground seems like obvious advice, but it's not easy to do during emotionally charged moments when you feel attacked. Yet it will help you accomplish two things. Emotionally, it lessens the perceived distance between you and the other person, and it may even lead to bonding. Rationally, it helps you analyze the issues in a way that will likely lead to mutually acceptable solutions. You can find common ground in a number of areas, including facts, conclusions, feelings, goals, and values.

DISAGREE DIPLOMATICALLY

Difficult conversations bring opposing perspectives together. To create a learning conversation rather than a defensive and judgmental one, and to lessen resistance to yourself and your views, find ways to disagree diplomatically. For instance, you can validate the views and feelings of others and use I-statements. **Validating** others means that you recognize their perspectives and feelings as credible or legitimate. It does not necessarily mean that you agree. As you learned in Chapter 3, *I-statements* begin with phrases such as *I think, I feel,* or *I believe.* During disagreements or difficult conversations, I-statements soften comments to sound more conciliatory and flexible and less blaming and accusatory (see examples in Table 7.1).

How good are you at distinguishing between diplomatic and undiplomatic ways of disagreeing? Take a look at the "Competent Communicator" box to find out.

AVOID EXAGGERATION AND EITHER/OR APPROACHES

As you navigate difficult conversations, avoid making them simplistic. Usually, you are encountering complex business and relationship issues. Oversimplifying these can inadvertently cause others to become defensive because you are in effect disputing their story or challenging their identity.

Two ways of oversimplifying are exaggerating and applying either/or approaches. If you find yourself using superlatives such as *always, never, most,* or *worst,* you might be exaggerating. Applying an either/or approach in a difficult conversation usually turns into a right-versus-wrong approach in which you are implying *I'm right, and*

To disagree with someone diplomatically, it helps to distinguish statements that have the characteristics of diplomacy—such as validating statements and I-statements—from those that do not. How well can you spot the difference? Read each of the following statements and indicate whether you think the statement is diplomatic or undiplomatic by placing a checkmark in the appropriate column.

	Diplomatic	Undiplomatic
1. You're making me really angry.	_____	_____
2. You seem upset right now.	_____	_____
3. I can see that you and I have different perspectives.	_____	_____
4. You don't know what you're doing.	_____	_____
5. I disagree with your viewpoint on this issue.	_____	_____
6. Please help me understand your position better.	_____	_____
7. I can't be friends with someone who thinks like you.	_____	_____
8. You obviously care deeply about this issue, as do I.	_____	_____
9. I respect your feelings.	_____	_____
10. The way you think is wrong.	_____	_____

Even though we have asked you to mark each statement as either diplomatic or undiplomatic, it is probably better to think of diplomacy as a continuum on which some statements are more diplomatic than others. In this instance, statements 2, 3, 5, 6, 8, and 9 are more diplomatic than statements 1, 4, 7, and 10.

you're wrong. This inevitably dooms the conversation. See examples of exaggeration and either/or approaches in Table 7.1.

INITIATE THE CONVERSATION, SHARE STORIES, AND FOCUS ON SOLUTIONS

Initiating a difficult conversation is stressful. You may have avoided bringing up the issue because you are nervous about how it will affect your working relationships with others, or how it will affect your career. Starting well is crucial because it offers a great opportunity to frame or orient the conversation for problem solving. Open with your sincere desire to understand and find a solution that works for each of you. This can help all participants avoid judging each other's motives unfairly. See Table 7.1 for examples of initiating a conversation.[35]

Once you've begun, listen to the story of others first, then share your story, and then create a shared story.[36] When you invite others to speak first, they recognize your sincere interest in understanding and cooperating with them. By telling your story, you allow others to see another version of reality and empathize with you. Finally, the **shared story** you create combines everyone's experiences, perspectives, and goals into a shared approach to work. The *their story–your story–shared story* process requires a substantial time commitment, but it is well worth it.

Table 7.1   Ineffective and Effective Approaches to Difficult Conversations

Approaches	Ineffective Examples	Effective Examples
Initiating the conversation	**Nancy:** "I want to go over your mishandling of the refunds several months ago. I have some ideas for how we can avoid this kind of problem in the future." This approach starts with blame. Worse yet, it frames the conversation as Nancy's story.	**Nancy:** "Kip, let's talk about how the refunds to business travelers were handled a few months ago. First, I want to apologize for speaking so harshly without hearing your side first. Since then, I feel like we haven't worked well together. I think we can figure out a better way to make sure we're on the same page, and I also think we can figure out ways to avoid misleading our customers. When you authorized the refunds, I never heard all the details. Do you mind telling me about some of the customers who were upset and what you did to address their concerns?" This approach is effective for several reasons. Nancy apologizes for her harsh words. She declares her intent: to work together better and come up with solutions. Nancy expresses her intent of discussing solutions that take into account both her own and Kip's perspectives (shared story). She invites Kip to tell his story.
Disagreeing diplomatically	**Nancy:** "Look, you clearly overstepped your authority. You refunded 10 customers nearly $400 each, but you are authorized to refund only $300 per customer without my say so. You were way out of line by authorizing these refunds prior to approval." Nancy does not recognize Kip's explanation or feelings as having any merit, which places Kip on the defensive and could lead him to feel resentment. Nancy projects a tone of blame by consistently using you-statements.	**Nancy:** "Thanks for telling me how you felt. I can see that you were looking out for the interests of the guests and trying to ensure these guests become loyal, repeat customers. I think you have a point that the guests rightfully thought they were overcharged because of miscommunication from us. In the computer reservation system, it's true you can refund up to $500 per traveler. Still, the hotel policy is clear that you should consult with me for refunds over $300. I view you as overstepping your authority because you made these refunds without checking with me first." Nancy validates Kip's perspective by understanding how he *felt*. She explains why she thinks he overstepped his authority with a variety of I-statements.
Avoiding exaggeration and either/or approaches	**Kip:** "I can never approach you with customer issues. You're always fixated on following the pricing policies to a tee, even when the guests have no way of knowing the costs they're incurring. You never try to understand the guest's perspective. Your approach is not working, and it's losing us money." Kip repeatedly exaggerates the frequency of Nancy's actions with words such as *never* and *always*. He takes an either/or approach by saying Nancy's approach doesn't work.	**Kip:** "I'm hesitant to bring up customer issues with you. I think you sometimes take a tough approach to guests, even when they have legitimate complaints. I can think of several cases in which guests have stopped coming here after you denied their claims. In each case, I agreed with their reasoning and understood why they were not aware of costs they were incurring. In the end, I think we end up losing revenues when we deny refunds to our guests who feel unfairly charged." Kip states his real feelings of frustration and explains his point of view. By using phrases such as *sometimes* and *I think*, he avoids a right-versus-wrong comparison between his and Nancy's approaches.

Kip and Nancy hold strong grievances because of a past disagreement about issuing refunds to business travelers. Their poor working relationship and avoidance of each other hinders productivity and makes work less pleasant for them and their team.

CHAPTER WRAP-UP

Whether conducted in person or online, meetings can be opportunities for engagement and productivity if they are planned and managed effectively. Here's a quick review of the chapter.

LO7.1 Describe approaches to planning meetings.

- Begin by asking essential questions about the meeting, its purpose, and its participants.
- Create and distribute an agenda that specifies the goals of the meeting and the topics to be discussed.

LO7.2 Apply principles for effectively running in-person meetings.

- Begin the meeting on time.
- Create traditions for starting the meeting.
- Set expectations for the meeting and follow the agenda.
- Encourage people to participate and express their ideas.
- Work to build consensus around a plan of action.
- End the meeting on time.
- Follow up after the meeting by distributing the meeting minutes.

LO7.3 Apply techniques for effectively conducting online meetings.

- Learn about the functions and limitations of meeting software.
- Help participants use meeting software effectively.
- Discuss ways of documenting and distributing the discussion.
- Begin the meeting with social chat or a lively question.
- Focus on your teammates and avoid multitasking.
- Use video whenever possible.

LO7.4 Recognize strategies for managing difficult conversations constructively.

- Embrace difficult conversations as opportunities.
- Assume the best in others.
- Adopt a learning stance.
- Stay calm and overcome noise.
- Work to find common ground.
- Disagree with others diplomatically.
- Avoid exaggeration and taking either/or approaches.
- Initiate the conversation, create a shared story, and find a solution.

A LOOK BACK

Now, let's review the opening scenario. Al appears to run meetings poorly, and everyone views them as a waste of time. Al says he'll mention several agenda items momentarily, revealing that he hasn't sent an agenda ahead of time. When instead he asks the team what they want to discuss, it may appear that he's trying to include everyone. In reality, he should have asked for agenda items at least a few days earlier when team members had time to give meaningful input. Al eventually decides to talk about assignments for a housing project. Apparently, the team has discussed this issue multiple times already. So it also appears Al rarely documents what they decide to do at their meetings.

KEY TERMS

CHAPTER REVIEW QUESTIONS

1. What are the most essential questions to ask when planning and preparing a meeting? **LO7.1**

2. At what time of the day are most employees at their peak performance level? Which day of the week is generally considered most productive? **LO7.1**

3. How are coordination meetings and problem-solving meetings similar? How are they different? **LO7.2**

4. What is an agenda, and when should an agenda be sent to a meeting's participants? **LO7.2**

5. What are some ways to reinforce the core values of your organization at the start of a meeting? **LO7.2**

6. Why is it beneficial to set expectations and follow an agenda when running a meeting? **LO7.2**

7. What are the most important tasks for a facilitator to accomplish? **LO7.2**

8. Why is it useful to take minutes or notes at a meeting? What details should they include? **LO7.2**

9. When is it especially beneficial to consider holding a meeting online, instead of face-to-face? **LO7.3**

10. What are the primary challenges of online meetings, according to research? **LO7.3**

11. How can online meeting software facilitate a productive interaction in an online meeting? **LO7.3**

12. What is social chat, and why is it advantageous in an online meeting? **LO7.3**

13. Why is it useful to avoid multitasking in an online meeting? **LO7.3**

14. In what ways is using video advantageous in an online meeting? **LO7.3**

15. For what reasons do most people prefer to avoid difficult conversations? **LO7.4**

16. What does it mean to "view conflict as an opportunity"? **LO7.4**

17. Why is it useful to commit to listening to people's stories? **LO7.4**

18. What types of noise are necessary to overcome in a difficult conversation? **LO7.4**

19. Why is it useful to find common ground with others? How do we validate the views and feelings of others? **LO7.4**

20. Why are exaggerating and taking either/or approaches counterproductive? **LO7.4**

21. What is a shared story? What makes it useful for managing difficult conversations? **LO7.4**

SKILL-BUILDING EXERCISES

Creating an Agenda (LO7.2)

Create an agenda for a meeting you recently took part in or a meeting you have coming up (work- or school-related). Feel free to make up details as necessary. Prepare the agenda with agenda items, time frames, goals, roles, and materials needed.

Being Friendly versus *Being Friends* for Difficult Conversations (LO7.4)

Kasper Rorsted, chief executive of Henkel, the consumer and industrial products company based in Düsseldorf, Germany, recently talked about the first time he had to be someone else's boss:

> [I first became someone else's boss] in 1989, right when I got promoted from being a sales rep in the Digital Equipment Corporation to being a sales manager at the age of 27. I had about 20 people at that point in time. All but two of them were older than I was. When you're 27, you're inexperienced, so you don't know what to fear. I didn't know what I probably should have known. The first time I realized it was serious was when, after about six months, I had to lay somebody off. And then suddenly you move from the sunny side of the deal to the real deal. I remember I was sleeping very poorly for almost a week. He had a family.
>
> So one of the lessons I learned from that, which I've been very aware of since, is to be friendly, but not a friend. I had grown up in the company and I knew everybody, so I was more a friend. But then I had to start having honest conversations with people about how they performed, and that taught me a lesson. I've always been friendly but never been friends anymore. When we have parties, I'm the one who will leave early.[37]

Based on Rorsted's comments, answer the following questions:

- What do you think Rorsted means that he could "be friendly, but not a friend" once he became a boss and had to have difficult conversations with others?

- Do you agree with his perspective about being friendly versus being friends? Do you think being friends makes having honest conversations in the workplace more difficult? Explain.
- How can a person prepare for the difficult conversations a boss or supervisor must have?

Describe a Difficult Conversation from a Movie or TV Episode (LO7.4)

Think about a recent movie or TV episode you watched. Select a scene that included an interesting but difficult conversation, one that might occur in the workplace if you can. Based on this scene, do the following:

- Summarize the scene in one paragraph.
- Analyze the difficult conversation. Explain how well the characters applied effective principles for communicating.
- Describe how you can apply two strategies from the scene as you approach difficult conversations in the workplace.

Assess a Recent Difficult Conversation (LO7.4)

Think about a recent difficult conversation you had, ideally, one that occurred at work or school. Then do the following:

- Summarize the conversation in one paragraph.
- Evaluate your and others' performance in terms of assuming the best in one another, staying calm, finding common ground, disagreeing diplomatically, avoiding exaggeration and either/or approaches, and sharing all stories (including a shared story).
- Describe three ways you would approach the conversation differently if you did it over again.
- Assuming you had the conversation again, what three questions would you ask to invite a learning stance?

Speaking Up in Meetings (LO7.2, LO7.3)

Barbara J. Krumsiek of the Calvert Group recently talked about the style of meetings that take place in her organization:

> I think it can be a little jarring actually for people who are used to perhaps a little more civility. I think we're civil, but we're direct. I don't like meetings if my direct reports leave the room and turn to somebody and say, "Can you believe someone said that?" And so I try to explain to them by example that if you find yourself doing that when you leave the room, or shaking your head, or kicking yourself for not having said something, or thinking that there were real problems with what somebody said, next time you have to say it in the room. You have to, or you will not be the most impactful member of this team. When I first got to Calvert, there was a lot of that. And I had one of my direct reports send me an email, complaining about something somebody else said. I just got back to them and said, "I'm not going to read this because I don't see the person you're talking about CC'd on it. So if you CC them on it and send it back to me, I will deal with it." Well, I never had to get it back, because once the person really dealt with it, it was fine.[38]

Based on Krumsiek's comments, answer the following:

- What types of expectations are there for meetings at the Calvert Group?
- What does Krumsiek say about the nature of directness and civility at meetings? Does this imply the meetings are not civil?
- How does Krumsiek deal with complaints about other team members?
- What are three principles from Krumsiek's comments that you can apply to the way you approach team communication?

Brainstorming at Meetings (LO7.2, LO7.3)

Susan Docherty, former president and managing director of General Motors, described how she and her team communicate at meetings:

> I love to brainstorm with my team around the table in my office. I like to use a big whiteboard for ideas, because when you make things visual, you encourage the team to get up there at the whiteboard and put their thoughts out there. It's one thing to say that you're inclusive, but it's a whole other thing to be inclusive. And when people come into my office, they feel welcome. My door is open. They can bring ideas. They begin to understand that, as a leader, I want to be collaborative. I don't have all the answers or all the best ideas, nor do I want to. The whiteboard also keeps great ideas in front of us, not buried in an email and not buried in a stack of papers on our desks. And it enables everybody to own what we've got to get done. People will grab a marker and put up there that we're going to do a deep dive to figure something out, and they put their name beside it. And there are lots of times where we put something on the board, and it requires a couple of people to get together to go work on it.[39]

Based on Docherty's comments and your own experiences, answer the following:

- What strategies can you use for making meetings more visual? What are the benefits of making meetings visual?
- What strategies can you use to make meetings more inclusive?
- What does it mean for "everybody to own what we've got to get done"? What are a few approaches you can take to help make this happen for work teams?

1. Mankins, M. (2014, April 29). This weekly meeting took up 300,000 hours a year. *Harvard Business Review.* Retrieved April 25, 2018, from https://hbr.org/2014/04/how-a-weekly-meeting-took-up-300000-hours-a-year.

2. Klubeck, J. S. (2018). The expense of ineffective meetings. *Wolf Management Consultants.* Retrieved April 25, 2018, from http://www.wolfmotivation.com/articles/the-expense-of-ineffective-meetings.

3. Ribbink, K. (2002, October). Run a meeting to fast-track your career. *Harvard Management Communication Letter, 3–4.*

4. Krattenmaker, T. (2003, May). How to make every meeting matter. *Harvard Management Communication Letter, 3–5.*

5. Ribbink, K. (2002, October). Run a meeting to fast-track your career. *Harvard Management Communication Letter, 3–4.*

6. Accountemps. (2010, August 17). Accountemps survey: Employee output is weakest late in the day. Retrieved August 10, 2017, from http://accountemps.rhi.mediaroom.com/least_productive.

7. Accountemps. (2008, February 7). Second day of the week remains most productive, survey shows. Retrieved August 10, 2017, from http://accountemps.rhi.mediaroom.com/tuesday.

8. Linsky, M. (2006, Spring). The morning meeting: Best-practice communication for executive teams. *Harvard Management Communication Letter, 3–5.*

9. *Corner Office.* "Meetings." *The New York Times.* Retrieved June 15, 2010, from http://projects.nytimes.com/corner-office/Meetings.

10. Bielaszka-DuVernay, C. (2004, Summer). Is your company as dull and unproductive as its meetings? *Harvard Management Communication Letter, 3–5.*

11. See, for example, http://timemanagementninja.com/2011/11/9-ways-to-start-the-9am-meeting-on-time.

12. Gargiulo, T. L. (2006). *Stories at work: Using stories to improve communication and build relationships.* Westport, CT: Praeger.

13. Obuchowski, J. (2005, Spring). Your meeting: Who's in charge? *Harvard Management Communication Letter, 3–5.*

14. Covey, S. R. (2013). *The 8th habit: From effectiveness to greatness* (workbook edition). New York, NY: Free Press.

15. Schulz-Hardt, S., Brodbeck, F. C., Mojzisch, A., Kerschreiter, R., & Frey, D. (2006). Group decision making in hidden profile situations: Dissent as a facilitator for decision quality. *Journal of Personality and Social Psychology, 91,* 1080–1093.

16. Bielaszka-DuVernay, C. (2004, Summer). Is your company as dull and unproductive as its meetings? *Harvard Management Communication Letter, 3–5.*

17. Snyder, L. G. (2009, March). Teaching teams about teamwork: Preparation, practice, and performance review. *Business Communication Quarterly, 77–78.*

18. *Personnel Today.* (2010, May 25). RW3 CultureWizard survey finds 40% of virtual teams underperform. Retrieved August 10, 2017, from http://www.personneltoday.com/hr/rw3-culturewizard-survey-finds-40-of-virtual-teams-underperform.

19. Majchrzak, A., Malhotra, A., Stamps, J., & Lipnack, J. (2004). Can absence make a team grow stronger? *Harvard Business Review, 82,* 131–137.

20. Martin, E. (2017, May 18). Why multi-millionaire Zappos CEO Tony Hsieh chooses to live in a trailer park. *CNBC.* Retrieved from https://www.cnbc.com/2017/05/08/why-multi-millionaire-zappos-ceo-tony-hsieh-lives-in-a-trailer-park.html.

21. Zappos 10 core values. (n.d.). Retrieved April 25, 2018, from https://www.zapposinsights.com/about/core-values.

22. De Smet, A., & Gagnon, C. (2017, October). Safe enough to try: An interview with Zappos CEO Tony Hsieh. *McKinsey Quarterly.* Retrieved from https://www.mckinsey.com/business-functions/organization/our-insights/safe-enough-to-try-an-interview-with-zappos-ceo-tony-hsieh.

23. Gelles, D. (2015, July 17). At Zappos, pushing shoes and a vision. *The New York Times.* Retrieved from https://www.nytimes.com/2015/07/19/business/at-zappos-selling-shoes-and-a-vision.html.

24. Ferrazzi, K. (2014, January 31). How virtual teams can create human connections despite distance. *Harvard Business Review Blog Network.*

25. Stone, D., Patton, B., & Heen, S. (2000). *Difficult conversations: How to discuss what matters most.* New York, NY: Penguin. Quote is from page xv.

26. Patterson, K., Grenny, J., McMillan, R., & Switzler, A. (2002). *Crucial conversations: Tools for talking when stakes are high.* New York, NY: McGraw-Hill; Myers, L. L., & Larson, R. S. (2005). Preparing students for early work conflicts. *Business Communication Quarterly, 68,* 306–317.

27. Patterson, K., Grenny, J., McMillan, R., & Switzler, A. (2002). *Crucial conversations: Tools for talking when stakes are high.* New York, NY: McGraw-Hill.

28. Patterson, K., Grenny, J., McMillan, R., & Switzler, A. (2002). *Crucial conversations: Tools for talking when stakes are high.* New York, NY: McGraw-Hill. Quote is from pages 9–10.

29. Evenson, R. (2012, September). Solutions for team conflict. *Toastmasters.* Retrieved from http://magazines.toastmasters.org/article/SOLUTIONS_FOR_TEAM_CONFLICT/1140168/121549/article.html.

30. Briant, A. (2009, July 20). The divine, too, is in the details. *Corner Office. The New York Times.* Retrieved from https://www.nytimes.com/2009/06/21/business/21corner.html.

31. Stone, D., Patton, B., & Heen, S. (2000). *Difficult conversations: How to discuss what matters most.* New York, NY: Penguin.

32. Baker, A. C. (2010). *Catalytic conversations: Organizational communication and innovation.* Armonk, NY: M.E. Sharpe.

33. Patterson, K., Grenny, J., McMillan, R., & Switzler, A. (2002). *Crucial conversations: Tools for talking when stakes are high.* New York, NY: McGraw-Hill.

34. Mayo Clinic. (2018). Anger management: 10 tips to tame your temper. Retrieved April 25, 2018, from https://www.mayoclinic.org/healthy-lifestyle/adult-health/in-depth/anger-management/art-20045434.

35. Covey, S. M. R. (2006). *The speed of trust.* New York, NY: Free Press.

36. Evenson, R. (2012, September). Solutions for team conflict. *Toastmasters.* Retrieved from http://magazines .toastmasters.org/article/SOLUTIONS_FOR_TEAM_ CONFLICT/1140168/121549/article.html.

37. Bryant, A. (2010, August 28). No need to hit the "send" key. Just talk to me. *The New York Times.* Retrieved from http:// www.nytimes.com/2010/08/29/business/29corner.html.

38. Bryant, A. (2010, May 22). It's not a career ladder, it's an obstacle course. *The New York Times.* Retrieved from http:// www.nytimes.com/2010/05/23/business/23corner.html.

39. Bryant, A. (2010, February 6). Now, put yourself in my shoes. *The New York Times.* Retrieved from http://www .nytimes.com/2010/02/07/business/07corner.html.

Learning Objectives

After reading this chapter, you should be able to do the following:

LO8.1   Formulate short-term and long-term career aspirations.

LO8.2   Understand principles for professional networking.

LO8.3   Develop a résumé, a cover letter, and a reference list.

LO8.4   Describe strategies for developing an online professional persona.

CHAPTER 8

Career Communication

Veronica was frustrated. She had submitted her résumé online for over a hundred positions in marketing, customer service, sales, human resources, and even finance. Yet she had received only three invitations to interview, and no job offers. What was going wrong?

Searching for jobs is a process nearly all of us go through many times during our lives. It can seem painfully drawn out in many cases, even for well-qualified, competent job applicants. By planning ahead, you can dramatically improve your success in job searches.

LO8.1

Formulate short-term and long-term career aspirations.

Goal Setting and Intentionality in Career Development

Most of us spend over half our waking hours at work. More importantly, many people gain deep satisfaction (or dissatisfaction) from their work lives. By carefully and intentionally thinking about your career interests and opportunities, you are likely to make choices that lead to rewarding career opportunities.

Early in your life, it's important to evaluate your career ambitions and qualifications. Clarify your professional goals for the short term (one to two years) and long term (five to ten years), identify the skills you have developed at school and work, and sort out the attributes that define who you are as a professional. As you seek better job opportunities, repeating this process will help you identify your most important and strongest features so you can develop a concise and compelling message about the value you bring to prospective employers.

To help you identify your interests, abilities, and attributes, consider completing a self-inventory (see Figure 8.1 with an example of Haniz's self-inventory). Start by writing your career goals. Even if you don't yet have clear ones in mind, do your best to imagine the type of work you would like to be doing in five and ten years. Allow yourself enough time to do some soul-searching and research about careers as you develop your goals.

Identifying your career goals helps you accomplish several things in the job search process. First, it helps you frame your résumé and cover letter to project your career hopes. Second, it helps you evaluate how well your abilities and attributes prepare you for your desired career. This process allows you to address those areas where you most need improvement. Finally, it shows employers that you are serious, because well-defined career goals imply seriousness in your approach to work.

Once you have written down your career goals, identify your abilities and attributes. **Abilities** are skills and knowledge you can apply to accomplishing work tasks,

Figure 8.1

Self-Inventory of Career Interests and Job-Related Abilities and Attributes

Setting goals and identifying your strengths and weaknesses will help you gain professional opportunities.

Haniz Zogby
April 1, 2019

My Career Goals
1. To act in a leadership role to develop and market financial services for credit unions
2. In five to ten years, to hold an influential marketing position within a credit union group

My Strongest Professional Abilities
1. Developing strong professional relationships with clients and vendors
2. Attracting new members to credit unions through referrals, seminars, mailings, and online social networking
3. Organizing members to participate in credit union–sponsored financial workshops and community events

My Strongest Professional Attributes
1. Trusted and reliable on important campaigns
2. Innovative and creative in approach to marketing and promotions
3. Passionate about the credit union industry

Areas Where I Need to Improve
1. Conducting customer surveys, statistical analysis, and survey reporting
2. Earning a reputation for excellence outside my local community

TECH TIP
Use Online Career Inventories to Help Identify Your Skills and Interests

To develop a goal-oriented, intentional career path requires some time and effort. You often need to try out various school subjects and work positions to help identify your interests. Conducting informational interviews and gaining advice from a variety of professionals can also help you shape your career goals. Also, consider taking some online career interest inventories. For example, the following free online inventories take between 10 and 30 minutes and provide a variety of recommendations based on your *clusters* of interests and capabilities:

- *The U.S. Department of Labor's Interest Assessment:* www.careeronestop.org/toolkit/careers/interest-assessment.aspx
- *The U.S. Department of Labor's Skills Matcher:* www.careeronestop.org/Toolkit/Skills/skills-matcher.aspx
- *Virginia Education Wizard Career Interests and Work Values Assessment:* www.vawizard.org/wizard/assessment-combined
- *Virginia Education Wizard Skills Assessment:* www.vawizard.org/wizard/skill-assess

careeronestop
your source for career exploration, training & jobs
Sponsored by the U.S. Department of Labor. A proud partner of the americanjobcenter network.

Explore Careers   Find Training   Job Search   Find Local Help   Toolkit   Resources For

Interest Assessment

Indicate your interest level for each activity below.

Activity	Strongly Dislike	Dislike	Unsure	Like	Strongly Like
1. Build kitchen cabinets		✓			
2. Develop a new medicine				✓	
3. Write books or plays				✓	
4. Help people with personal or emotional problems					✓
5. Manage a department within a large company			✓		
6. Install software across computers on a large network		✓			
7. Repair household appliances		✓			
8. Study ways to reduce water pollution					
9. Compose or arrange music			✓		
10. Give career guidance to people				✓	

Back   Page 1 of 3   Next

Online career inventories can help you identify your interests and abilities.
Source: State of Minnesota, https://www.careeronestop.org

The process will assist you in making more informed career decisions. It will also help you develop your résumé to more effectively tell your professional story.

such as using accounting software or conducting marketing surveys. **Attributes** are personal traits or characteristics. In the job application process, employers are often looking for more than your abilities. They're trying to figure out what kind of person you are. These judgments often come in the form of adjectives, such as *reliable, analytical,* or *people-oriented.* These attributes are difficult to measure precisely, but they indicate how well you'll fit into the company culture, how much effort and commitment you'll put into your work, and how you'll influence the work of others.

One useful way of analyzing your *abilities* and *attributes* is in terms of credibility, which is composed of competence (ability to accomplish work tasks), caring (ability to maintain effective workplace relationships), and character (personal integrity and ability to uphold corporate norms and standards). Consider drafting a list of your key abilities and attributes. Table 8.1 will help you get started. To be most effective, draft a list of 10 to 15 professional abilities and attributes. Once you start developing a résumé (discussed later in this chapter) and preparing for job interviews (discussed in the next chapter), you should winnow this list down to 2 or 3 abilities and 2 or 3 attributes that you want to highlight.

Table 8.1 **Abilities and Attributes That Establish Credibility in the Job Application Process**

	Abilities (Skills and/or Knowledge)	Attributes (Enduring Approaches to Work)		
Competence (Task)	Function-specific (such as marketing, finance) Company/industry Technology Analysis/research	Achievement-oriented Ambitious Analytical Assertive Creative Can-do attitude Curious	Decisive Detail-oriented Entrepreneurial Independent Inquisitive Passionate	Problem solver Resourceful Results-oriented Seeks challenges Takes initiative Visionary
Caring (Relationships)	Communication/interpersonal Teamwork Emotional intelligence Leadership Intercultural	Customer-oriented Diplomatic Empathetic Flexible Generous	Inspiring Loyal Motivational People-oriented Persuasive	Responsive Sensitive Supportive Team-oriented Tolerant
Character (Values)	Familiarity with corporate culture and values Dedication to the success of the company Knowledge of business ethics	Accountable Committed Constant Dedicated Dependable	Fair Hardworking Honest Open-minded Optimistic	Reliable Responsible Straightforward Trustworthy Unbiased

LO8.2

Understand principles for professional networking.

Professional Networking

Networking can open many learning and professional opportunities. Some people think of networking as focused on selfish, short-term gains for the person building the network. A better view of **networking** sees it as a proactive approach to building professional relationships to achieve shared company, career, and professional development goals. The most effective networkers seek to help others in their networks in many ways, including providing advice, sharing information, giving referrals, and coaching and mentoring. They often receive professional opportunities in return but do not expect these to materialize at any given time. In other words, they view networking as relational but not as transactional.[1]

During school and early in your career, networking may seem challenging. Your network is generally smaller, and you often have less to offer people in your school and professional networks. Yet, you can still begin the process. As a student seeking new positions and opportunities, consider adding to your network by conducting informational interviews with people in your field of interest, attending campus job fairs and career networking events, joining clubs and other professional interest groups, attending campus speeches and other professional development events, and volunteering at a local nonprofit.

CONDUCT INFORMATIONAL INTERVIEWS

In an **informational interview**, you speak with a successful and accomplished professional to seek out career advice. It is an excellent opportunity to learn about career choices and career paths.

Most professionals are honored and flattered when asked to give career advice. So, aim to make conducting informational interviews a regular practice. Since your interviewees are granting you a favor, keep the conversation short—20 to 30 minutes is typical. Learn as much as you can about the person before meeting, and go prepared with questions such as the following:

- What are your daily activities in this position?
- What do you enjoy most about this position?

- How did you get this position? What are some of the qualifications for this position?
- What are typical career paths in your area of expertise? In your company? In your industry?
- How do you continue to grow and learn in your area of expertise? What sources of information do you use? Do you recommend any books?
- What advice would you give to someone like me who's just starting a career?

You can ask dozens of other questions. The key is to think about what you want to learn and then draft questions accordingly.

Avoid using informational interviews to directly ask for position openings or job leads. These interviews are intended for learning and growth only. However, if your interviewee offers some jobs leads without your asking, feel free to follow up.[2]

ATTEND JOB FAIRS AND OTHER CAREER NETWORKING EVENTS

Make sure to go your school's career office or use other information sources to find out about various job fairs and career networking events on your campus. Even if you're not looking for opportunities for another year or two, go to these events to get accustomed to the way people interact and socialize. Even if a networking event is outside your professional interests (for example, you're a marketing student but you see a networking event for students interested in consulting), consider attending to meet others and practice holding conversations in these important situations.

ATTEND CAMPUS SPEECHES AND OTHER PROFESSIONAL DEVELOPMENT EVENTS

Be on the lookout for speeches by accomplished professionals and other professional development events. Not only can you learn a lot, but you'll often meet interesting people from inside and outside your school. You never know how showing interest in the speakers, trainers, and attendees at these events can lead to continued professional interactions over the years.

JOIN CLUBS AND OTHER PROFESSIONAL INTEREST GROUPS

By joining clubs, especially those in functional areas (data analytics club, developers club), you can learn a lot of skills that make you marketable. The networking aspects of joining clubs, however, is often even more important for your career. Many club members enjoy friendships and professional relationships that endure for years and decades. It's not uncommon for their interactions to result in job leads.

VOLUNTEER AT A LOCAL NONPROFIT

When you stretch yourself to volunteer in community organizations, you place yourself within a whole new network of people. In nonprofit organizations, you often meet many generous people. You shouldn't view these efforts as ways to get new professional opportunities, but you'll be surprised how often professional opportunities arise.

These networking activities require some initiative and persistence. You may need to get out of your comfort zone and be a bit more outgoing, but you'll be in good company: 40 to 50 percent of adults say they are shy.[3] By forcing yourself into these situations, you'll improve at small talk and quickly building rapport with others. Taking a sincere interest in others will also help you succeed.[4] Finally, remember networking takes time, often months or years.[5]

CAREER TIP
Find Mentors to Help You Develop Your Career

Geisha Williams has been CEO and president of Pacific Gas and Electric (PG&E) for nearly the past decade. As a Cuban immigrant, she has relied on education, entrepreneurialism, preparation, and hard work to develop a satisfying and productive career. She's also depended on the advice and support of others.

As an early-career professional in her early 20s, Williams made one of her best decisions: find a mentor. She explains, "My career aspirations were not very lofty. I thought, if I worked really hard, someday maybe I could be a manager.... Clark Cook [my mentor], looked at me, and said, 'Geisha, you know, someone has to run this place. Someone has to be in charge. Why not you?' What he meant was that I should aim for CEO or president of the company. I remember saying something like, are you kidding me?"[6]

Clark Cook became Williams's lifelong mentor. He believed in her potential, and he consistently shared ideas with her about how to move to the next stage of her career and develop her leadership skills. She explains, "[He] inspired me in a way that I had never been inspired before." Thirty years after Clark opened her eyes to her own potential, Williams became a company president. And she continues to go to lunch with Clark and discuss professional matters.

Geisha Williams, CEO and president of Pacific Gas and Electric
©Bloomberg/Getty Images

Like Williams, you should seek out people who can act as mentors, especially early in your career. Most companies now have formal mentoring programs. As you take new positions, make sure to inquire about options for new employees. Mentors can help you identify and pursue your interests, connect you with new opportunities, and guide you in career decisions.[7]

Preparing a Résumé and Cover Letter

One of the first steps job seekers take is to identify open positions of interest. When you find job postings that catch your interest, the next step is to communicate that interest to employers. Because many employers receive dozens or even hundreds of applications for each available position, you need to ensure that your cover letter and résumé make a positive first impression. In this section, you will learn to set up the message structure for résumés and cover letters; pay attention to tone, style, and design; create chronological and functional résumés; develop a reference list; and construct a cover letter.

LO8.3

Develop a résumé, a cover letter, and a reference list.

SET UP THE MESSAGE STRUCTURE FOR RÉSUMÉS AND COVER LETTERS

Your résumé should tell a story of the value you can provide to an employer. Like other persuasive messages, it is stronger if you have a central sales theme. By choosing two or three abilities and attributes to highlight, you can craft a compelling document that shows how you meet the employer's needs.

Companies generally prefer single-page résumés, although it is increasing acceptable to create two-page résumés.[8] As a university student, you will likely aim for a one-page document. A typical résumé contains the following major sections: a name block, summary statement, education, and experience.

Name block. Most résumés begin with your name and contact information. This section allows recruiters to easily find your address, phone number, and email address when they need it. This section should not contain any distracting information, such as an unprofessional email address.

Summary statement (optional). Many professionals now create a short section just below the name block describing their overall qualifications. They often label this section "Qualifications Summary," "Skills Summary," "Career Summary," or something similar. In five to ten sentences (often in bulleted style), this section generally states the candidate's primary accomplishments, abilities, and attributes.

Education. This section summarizes your experiences in higher education and professional training. If your education section highlights studies in a discipline related to the jobs you are seeking, put it before your work experience.

In addition to listing the schools you have attended, the degrees you have earned (or anticipate earning), your field of study, and the dates of your degrees, consider including some information about the uniqueness and value of your education. If you have room, a short list of courses related to the job you are seeking helps employers understand the content of your program. You might also include class projects, practicum experiences, service learning activities, or other educational experiences that highlight your key abilities and attributes.

Include your grade point average (GPA) if it is high (3.5 or higher on a 4-point scale) or if it is required by the employer. If you have achieved any academic credentials or awards, mention those, too. For example, being on the dean's list or graduating with honors are well-recognized distinctions. If you received scholarships or other academic awards that employers may not recognize, include a short explanation of their significance.

Work experience. In this section, sometimes called "Employment History" or "Experience," list your accomplishments and responsibilities from previous jobs in reverse chronological order, beginning with your current or most recent job. Some students wonder if they should include unpaid internships in this section. Typically, you should, because they are relevant and legitimate professional experiences. In fact, the abilities and attributes students gain from internships are often more relevant and transferable to sought-after positions than those from their previous paid positions.

Additional information. Education and work experience often account for the majority of your résumé content. You can provide a variety of other information, however, to accentuate your key abilities and attributes. For example, you might consider including some of the following:

- Technology skills
- Professional associations
- School clubs
- Honors and awards
- Certifications
- Community activities
- Volunteer work
- Specialized training
- Foreign language abilities

As you think about additional information to provide, the question to ask yourself is: *Does providing this information carry on a narrative of my key abilities and attributes?* Many employers are looking particularly for job candidates with strong technology and interpersonal skills.[9] You can highlight those skills when you showcase your community and volunteer work, professional and student affiliations, and computer skills.

PAY ATTENTION TO TONE, STYLE, AND DESIGN

Once you have gathered information for your résumé, you're ready to present the information in a compelling and concise manner. The tone, style, and design must be perfect. Employers often skim your résumé on the first pass; unless you can present your main credentials within 15 to 30 seconds, you may be eliminated from the job pool. Even if potential employers reward your well-designed résumé with a second look, they are unlikely to spend a lot of time focusing on it. In one survey of hiring managers, nearly 20 percent said they spent less than two minutes reviewing a résumé.[10] In some cases, your résumé is screened by software to ensure you meet minimum qualifications. To pass this screening, your résumé must contain the right keywords (see the "Preparing Résumés for Electronic Screening" section later in this chapter).

The crucial point is developing your résumé so that you can make the most of the small window of opportunity you have with potential employers. What can you do to show your distinctive combination of abilities and attributes? What can you do to make your experience stand out? How can you persuade prospective employers that you will be a good investment for them? Several pieces of advice are key.

Emphasize accomplishments with action verbs. As you describe your accomplishments and experiences, begin your statements with action verbs (see Table 8.2

Table 8.2 Action Verbs for Résumés

Management/Supervision	Decided	Contracted	Balanced
Assigned	Delegated	Demonstrated	Budgeted
Evaluated	Directed	Developed	Controlled
Executed	Enabled	Exceeded	Corrected
Facilitated	Encouraged	Excelled	Cut
Hired	Enlisted	Gained	Earned
Managed	Executed	Generated	Estimated
Mentored	Formed	Improved	Evaluated
Monitored	Guided	Increased	Forecasted
Motivated	Implemented	Launched	Interpreted
Organized	Influenced	Marketed	Prepared
Oversaw	Initiated	Proposed	Preserved
Planned	Instituted	Raised	Projected
Scheduled	Led	Secured	Reconciled
Screened	Set goals	Sold	Reduced
Selected	**Marketing/Sales**	**Finance/Accounting**	**Teamwork/Communication**
Strengthened	Accumulated	Allotted	Arranged
Supervised	Advertised	Appraised	Coached
Trained	Attained	Assessed	Collaborated
Leadership	Boosted	Audited	Coordinated
Authorized	Broadened	Averted	Described

for a list of examples). By doing so, you highlight your abilities and attributes in a way that emphasizes action and results.

Select your action words strategically. Without exaggerating, choose verbs that make your key abilities and attributes jump off the page. For example, if you want to show that you are a leader, a series of statements beginning with action verbs such as *guided, initiated,* and *led* paint a more vivid picture than the statement *I am a good leader.*

Avoid verbs that undersell your abilities and attributes. Phrases such as *answered calls, entered information in the computer,* and *waited tables* do not emphasize transferable abilities and attributes. Rather, they focus on menial duties and do not focus on professional outcomes. Read through some of the less and more effective statements in Table 8.3 and notice how action verbs can bolster your credibility.

Quantify your accomplishments whenever possible.   Your potential employers want to know how valuable your contributions have been in your prior jobs. So, when possible, describe key contributions and how their impact on the bottom line. Often, even when you can't say for certain how much you affected a company's financial results, you can provide numbers that show the significance of your work. Notice the contrasts between less and more effective examples in Table 8.4 and how quantification strengthens the more effective statements.

Table 8.2 *continued*

Teamwork/Communication (cont.)	Explored	Processed	Resolved
Encouraged	Gathered	Purchased	Responded
Explained	Identified	Recorded	Served
Informed	Inspected	Reorganized	Settled
Mediated	Interpreted	Reviewed	Treated
Negotiated	Operated	Screened	Worked with
Persuaded	Performed	Streamlined	**Innovation/Creativity**
Presented	Proved	Systematized	Built
Promoted	Quantified	Updated	Completed
Publicized	Researched	**Customer Service**	Conceptualized
Reported	Reviewed	Assisted	Created
Specified	Solved	Clarified	Defined
Summarized	Studied	Confronted	Designed
Supported	Surveyed	Delivered	Developed
Teamed with	Tested	Greeted	Devised
Analysis/Research	**Administration**	Handled	Formulated
Analyzed	Administered	Maximized	Innovated
Compiled	Edited	Met	Invented
Conducted	Installed	Minimized	Ranked
Detected	Maintained	Performed	Received
Diagnosed	Modernized	Provided	

Table 8.3   Using Action Words to Emphasize Accomplishments

Less Effective	More Effective
Responsible for marketing efforts for younger members	Developed and ran marketing campaigns targeting young professionals and university students that resulted in approximately 55 new members in the past year
Without an action word, this statement sounds unnecessarily weak and passive	By starting with strong action words, this statement illustrates a sense of goal setting and achievement
Answered phones	Greeted clients and scheduled appointments in person and by phone
Although this statement starts with an action word, it emphasizes a menial, nonskilled effort	This action word immediately draws attention to the candidate's focus on customer orientation and value for a business
Kept track of tanning products	Took inventory of all items sold in the store
This statement emphasizes a duty without any reference to the business importance of the task	This statement illustrates a sense of purpose in accomplishing an important business task

Table 8.4   Quantifying Accomplishments

Less Effective	More Effective
Supervised other tellers in the teller department	Supervised six tellers, and was responsible for the overall direction, coordination, and evaluation of my unit
Without a quantity, potential employers might assume a rather inconsequential set of supervision duties	With the number of tellers noted, potential employers see that the applicant has supervised a team
In charge of effort to support local breast cancer awareness event	Organized a group of 83 members to participate in a local breast cancer walkathon
Without quantification and an action word to begin this statement, this phrase emphasizes responsibilities rather than accomplishments	By quantifying the performance (recruiting 83 members), this accomplishment stands out as exceptional

Position your most important contributions first.   The supporting details you place first or second under each heading in your résumé form the deepest impressions about your abilities and attributes. And because most potential employers skim, they may see only the first one or two items under each heading. So, strategically arrange this information to highlight your best features (see Table 8.5).

Remove irrelevant details.   Writing résumés and cover letters requires the discipline to tell a story of how your key abilities and attributes will provide value to an employer. Avoid details about your personal life, especially those that some people might find unprofessional (your political or religious views). Omit personal interests and hobbies unless they take up little space and accentuate your key abilities and attributes (see Table 8.6).

Avoid clichés.   Many clichés, such as *dream job* or *track record of success*, fail to highlight your abilities and attributes for a few reasons. First, they do not communicate your specific accomplishments. Second, many potential employers perceive these statements as showing unrealistic or naive expectations about a job or inflated beliefs about abilities.

Table 8.5 **Quantifying Accomplishments**

Less Effective	More Effective
▲ *Greeted clients and scheduled appointments in person and by phone*	▲ *Managed financial bookkeeping for the company using QuickBooks*
▲ *Assisted with purchasing of medical supplies and processing of client orders*	▲ *Assisted with purchasing of medical supplies and processing of client orders*
▲ *Managed financial bookkeeping for the company using QuickBooks*	▲ *Greeted clients and scheduled appointments in person and by phone*
This list emphasizes customer skills and de-emphasizes financial bookkeeping skills. If the goal is to display financial abilities, this list is not effective.	This list emphasizes financial abilities with less emphasis on purchasing and customer service.

Table 8.6 **Removing Unnecessary Details**

Less Effective	More Effective
Community Activities and Accomplishments Volunteer, VITA, Columbia, SC (giving up my Saturdays in support of a good cause) Church Choir (my church choir contains professional-level talent and tours internationally) Member of the National Association of Federal Credit Unions Volunteer Gymnastic Coach, Columbia, SC Varsity Basketball Overall MVP (2011–2012), Team Captain (2010–2012)	**PROFESSIONAL ASSOCIATIONS AND COMMUNITY ACTIVITIES** **Member,** National Association of Federal Credit Unions, Arlington, VA, 2016 to present **Volunteer Tax Consultant,** Volunteer Income Tax Assistance (VITA) program, Columbia, SC, 2015 to present **Volunteer Coach,** Elite Gymnastics Summer Camp, Columbia, SC, 2009 to 2013 (summers)
This list contains several unnecessary pieces of information. The references to the church choir and high school sports are interesting; however, in limited space, they do little to highlight the candidate's key abilities and attributes.	This condensed list better frames the candidate's activities in a professional light and in terms of key abilities and attributes. The candidate retains one sports item (gymnastics coach) to show her leadership abilities and commitment to the community.

FOCUS ON ETHICS
Fudging the Facts on Your Résumé

As you prepare to finish your college degree and look for your first job, you become increasingly aware of your limited work experience and worry about your ability to compete with other applicants. To make yourself sound more qualified, you consider exaggerating the level of responsibility you had in some of your previous positions. Although your job at the college library consisted mainly of reshelving books, you think about saying on your résumé that you were "responsible for data reacquisition." Even though you worked as part of a team, you consider using terms that imply others on the team reported to you. You even think about stretching your employment dates to make it seem as though you worked longer than you did. *What's the big deal,* you wonder. *Everyone exaggerates on a résumé,* you think to yourself; plus, your supervisor from the library took another job long ago, so she can't be contacted to verify the details you've listed.

CONSIDER THIS: Most of us would agree that deception is unethical, so at what point does exaggerating or stretching the truth on a résumé constitute deception? Even if your exaggerations were never discovered, how might they end up harming an employer who took you at your word and hired you? How might your exaggerations end up harming you in the long run?

Table 8.7 **Proofreading for Typos and Misspellings**

Less Effective	More Effective
Increased the moral of the unit and gained incite into managing frontline employes.	*Increased the morale of the unit and gained insight into managing frontline employees.*
These spelling errors (moral, incite) would not be detected with spell-check software. Also, notice the typographical error on the word "employees."	The spelling is correct in this case, and there are no typographical errors.

Table 8.8 **Formatting to Distinguish Key Pieces of Information**

Less Effective	More Effective
Work Experience	**WORK EXPERIENCE**
Better Horizons Credit Union, Pescaloosa, FL	BETTER HORIZONS CREDIT UNION, Pescaloosa, FL
Marketing Specialist/Loan Officer Jan 2017 to present	**Marketing Specialist/Loan Officer, Jan 2017 to present**
With all formatting the same, the company, position, and dates are difficult to pick out quickly. This problem is amplified over an entire document.	With unique formatting applied to section headings (centered, capitalized, bolded), company (capitalized, left aligned), position (bolded, left aligned), and dates (bolded), employers can pick out key pieces of information rapidly and within seconds gain a good sense of employment and education histories.

Be exact and avoid errors.   Once you make the first cut, potential employers scrutinize your résumé with intensity. Many will discard it immediately if it contains typos or other careless errors. In one recent survey, roughly three of four financial executives (76 percent) said they would eliminate job applicants with just one or two typos on their résumés.[11] In other words, the standard is high, and few potential employers are forgiving. For an example of poor proofreading, see Table 8.7.

Potential employers will pay exacting attention to all the information in your documents and interviews. Any inconsistency or questionable information may reflect poorly on your character and damage your chances or disqualify you. So, be accurate and precise in setting out dates of employment, job responsibilities and accomplishments, educational background, and all other aspects of the résumé and cover letter.

Format to distinguish pieces of information.   As you format your résumé, focus on ease of processing and consistency. Imagine recruiters who are reviewing dozens if not hundreds of résumés in a day. They are likely skimming on the first pass to see whether your résumé deserves more attention. So, make sure they can gather the most pertinent information quickly. By formatting your document effectively with bold, italics, spacing, and other features, you can help recruiters understand your primary abilities and attributes within 20 to 30 seconds (see Table 8.8).

Select a simple yet visually appealing layout.   The last step in the résumé process is choosing a layout. Many job candidates instinctively worry about the appearance in the early stages of résumé writing, especially when they are working from model documents or templates. Resist this natural urge and focus on planning your message first and fine-tuning its tone and style. Then, select an appealing layout.

You can choose from dozens of options and even design your own. Generally, use a lot of white space so your résumé does not appear cluttered, and choose designs

THE COMPETENT COMMUNICATOR *Résumé Checklist*

Make sure your résumé is as strong as possible by evaluating it according to the following checklist. Place a checkmark next to each applicable statement.

1. ____ I have included all relevant contact information, including my name, address, email address, and telephone number.

2. ____ The email address listed on my résumé is professional (robert.wilmot@gmail.com vs. bobby_cuddlebear@gmail.com).

3. ____ I have included all my relevant education and work experience.

4. ____ I emphasized my accomplishments with appropriate action verbs.

5. ____ I have positioned my most important contributions first and removed irrelevant details.

6. ____ The format of my résumé is simple yet visually appealing.

7. ____ I have acquired permission from each of my references to use his or her name and contact information.

8. ____ I quantified my accomplishments wherever possible.

9. ____ Everything I say on my résumé is accurate.

10. ____ I have thoroughly proofread my résumé to make sure there are no mistakes.

Your goal should be to create a résumé that meets all these criteria.

that contain a clear scheme for headings and formatting. Make sure the content is balanced across the page rather than clustered to one side.

Also, make sure to have several trusted people proofread your résumé. Ask them to give feedback on the details (i.e., typos, possible inconsistencies), the overall messaging (i.e., alignment with employer needs, emphasis of key selling points), and appearance. Does your résumé make the grade? Use the checklist in "The Competent Communicator" box to find out.

CREATE CHRONOLOGICAL AND FUNCTIONAL RÉSUMÉS

Most people, by default, assemble their résumés in chronological format. Yet, there are other options. The two major options are **chronological résumés,** which present the information grouped by work and education over time, and **functional résumés,** which present the information in terms of key skills. The most common and generally preferred format, especially for young professionals, is the chronological résumé. One recent survey showed that 75 percent of hiring managers preferred them, whereas 17 percent preferred functional résumés, and 8 percent had no preference.[12]

Functional résumés draw special attention to your key skills. They are most often used by professionals with extensive experience and individuals with little or no work experience. Experienced professionals use them as a way to streamline a lengthy list of jobs offering similar accomplishments and experiences. Inexperienced individuals often use them to emphasize key skills developed through a combination of school, community, volunteer, and other types of activities while de-emphasizing lack of work experience.

Consider creating both a chronological and a functional résumé to see which is more effective at selling your key abilities and attributes. The process of creating both types may even give you insight about how to present your selling points. Suppose Haniz has worked for Better Horizons Credit Union for five years but now wants a position in

Figure 8.2 An Ineffective Chronological Résumé for an Applicant with More Experience

Potential employers may not see your potential if your résumé doesn't highlight and effectively promote your strengths.

Haniz Zogby
164 Founders Ridge Court, Havana, FL 32333
Phone: 850-784-7391; email: hanizzogby@gmail.com

Education
Florida State University, Tallahassee, Florida, Graduation: May 2019, BS in Finance, Minor in
Event Management GPA: 3.714 (Magna Cum Laude)
Major coursework: ECON 2013, 2023; ACG 2021, 2071, 3171, 3331; FIN 3244, 4424, 4324, 4329,
4453; MAN 3240, 4720 3.924 GPA at Woodbridge High School (7th in Class), Palmetto Scholarship

Work Experience
Better Horizons Credit Union, Irmo, SC
Marketing Specialist/Loan Officer, Oct 2017 to present
  •Extend business and personal loans to credit union members
  •Assist with promotional programs
  •Responsible for marketing efforts for younger members
  •In charge of effort to support local breast cancer awareness event
Teller Supervisor, Oct 2016 to Oct 2017
  •Responsible for all cash reserves at the credit union
  •Helped with referral and sales programs
  •Balanced monthly general ledgers
  •Supervised other tellers in the teller department
  •In charge of the entire unit and its activities
Teller, July 2014-Oct 2016
  •Managed banking transactions for members in a helpful and efficient manner
  •Recognized as the top referral getter among the tellers
Palmetto Home Medical, Columbia, SC
Receptionist/Billing Assistant, May 2011–May 2014 (summers)
  •Answered phones
  •Data entry into the computer
Ultra Tan, Blythewood, SC
Salon Attendant, September 2013 to May 2014
  •Cleaned the salon
  •Answered questions that customers had
  •Kept track of tanning products
Computer Skills
MS Word, MS Excel, MS Access, MS PowerPoint, Prezi, MS Publisher, MS Project, QuickBase,
MS Outlook, QuickBooks, Powerscan Loan Display, WebEx

Community Activities and Accomplishments
Volunteer, VITA, Columbia, SC (giving up my Saturdays in support of a good cause)
Church Choir
Member of the National Association of Federal Credit Unions
Volunteer Gymnastics Coach, Columbia, SC
Varsity Basketball Overall MVP (2011-2012), Team Captain (2011-2012)

Study Abroad
Cass Business School, Dubai, United Arab Emirates
  •Took business classes in a multicultural environment
  •Observed one of the most dynamic business environments in the world
  •Took Arabic language courses

The excessively plain appearance of this résumé does not create a positive initial impression.

Recruiters will have a challenging time identifying key attributes and abilities.

Text appears cluttered because it is mostly on the left-hand side of the page without space in between.

The lack of **bold,** *italics,* or other formatting features makes it difficult to rapidly identify key pieces of information.

The focus on responsibilities as opposed to accomplishments fails to sufficiently highlight abilities.

Weak verbs do not emphasize high-order thinking and transferable skills for business.

Sections with additional information do not effectively highlight key attributes and abilities.

which she will have more responsibility and spend more of her time working in innovative marketing campaigns. Notice her ineffective chronological résumé in Figure 8.2 and the improved, more effective chronological résumé in Figure 8.3. Then, study the example of an effective functional résumé in Figure 8.4. Also, note the effective functional résumé for an applicant with less professional experience in Figure 8.5.

Figure 8.3   An Effective Chronological Résumé for an Applicant with More Experience

Effective chronological résumés help your potential employers understand your professional narrative and your professional strengths rapidly.

Haniz Zogby | 164 Founders Ridge Court, Havana, FL 32333 • 850-784-7391 • hanizzogby@gmail.com
LinkedIn: linkedin.com/in/hanizzogby • *Online Portfolio*:
sites.google.com/site/hanizzogby

EDUCATION

FLORIDA STATE UNIVERSITY, Tallahassee, FL
Bachelor of Science in Finance, Minor in Event Management   **Graduation: May 2019**
- *Primary coursework*: bank administration, investments, marketing of financial services, event management
- *Study abroad*: one semester at Cass Business School in Dubai focusing on international finance and marketing
- *GPA*: 3.7; *Awards*: Magna Cum Laude

WORK EXPERIENCE

BETTER HORIZONS CREDIT UNION, Pescaloosa, FL
Marketing Specialist/Loan Officer   **Jan 2017 to present**
- Developed and ran marketing campaigns targeting young professionals and university students that resulted in approximately 55 new members in the past year
- Established a reward points program that was adopted by nearly 30 percent of members
- Organized a group of 83 members to participate in a local breast cancer walkathon
- Extend business and personal loans to credit union members

Teller Supervisor   **Dec 2015 to Jan 2017**
- Implemented and tracked referral and sales programs in the teller department
- Balanced monthly general ledgers, including branch and teller over/short
- Managed all cash reserves at the credit union
- Supervised six tellers; responsible for the overall direction, coordination, and evaluation of unit

Teller   **July 2014 to Dec 2015**
- Handled banking transactions for members in a helpful and efficient manner
- Obtained the most referrals in the teller unit during the entire year (2015)

PALMETTO HOME MEDICAL, Columbia, SC
Receptionist/Billing Assistant   **May 2012 to July 2014 (summers)**
- Managed financial bookkeeping for the company using QuickBooks
- Assisted with purchasing of medical supplies and processing of client orders
- Greeted clients and scheduled appointments in person and by phone

ULTRA TAN, Blythewood, SC
Salon Attendant   **Sept 2013 to May 2014**
- Sold tanning packages and tanning lotions
- Took inventory of all items sold in the store
- Resolved customer concerns related to products, billing, and scheduling

COMPUTER SKILLS

Project Management/Scheduling: QuickBase, MS Project, MS Outlook
Presentations/Publishing/Word Processing: WebEx, MS PowerPoint, Prezi, MS Publisher, MS Word
Finance/Accounting: QuickBooks, Powerscan Loan Display
Spreadsheets and Databases: MS Excel, MS Access

PROFESSIONAL ASSOCIATIONS AND COMMUNITY ACTIVITIES

Member, National Association of Federal Credit Unions, Arlington, VA, 2016 to present
Volunteer Tax Consultant, Volunteer Income Tax Assistance (VITA) program, Pescaloosa, FL, 2014 to present
Volunteer Coach, Elite Gymnastics Summer Camp, Columbia, SC, 2009 to 2013 (summers)

This simple but nicely formatted résumé allows recruiters to rapidly identify key abilities and attributes.

Distinctive and consistent formatting for headings (centered **BOLD CAPS**), organizations (CAPS), position (**bold**), and dates (right-aligned **bold**) make information easy to identify.

Specific accomplishments enhance credibility of claims.

Strong action verbs emphasize transferable management and marketing abilities.

Grouping helps rapidly display key computer skills.

Selective display of associations and community activities highlights key abilities and attributes.

PREPARING RÉSUMÉS FOR ELECTRONIC SCREENING

Increasingly, employers use various automated tools during the hiring process. These tools may include software that screens résumés for minimum qualifications, matches résumés to open positions, and even automates communication

Figure 8.4 **An Effective Functional Résumé for an Applicant with More Experience**

Effective functional résumés prominently display your key skill sets.

Haniz Zogby

164 Founders Ridge Court, Havana, FL 32333 ● 850-784-7391 ● hanizzogby@gmail.com
LinkedIn: www.linkedin.com/hanizzogby ● *Online Résumé*: https://sites.google.com/site/hanizzogby

Qualifications Summary

Ambitious credit union professional with record of successful marketing through local events, seminars, mailings, online social networking, and referrals. Knowledgeable of best practices in marketing for credit unions and innovative financial services for credit unions. Committed to leading marketing efforts to increase credit union membership and empower those who use local credit unions.

Skills

Marketing for Credit Unions
- Developed and ran marketing campaigns targeting young professionals and university students that resulted in approximately 55 new members in the past year
- Established a reward points program that nearly 30 percent of members adopted
- Implemented and tracked referral and sales programs in the teller department

Event Management
- Organized a group of 83 members to participate in a local breast cancer walkathon
- Set up regular seminars about retirement plans, investing, and business loans for credit union members
- Minored in Event Management and completed team projects for a charity fund-raiser (organized a music concert), a sports event (set up a kids' night), and a wedding

Leadership
- Participated in all major decisions for Better Horizons Credit Union during the past year as assistant manager
- Supervised six tellers; responsible for the overall direction, coordination, and evaluation of entire teller unit
- Involved in leadership roles at work, school, and community for the past ten years

Technology
- Excel at using software to facilitate project management and scheduling (QuickBase, MS Project, MS Outlook)
- Comfortable with a variety of online and face-to-face presentation software platforms (WebEx, MS PowerPoint, Prezi)
- Advanced-level use of a variety of finance, accounting, spreadsheet, and database software (QuickBooks, Powerscan Loan Display, MS Excel, MS Access)
- Expert at word processing and publishing software (MS Publisher, MS Word)

Employment History

07/2014–present	BETTER HORIZONS CREDIT UNION, Pescaloosa, FL *Marketing Specialist/Loan Officer* (01/2017–present), *Teller Supervisor* (12/2015–01/2017), *Teller* (07/2014–12/2015)
05/2011–07/2014 (summers)	PALMETTO HOME MEDICAL, Columbia, SC, *Receptionist/Billing Assistant*
09/2013–05/2014	ULTRA TAN, Blythewood, SC, *Salon Attendant*

Education

Bachelor of Science in Finance, Minor in Event Management, FLORIDA STATE UNIVERSITY, Tuscaloosa, FL, Graduation: 05/2019.

Study Abroad, one semester of business classes at CASS BUSINESS SCHOOL, Dubai, UAE

Community Involvement

Volunteer Tax Consultant, VOLUNTEER INCOME TAX ASSISTANCE (VITA) PROGRAM, Columbia, SC, 2014–present.

Volunteer Coach, ELITE GYMNASTICS SUMMER CAMP, Columbia, SC, 2009–2013 (summers).

This cleanly formatted résumé sends signals of professionalism and orderliness.

The "Qualifications Summary" section contains a concise statement that highlights key abilities and attributes.

By grouping skills, Haniz demonstrates what she has to offer in a matter of seconds.

A brief "Employment History" section helps recruiters judge the depth and consistency of her experience.

The "Education" and "Community Involvement" sections contain only a few strategically selected items that focus on her key messages.

(e.g., sending thank-you notes, answering questions with chatbots). These software tools are becoming more sophisticated with the use of artificial intelligence. Most large companies use this type of software as part of the hiring process.[13]

When you submit your résumé to platforms with many open positions (e.g., CareerBuilder job application platform; a Fortune 500 company), you should consider

Figure 8.5   An Effective Functional Résumé for an Applicant with Less Experience

Even without much work experience, you can effectively highlight your skills and interests to potential employers.

Jaclyn Peha
1832 Weston Avenue, Pescaloosa, FL 32333
Email: jpeha@betterhorizons.net

WEB DEVELOPMENT SKILLS

Creative and talented web developer with skills in the following areas:
- *Web specialties*: Website design, web analytics, user interaction, search engine optimization
- *Programming languages*: JavaScript, Java, CSS, HTML, XHTML
- *Adobe Suite*: Dreamweaver, Muse, Fireworks, Flash Professional, Photoshop

EDUCATION AND COURSEWORK

Associate of Applied Science in Information Technology
Pescaloosa Community College, Pescaloosa, FL
September 2017 to April 2019

Web Development Coursework:

- Web & Multimedia Development
- Web Analytics & Search Engine Optimization
- Interactive Web Design
- Web Security
- Internet Commerce
- ActionScript Programming

- Web Content Management
- Advanced Website Design
- Audio-Video Editing
- HTML Programming
- Web Scripting
- Server-Side Programming

WORK EXPERIENCE

IT Intern

Better Horizons Credit Union, Pescaloosa, FL
April 2019 to present

- Assist in developing the branding and communication strategies for the website
- Develop multimedia content for the "Members" section of the website
- Identify strategies for search engine optimization
- Provide tech support for public relations events

PROJECTS

- Co-developed the "Career Resources" section on the Pescaloosa Community College website
- Developed the website of a local nonprofit (*Foundation for Consumer Fairness*)
- Created and maintained Joaquin Jacobi High School's Debate Club website for two years

PERSONAL INTERESTS

Sudoku and crossword puzzles, travel photography, travel documentaries, hiking

---

Formatting allows recruiters to rapidly identify key abilities and attributes. Recruiters can gather the main messages (Jaclyn's abilities and attributes) in each section in a matter of 10 to 15 seconds.

Despite relatively limited experience, Jaclyn portrays herself as skilled in many areas of web development. Her confident, but not exaggerated, language shows her strong potential.

Compared to the ineffective example, this résumé provides far more relevant details, particularly in the "Work Experience" and "Projects" sections.

---

developing a résumé version that will perform well with electronic screening. To ensure you pass this first electronic screening so people actually read your résumé, consider the following strategies:[14]

- *Maintain simple formatting.* Complicated or less used formatting—including fonts, symbols, and graphics—can confuse some software applications.
- *Use keywords strategically.* Make sure to include keywords that capture your key abilities and attributes and that match requirements from related job positions (you'll notice this aligns with the advice you've read about already as you evaluated a job

post and thought carefully about your key selling points; make sure to emphasize key-words even more for automated screening—up to two or three times in your résumé).

- *Avoid exclusive use of acronyms.* Make sure to spell out words so the screening software catches everything.

DEVELOP A REFERENCE LIST

You will need to provide a list of personal references as part of most job applications. Some job applications put off this task until the last minute because they under-estimate its significance. In fact, your references may be among the most important factors in gaining a new position.

Develop relationships with potential references over time. Well before you need to apply for a position, compile a list of people who can provide credible accounts of your qualifications. Consider people who know you and work in fields and indus-tries that interest you. Also consider professors with whom you have established a pos-itive relationship, ideally in classes directly related to the positions you seek.[15]

Contact your reference ahead of time. Before you place any names on your list, reach out to those individuals and, as a courtesy, ask permission to use their names. A short email may be enough, but consider meeting in person or calling to explain the positions you are applying for and recent experiences you've had. These short conver-sations allow your references to speak to employers about you with enthusiasm and provide up-to-date information. And they give you a chance to seek advice about how to handle the job application process. Also send these individuals your current résumé so they are aware of the information potential employers have.

Thank your references. Your references will undoubtedly wonder how your job search is going. Stay in touch with them about the progress you've made. When your job search is complete, thank them for their participation. These shows of goodwill may come in handy over the years as you ask the same individuals for assistance in future job searches. For further tips on maintaining positive relationships with your references, take a look at the "People First" box.

Complete a consistently formatted, well-detailed reference list. When you construct a list of references, check the job announcement to see how many are required. If it does not provide a number, list three to five with current contact information. In addition, consider providing a brief (one or two sentences) descrip-tion of your professional or school relationship to each reference. Finally, format the list of references to be compatible with your résumé (see Figure 8.6). In many cases, you'll enter information about your references into a digital job-application plat-form. Having a document with references helps you do this efficiently and allows you to provide the document if requested by hiring managers.

CONSTRUCT A COVER LETTER

Cover letters (often sent in email form) describe your interest in and qualifications for a position. You must uniquely tailor each cover letter to a particular position; no two cover letters should be the same. Not all job postings require a cover letter. However, a well-written cover letter can often give you an advantage even when it is not formally required.

The primary goal of your cover letter is to sell your key abilities and attributes in a way that matches the needs of the employer for a particular position. Keep in mind the following advice.[16]

Remember that the cover letter makes a first impression. You want an employer's first impression of you to be entirely positive. A perfect, error-free cover letter can immediately place you in the upper echelons of job applicants. A New York tutoring company, Inspirica, recently sought writing tutors and received 220 cover letters. About 93 percent contained writing errors.[17]

PEOPLE FIRST

Treating References with Respect

IMAGINE THIS: Your neighbor calls you to let you know about a great job opportunity at the company where he works. The job is perfectly suited to your skills and experience, and it comes with terrific benefits and opportunities for advancement. The only catch is that the application deadline is tomorrow, and the company needs a list of professional references along with your résumé.

Now, consider this: You have a résumé, but it doesn't include a list of references, so you need to construct a list before tomorrow's application deadline. You identify a manager from one of your former jobs, a professor from a class you took two years ago, and your neighbor himself as potential references, and because you're pressed for time, you consider simply listing these names on your résumé and hoping everyone would agree to provide you a positive reference if asked. A more respectful approach, however, is to

- Consider whether each reference has something worthwhile and relevant to say about you. A manager from a former job can speak to your attributes as an employee, but if you were only one of several dozen students in a class two years ago, the professor may not know you well enough to provide an informed reference. Similarly, a neighbor can attest to your personal attributes, such as your character or integrity, but cannot speak to your merits as an employee without direct experience working with you.

- Ask each person's permission to be listed as a reference, even if time is short. You don't want your references to be caught off-guard or feel that you provided their names and contact information without their knowledge.

- When you ask to include someone as a reference, tell that person about the job you are seeking and the kinds of qualifications it would be advantageous for him or her to highlight about you. Most references want to be as helpful as possible in your job search, so equip them with details they can use in a reference call or letter of recommendation.

Many people you approach to serve as references are busy, and their time is in high demand. Take a people-first approach by showing them the courtesy of asking their permission and respecting their time. This investment in goodwill can pay big dividends in the form of personal and professional support in the long run.

> **THINK ABOUT THIS:**
> How would you feel if someone listed your name, telephone number, and email address on his or her résumé without asking you first? If an employer called on you to provide a reference for that person, how would that behavior color your evaluation?

Clearly identify the position you are seeking. Your potential employer is likely reviewing applications for several—sometimes hundreds of—positions at the same time. Many employers use electronic application systems to clearly identify the positions that applicants are seeking. In any case, clearly and prominently identify the position you are applying for in your cover letter. The subject line is often a good location for this information.

Be focused and concise. Given large applicant pools for every opening, potential employers prefer shorter, more concise cover letters. Aim for three to five targeted paragraphs that focus on your main selling points—your key abilities and attributes—and how they match the employer's needs. This focused approach can create a prism through which the employer will interpret your résumé, strengthening the story of your qualifications it will tell.

Use a tone that is confident but not arrogant. One of the most challenging aspects of the cover letter is getting the tone right. Employers are looking for employees who can contribute, so you should mention how your unique abilities can help

Figure 8.6   **Reference List**

Your reference list should include credible contacts who can speak candidly and positively on your behalf.

Haniz Zogby | 164 Founders Ridge Court, Havana, FL 32333 ● 850-784-7391 ● hanizzogby@gmail.com
LinkedIn: linkedin.com/in/hanizzogby ● *Online Résumé*: sites.google.com/site/hanizzogby

REFERENCE LIST

Christine Russo
CEO and President
BETTER HORIZONS CREDIT UNION
Address: 1488 Altura Dr.
Pescaloosa, FL 32315
Phone: 850-971-0234
Email: russo@betterhorizons.com
Relationship: Ms. Russo has been my supervisor for the past five years. She is intimately familiar with my work in the following positions: marketing specialist, loan officer, teller supervisor, and teller.

Jim Harrill, CPA
Owner
HARRILL TAX ASSOCIATES
Address: 3419 Main Street
Havana, FL 32333
Phone: 850-972-3188
Email: jamesharrilljr@harrilltax.com
Relationship: Mr. Harrill trained me and supervised my work as a volunteer tax consultant for the VITA program. He is familiar with my work ethic and commitment to the community.

Jamie McPherson, PhD
Associate Professor of Finance
FLORIDA STATE UNIVERSITY
Address: 719-C Thurmond Tower
Tallahassee, FL 32302
Phone: 850-777-1848
Email: mcpherson@fls.edu
Relationship: Dr. McPherson taught two of my courses and served as an advisor for my honors thesis about emerging financial services in credit unions.

Jack Gerardi
Owner and President
PALMETTO HOME MEDICAL
Address: 18 Foxborough Lane
Columbia, SC 29201
Phone: 803-798-1312
Email: jgerardi@palmettohomemed.com
Relationship: Mr. Gerardi supervised my work as a receptionist and billing assistant for 3-1/2 summers.

Consistent formatting allows recruiters to quickly gather key information.

Formatting that matches the résumé formatting shows attention to detail and a touch of class.

A brief statement about relationships with references demonstrates professionalism and helps recruiters make judgments about the value of each one.

SHARPEN YOUR SKILLS

Proofreading for Precision

As tedious as it can be to proofread someone else's writing, it can be even more difficult to proofread something you have written yourself. A résumé or cover letter containing mistakes can be enough to prevent you from getting the job you want, though, so effective proofing is essential. One way to sharpen your proofreading skills is to look for one type of problem at a time. Instead of reading your document from start to finish and trying to catch everything at once, concentrate only on spelling the first time through. Then go through your document again to focus only on grammar. Finally, read carefully to focus only on punctuation. Breaking up the proofing process in this way can help you be more precise and find errors you might otherwise miss. Also, always remember to ask trusted colleagues and friends to proofread your résumé and likewise break up the process.

the company. Yet, hiring managers may view excessive self-praise as arrogance. You should also show your interest in the position and the company, because hiring managers will be trying to gauge your enthusiasm and commitment. But avoid flowery language, which hiring managers may find off-putting and not businesslike.

Tailor your cover letter to the job posting and the employer's needs. By carefully reading the job announcement, you can prioritize your selling points so they are tailored to the position of interest. This approach not only accentuates your ability to do the job; it also shows you have researched the position and are responsive to the needs of the company. The Internet provides many ways to learn about specific companies.

Figure 8.7   **An Unsolicited Cover Letter**

Unsolicited cover letters should concisely state your potential value and demonstrate your understanding of the potential employer.

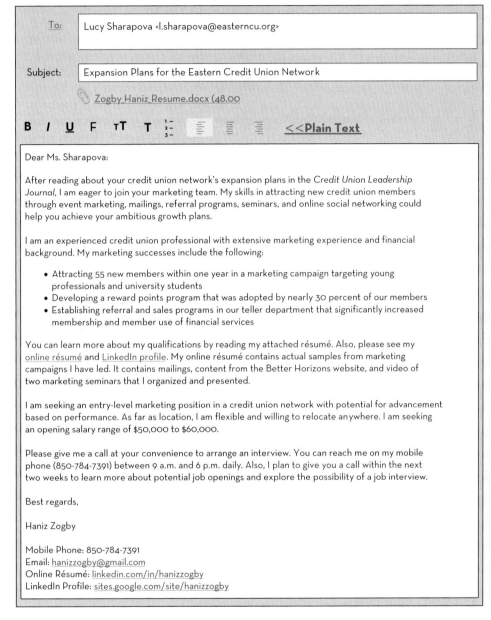

To: Lucy Sharapova <l.sharapova@easterncu.org>

Subject: Expansion Plans for the Eastern Credit Union Network

Zogby_Haniz_Resume.docx (48.00

B *I* <u>U</u> F ᴛT T <<**Plain Text**

Dear Ms. Sharapova:

After reading about your credit union network's expansion plans in the *Credit Union Leadership Journal*, I am eager to join your marketing team. My skills in attracting new credit union members through event marketing, mailings, referral programs, seminars, and online social networking could help you achieve your ambitious growth plans.

I am an experienced credit union professional with extensive marketing experience and financial background. My marketing successes include the following:

- Attracting 55 new members within one year in a marketing campaign targeting young professionals and university students
- Developing a reward points program that was adopted by nearly 30 percent of our members
- Establishing referral and sales programs in our teller department that significantly increased membership and member use of financial services

You can learn more about my qualifications by reading my attached résumé. Also, please see my online résumé and LinkedIn profile. My online résumé contains actual samples from marketing campaigns I have led. It contains mailings, content from the Better Horizons website, and video of two marketing seminars that I organized and presented.

I am seeking an entry-level marketing position in a credit union network with potential for advancement based on performance. As far as location, I am flexible and willing to relocate anywhere. I am seeking an opening salary range of $50,000 to $60,000.

Please give me a call at your convenience to arrange an interview. You can reach me on my mobile phone (850-784-7391) between 9 a.m. and 6 p.m. daily. Also, I plan to give you a call within the next two weeks to learn more about potential job openings and explore the possibility of a job interview.

Best regards,

Haniz Zogby

Mobile Phone: 850-784-7391
Email: hanizzogby@gmail.com
Online Résumé: linkedin.com/in/hanizzogby
LinkedIn Profile: sites.google.com/site/hanizzogby

The message is concise. The body has just 276 words. Further, the short paragraphs and bulleted items allow the recruiter to get the gist within 15 to 30 seconds.

The subject line focuses on the needs and ambitions of the employer.

Links to Haniz's online résumé and LinkedIn profile allow the recruiter to learn more if she is interested.

The tone is confident and assertive without being demanding.

As an unsolicited request for a job interview, this message is more up front about issues such as salary and promotional opportunities.

Adapt your approach for unsolicited letters.   Most people gain their positions through formal job announcements—that is, jobs *solicited* by companies. A **solicited cover letter** is a cover letter for an open position that a company advertises. An **unsolicited cover letter,** in contrast, states your interest in working for a company that is not actively requesting job applications.

When writing unsolicited cover letters, you'll make several modifications. First find out as much as possible about the employer so you can explain how your qualifications fit the organization's needs. Begin with a proposition about how you can add value, and then summarize your key abilities and attributes quickly, perhaps in bulleted form. Figure 8.7 displays an example of an effective unsolicited cover letter in email form.[18]

LO8.4

Describe strategies for developing an online professional persona.

Developing Your Online Professional Persona

Social media platforms give you many opportunities to network and reach your professional goals. LinkedIn is the most popular professional networking platform.

A strong presence on LinkedIn can help you in a variety of ways in the job search process. Many HR professionals will view your LinkedIn profile after seeing your cover letter or résumé. Just before a job interview, your interviewer may look at your profile to learn more about you. The company representative you met at a job fair may look at your profile to decide whether to follow up with you. In some cases, HR professionals may contact you after seeing that you match what they're looking for in certain positions.

You can expect that many of your professional contacts—colleagues, partners, clients, customers, and others—will check your profile to learn more about you. But you should consider using LinkedIn for many purposes, not just to find job opportunities. Increasingly, LinkedIn is also a professional learning platform. By following the posts of thought leaders, business leaders, companies of interest, and curated newsfeeds in specific topics, you can consistently learn and stay up to date with business and industry knowledge.

Approach your LinkedIn profile in the same way you approach your résumé. Identify a professional narrative of your key selling points to set up a profile that is persuasive to your professional contacts. With fewer space constraints than on your résumé, you can provide additional types of information. Notice Haniz's LinkedIn profile in Figure 8.8. In addition to providing information about her education and work experience, she has dedicated space to list personal interests, languages, volunteer experience, certifications, courses, and other items. She also displays the people, organizations, and curated newsfeeds she follows. As long as these additional items reinforce her intended professional narrative, she should include them.

PROVIDE A PROFESSIONAL PHOTO

Unlike résumés, the first item most LinkedIn viewers see is your profile picture. Make sure you upload a high-resolution, warm, and professional photo.

CREATE A PERSONALIZED URL

LinkedIn allows you to create a unique web address. Personalizing your link to include your name makes your profile more memorable and professional.

COMPLETE THE SUMMARY SPACE

A common missed opportunity among LinkedIn users is failing to use the summary space. In one to three paragraphs, you can brand yourself with your key abilities and attributes and major accomplishments. Use concise, confident, natural, and cliché-free language.

USE MULTIMEDIA

LinkedIn allows you to upload a variety of file types, including video and pictures. If you have appropriate multimedia to highlight your accomplishments, you can set yourself apart from others on LinkedIn.

CHOOSE SECTIONS WISELY

LinkedIn allows you to choose from well over 20 types of sections, including causes you care about, test scores, projects, honors and awards, publications, and so on. Add information when it reinforces your professional narrative. While you have more space than on a résumé, you should still choose selectively to highlight your key selling points.

Figure 8.8   **An Example of a Well-Developed LinkedIn Profile**

You can use your LinkedIn profile to supplement your résumé in the job application process.

Photos: *(left) ©Ingram Publishing; (right) ©Images-USA/Alamy*

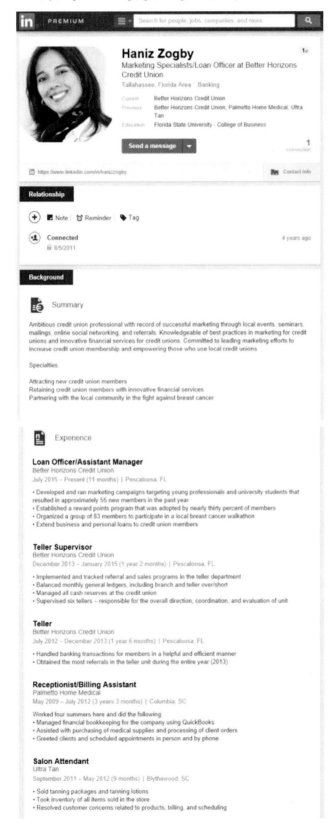

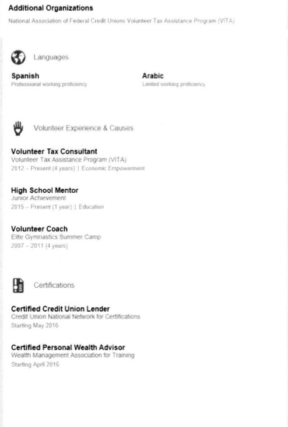

Figure 8.9

A Less Effective, Nonpersonalized LinkedIn Invitation

Avoid using the default invitation in LinkedIn.

Source: LinkedIn Corporation

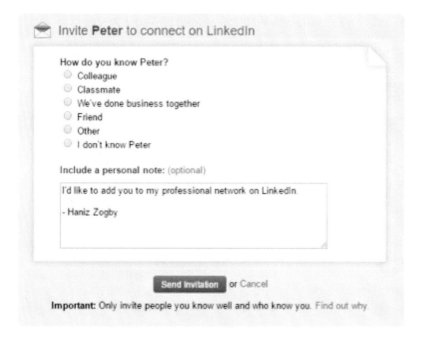

MANAGE YOUR RECOMMENDATIONS AND ENDORSEMENTS STRATEGICALLY

LinkedIn allows you to give and receive recommendations and endorsements. If you choose to display them, you should generally limit the number of recommendations to two or three per position or section. LinkedIn automatically gives your connections the option to endorse you for various skills. You can choose to display only those endorsements that are most accurate and that align with your key selling points.

BUILD A NETWORK OF IMPORTANT CONNECTIONS

LinkedIn prominently displays the number of connections you have in your network. As you build your network, resist the urge to focus on the quantity rather than the quality. Typically, connect with professionals and peers with whom you share professional interests. Make sure to personalize your invitations when you hope to connect with others. Notice Figure 8.9 in which the invitation is generic and nonpersonalized. By contrast, the invitation in Figure 8.10 is personalized. Taking a minute to personalize the invitation shows your genuine interest in connecting with others.

SHOW SOME PERSONALITY AND BE POSITIVE

While you should maintain professionalism on LinkedIn, you have more flexibility in the way you portray yourself and interact with others than with résumés and cover letters. Find ways to show your personality in positive and warm ways.

MAINTAIN A GIVER MENTALITY

An important principle of networking is being a giver rather than a taker. LinkedIn allows you to provide others with recommendations, endorsements, likes, and lots of helpful information. As you gain a reputation for helping and providing value to others, you will find many opportunities open up to you.

Figure 8.10

A More Effective, Personalized LinkedIn Invitation

Sending a short, personalized LinkedIn invitation demonstrates your sincere interest in others.

Source: LinkedIn Corporation

STAY ACTIVE ON LINKEDIN

Make sure to consistently update your LinkedIn information. Use LinkedIn as a professional learning platform. Pay attention to the accomplishments of those in your network and congratulate them. Periodically share status updates. Join some communities and groups. As you invest an hour or two per week on LinkedIn, you'll find that professional opportunities will arise through your networking and learning.

SHARPEN YOUR SKILLS

Creating an Effective Online Persona

One of the most effective ways of creating an effective persona in an online venue such as LinkedIn is to emulate good examples. If you're already on LinkedIn, peruse other users' profiles and identify three that strike you as especially effective. Or Google "best LinkedIn profiles" to find examples with impact. Pay attention to what makes each profile so compelling to you, and list the attributes effective profiles seem to have in common. Then edit your own profile to include the same attributes.

CHAPTER WRAP-UP

Many of your professional opportunities depend on you carefully developing your professional reputation. You can use use professional networking, cover letters and resumes, and online professional social networking sites to help you develop your professional reputation. Here's a quick review of the chapter.

LO8.1 Formulate short-term and long-term career aspirations.

- Complete a self-inventory of career goals, professional abilities and attributes, and areas to improve.

LO8.2 Understand principles for professional networking.

- View professional networking as a relationship-oriented process with a focus on shared opportunities and success.
- Tap into formal and informal networks.
- Conduct informational interviews.
- Attend job fairs and other career networking events.
- Attend campus speeches and other professional development events.

- Join clubs and other professional interest groups.
- Volunteer at a local nonprofit.

LO8.3 **Develop a résumé, a cover letter, and a reference list.**

Résumés

- Create a structure that tells a story.
- Gather information about your education, work experience, and other areas relevant to your professional abilities and attributes.
- Emphasize accomplishments with action verbs.
- Quantify your accomplishments whenever possible.
- Position your most important contributions first.
- Remove irrelevant details.
- Avoid clichés.
- Be exact and avoid errors.
- Format to distinguish pieces of information.
- Select a simple yet visually appealing layout.
- Create both a chronological and functional résumé.

Reference Lists

- Develop relationships with potential references over time.
- Contact your references ahead of time.
- Thank your references.
- Complete a consistently formatted, well-detailed reference list.

Cover Letters

- Remember that the cover letter makes a first impression.
- Clearly identify the position you are seeking.
- Be focused and concise.
- Use a tone that is confident but not arrogant.
- Tailor your cover letter to the job posting and the employer's needs.
- Adapt your approach for unsolicited letters.

LO8.4 **Describe strategies for developing an online professional persona.**

- Provide a professional photo.
- Create a personalized URL.
- Complete the summary space.
- Use multimedia.
- Choose sections wisely.
- Manage your recommendations and endorsements strategically.
- Build a network of important connections.
- Show some personality and be positive.
- Maintain a giver mentality.
- Stay active on LinkedIn.

A LOOK BACK

Now, let's return to the opening scenario. Veronica has been unsuccessful in her job search. Sometimes, it takes a while to find a job out of college. It's not always the job applicant's fault. But we can immediately recognize some likely reasons for Veronica's failures. She's applied for positions in so many areas that she likely hasn't developed any clear career focus. That lack of focus is probably reflected in her job application packages. Furthermore, she's likely taken a passive approach to the job search without developing any networking orientation. She appears to have relied entirely on online submissions. Veronica should reevaluate the approach she's taken to her job searches, take time to create an inventory of her goals, develop a networking orientation, and redevelop her job applications with a more targeted approach.

KEY TERMS

CHAPTER REVIEW QUESTIONS

1. How can identifying your job interests, abilities, and attributes help you develop an effective résumé? LO8.1

2. In what ways can you categorize your key abilities and attributes to project credibility? LO8.1

3. What exactly is meant by networking in a professional sense? LO8.2

4. How can you use informational interviews to learn about career options? LO8.2

5. What are some networking strategies you can begin implementing immediately? LO8.2

6. How can you use résumés to tell your professional story? LO8.3

7. What are the key sections of résumés and what are the purposes of these various sections? LO8.3

8. Why should you use action words on your résumés? LO8.3

9. What are some ways you might undersell yourself on résumés? LO8.3

10. Why should you try to quantify accomplishments when possible? LO8.3

11. What does it mean to position your most important accomplishments first and why is this important? LO8.3

12. What do you think are common irrelevant details that college students place on résumés? LO8.3

13. What are the benefits and drawbacks of chronological and functional résumés? LO8.3

14. What is the purpose of grouping and labeling data on your résumé? LO8.3

15. What strategies can you use to develop a reliable reference list for your job searches? LO8.3

16. What strategies can you use to project competence and confidence but not arrogance in your job application messages? LO8.3

17. What strategies can you use to develop an effective online professional persona? LO8.4

SKILL-BUILDING EXERCISES

Evaluating Your Key Selling Points (LO8.1)

Using Table 8.1 and Figure 8.1 as guides, do the following:

- State your career goals.
- Describe the three or four abilities and three or four attributes that you want to stand out most prominently in your job application package. Why do you want these skills and attributes to stand out?
- Name the two or three abilities and attributes you most want to develop.

Networking Presentation (LO8.2)

Conduct between one and three informational interviews. Identify some professionals who work in positions you aspire to hold or who do work that you aspire to engage in. Set up 30-minute to 1-hour informational interviews with these individuals. (For some good guidance on informational interviews, see *The New York Times* post by Marci Alboher at https://shiftingcareers.blogs.nytimes.com/2008/01/29/mastering-the-informational-interview.)

You should approach these informational interviews with real questions in mind, some issues you really want to understand better. Reach out to people you don't know. Ideally, you'll meet in person, but online video conversations work as well.

From your informational interviews, you'll develop a presentation to help your classmates understand professional opportunities. Identify one or two interesting themes from your interviews to share in your presentation.

Ideally, you'll make your presentation story-based. Talk about the individuals you chose to interview (What are their areas of expertise? What are their accomplishments? Why do you admire or respect them? What are their personalities like? What drives them?). Spend most of your time providing key insights about professional insights and opportunities you learned from your interviewees. Make sure to clearly identify the take-away points while sharing examples shared by your interviewees.

Getting Feedback on Your Résumé and Cover Letter (LO8.3)

To determine how well you are promoting your selling points (your two or three key abilities and two or three key attributes), do the following in this order:

1. Write down your key selling points.
2. Create your résumé and cover letter to highlight these key selling points.
3. Without providing what you believe are your key selling points, ask a trusted classmate/colleague/

professor to review your résumé and cover letter. Specifically, ask your peer to answer the following questions:

- Based on these documents, what do you think my key selling points are? Ask your peer to mention abilities or skills and attributes or traits.
- Do my key selling points stand out clearly? Do you think my résumé and cover letter provide a consistent message about my selling points?
- What suggestions do you have for me to improve these documents?

4. After getting responses from your peer, answer the following questions:
   - What did your peer say were your key selling points? What did your peer say about how well your selling points stood out?
   - How closely aligned were your peer's observations with what you intended to be your key selling points?
   - Based on your peer's observations, what modifications should you make to your résumé and cover letter to better highlight your selling points?

Getting Feedback on Your Résumé from a Professional in Your Desired Discipline/Industry (LO8.3)

Find a professional in the discipline and/or industry that interests you. Ask this person to review your résumé and give you feedback about the following: (a) strength of your résumé in gaining the position you seek; (b) advice for improving the résumé; (c) areas of your résumé that may appear less credible or perhaps even exaggerated; and (d) advice for increasing career opportunities. Turn in the following:

- Revised résumé.
- Document detailing what you learned from the business professional and what changes you made to your résumé as a result.

Getting Feedback on Your Résumé from Classmates (LO8.3)

Form a group of three to four classmates. Read one another's résumés, spending three to five minutes per résumé. As you read, focus on how well the person communicates key abilities and attributes. Debrief by explaining the following:

- Key abilities and attributes communicated by the résumé.
- Two or three areas in which the résumé could be improved.
- Any areas in the résumé that seem less substantiated than others.

Individually, write two to three paragraphs about the comments and advice you received from the other members in your group.

Using Action Words (LO8.3)

Using Tables 8.2, 8.3, 8.4, and 8.5 as guides, do the following:

- Choose ten of the action words and create statements that you could use on your résumé with your accomplishments.
- Make five statements of accomplishments that you could place on your résumé that include quantification (e.g., increased sales by 12 percent).

Creating Functional and Chronological Résumés (LO8.3)

Create two versions of your résumé—a chronological and a functional résumé. In addition to these two documents, create a separate document that describes the advantages and disadvantages of using each type.

Creating a Reference List (LO8.3)

Create a reference list with five individuals whom you could trust to provide good professional endorsements of your abilities. Provide all contact information and a brief statement about how each person knows you.

Creating a Cover Letter (LO8.3)

Choose a job announcement that interests you. Write a cover letter that is addressed to the contact person/organization in this announcement.

LinkedIn Profile Evaluation (LO8.4)

Based on your LinkedIn profile, respond to the following items:

- What is your LinkedIn profile address?
- What are the main traits that stand out about you on your LinkedIn page?
- What are the main abilities that stand out about you on your LinkedIn page?
- Which parts of your LinkedIn profile best promote who you are as a professional?
- Which parts of your LinkedIn profile least promote who you are as a professional?
- What are three changes you intend to make to improve your LinkedIn profile?
- What three groups would you like to join and participate in?
- Which three organizations should you follow? Why?
- Which three professionals should you follow? Why?

ENDNOTES

1. Casciaro, T., Gino, F., & Kouchaki, M. (2016, May). Learn to love networking. *Harvard Business Review, 94*(5), 104–107; de Janasz, S. C., & Forret, M. L. (2007). Learning the art of networking: A critical skill for enhancing social capital and career success. *Journal of Management Education, 32*(5), 629–650; Grayson, C., & Baldwin, D. (2007). *Leadership networking: Connect, collaborate, create.* Greensboro, NC: Center for Creative Leadership; Misner, I., Alexander, D., & Hilliard, B. (2009). *Networking like a pro: Turning contacts into connections.* Canada: Entrepreneur Press.

2. Alboher, M. (2008, January 29). Mastering the informational interview. *The New York Times.* Retrieved from https://shiftingcareers.blogs.nytimes.com/2008/01/29/mastering-the-informational-interview.

3. Baber, A., & Waymon,L. (2007).*Make your contacts count: Networking know-how for business and career success* (2nd ed.). New York, NY: American Management Association.

4. Casciaro, T., Gino, F., & Kouchaki, M. (2016, May). Learn to love networking. *Harvard Business Review, 94*(5), 104–107; Krattenmaker, T. (2002, April). A blueprint for constructing a personal and professional network. *Harvard Management Communication Letter, 3–4.*

5. Misner, I., Alexander, D., & Hilliard, B. (2009). *Networking like a pro: Turning contacts into connections.* Canada: Entrepreneur Press.

6. Caley, C. (2014, February 17). Geisha Williams: Set your sights high, take charge and keep the lights on. *Leadership California.* Retrieved from https://www.leadershipcalifornia.org/i4a/pages/index.cfm?pageID=3587.

7. Caley, C. (2014, February 17). Geisha Williams: Set your sights high, take charge and keep the lights on. *Leadership California.* Retrieved from https://www.leadershipcalifornia.org/i4a/pages/index.cfm?pageID=3587.

8. Lawler, M. (2018, April 18). The one-page resume vs. the two-page resume. *Monster.* Retrieved from https://www.monster.com/career-advice/article/one-page-or-two-page-resume.

9. Accountemps. (2009, October 29). Most wanted: "People" people: Survey shows interpersonal skills can trump technical knowledge in job search. Retrieved July 15, 2017, from http://accountemps.rhi.mediaroom.com/people_skills.

10. Accountemps. (2012, September 18). "You had me at hello": Survey finds most employers form opinions of job interviewees within 10 minutes. Retrieved July 15, 2017, from http://accountemps.rhi.mediaroom.com/interview-time.

11. Accountemps. (2014, May 15). Survey: One or two resume mistakes enough for majority of managers to pass on a job candidate; still, managers are more lenient than they were five years ago. Retrieved July 15, 2017, from http://accountemps.rhi.mediaroom.com/index.php?s=189&item=1730.

12. Accountemps. (2010, January 10). Form over function: Three-quarters of executives surveyed prefer chronological resumes from job seekers. Retrieved July 16, 2017, from http://accountemps.rhi.mediaroom.com/chronology?_ga=1.143833717.1115341173.1472658477.

13. Zielinksi, D. (2017, May 4). Today's ATS solutions go well beyond resume storage. *Society for Human Resource Management.* Retrieved from http://www.shrm.org/resourcesandtools/hr-topics/talent-acquisition/pages/ats-solutions-buyers-guide-shrm.aspx.

14. Slack, M., & Bowitz, E. (n.d.). Beat the robots: How to get your resume past the system & into human hands. *The Muse.* Retrieved from https://www.themuse.com/advice/beat-the-robots-how-to-get-your-resume-past-the-system-into-human-hands.

15. Isaacs, K. (2011, October 6). Get your references together for your job search. *Monster.* Retrieved July 16, 2017, from https://www.monster.com/career-advice/article/prepare-your-references.

16. Isaacs, K. (2011, January 20). Cover letters to recruiters. *Monster.* Retrieved July 16, 2017, from https://www.monster.com/career-advice/article/Cover-Letters-to-Recruiters.

17. Lublin, J. S. (2010, July 6). The keys to unlocking your most successful career. *The Wall Street Journal.* Retrieved July 16, 2017, from https://www.wsj.com/articles/SB10001424052748704293604575343322516508414.

18. Isaacs, K. (2011, January 20). Cold cover letters. *Monster.* Retrieved January 16, 2017, from https://www.monster.com/career-advice/article/cold-cover-letters.

Learning Objectives

After reading this chapter, you should be able to do the following:

LO9.1 Differentiate types of interviews.

LO9.2 Formulate strategies for conducting a job search.

LO9.3 Identify tactics to respond to employment interview questions.

LO9.4 Outline approaches to succeeding in a web conference interview.

LO9.5 Explain etiquette for following up after job interviews.

CHAPTER 9

Interviewing Successfully

Jalen sat down nervously. He immediately felt out of place in his buttoned shirt and casual slacks because his interviewer, Ana Bacud, was dressed in a formal suit. Ana started the conversation, "So, Jalen, perhaps you could tell me a bit about yourself and why you'd like to work here."

Jalen took about five minutes to talk about the finance program he was enrolled in, how much he enjoyed sports, how convenient the location of this company was for him, and how much this job would mean to his career. After the 30-minute interview ended, he left the office wondering how well he had done. He considered sending a thank-you note but thought it might seem presumptuous. After a week passed during which he didn't hear anything, he drafted an email message to Ana to ask about the position, but then he decided emailing her was too intrusive. A month later, he received an official rejection from the company. What had gone wrong?

Preparing for a Successful Interview

Your ability to participate successfully in interviews can be an asset when communicating in the workplace, and not just when you're applying for a job. Interviews are conducted for many reasons. We'll begin this section by exploring some of them. We'll then consider how you can land, and subsequently prepare for, a successful job interview, and how you should respond to discriminatory questions if you encounter them.

WHAT IS AN INTERVIEW?

An **interview** is a structured conversation that focuses on questions and answers.[1] The job interview—which we examine below as an example of a *selection interview*—is critical in the workplace; after all, most of us won't be hired unless we succeed in the job interview. There are many uses of interviews in the workplace, however. Let's look at the main ones.

LO9.1

Differentiate types of interviews.

TYPES OF INTERVIEWS

Interviews at work can take the following forms:

- *The appraisal interview:* Whenever you sit down with someone to discuss your performance and goals, you're taking part in an **appraisal interview**. In many lines of work, managers and supervisors conduct appraisals of all their employees on an ongoing basis, whether quarterly, semiannually, or annually. The appraisal interview can encourage you to continue what you're doing well and guide you to improve.[2]

- *The problem-solving interview:* A **problem-solving interview** helps participants understand the nature of a problem and identify potential solutions. You take part in problem-solving interviews, for instance, when you discuss treatment options for an illness with your physician or financial options for a mortgage with your banker.[3]

- *The exit interview:* If you've resigned from an organization to take a job elsewhere, you may be asked to complete an **exit interview**, a conversation about your experiences with the organization you're leaving. During this interview, you usually describe both positive and negative aspects of your job, your supervisors, and the organization.

- *The counseling interview:* If you go through a difficult time, you might reach out to close friends, relatives, or a professional therapist to express your feelings, receive empathy, and gain an outside perspective on your situation. This conversation is a **counseling interview**, an interaction aimed at supporting an individual through a personal problem.

- *The service-oriented interview:* A **service-oriented interview** is a conversation meant to help you with a product or service you have purchased. When you tell the customer service representative you've discovered a torn lining in a jacket you just bought, he may examine the jacket and offer you a refund or exchange.

- *The persuasive interview:* If you've ever received a telephone call asking you to vote for a political candidate or a proposition, you've participated in a **persuasive interview**, a conversation intended to affect your belief, opinion, or behavior. You also take part in persuasive interviews when people try to convince you to donate money or volunteer your time.

- *The survey interview:* Each decade, the federal government conducts a *census*, a survey to count and gather information about the U.S. population. To collect census data, government workers may visit or call households and businesses to ask a variety of questions, including "How many people live in your household?" and "How many of you are employed full-time?" Your conversation with

When you leave a position, you may be asked to do an exit interview to describe your experiences with that organization.

©stockfour/Shutterstock

the census worker constitutes a **survey interview,** an interaction aimed at gathering information. Survey interviews can also occur as part of a research study or public opinion poll.

- *The selection interview:* A **selection interview** is a conversation intended to help the interviewer choose the most appropriate person for a position, an assignment, a promotion, or an award. When you interview for a job, you are taking part in a selection interview, one that is critical to your chances for employment.

Although people take part in many types of interviews, one type that nearly everyone will encounter is a selection interview for employment, which is part of the process of searching for a job. Let's look at some strategies for locating jobs for which to apply and then for preparing to succeed in an employment selection interview.

CONDUCTING A JOB SEARCH

The first step in landing a job interview is to identify positions for which to apply. It helps to start by considering which types of jobs are right for you. You should then complete a thorough job search first and analyze the needs of potential employers. Before contacting a potential employer, you should also check your online persona.

Decide which jobs are right for you. Before you begin looking for job announcements, it helps to know what kind of job you are seeking. To narrow your options, focus on the *characteristics* of your ideal job. Do you enjoy working with others or do you prefer working alone? Do you prefer a 9-to-5 schedule or do you require flexibility with your hours? Do you enjoy doing work that is similar every day or different every day? Would you like to work in a large corporation or a small organization? Do you need to stay in your current city or do you have the ability to relocate? What kind of opportunities for career advancement are important to you?

Make a list of seven to ten criteria that are most important to you in a job. As you encounter job announcements, refer to your list and prioritize job opportunities that meet most of your criteria. As you do so, consider the types of work that will not only be fulfilling to you now but will also allow you to grow. As the "Career Tip" box explains, Indra Nooyi, former CEO of PepsiCo, recommends seeking work that will challenge you and provide opportunities for lifelong learning.

LO9.2

Formulate strategies for conducting a job search.

CAREER TIP

When Indra Nooyi was promoted to the CEO position at PepsiCo in 2006, her mother immediately told her, "You might be president of PepsiCo, but when you come home to your family, leave that damned crown in the garage."[4] Nooyi has followed that advice and tried to maintain a sense of humility in all her work.

Nooyi is often asked for career advice. She consistently tells people to go after challenging work:

Embrace tough assignments. Conventional wisdom suggests that it's easier to take the path of least resistance by signing up for an easy job, doing it well, and moving on to something bigger. The problem with that theory is that nobody notices when you do an easy job well. It's far better to challenge yourself by raising your hand for the toughest assignments and work to solve problems that no one else has been able to solve. That's how you truly become a trusted leader inside an organization.[5]

Similarly, she has encouraged young professionals never to stop learning: "Whether you're an entry level employee fresh out of college or a CEO, you don't know it all.

Indra Nooyi, former CEO of PepsiCo
©Monica Schipper/Getty Images Entertainment/Getty Images

Admitting this is not a sign of weakness. The strongest leaders are those who are lifelong students."[6] As you choose new positions and roles early in your career, take Nooyi's advice to heart by seeking challenging work and constantly learning.

Complete a thorough job search process.   Looking for jobs takes a lot of time. It's not uncommon for three to six months to elapse between the time you find a position announcement and are offered the job. A thorough search for the best potential positions at the initial stages can save you a lot of time and increase your likelihood of getting a position that reflects your long-term interests.

An excellent place to start is with your friends, family members, instructors, and anyone you know who works in your area of interest. Tell those people the kind of work you want to do and ask for ideas about where to look. They may be able to put you in touch with employers in your field who are looking for people to hire and also give you pointers for connecting with other potential employers.

Use all the resources available to learn about your options. Spend some time talking to experts at your school's career center and make a plan for exhaustively searching for jobs that match your interests and qualifications. When possible, contact and get involved with professional organizations and visit organizational websites to learn about options. Go to job fairs on and off campus to see what opportunities are open and to practice networking in a competitive environment.

You can also search for job openings online. Websites such as Indeed.com, Monster .com, CareerBuilder.com, and CollegeRecruiter.com help you search for jobs by location, field, or company. They describe available openings and allow you to apply for the jobs online. Some websites specialize in advertising positions within a specific field. For instance, TeacherJobs.com posts vacancies for educators, and MedicalJobs .org lists openings for positions in a variety of health care fields. You can also identify vacancies at specific companies by looking at their individual websites, often at the page called "Employment" or "Careers."

Analyze the needs of potential employers.   When hiring you, employers are making a huge investment, so they want to ensure that they make the right decision. According to London-based recruiter Jörgen Sundberg, it costs as much as $240,000 to recruit, hire, and train a new employee, so companies are careful about whom they bring on board.[7] They will be willing to make that investment in you only when you demonstrate that you meet *their* needs, so carefully read and analyze the job position announcement to understand those needs. Then, group the requests in the announcement in terms of abilities and attributes. For an example, see Figure 9.1, in which a posting for a marketing specialist is analyzed for the key abilities and attributes being sought. Once you've done this, you're in a good position to decide whether you match these criteria and, if so, to frame your résumé and cover letter to highlight these abilities and attributes.

Some job announcements include contact information for a company representative. If you have questions that the job announcement does not answer, you might call or email this person before applying, to express your interest and find out more. By doing this, you connect with an influential person in the organization and gain insight not provided in the job announcement.

Before an interview, you will also want to find out about the company's size, the location of its headquarters and major divisions, its top officers, and its past and recent history. Explore the company's website and other sites that discuss the firm for that information, or look for it in the company's annual report, which you may be able to download. You can also get a sense of the company's culture by searching online for recent news stories about it.

Check your online persona.   As Chapter 8 discussed, you will carefully draft your résumé and cover letter to portray yourself as competent, professional, and responsible. Don't make the mistake, however, of believing those documents constitute all the information a potential employer could find about you. In fact, a 2015 survey found that 52 percent of employers log onto social media sites to research job candidates.[8] What would a human resources director learn about you by Googling your name? Have you posted overly revealing comments on Twitter? Do the interests in your Facebook profile include "getting smashed every weekend"? There's a simple way to find out. Google your own name and see what comes up. Anything you can find about yourself online will be just as accessible to any potential employer. You may consider it an invasion of your privacy for employers to consult the Internet for information about you. Once you post something online, however, it becomes accessible not only to your friends but also to anyone seeking information about you, including a prospective employer.

If your Google search returns anything you wouldn't want a potential employer to see, take it down or make it accessible to authorized viewers only (such as your closest Facebook friends). Or change your name on social media—temporarily, at least—so prospective employers will have a more difficult time finding you online. The last thing you want is to lose a job opportunity because a hiring manager sees your spring break pictures on Facebook and concludes that you don't have the character or maturity to perform competently in the job.

Displaying Your Best Self during a Job Interview

Your cover letter, résumé, and other job documents set the stage for the most consequential part of the process—the interview. Once you have secured an interview, you have made the initial cut and are likely deemed a good candidate. You are now competing against the best candidates for the position.

Many job applicants spend little time preparing for the interview, essentially "winging it." But preparation often distinguishes those who receive offers from those who do not. In this section, we survey some crucial strategies for winning the job.

Figure 9.1 **Analyzing a Job Posting for Key Needs**

This is one way to analyze a job posting for the most important abilities and attributes that the employer is seeking.

Job Summary	Credit Union Field Marketing Specialist
Location 84341 **Job Type** Full-time **Reference Code** 831481809	**Organization:** Anchor Federal Credit Union Network **Education Required:** College degree **Experience Required:** 1–3 years **Position Description:** Works with managers throughout the Anchor Federal Credit Union network to develop local marketing events to promote Credit Union membership. Coordinates all activities for each event, including supply distribution, prizes, and duration of campaign, budget, marketing support, and staffing. Responsible for tracking results and providing recommendations for future events. Also is responsible for collecting and maintaining data related to market conditions of each proposed site. Performs various other marketing and support functions when not traveling, including general promotional development, membership surveys, collateral production and tracking, retiree package mailings, and other projects as assigned by the VP of Marketing. **Position Requirements:** Develops individual marketing activities to support branch growth and/or agency events. Travels to various locations throughout the country to organize events. Analyzes market conditions to ensure that the marketing activity is in line with the demographics of that particular region. Provides annual profile of demographics for each region. Oversees budget for each activity. Is responsible for reporting variances on a monthly basis. Works with outside vendors to solicit participation in marketing activities. Actively promotes the participation of both staff and monetary contributions from these outside sources. Works with VP and AVPs of branches to set priorities and establish goals for each event. Tracks results of each event and analyzes the success/shortfall of each. Distributes reports for review. Tracks marketing collateral inventory for branches and DMs. Ensures timely distribution and proper inventory controls. Develops mailings for account generation and retention. Develops ongoing mail programs to DMs and BCO managers for relationship development throughout the agency side of the business. Makes routine phone calls to HR managers, DMs, and BCO managers to establish event schedules, coordinate Financial Finesse seminars, and maintain relationships throughout the organization. Performs other duties as assigned. **Position Attributes:** *Candidate must be able to travel 25–30% domestically. *A minimum of 2 years of field marketing and sales experience. *Candidate must have presentation skills and experience.

Abilities wanted

Marketing: local marketing events, market analysis, marketing reports (written and oral), sales letters and other mailings to generate membership, seminars.
Relationship management: work with branch managers to organize local events and set marketing strategies; staffing for events; maintain intra-organizational relationships and relationships with outside vendors.
Communication: distribute event schedules, disseminate marketing reports, encourage participation, make sales presentations.

Attributes wanted

Ambitious: must be able to take initiative on organizing many events and meet deadlines.
Creative: must develop attractive and compelling marketing events and campaigns.
Organized: must be able to manage many simultaneous projects, events, and relationships.

TECH TIP

Getting an Insider's View of Potential Employers

Few job seekers get an inside look at the companies that interest them. A variety of websites can help you find this invaluable perspective, however. One is Glassdoor.com, where you can find reviews about a company of interest posted by its current and former employees. You can learn how satisfied employees are with the company, what the company culture is like, what advancement opportunities are there, and even what the salary ranges are for various positions.

By getting as much inside information about a company as possible, you can decide whether the company culture and job opportunities match your expectations before you even apply. You can also better prepare for the job application and interview process, and perhaps even for salary negotiations once you have a job offer.

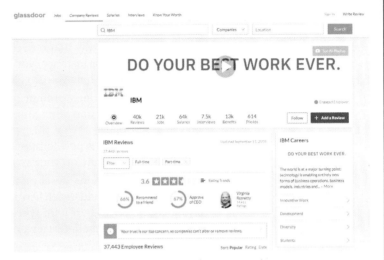

Glassdoor.com's inside look at IBM's profile as an employer

Source: https://www.glassdoor.com

PAY ATTENTION TO APPEARANCE AND ETIQUETTE

One of the first signals of professionalism you give at a job interview is your appearance. As much as possible, gain a sense ahead of time about dress standards at the company where you are interviewing. To do so, you might ask people who are familiar with the company's culture, or you might consult the company's website and pay attention to photos of employees. Generally, you should dress up even when the company has a fairly casual environment—that is, wear well-pressed, clean, and nicely fitted businesslike clothes. Avoid over-accessorizing with too much jewelry, flashy glasses, or other items. Consider a dress rehearsal at home to feel at ease in your chosen outfit.[9]

Greeting an interviewer with a handshake and a smile is an excellent way to make a positive first impression.

©monkeybusinessimages/Getty Images

During your visit to the company—before, during, and after the formal interview—pay attention to appropriate etiquette. Most hiring managers expect you to maintain a certain level of formality. Greet those you meet with handshakes and enthusiasm, and be sure you know (and can spell) their names and titles so you can write to thank them afterward for taking the time to meet with you.

DISTINGUISH BETWEEN TYPES OF QUESTIONS

One reason job selection interviews are stressful is that you don't usually know beforehand what questions the interviewer will ask. However, you can anticipate many questions and prepare for them. Let's first briefly examine the most common types of questions and identify successful responses to each.

- **Open-ended questions** invite a broad range of answers. Questions such as "Tell me about yourself" and "What are your goals for the future?" give you the opportunity to reply in a way that reflects positively on you. In response to a question about your goals, for instance, you can focus on two or three that are relevant to the job and explain how you are already working toward attaining them.

- **Closed-ended questions** prompt brief, specific answers. Some call for a simple yes or no, such as "Can you work weekends?" Others elicit particular pieces of information, such as "What was your college major?" When you're asked closed-ended questions, it is best to provide short, direct answers. An interviewer who wants you to elaborate on your answer will ask you to do so.

- **Hypothetical questions** describe a realistic situation and ask you to speculate about how you would react. An interviewer might ask, "Suppose a customer asked you to refund an item without a receipt. How would you handle that?" Your answer helps the interviewer see how you would manage the situation.

- **Probing questions** request more detail on answers you have already provided. Let's say you are asked why you left your previous job, and you cite the lack of opportunities for advancement as the reason. A probing question could ask "What opportunities for advancement make a job more appealing to you?" Now you can elaborate on what you've said.

Most job selection interviews include a mix of general and position-specific questions. Interviewers commonly begin with broad, open-ended questions, such as "Tell me a little about yourself." From there, they typically move to more specific, closed-ended, hypothetical, and probing questions about the candidate's education, work history, skills and talents, and qualifications for the job.

RESPOND EFFECTIVELY TO INTERVIEW QUESTIONS

The moment of truth for hiring managers generally occurs during the job interview. Many make fairly quick judgments about your abilities and attributes. In a recent analysis of more than 200 job interviews, 25 percent of employers reported deciding whether or not to hire a candidate within 5 minutes, and another 35 percent reported making that decision within 15 minutes.[10] Your window may be brief to make the case that you are a good fit for the company. To prepare for the questions you may be asked, consider the following tips.

Respond to questions strategically and concisely.   Find ways throughout the interview to emphasize the selling points you highlighted in your cover letter and résumé. Avoid bragging, but do claim credit for what you have accomplished by saying "I" rather than "we" when discussing past work. Of course, balance this confidence by also highlighting your team orientation.[11]

Finally, give concise answers that take between about 30 seconds and two minutes so they are neither abrupt nor unfocused. Longer answers can disrupt the give-and-take rhythm of the interview.

In Table 9.1, you'll find many common types of interview questions. Be prepared to respond to any of them strategically, confidently, and concisely.

It's one thing to review commonly asked questions, but it's another to consider how best to answer them. Suppose Haniz wants a position at her current employer, Better Horizons Credit Union, in which she will have more responsibility and spend more of her time working in innovative marketing campaigns. Take a look

Table 9.1   Common Job Interview Questions for Entry-Level Business Positions

Type of Question	Examples
Introductory	• Tell me about yourself. • How was your trip here? Did you find our office easily? • How do you like living in ___?
Education and training	• Why did you choose your school? • Why did you choose your major? • What was your favorite part of your program? Least favorite?
Knowledge of company and industry	• How much do you know about our company? • What do you think are some of our main business challenges? How can you help? • What trends do you see in this industry?
Work experience	• How did you get your last job? • Why did you leave your last job? Have you ever been fired? • What did you like least about your last job? • Why did you apply for this job? • What are you looking for in a job? • How will you be successful in this position? • What were some tough decisions you had to make in your last job?
Approaches to work, goals, and success	• What are your biggest accomplishments? • Tell me about a project you worked on in your most recent job. How did you contribute to its success? • What do you wish you had accomplished but were unable to? • Can you tell me about a difficult situation you encountered at work? How did you respond? How did you get your team to work effectively? • Can you tell me about a situation when you had to work under pressure and deal with deadlines?
Personal attributes	• What are your strengths? Weaknesses? • What would your current boss say are your greatest strengths and weaknesses? • Are you creative? Hardworking? Ambitious? Can you give examples? • What have you learned from your previous jobs?
Interpersonal, team, management, and leadership skills	• What types of people do you like to work with? • What types of people do you find the most difficult to work with? • What is your leadership/management style? • Do you have top management potential? • How well do you work in teams? • What is your communication style when working with others? • Have you had to make an unpopular decision or announcement? How did you do it?

at Table 9.2 for some examples of effective and less-effective ways in which she might respond to commonly asked questions in her interview.

Be perceptive about what hiring managers are evaluating. Hiring managers ask most questions with specific goals in mind. They are trying to evaluate how well your abilities and attributes match the needs of the position and fit into the

SHARPEN YOUR SKILLS

Preparing to Answer Interview Questions

Think of a job you would like to have when you graduate. Review the questions in Table 9.1 and write out a short answer for each. Afterward, role play an interview with a trusted relative or advisor to practice answering those questions and ask that person for feedback about how you might improve your performance.

Table 9.2   **Responses to Common Job Interview Questions**

Less Effective	More Effective
Q. *Tell me about yourself.*	**Q.** *Tell me about yourself.*
A. Well, I'm a recent graduate with a degree in finance. I also minored in event management. I have worked for a credit union for the past five years. I started out as a teller and moved up from there. Prior to working at the credit union, I worked at a medical supplies company and a tanning salon. Outside that, I've been heavily involved in sports my whole life. And, that brings me right up to now, ready to move into a new position.	**A.** About five years ago, I took a position as a teller at a credit union. I found that I really loved the credit union approach to providing financial services. Within months, I realized that this was a career direction for me. I was fairly quickly promoted into other positions—first as a teller supervisor and then a loan officer and marketing specialist. While working at the credit union, I also went to Florida State University, where I majored in finance and minored in event management. I focused all my studies on my deep interest in marketing financial services for credit unions. One reason I'm so intrigued by the position here is that it combines several of my key interests.
Evaluation: This response is factual but does not directly lead into a coherent, inspiring account of Haniz's selling points.	**Evaluation:** This statement captures Haniz's background, naturally describes several of her selling points, and ties her selling points to the needs of the position. At 120 words, this statement would take roughly 45 seconds to one minute to state.
Q. *It looks like you just graduated. Tell me about your university experience.*	**Q.** *It looks like you just graduated. Tell me about your university experience.*
A. I had a great time in school. I had great professors all the way through my program in finance. I made great friends. One of the most exciting parts of my schooling was studying in Dubai for a semester, which really opened my eyes to the world. The only part I didn't like about school was the pressure of working for most of my four years and also studying on the side. But, I think I grew a lot from the experience.	**A.** Going to Florida State University was a great experience and helped me improve my skills in marketing financial services. Early in my finance program, I took a variety of classes about banking and investments that helped me think about financial services we could offer at Better Horizons. Also, I used a lot of what I learned in my event management minor to think about events we could run at the credit union. I think my favorite semester was the one in which I went abroad to Dubai. I was fascinated to see that the businesses in that country are using so many creative and innovative approaches to event marketing. I've tried to use some of those techniques I saw in Dubai at Better Horizons.
Evaluation: This response provides a general overview of Haniz's experience but fails to provide a sense that she was pursuing a set of goals. It does not contain her selling points.	**Evaluation:** This response ties Haniz's university experiences to her professional goals and accomplishments. It highlights her key selling points and shows her goal-directed approach to work.
Q. *Why do you want to leave your current job?*	**Q.** *Why do you want to leave your current job?*
A. My job at Better Horizons Credit Union has given me many opportunities, but I am often frustrated with the conservative approach that our board has taken to developing new services. My immediate supervisor usually agrees with my ideas, but she understands that the board will not approve our most ambitious suggestions. So, she falls in line. Better Horizons has been a great learning experience, but I'm simply ready to have a more ambitious position.	**A.** I've enjoyed working closely with so many of my colleagues, and getting to know the community has been wonderful. Last year, when I helped run our campaign that brought in so many younger members, I realized that I wanted to be part of a larger credit union network in a position where I could spend more of my time developing marketing events and facilitating coordination between branches. I think this is where my strengths lie, and as far as I can tell, they would be a good match for your position.
Evaluation: By stating her displeasure with the board and the less-than-ambitious work culture, Haniz makes a risky statement. Some hiring managers will worry that she does not work well with others.	**Evaluation:** By focusing on the satisfying aspects of the position she intends to leave, Haniz is more likely to give the impression that she is a committed, team-oriented employee. She segues her response into the needs of the current position.

Less Effective	More Effective
Q. *How well do you work in teams?*	**Q.** *How well do you work in teams?*
A. I take a win–win mentality into all team projects. I really believe that one plus one can make three if you work together as a team. I think if you ask anyone I've worked with, they'll tell you that I facilitate a productive work environment where we're feeding off one another's ideas and where the end result is a creative and effective solution.	**A.** I enjoy working in teams to meet marketing objectives. Last year's marketing campaign that resulted in 55 new members was the result of a five-member team at Better Horizons. I was asked to head up the team and focused on events and social media, while the other team members worked on their specialty areas, such as market research, print advertising, and radio spots. Even though we each had our specialties, we had to work together extensively to make sure we created a unified marketing message. We also pushed one another to come up with better ideas. I don't think we could have achieved such a successful campaign without one another.
Evaluation: This clichéd, vague response does little to convey Haniz's real ability to work in teams.	**Evaluation:** This response shows Haniz's ability to work in teams through a concrete example. It inspires confidence that Haniz is a team player and genuinely understands the economic value of working in teams.
Q. *Do you have management experience? What is your approach to managing others?*	**Q.** *Do you have management experience? What is your approach to managing others?*
A. Yes. As a teller supervisor, I supervised a unit of six tellers. I was responsible for coordinating, scheduling, and managing the overall performance of the group. I think the most important part of managing is being open. The tellers always knew where I was coming from and vice versa.	**A.** Yes. At Better Horizons, I've managed the teller department and led a variety of marketing campaigns that required bringing together the ideas and resources of credit union employees and members. I have been most successful when I've followed several principles. First, I think it's important to set a vision and articulate the big goals. Second, I think it's critical to get everyone's ideas about how to achieve the goals. Finally, I think you have to find ways to gain buy-in and create incentives for others to engage in the goals. Here's how I did this with our mailing campaign to attract more members. . . .
Evaluation: This response is too short. Although it is positive, it fails to lead into Haniz's selling points of developing marketing campaigns.	**Evaluation:** This response answers the question and also transitions to Haniz's selling points.
Q. *What are your weaknesses?*	**Q.** *What are your weaknesses?*
A. I can't really think of any weaknesses off the top of my head. Well, I guess one thing is that I never settle for anything less than excellence. Some people who accept mediocrity say I'm a control freak, but I get the job done. So, in one way you could view this as a weakness, but from the business viewpoint, it's a net plus.	**A.** One of the things I noticed in the job posting is that you are looking for someone with the ability to conduct member surveys. I wish I could say that I had experience doing surveys in my current job. I think it is critical to include surveys as part of market analysis. I took several courses about conducting surveys and statistical analysis, but so far I haven't applied this knowledge to real business problems. I look forward to developing my abilities in this regard and would welcome any training or mentoring.
Evaluation: This question is common in job interviews. Many job candidates view it as a trick question and evade it or state a weakness that could really be viewed as a strength. This response does not show that Haniz is self-aware enough to improve quickly on the job.	**Evaluation:** This response shows that Haniz is self-aware. It also reveals her ambitious, goal-setting nature and recognizes what she needs to do to provide value for her potential employer.

organization's culture. Thus, they will ask a variety of questions about your education, work experience, and knowledge of their company. You can fairly easily discern what most questions are designed to find out about you.

When you can't, think about what kinds of judgments the interviewer might make. For example, when hiring managers ask you to introduce yourself, they want

Discussing Your "Greatest Weakness"

Interviewers often ask applicants to identify their greatest strengths and weaknesses—and although talking about our strengths is often easy, many of us find discussing our weaknesses to be discomforting. To avoid appearing weak, we may say we have no significant weaknesses, or we may decide to divert attention from our true weaknesses by attempting to disguise a strength as a weakness, such as by saying "I'm a perfectionist." Instead, it helps to select weaknesses that you have already started to improve but that are not essential for success in the job you are seeking. If you are applying for an accounting position, for instance, you might mention how you have always been intimidated by public speaking—likely not a large requirement of an accounting job—and the steps you have taken to become more comfortable with it. If you're seeking a job as an editor or proofreader, you might discuss how you have struggled with math but have worked to overcome that challenge. The point is to identify a weakness that (1) you are working to improve and (2) will not prevent you from succeeding in the job you're after. Imagine interviewing for a coveted position when you graduate from college and being asked to identify your greatest weakness. With a classmate or trusted mentor, practice offering an answer that identifies an honest weakness and then discussing what you are doing to overcome that weakness.

to know how you see yourself. This gives them a glimpse into your sense of your life and career direction, your priorities, and your work values. When they ask you what your weaknesses are, they are generally less concerned about what you can't do now than about what you can do later (see the "Sharpen Your Skills" box for strategies on answering this question constructively). They are trying to see how self-aware you are and whether you are likely to improve over time. Even small talk—such as polite chat about the weather or how your football team is doing—helps hiring managers make judgments about your emotional intelligence.

Tell success stories.   During job interviews, stories about your successes can create a positive connection between you and your potential employers. They provide specific and concrete evidence of your abilities and attributes and a glimpse into who you are as a person.[12]

One approach to telling success stories is the **STAR method** (Situation–Tasks–Actions–Results). Table 9.3 shows how Haniz uses the STAR method to briefly but convincingly respond to the question "How well do you work with deadlines?"

Read through this example and compare its specificity to an abstract, nonspecific response, such as "I work well under pressure and deadlines. In fact, I thrive under these conditions and often produce my best results."

As you tell success stories, make sure they respond directly to interview questions and reveal your best selling points. Also, keep them relatively brief. Generally, responses that are longer than a few minutes are too long. You might consider writing out five or six success stories you could use in a job interview and timing yourself as you recount them.

One strategy for succeeding in a job interview is to tell stories about your successes.

©EDHAR/Shutterstock

Avoid criticizing your former organizations, supervisors, and colleagues. Among the worst offenses in job interviews is speaking negatively of your current or past employers. That will make hiring managers wonder how well you get along with others and what attitude you bring to work. When you are asked questions such as "Why do you want to leave your current job?" or "What is your least favorite part of your job?" be prepared with an honest response that is constructive, forward-looking, and complimentary of your job if possible. For instance, you might mention how much you appreciate your previous employer but felt you were ready for bigger responsibilities than you had in your previous position.

Table 9.3 **The STAR Approach to Responding to Interview Questions**

	Example Statements
Situation in which you created a positive outcome	**Q.** *How well do you work with deadlines?* **A.** I'm quite used to meeting deadlines, and actually, I've done some of my best work when I had to hit a deadline. One example occurred recently in organizing a group of credit union employees and members to participate in a local walkathon to support breast cancer. For over a decade, our credit union has been a prominent supporter of the event, but our participation has decreased almost every year. Last year, our group was composed of just 15 people, most of whom were employees. Altogether, we raised only around $600.
Tasks you were assigned as part of a process	Two weeks before the deadline for signing up, our president approached me and asked me whether I could head up a promotional effort to get a larger group from the credit union. She suggested that I aim for at least 30 people and focus on getting more of our members on the walkathon team, especially newer members.
Actions you took that led to outcome	Within a few days, another marketing specialist and I had set up some incentives for members to participate, such as free T-shirts and water bottles. We developed promotional messages that we sent out by email and via our Facebook page and our website. I think what made the most difference is that we asked tellers to distribute flyers each time a member came in for a transaction.
Results that occurred	Ultimately, we recruited 83 walkers and raised nearly $10,000 for our local breast cancer center. We also were able to get a variety of new members to join our walkathon team and connect on a deeper level with our credit union community.

Know what can and cannot be asked. In the United States, the Equal Employment Opportunity Commission (EEOC) is the federal agency that monitors unfair discrimination in hiring and firing decisions. For the last four decades, the EEOC has enforced guidelines that specify what an employer may and may not ask prospective job candidates during employment interviews and on application forms. The guidelines are intended to ensure that employers ask only for information relevant to the position being sought.

FOCUS ON ETHICS
Criticizing a Former Employer

Imagine that, a year and a half ago, you were thrilled to land a coveted position at one of the most respected public relations firms around. What you hoped would be a dream job, however, quickly turned into a nightmare because of your supervisor. Although widely known and respected in the public relations field, he is ruthless and inconsiderate in the office. At times, his behavior toward you even bordered on discriminatory. You now find yourself interviewing for a job at a new company, where the interviewer asks you why you want to leave such a prestigious firm. You consider whether to respond honestly—by describing how terrible your current supervisor is—or simply to say you're looking for a new career opportunity.

CONSIDER THIS: Are you lying to the interviewer if you don't describe your *real* reason for wanting a new job? Do you think the interviewer would find it ethical for you to bad-mouth your current employer? What do you think is the most ethical way to respond to the interviewer's question?

The law specifies that some questions can be asked only if there is a bona fide reason for asking them.

©imtmphoto/Getty Images

In most cases, federal law prohibits employers from considering factors such as a person's sex, age, ethnicity, sexual orientation, religion, marital status, political orientation, or disability status in decisions to hire, promote, or fire. Some cities and states also prohibit employers from asking about a candidate's salary history.[13] Exceptions are allowed only when there is a *bona fide*, or legally legitimate, reason for them. For instance, if the position legitimately requires someone of a certain sex (such as a women's locker room attendant), a certain ethnicity (such as an actress playing an ethnic-specific movie role), or a certain physical ability (such as a firefighter, who must be able to walk and carry loads of a certain weight), these factors may be considered in employment decisions.

Most jobs, however, require only the skills and training necessary to perform the assigned tasks. If there is no bona fide reason to require applicants to fit a specific demographic profile (such as being of a particular age, marital status, or religion), employers cannot legally ask about those characteristics during a job selection interview. Even if one characteristic, such as ethnicity or physical ability, is a bona fide job requirement, the employer can ask only about *that* attribute, not the others.

As a job applicant, you benefit by knowing the laws regarding employment and illegal discrimination. Table 9.4 offers a list of questions that are generally illegal for employers to ask in an interview, alongside similar, job-related questions that *are* legal to ask.

If you are asked an illegal question during a job interview, whether through the interviewer's ignorance or in an intentional attempt to gain information about you

Table 9.4   **What Can and Can't Be Asked during a Job Interview**

Legal to Ask	Illegal to Ask
Are you authorized to work in the United States?	Are you a citizen of the United States?
What languages do you speak, read, or write fluently?	What is your native language?
Are you available to work on the days this job requires?	What religious holidays or days of worship do you observe?
Are you 18 years of age or older?	How old are you?
Have you worked or earned a degree under another name?	Is this your maiden name?
What is your experience working with children?	Do you have children?
Are you able to perform the specific duties of this position?	Do you have any disabilities?
Do you have upcoming events that would require extensive time away from work?	Are you a member of the National Guard or military reserves?
Are you willing to relocate if necessary?	Do you live nearby?
Tell me about your experience managing others.	How do you feel about supervising men or women?

Source: HR Toolbox, https://hrworld.com/features/30-interview-questions-111507.

PEOPLE **FIRST**

Keeping Your Cool When Asked an Illegal Question

IMAGINE THIS: You're interviewing for a job you really want. You have prepared three questions to ask at the end—but the interviewer answers all of them during your interview, leaving you with nothing new to ask. Therefore, you're already flustered when the interviewer tries to fill the gap by asking you a question that you recognize as illegal for an employer to ask.

Now, consider this: Even though you realize the question is inappropriate, you want this job and you don't want to cause a scene by pointing that out. Instead, try these strategies:

- Answer directly but briefly. "Do you go to church?" "Yes, I do."

- Pose a tactful inquiry. "What is your political orientation?" "Why do you ask?"

- Tactfully refuse to answer. "Do you plan to have children?" "My family plans won't interfere with my ability to do this job."

- Neutralize the question. "What happens if your spouse gets called for military duty?" "My spouse and I would discuss the logistical requirements of any change in our circumstances."

- Take advantage of the question. "Do you have any disabilities?" "As someone with mild dyslexia, I've learned to treat people with a wide range of abilities empathically and respectfully."

Although you may feel uncomfortable or even offended when asked an illegal question, it is seldom best to respond defensively ("You can't ask me that; it's none of your business"). Instead, use one of these strategies to defuse the tension and show that you can react tactfully and professionally in an uncomfortable situation.

THINK ABOUT THIS:

Why is it to your advantage to respond tactfully to an illegal question? How can you avoid getting flustered in this situation?

the employer doesn't need, there are ways you can provide the necessary information without embarrassing the interviewer or causing everyone discomfort. Communication professors Charles Steward and William Cash suggest five potential ways of responding effectively to illegal questions, which you can read about in the "People First" box.[14]

Generate questions of your own.   Generally, your interviewer will end the interview by asking you what questions you have. Come prepared with some. When interviewees do not ask questions, hiring managers often view them as uninterested or inexperienced. Some strategies for formulating good questions are these:

- Ask the interviewer to reflect on his or her own experiences. An excellent question is, "What have you most enjoyed about working here?" This allows the interviewer to tell you about himself or herself and also to identify the aspects of the company he or she most appreciates.

- Ask questions that indicate your long-term interest in the job. A question such as "What opportunities would this position offer for someone who is interested in growing with this company?" suggests you are thinking about your career in the long term and will be serious about your commitment to your employer.

- Don't ask for details about the company that you should already know. Recall that part of preparing for a job selection interview is researching your potential employer. Therefore, you don't want your questions to reveal ignorance about the company, such as "Where is this company's headquarters located?"

Table 9.5 **Questions by Job Candidates in First Interviews**

Less Effective	More Effective
▲ What kind of salary are you offering for this position?	▲ What are you looking for in the person who takes this position?
▲ How often can I work from home?	▲ Can you tell me about the company culture?
▲ Is there a strong benefits package?	▲ If there were any one thing you could change about the company culture, what would it be?
▲ How much vacation time will I get?	▲ How do you evaluate employees' performance?
▲ Do you cover medical, dental, and vision insurance?	▲ Whom would I report to in this position? What is that person's management style?
	▲ Do you have any concerns about my ability to succeed in this position?
	▲ What are the next steps in this process?

- Never ask about salary or benefits unless the interviewer has brought up those subjects. Some interviewers may ask you about your salary requirements. However, unless the interviewer introduces the topic, don't inquire about the salary, vacation time, or medical benefits. Those are questions to be posed after you have a job offer.

In Table 9.5, you will notice several questions that are not effective and others that are generally effective.

LO9.4

Outline approaches to succeeding in a web conference interview.

Succeed in Web Conference Interviews

Many companies are using web conferences for initial job interviews. Using Skype, Google Hangouts, or other platforms is far more convenient and less expensive—in time and money—than flying in job candidates for on-site interviews. Consider the following strategies for these types of interviews.

DO SEVERAL TRIAL RUNS

Make sure to do several mock job interviews via web conference with a parent, friend, or professional in your field. Within 20 to 30 minutes, you'll learn a variety of ways to act professionally and feel natural. Test your equipment each time to make sure your video and audio work well.

MAKE SURE YOUR PROFILE CREATES THE RIGHT IMPRESSIONS

The first thing many recruiters will see is your profile on Skype or Google Hangouts. You can make a great first impression by including a professional-looking photograph and a biography that highlights your skills, education, experience, and career goals.

LOOK PROFESSIONAL

Some job candidates view web conference job interviews as less formal than in-person job interviews. That's not the case. Wear a suit or appropriate professional dress to show your interest in the job. Consider adjusting the temperature in your room to ensure you're comfortable with a suit on during the interview.

TIDY YOUR ROOM OR OFFICE

Many job interviewers form impressions of you based on the surroundings in your room or office. Make sure your room is clean, organized, and attractive. Remember that an interviewer will be able to see everything behind you that is in the camera frame, so make sure your surroundings are neat and that there are no inappropriate photos or other objects that would attract negative attention.

LOOK DIRECTLY AT THE CAMERA

During your interview, remind yourself to *look at your web cam* most of the time, especially while listening. Don't focus on the image of the interviewer or the image of yourself. Looking at your web cam may feel unnatural to you, but it will appear natural to the other party. When you look directly at your camera, you appear to the interviewer to be looking at him or her.

SMILE AND EXPRESS YOURSELF NONVERBALLY

Many people find it challenging to express themselves nonverbally in web conferences. Initially, you may need to make a conscious effort to smile and use gestures. Many people use gestures less often during a web conference because they rest their elbows on a desk or armchair, which hinders natural movement. You might consider not doing that, to free up your hands and arms.

USE NOTES STRATEGICALLY

A major advantage of web conference interviews is that you can have notes—on paper or in an open file on your computer—to give you cues during the interview. For example, you might have a list of points you want to emphasize or a few questions to ask. Use these notes sparingly, however, so that you can maintain eye contact with your interviewer and avoid the impression you're not prepared for the interview.

AVOID DISTRACTIONS

Remove clutter from your desk, close all unneeded files on your computer, and make sure there aren't any interruptions. If you have roommates, ask them to be quiet

Interview Preparation Checklist

Think about either an upcoming interview or one you can envision. Use this checklist to make sure you've given adequate attention to the necessary preparation steps. Read each of the following statements and indicate whether the statement is true or false by placing a checkmark in the appropriate column.

	True	False
1. I have thoroughly researched the employer.	_____	_____
2. I have practiced answering various types of interview questions.	_____	_____
3. I know exactly how to get to the interview site.	_____	_____
4. If the interview is online, I have checked my Internet connection prior to the interview.	_____	_____
5. I am wearing attire that is appropriate for the job I want.	_____	_____
6. I have thought carefully about what this employer is seeking.	_____	_____
7. If the interview is online, I have made certain that my surroundings are tidy and look professional, and that there will be no interruptions or distractions.	_____	_____
8. I have prepared at least three questions to ask the interviewer.	_____	_____
9. I am aware of what can and cannot be asked.	_____	_____
10. I am well rested and ready for success.	_____	_____

It should be evident that the best response to each statement is "True." If you are less confident about any of the items, use this checklist as a reminder of what you most need to work on prior to your interview, in order to communicate as competently as possible.

during your interview. If you have a pet, make sure it's not close enough to your room or office that the interviewer might hear it. If car horns, police sirens, or other distracting noises are frequent where you live, consider finding a better location for the interview.

How prepared are you to face the challenges of an interview? Check out the "Competent Communicator" box to assess your readiness.

LO9.5

Explain etiquette for following up after job interviews.

Following Up after the Job Interview

Your work is not over when you walk out of the interview. It is also worth your while to send a thank-you note to the interviewer and follow up with him or her later.

SENDING A THANK-YOU NOTE

Send your interviewer a thank-you note—either handwritten or electronic—shortly after your interview. As illustrated in Figure 9.2, indicate that you appreciate the interviewer having taken time to speak with you, note how you benefited from the interview experience, and express your excitement about the position. You might want to close by saying you look forward to hearing back. Sending a thank-you note requires only a few moments but may be the one gesture that sets you apart from equally qualified competitors.

Figure 9.2

A Sample Thank-You Note

Sending an interviewer a sincere thank-you note can help you stand out from your competition and increase your likelihood of success.

Photo: *©KQS/Alamy*

Sending a note of appreciation following an interview is a good strategy. In a poll of 150 senior executives, 88 percent stated that sending a thank-you note could increase the chances of employment. When asked how many job applicants actually *do* send thank-you notes, however, the executives estimated that only half of candidates do so.[15]

CONTACTING THE INTERVIEWER

Unless the interviewers tell you to wait until they contact you, feel free to follow up with their progress in making a selection. Many job applicants hesitate, assuming they may annoy or nag hiring managers. But 48 percent of HR managers say they view job candidates more favorably when they follow up.[16] Your polite follow-ups show that you want the position and that you are persistent. As shown in Figure 9.3, most hiring managers expect you to follow up, with nearly half (43 percent) saying you should check back at least once per week.

Figure 9.3 How Often Should You Check Back after Being Interviewed?

Most hiring managers expect applicants to check back with an interviewer after completing a job interview.

Source: Society for Human Resource Management. (2009, September 15). *SHRM poll: Interviewing do's and don'ts for job seekers.* Copyright © 2009. Alexandria, VA: Society for Human Resource Management.

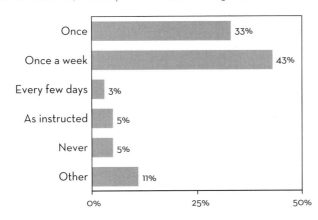

Landing a job almost always requires succeeding in a job interview. Here's a quick review of the chapter.

LO9.1 Differentiate types of interviews.

- Appraisal interviews involve discussing past performance and future goals.
- Problem-solving interviews occur to identify problems and consider possible solutions.
- Exit interviews are conversations about your experience with a job you are leaving.
- Counseling interviews focus on supporting an individual through a personal problem.
- Service-oriented interviews are conversations about a product or service you have purchased.
- Persuasive interviews attempt to affect your beliefs, opinions, or behaviors.
- Survey interviews are interactions aimed at gathering information.
- Selection interviews are conversations focused on helping an interviewer choose the appropriate candidate for a position, assignment, promotion, or award.

LO9.2 Formulate strategies for conducting a job search.

- Begin by considering the characteristics you most value in a job.
- Complete a thorough search process to identify positions that match your criteria.
- Analyze the needs of your potential employers.
- Check your online persona and make adjustments as necessary.

LO9.3 Identify tactics to respond to employment interview questions.

- Practice answering common interview questions in ways that are strategic, confident, and concise.
- Be perceptive about what hiring managers are evaluating.
- Tell stories of your successes.
- Practice the STAR method for responding to questions.
- Avoid criticizing former employers, supervisors, and colleagues.
- Be aware of what types of questions are illegal to ask.
- Generate questions to ask the interviewer.

LO9.4 Outline approaches to succeeding in a web conference interview.

- Do several trial runs for practice.
- Ensure that your profile creates a positive impression.
- Look professional.
- Make sure your room or office is tidy.
- Look directly at the camera, especially while listening.
- Smile and express yourself nonverbally.
- Use notes strategically.
- Avoid distractions.

LO9.5 Explain etiquette for following up after job interviews.

- Send a thank-you note to the interviewer shortly after your interview.
- Feel free to contact the interviewer about his or her progress in making a hiring decision.

A LOOK BACK

Now, let's return to the opening scenario. Jalen was unsuccessful in his job interview for several reasons. He immediately recognized he was underdressed, and the interview went in the wrong direction at the start when he spent five minutes responding to the first question. Jalen also appeared directionless in his response and didn't tie his abilities to the needs of the employer. After the interview, he failed to send a thank-you note or contact Ana again. The next time Jalen gets an opportunity for an interview, he should prepare more strategically and ensure he follows up.

appraisal interview   206
closed-ended question   212
counseling interview   206
exit interview   206
hypothetical question   212

interview   206
open-ended question   212
persuasive interview   206
probing question   212
problem-solving interview   206

selection interview   207
service-oriented interview   206
STAR method   216
survey interview   207

CHAPTER REVIEW QUESTIONS

1. How is a selection interview different from other types of interviews? **LO9.1**

2. What strategies are useful when searching for a job? **LO9.2**

3. What can you learn about an employer's needs by examining job postings? **LO9.2**

4. What are some additional ways of learning about an employer's needs aside from job postings? **LO9.2**

5. What are some ways of identifying the key abilities and attributes employers are seeking for unfilled positions? **LO9.2**

6. Why is it important to check your online persona? **LO9.2**

7. What do you think interviewers are trying to learn with the various types of interview questions listed in Table 9.1? **LO9.3**

8. Why is it important to be concise with many of your responses during interviews? **LO9.3**

9. How does the STAR approach to answering interview questions help you display your key abilities and attributes? **LO9.3**

10. How should candidates respond to illegal questions during a job interview? **LO9.3**

11. What strategies should you use to succeed in online job interviews? **LO9.4**

12. Why is it advantageous to send a thank-you note after an interview? **LO9.5**

13. When is it advisable to contact a hiring manager after an interview? **LO9.5**

SKILL-BUILDING EXERCISES

Analyzing a Job Announcement of Interest to You (LO9.2)

Find a job announcement for a position of interest to you. Using Figure 9.1 as a guide, do the following:

- Group and categorize the key abilities and attributes that are being sought.
- Describe your fit with these abilities and attributes.
- Explain how you can compensate for abilities or attributes that you have not yet fully developed.

Telling Stories with the STAR Method (LO9.3)

Write down how you would answer one of the following interview questions using the STAR method: (a) Can you tell me about a challenge you overcame at work? (b) Can you give me an example of how you showed leadership at work? or (c) Can you tell me about one of your recent successes at work? You can substitute school experiences for work experiences if you'd like.

Writing a Thank-You Note (LO9.5)

Choose a job position that interests you. Assume you have just completed the job interview. Write a thank-you message that you think appropriately expresses gratitude and improves your chances in the hiring process.

Interviewing with a Hiring Manager about Job Application Best Practices (LO9.2, LO9.3, LO9.5)

Contact a hiring manager (consider any person you know who is engaged in the hiring process) and arrange a time to interview that person for 30 minutes to one hour. Ask him or her about the following:

- Keys to successful interviews.
- Common mistakes in job interviews.
- Appropriate ways to follow up after interviews.

After the interview, write a thank-you note, and then write a two-page report detailing best practices for successfully navigating the job application process and getting a job. Tailor your report to undergraduate students who are seeking entry-level professional positions.

ENDNOTES

1. Stewart, C. J., & Cash, W. B. (2013). *Interviewing: Principles and practices* (14th ed.). New York, NY: McGraw-Hill.

2. Rockoff, J. E., Staiger, D. O., Kane, T. J., & Taylor, E. S. (2010, July). Information and employee evaluation: Evidence from a randomized intervention in public schools. National Bureau of Economic Research working paper no. 16240. Retrieved July 15, 2017, from http://www.nber.org/papers/w16240.

3. Coulehan, J. L., & Block, M. L. (2006). *The medical interview: Mastering skills for clinical practice.*Philadelphia, PA: Davis.

4. Baer, D. (2014, October 31). Pepsi CEO Indra Nooyi gave the perfect advice for getting noticed at work. *Business Insider.* Retrieved April 25, 2018, from http://www.businessinsider.com/pepsi-ceo-indra-nooyi-career-advice-2014-10.

5. Tkaczyk, C., & Olster, S. (2014, October 29). Best advice from CEOs: 40 execs' secrets to success. *Fortune.* Retrieved April 25, 2018, from http://fortune.com/2014/10/29/ceo-best-advice.

6. Tkaczyk, C., & Olster, S. (2014, October 29). Best advice from CEOs: 40 execs' secrets to success.*Fortune.* Retrieved April 25, 2018, from http://fortune.com/2014/10/29/ceo-best-advice.

7. Frye, L. (2017, May 9). The cost of a bad hire can be astronomical. *Society for Human Resource Management.* Retrieved April 25, 2018, from https://www.shrm.org/resourcesandtools/hr-topics/employee-relations/pages/cost-of-bad-hires.aspx.

8. Perkins, O. (2015, May 14). More than half of employers now use social media to screen job candidates, poll says; even send friend requests. *Cleveland Plain Dealer.* Retrieved April 25, 2018, from http://www.cleveland.com/business/index.ssf/2015/05/more_than_half_of_employers_no_1.html.

9. Gurchiek, K. (2010, November 1). Dress to impress, not stress, the hiring manager. *Society for Human Resource Management.* Retrieved July 16, 2017, from https://www.shrm.org/hr-today/news/hr-news/Pages/dresstoimpress.aspx.

10. Frieder, R. E., Van Iddekinge, C. H., & Raymark, P. H. (2016). How quickly do interviewers reach decisions? An examination of interviewers' decision-making time across applicants. *Journal of Occupational and Organizational Psychology, 89,* 223–248.

11. Barnes, H. (2011, January 10). Use personal stories to connect with an employer and get a job. Retrieved July 16, 2017, from http://www.hb.org/use-stories-to-get-a-job-and-connect-with-an-employer.

12. Johnson, T. (2010, April 19). Land that job: What interviewers really want you to ask them. Retrieved July 16, 2017, from http://abcnews.go.com/GMA/JobClub/questions-job-interview/story?id=10409243.

13. Cain, Á., & Pelisson, A. (2018, April 10). 9 places in the US where job candidates may never have to answer the dreaded salary question again. *Business Insider.* Retrieved April 25, 2018, from http://www.businessinsider.com/places-where-salary-question-banned-us-2017-10.

14. Stewart, C. J., & Cash, W. B. (2007). *Interviewing: Principles and practices* (12th ed.). New York, NY: McGraw-Hill.

15. Society for Human Resource Management. (2014). *SHRM survey findings: Résumés, cover letters and interviews.* Alexandria, VA: Author.

16. Bryant, A. (2009, April 11). Knock-knock: It's the C.E.O. *The New York Times.* Retrieved July 16, 2017, from http://www.nytimes.com/2009/04/12/business/12corner.html.

Learning Objectives

After reading this chapter, you should be able to do the following:

LO10.1 Recall principles for writing effective emails and digital messages.

LO10.2 Describe how to effectively manage emotion in online communications.

LO10.3 Identify approaches to develop shared knowledge and make decisions in online forums and communities.

LO10.4 Explain strategies to develop mass communications in digital environments.

CHAPTER 10

Writing across Media

Siddarth put his hand against his head in frustration as he read the latest email from his supervisor, Jerry. Over the past three days, the two had exchanged nearly 20 email messages on the same subject, starting with Siddarth's "Can you tell me how to get my travel expenses reimbursed?" Each reply from Jerry had only left him more confused. In the last, Jerry had written, "PLEASE READ CAREFULLY!!!" Siddarth quickly wrote back, "This is getting more and more confusing." What are the signals that Siddarth and Jerry are not using email effectively?

You'll likely read and send thousands of emails and other digital messages during your career, so it's worth thinking carefully about how to write these messages effectively.

LO10.1

Recall principles for writing effective emails and digital messages.

Creating Effective Emails

Email communication is the primary form of written business communication. Many business professionals spend well over ten hours per week reading and writing emails (see Figure 10.1).[1] There are many other digital forms of written communication, such as texting and messaging. Yet, many of your colleagues, clients, and other contacts will likely prefer to use email for most important messages for many years to come. The following strategies, which we expand on next, will help you craft effective emails: use email for the right purposes, ensure ease of reading, show respect for others' time, protect privacy and confidentiality, respond promptly, and maintain professionalism and appropriate formality.

USE EMAIL FOR THE RIGHT PURPOSES

Email is easy and convenient. Before choosing it for your message, however, consider whether it is the best communication channel for your work purposes. Because emails usually lack the verbal and nonverbal cues associated with face-to-face communication, they are best suited for routine, task-oriented, fact-based, and nonsensitive messages. Emails may be used to praise others but should rarely be used to criticize. If an email chain (extended email conversations) has stretched to four or five replies, you should probably switch to a phone call or in-person conversation to conclude the matter more efficiently.

ENSURE EASE OF READING

Your audience is unlikely to read your written message unless you make it easy for them. Compare the emails in Figures 10.2 and 10.3 and think about how quickly a reader can process the information in each case. Use the following tips to ensure your emails are easy to read.

Figure 10.1 **Time Devoted to Emails by Business Professionals**

Professionals spend a significant amount of their time reading and writing emails each week.

Source: Based on December 2015 survey of 1,004 marketing, R&D, and IT managers in the following industries: Finance, Banking, and Insurance; Health Care and Social Assistance; Manufacturing; and Retail and Wholesale Trade. Findings of this survey first presented at the following academic conference: Cardon, P. W. (2016, April 23). *The role of leadership communication and emotional capital in driving internal social media use.* Presentation at the Association for Business Communication Southeast/Midwest Regional Conference, St. Louis, MO.

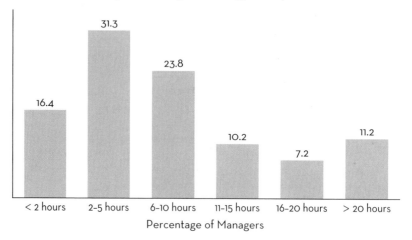

Time Spent Reading and Writing Emails per Week

Figure 10.2 **A Less Effective Email**

Message recipients are less likely to read and respond to poorly written emails.

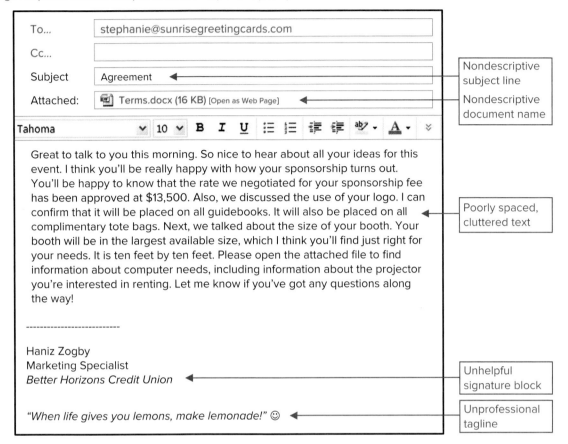

To... stephanie@sunrisegreetingcards.com

Cc...

Subject Agreement ← Nondescriptive subject line

Attached: Terms.docx (16 KB) [Open as Web Page] ← Nondescriptive document name

Tahoma 10 **B** *I* <u>U</u>

Great to talk to you this morning. So nice to hear about all your ideas for this event. I think you'll be really happy with how your sponsorship turns out. You'll be happy to know that the rate we negotiated for your sponsorship fee has been approved at $13,500. Also, we discussed the use of your logo. I can confirm that it will be placed on all guidebooks. It will also be placed on all complimentary tote bags. Next, we talked about the size of your booth. Your booth will be in the largest available size, which I think you'll find just right for your needs. It is ten feet by ten feet. Please open the attached file to find information about computer needs, including information about the projector you're interested in renting. Let me know if you've got any questions along the way! ← Poorly spaced, cluttered text

----

Haniz Zogby
Marketing Specialist
Better Horizons Credit Union ← Unhelpful signature block

"When life gives you lemons, make lemonade!" ☺ ← Unprofessional tagline

Provide a short, descriptive subject line. Message recipients make immediate judgments about the importance of a message based on the subject line. If it is not clear and compelling, they may not open the message right away, and if it is not descriptive enough, they may have trouble finding it later. Good subject lines are generally 5 to 10 long. In contrast, poor subjects are either too short (1 or 2 words), and thus nondescriptive, or too long (12 words or longer), and thus difficult to process. Subject lines frame your entire message, serving almost the same role that headlines do on news stories.

Keep your message brief yet complete. Get to the point within three or four sentences and keep your paragraphs about half the size of those in business documents—ideally 30 to 50 words long. Consider placing the most critical information at the beginning so readers gather the most relevant information immediately. Most people are inundated with messages and often pay more attention to the beginning of those they read, skimming or even skipping the rest, especially if they are reading on a mobile device.

SHARPEN YOUR SKILLS

Compose an *Effective Subject Line*

Locate a few email messages you recently sent for work. For each, rewrite the subject line so that it is simple and focused, presents the most important words first, and includes no unnecessary words. Take note of how much revision each subject line required and apply the same priorities to the subject line you compose for your next email message.

Figure 10.3 A More Effective Email

As you write effective emails, you'll find that you build better professional relationships and accomplish work tasks more efficiently.

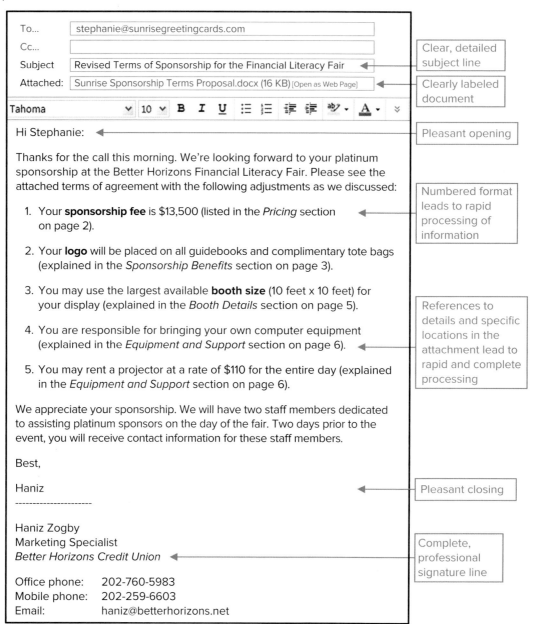

Clearly identify expected actions. Many emails are intended to spur action. Make your requests clear and specific so recipients know exactly how to respond. Often you can place these directions in the subject line for greatest clarity; for example, "Submit expense reports by Friday."

Provide a descriptive signature block. Signature blocks should provide clear contact information so recipients can easily reach you through richer communication channels if needed. A helpful signature block also enhances your professional image.

Use attachments wisely. Attachments allow business professionals to share documents, graphics, spreadsheets, databases, and other types of files that do not display effectively in an email window. Very large documents may be more easily shared on a company intranet or another location (such as Google Drive or Dropbox). Make sure to share only relevant files so you don't create information overload for others.

SHOW RESPECT FOR OTHERS' TIME

Ironically, its very convenience makes email communication easy to overuse. You can show respect for your colleagues by imagining the long line of emails that are likely already awaiting their response. Assume they therefore have low tolerance for poorly written, sloppy, unclear emails. Consider the following tips for earning their good-will with your own messages.

Select message recipients carefully.   Before sending an email, think about the workload you are creating for others. Not only do they commit time to reading your email, but they also often interrupt another work task to do so. If you are requesting information or action, your colleagues are further committed in terms of time. So, make sure the email is necessary and relevant for each of your message recipients.

Provide timelines and options.   If you use email to set up group meetings or coordinate tasks with deadlines, provide detailed information about your availability and give several options. In this way you minimize the number of emails needed to coordinate your efforts and show respect for your colleagues' schedules. Also, make use of scheduling tools such as Doodle.

Be careful about using the priority flag.   You will routinely make requests of others that are time-sensitive. If you too often set the priority flag on such emails, your colleagues may become annoyed, perceiving you as pushy. In fact, some business professionals are more likely to ignore emails when the priority flag is set. If you need something urgently, mention it politely in the subject line or use a rich communication channel such as a phone call to gain buy-in.

Let others know when you will take longer than anticipated to respond or take action.   If you can't respond to a request made in an email, reply immediately and explain how soon you can respond in full. You might use phrases such as "I will respond to your email by next Tuesday," or "I can take care of this by the end of next week."

Avoid contributing to confusing and repetitive email chains.   Email chains are groups of emails that are sent back and forth among a group of people. As the number of messages and people involved in an email chain increases, confusion can build.

Three features contribute to email chains: *forward, copy,* and *reply all.* The forward feature allows you to send any message you receive to others with the click of the mouse. As always, make sure those to whom you are forwarding the message *need* to see it. Also, consider whether the original sender would find it appropriate for you to forward the email; after all, he or she did not place those people on the original message. For the same reason, many business professionals consider use of the *blind carbon copy (bcc)* feature a breach of privacy. Another reason for caution is that once you send an email, you have no control over whether others will forward it, and to whom, which leads to this good advice from Tony DiRomualdo, strategy and IT researcher: "Don't say anything you would not want the entire planet to read at some point."[2]

Many business professionals use the *copy* feature liberally to let everyone in a department in on the conversation. Of course, one of your goals is transparency, achieved by allowing relevant others in your group know how decisions are being made. But copying too many people can lead to information overload and also dilute responsibility by making it unclear exactly who among the recipients is supposed to do what. The more people you copy, the less likely you will get a response. Also,

PEOPLE **FIRST**

Mistakenly Hitting Reply All

IMAGINE THIS: You receive an email from a co-worker announcing that your colleague Dina has received a coveted promotion. You have not found Dina to be particularly good at her job, and you suspect that your manager promoted her largely because she is a minority. Although you would never express these thoughts aloud in your workplace, you believe your co-worker shares these perceptions, so you reply to the email saying that "competence obviously takes a back seat to diversity around here, huh?"

Now, consider this: To your surprise, you receive a copy of your own email moments after you sent it. At that point, you realize that your co-worker's message had been sent to a company listserv, and instead of replying only to your co-worker, you sent your response to your entire division, including Dina. How can you manage this situation with a "people first" focus? Take a look at the following tips:

- "Unsending" an email is virtually impossible. Even if your email system allows you to "recall" a message, that won't remove it from anyone's inbox; it will simply call more attention to it.

- Ask for a face-to-face meeting with Dina and your manager. After all, your message insulted them both. Don't try to justify your behavior or argue about the merits of Dina's promotion. Rather, own up to the fact that you were surprised, and perhaps a bit envious, of Dina's advancement in the company and that you reacted emotionally. Admit that you exercised extremely poor judgment, and that your mistake in replying to the entire listserv was irresponsible and unprofessional.

- Ask your manager's advice on how to address the mistake with the rest of your division. If your manager feels that an apology to other co-workers is in order, respect your co-workers enough to apologize in person, rather than through another mass email.

Responding to an email mistake in a professional and "people first" manner can help preserve valuable relationships and ensure that an already awkward situation doesn't become worse.

> **THINK ABOUT THIS:**
>
> Why is it useful to apologize to Dina and your manager face-to-face? Under what conditions could mistakenly hitting *reply all* cause problems that go beyond embarrassment and hurt feelings? What concrete steps can you take to avoid making a similar mistake in the future?

some people perceive copying a direct supervisor or boss on emails between peers as a subtle power play.[3]

The *reply all* feature can contribute to confusing email chains in many of the same ways as the *forward* and *copy* features. In an email conversation among more than four or five people, some recipients can lose track of the sequence of messages or miss some messages altogether. Reply email chains become especially confusing when some colleagues are using just the *reply* feature whereas others are using the *reply all* feature. One advantage of team blogs and wikis in the workplace (discussed later in the chapter) is that they remove some of these inefficiencies by placing messages and shared content in a central location rather than in various, separate email boxes. The *reply all* feature has its uses, but check out the "People First" box for suggestions about what to do if you click it by accident.

PROTECT PRIVACY AND CONFIDENTIALITY

Be careful not to share sensitive or confidential information, accidentally or on purpose. Even a mistake in an address line can have damaging professional consequences. Consider, for example, that eight in ten marketing and advertising executives say they have made mistakes via email, such as sending job offers to the wrong people or revealing confidential salary information to the entire company.[4] Double-checking that you have placed the correct people in the address line before you hit the send button is a worthwhile habit that requires just a few extra moments.

RESPOND PROMPTLY

One recent study of business professionals found that nearly all expect an email response within one day.[5] Most prefer to hear back within an hour or two; younger professionals are more likely to expect a response even sooner. The majority of business professionals in all age groups expect a response within one to two hours. If you choose not to check your email more than four to five times a day (a good strategy to maintain your productivity), let others know how soon to expect replies.

MAINTAIN PROFESSIONALISM AND APPROPRIATE FORMALITY

Email communication is typically considered fairly formal. Management consultant Beverly Langford reported what thousands of business leaders have observed about an overly casual attitude toward email use:

> Many people seem to forget that email is, in fact, written communication, and, consequently, treat it much less carefully. Workplace email messages often contain terse and offhand remarks and project a flippant attitude that is sometimes excessive, even bordering on the unprofessional. Those who write the emails often seem to be overlooking how their message is coming across to the receiver. Further, when composing emails, many people don't seem to be nearly as concerned with structure and correctness as they would be when putting something on paper. This . . . is ironic because often many more people see an email than would ever see a hard copy of a memo or letter because it's so easy for the recipient to forward an email to anyone he or she chooses.[6]

Generally, you are better off erring on the side of formality. Consider the following recommendations.

Avoid treating email as casual communication.   Certain casual ways of writing and formatting appear unprofessional—for example, using all lowercase letters or nonstandard spelling (*hey barbara, how r u*), using excessive formatting (flashy background colors, unusual fonts), providing extraneous information in the signature line (favorite quotations), and typing in all caps (IMPLIES ANGER). Humor and sarcasm, too, can be misinterpreted in digital communications, even among close colleagues. Furthermore, even when considered funny, they can draw attention away from your central message.

Apply the same high standards as for other written documents.   Carefully review your message for typos, spelling, punctuation, or grammatical problems before sending it. For important messages, consider first composing with word processing software. This will help you apply a higher level of seriousness. In addition, you'll be able to use spell-check and grammar-check features that are more reliable than those within email systems.

Use greetings and names.   One of Dale Carnegie's most famous pieces of networking advice says, "A person's name is to that person the sweetest most important sound in any language."[7] Although short greetings and names are not technically required, consider using them. A communication researcher was recently given access to emails from two organizations, one with high and one with low morale. She found that the presence or absence of greetings and names at the beginning of emails was a strong indicator of company climate (see Figure 10.4).[8] In the low-morale organization, just 20 percent of the emails contained greetings, and just 36 percent contained names. In contrast, in the high-morale organization, 58 percent contained greetings, and 78 percent contained names. The same trend was shown in closings. In the low-morale organization, just 23 percent of the emails contained a polite closing and a name compared to 73 percent in the high-morale organization.

TECH TIP
Using Grammar Checks

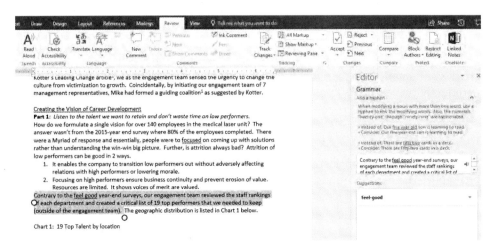

Grammar checks can help you polish your writing.

Source: Microsoft Corporation

Most word processing software programs contain spelling and grammar checks to help you avoid basic mistakes. Many of these programs, such as Microsoft Word, also have tools to evaluate writing style and ease of reading. Typically, these tools are not set by default. You will need to manually select them. (In Microsoft Word, you can access them by changing settings in the *Proofing* area of *Word Options*.)

When you run spelling and grammar checks, you can review your document sentence by sentence for passive voice, noun clusters, and other elements. Once you finish the check, you will see a final calculation of readability statistics (based on Flesch and Flesh-Kincaid measures). Keep in mind that the software is not perfect. Generally, however, it will help you improve your writing style.

Readability Statistics	? ✕
Counts	
Words	2,244
Characters	11,719
Paragraphs	142
Sentences	118
Averages	
Sentences per Paragraph	2.3
Words per Sentence	17.3
Characters per Word	5.1
Readability	
Flesch Reading Ease	40.0
Flesch-Kincaid Grade Level	11.9
Passive Sentences	17.7%

OK

Word processing software generally includes tools to help improve your writing style.

Source: Microsoft Corporation

LO10.2

Describe how to effectively manage emotion in online communications.

Manage Emotion and Maintain Civility

Many managers cite the lack of emotion in emails as a benefit of the medium. They see email as a channel that allows the exchange of messages in minimal form—objective, task-based, and straightforward. As one manager explained, "With email I find myself answering without all the kindness necessary to keep people happy with their job."[9]

Yet, avoiding emotion entirely, even for task-based messages, is nearly impossible. Business professionals often want to invoke some emotion—perhaps enthusiasm or

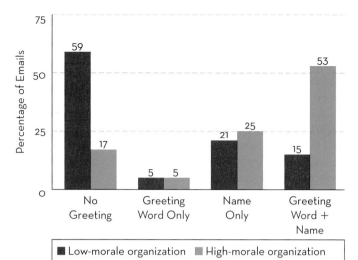

Figure 10.4

The Use of Email Greetings and Names in a Low-Morale and a High-Morale Organization
Using greetings and names in emails typically leads to a better work environment.

Source: Data from Waldvogel, J. (2007). Greetings and closings in workplace email. *Journal of Computer-Mediated Communication, 12*(2).

a sense of urgency. Even when senders intend to convey a relatively nonemotional message, recipients may experience an emotional reaction.

In the absence of face-to-face communications, emails tend to elicit either the neutrality effect or the negativity effect. The **neutrality effect** means that recipients are more likely to perceive messages with an intended positive emotion as neutral. That is, the sender may wish to express enthusiasm about an event, but the receiver decodes the information without "hearing" the enthusiasm. The **negativity effect** means that recipients are more likely to perceive messages as negative that are meant to be neutral. The neutrality and negativity effects can lead to conflict escalation, confusion, and anxiety. Expert business communicators remain aware of these tendencies.[10]

Two characteristics of non-real-time electronic communications can lead to feelings of anger and frustration more so than in face-to-face communications. First, people often feel comfortable writing things they would not say in person. In some cases, this sense of freedom leads to **flames**, emails or other digital communications with "hostile intentions characterized by words of profanity, obscenity, and insults that inflict harm to a person or an organization."[11]

The second aspect of non-real-time electronic communications that can lead to anger and frustration is **cyber silence**, which is nonresponse to emails and other digital communications. Senders may wonder whether recipients are purposely avoiding or even ignoring them. As the length of time between messages increases, they often experience more frustration and anger.[12]

As a message sender, grant the benefit of the doubt to your recipients when responses take longer than you expected. Instead of getting frustrated, consider giving them a phone call. Keep in mind that they may have different expectations about a reasonable time frame to respond to your email. If they routinely take longer than you expect, politely mention that you would appreciate quicker responses and explain why this would be helpful.

Cyber incivility is the violation of respect and consideration in an online environment based on workplace norms. Research has shown that "fast-paced, high-tech interactions may add to incivility, as people believe that they do not have time to be 'nice' and that impersonal contacts [such as electronic communications] do not require courteous interaction."[13]

Research shows that 91 percent of employees reported experiencing either active or passive cyber incivility from supervisors in the workplace. **Active incivility** includes direct forms of disrespect (being condescending or demeaning, saying something hurtful). **Passive incivility** is indirect (using emails for time-sensitive messages rather than more direct and efficient forms of communication, not acknowledging or replying to emails). Cyber incivility has been shown to lead to lower job satisfaction and organizational commitment. Active incivility was the more damaging of the two forms.[14]

If you receive uncivil electronic communications, avoid escalation. You can take several steps to constructively address uncivil emails: reinterpretation, relaxation, and defusing. **Reinterpretation** involves adjusting your initial perceptions by making more objective, more fact-based, and less personal judgments and evaluations. When people are distressed, they often make extreme, subjective, and overly personal judgments. By reinterpreting the event, you allow yourself to take the communication less personally. This is easier said than done. Many people engage in relaxation techniques to help constructively reinterpret the event. **Relaxation** involves releasing and overcoming anger and frustration so that you can make a more rational and less emotional response. People use a variety of methods to alleviate the physiological impact of anger, including counting to ten, taking time-outs, engaging in deep breathing, and looking for the humor in the situation.[15]

Notice two responses—a less effective one in Figure 10.5 and a more effective one in Figure 10.6—to an angry email. Jaclyn expressed frustration with a conversation she had with Haniz. Jaclyn, perhaps unwisely, fired off an angry email (see the bottom message in

Figure 10.5 A Less Effective Response to an Angry Email

Professionals who inject anger and other negative emotions into email messages rarely accomplish their relationship and task goals.

Reply   Reply All   Forward

Re: Issues

Zogby, Haniz

To: Jaclyn Peha

Cc: Christine Russo

We need to talk about this email when I get back in a week after the holiday. I thought we had a productive conversation but you obviously were not candid or professional. Also, please empty your voice mail. I tried reaching you several times only to get your full voice mail box.

From: Jaclyn Peha [jaclyn@betterhorizons.net]
Sent: Saturday, July 1 9:54 PM
To: Haniz Zogby [haniz@betterhorizons.net]

Subject: Issues

Haniz, the other day when we discussed the new website, you didn't give me a chance to explain my ideas, and I don't think you made the conversation fair. I tried to explain that your goal of attracting younger customers is good, but we need to create a more interactive website that's plugged into social media if we're going to make this happen. You seem to just want the easiest, quickest solution. Before we start developing the site any more, let's meet and change things up a bit. Jaclyn

Impersonal. Leaves out greeting and name.

Confrontational. Immediately creates a *me-versus-you* approach with the phrase "We need to talk."

Defensive/attacking. Focuses on defending rather than understanding Jaclyn's point of view.

Accusatory. Jaclyn lays blame on Haniz in every regard. The repeated use of *you-voice* increases the accusatory tone.

Figure 10.5), and Haniz responded (the top message in Figure 10.5). Regardless of whether Jaclyn was correct about Haniz's approach to developing the website, email is rarely an effective communication channel to air complaints or to discuss emotionally charged issues. Figure 10.6 presents a more effective response from Haniz to this exchange.

To **defuse** the situation when you receive an uncivil email, focus on task-related facts and issues in your reply. Recap your shared objectives and agreements and suggest meeting in person, or via phone or videoconference. Such a meeting is nearly always essential to renewing cooperation on shared work efforts.

You often will need to respond to electronic messages that you feel are unfair or inappropriate. Notice how Haniz escalates the problem in the less effective response by writing in an impersonal, defensive, and confrontational manner. By contrast, notice how she defuses the situation in the more effective response by avoiding defensiveness, focusing on shared interests, and arranging for a time to meet face-to-face. The ability to defuse uncivil electronic communications requires high emotional intelligence. It will pay off in many ways during your career: It will help your colleagues and team members stay on task and perform better; it will help you develop a reputation for constructively resolving differences; and it will lead to more satisfying work experiences.

Figure 10.6 A More Effective Response to Defuse an Angry Email

In tense email exchanges, you'll build your professional relationships by maintaining professionalism and seeking richer communication channels, such as face-to-face conversations.

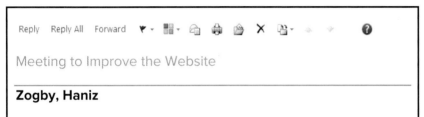

Reply   Reply All   Forward

Meeting to Improve the Website

Zogby, Haniz

To: Jaclyn Peha

Hello Jaclyn,

I'm sorry to hear that you did not think our conversation was fair. I'm glad you're thinking about how we can use the website to better attract younger customers.

When we're both back in the office, let's set up a time to discuss plans for the website. Would you be willing to come up with your three major ideas to make the website more interactive and connected to our social media platforms?

When we meet, I'd like to get a sense of the resources we would need to commit to your ideas. We need to make sure these ambitious plans make business sense.

Would you like to include anyone else in our meeting? Do you think the entire marketing team should participate in this discussion?

Enjoy your holiday weekend!

Haniz

Cordial and personal. Uses Jaclyn's name and extends warm wishes.

Validating. Compliments Jaclyn on her desire to improve the website.

Inviting. Asks for Jaclyn's input in terms of ideas and people who should be included in the decision-making process.

Nondefensive. Haniz makes it clear that making "business sense" is an important part of the discussion. Yet, she does so without sounding defensive or intimidating (she is in the position of a superior).

Focus on rich communication. Haniz temporarily defuses the situation by email but realizes these issues require rich communication. So, she identifies a meeting as the next step in the process.

Defusing Tension before Responding to a Message

When they encounter a message that provokes anger, some people are better than others at defusing tension. How skilled are you at defusing tension before you respond to a message? Read each of the following statements, and indicate how accurately it describes you by assigning a number between 1 ("not at all") and 7 ("very much").

1. ____ I recognize the signs of stress when I feel them.

2. ____ When I receive a message that makes me angry, I am able to resist responding immediately.

3. ____ When I feel tense, I remind myself that my tension is affecting the way I think.

4. ____ When a message makes me angry, I tell myself that I could be misinterpreting or misunderstanding it.

5. ____ I take deep breaths and try to calm myself down when I feel tense.

6. ____ During experiences of tension, I avoid arguing with others in my mind.

7. ____ I never respond to a message when I'm feeling angry.

8. ____ I recognize that it is hard to think and communicate clearly when I'm distressed.

When you're finished, add up your scores and write the total on this line: ____. The ranges below will help you see how skilled you are at defusing tension.

- 8–24: You struggle with defusing tension when you feel it, so that is a skill worth improving.
- 25–48: You are moderately good at defusing tension. Continued practice will strengthen that skill.
- 49–56: You are skilled at defusing tension, which helps you respond effectively to anger-inducing messages.

How good are you at defusing tension before responding to an email message? Check out "The Competent Communicator" box to find out.

Working on Internal Digital Platforms

Most organizations provide an **internal digital platform** to organize communication among employees; many are based on the Facebook model and can be called corporate intranet, enterprise social networking platform, or enterprise social software. They include many tools, including a dashboard, blogs, and discussion forums. In this section we highlight a few of these tools—particularly those that use written communication.

FOLLOW YOUR COMPANY'S DIGITAL COMMUNICATION AND SOCIAL MEDIA GUIDELINES

Most companies have guidelines for digital communication within your organization and social media posts outside your organization. Make sure to learn about the expectations your organization has for your communication. Generally, these guidelines provide broad principles for communicating effectively. For example, Intel's social media guidelines are based on three principles: disclose (be transparent), protect (protect yourself and the company), and use common sense (use "professional, straightforward and appropriate communication").[16]

CAREER TIP
Always Work on Your Writing Skills

Jason Fried, CEO of Basecamp
©Bergatron

Jason Fried, CEO of the software company Basecamp, embraces the use of traditional and social media to build an effective professional persona that aligns with the reputation of his organization. As a TED Talks speaker and a prolific writer and contributor on platforms such as Twitter (twitter.com/jasonfried), Medium (medium.com/@jasonfried), LinkedIn (www.linkedin.com/in/37signals), Inc. (www.inc.com/author/jason-fried), and BigThink (bigthink.com/experts/jasonfried), he brings attention to issues such as productivity, project management, collaboration, workplace satisfaction, diversity, and business strategy. He is known for building a great workplace where all employees are encouraged not to work more than 40 hours per week.

Jason frequently talks about the importance of excellent writing skills. Here is his approach to hiring:

> Our top hiring criteria—in addition to having the skills to do the job—is, are you a great writer? You have to be a great writer to work here, in every single position, because the majority of our communication is written, primarily because a lot of us work remotely but also because writing is quieter. And we like long-form writing where people really think through an idea and present it. This is one of the reasons I don't like chat services. When companies start thinking one line at a time and everyone's rushed and you have to get your conversation in before it scrolls off the screen, I think it's a terrible, frantic way to work, and people are burning out because of it.

Jason explains that the company evaluates job candidates' cover letters, résumés, and email correspondence to determine whether they are strong writers. He views clear writing as a demonstration of clear thinking. So, remember to consistently improve your writing skills and, like Jason, find ways to build your professional reputation through traditional and social media.

SOURCES: Orin, A. (2016, December 28). I'm Jason Fried, CEO of Basecamp, and this is how I work. *LifeHacker.* Retrieved from https://lifehacker.com/im-jason-fried-ceo-of-basecamp-and-this-is-how-i-work-1790556608; Bryant, A. (2017, September 1). Jason Fried of Basecamp on the importance of writing skills. *The New York Times.* Retrieved from https://www.nytimes.com/2017/09/01/jobs/corner-office-jason-fried-basecamp.html.

ORGANIZE YOUR DASHBOARD TO CONTROL YOUR COMMUNICATION AND INFORMATION FLOW

Nearly all internal digital platforms contain a **dashboard**, your front page when you log in, which operates as your communication and information hub. Your dashboard gives you many opportunities to learn about and connect with others. You can also allow others to learn more about you and enhance your credibility within your organization. In most cases, status updates and other project notifications should be most prominent. You can also display your mail, your schedule, the communities you belong to, and people you follow in the organization.

Figure 10.7

A Profile on an Internal Digital Platform

Providing a complete profile on internal digital platforms can help you network within your company and get involved in meaningful projects.

©Kate Kunz/Glow Images

CREATE A COMPLETE AND PROFESSIONAL PROFILE

Much as you would on a social network like LinkedIn, in your profile you provide information about yourself, such as your position, contact information, professional interests, and current projects. You can usually provide a picture and list personal interests outside work. Colleagues who do not know you well may be more likely to contact you for projects and other opportunities based on what they learn from your profile, and other people's profiles are an excellent way for you to find people with needed expertise or shared professional interests. Notice in Figure 10.7 how Jeff edits his profile by uploading a professional picture, concisely stating his skills and interests, and providing tags to make his profile more easily searchable.

USE BLOGS AND STATUS UPDATES FOR TEAM COMMUNICATION

Blogs are posts that are arranged chronologically, similar to a journal format. Traditionally, most blogs have included entries by just one or a few individuals, although many allow reader comments. Increasingly, teams and other professional groups write blogs, allowing business professionals to share their ideas and experiences and connect with other employees with similar professional interests.[17] A variety of blog types has emerged in the workplace, including individual expert blogs, company executive blogs, company team blogs, company update blogs, company crisis blogs, and internal company blogs.[18]

Blog posts are excellent opportunities for leaders, managers, and supervisors to keep employees aware of announcements and updates. By using the comment features on these blogs, employees can ask questions and share their opinions. This helps create a more interactive, transparent decision-making process within organizations, business units, and teams. Notice in Figure 10.8 how Andrea makes a short announcement via a blog post. Kip has a question and Andrea quickly responds. This process helps Andrea get input from her colleagues to make better decisions. It also gives all employees the sense that their concerns and opinions matter.

Status updates, also known as **microblogs**, are short comments that typically contain just a few sentences. As part of internal digital platforms, status updates are tools for broadcasting quick announcements and urgent information. Members of a network can also use them to ask questions that need immediate responses. They

Prestigio Marketing Team

| New Entry | View All Entries |

Update about Seasonal Employees

Andrea Garcia ⊡ | Today 3:18 PM | Tags: seasonal employees | 2 Comments | 6 Views

☺ 1 You like this - Unlike

Each holiday season we depend on hiring 15 to 20 seasonal employees. Most of our seasonal employees are young adults from the local community. Until about five years ago, we generally received 50 to 60 applications each holiday season. We could easily choose employees who we were happy with.

We've struggled in the past few years to attract applicants. Now we receive just 20 to 30 applications each holiday season. We've only hired 10 to 15 of these applicants during the past few holiday periods. This has left us strained and understaffed for some important events.

This week I met Jade Kim, president of PT Temp Services. She shared the following pieces of information with me:

- Nearly all hotels and resorts in our regions are facing a similar situation. Compared to five years ago, there are 40 percent fewer 18-to-25-year-olds looking for temporary work.
- Her agency specializes in attracting temporary workers for retail and hospitality businesses.
- She is preparing a proposal to represent the Prestigio for the upcoming hiring season.

I will keep you updated about this situation. I'm cautiously optimistic that PT Temp Services can help us adequately staff our holiday season needs. That should take some stress off each of you.

Add a Comment | More Actions ⌄

Comments (2)

Andrea Garcia ⊡ commented Today 3:26 PM   ☺ 2 You like this - Unlike

Kip, that's an important question. My understanding is that we can ask PT to do all screening and hiring OR we can have them do only screening and we make the final decisions. I will follow up to better understand our options.

Comment Permalink | Reply | More Actions⌄

Kip Yamada ⊡ commented Today 3:22 PM   ☺ 3 You like this - Unlike

Andrea, in the past, I've enjoyed the process of selecting a few of the seasonal workers to work on my projects. If we outsource our hiring to PT, will we still be able to provide any input into which seasonal employees are selected?

Comment Permalink | Reply | More Actions⌄

---

are particularly useful in teams so team members can coordinate their efforts effectively. Notice in Figure 10.9 how a marketing team uses updates throughout the day to ensure they work well together. The most popular public microblogging platform is Twitter.

Organizations are increasingly using team blogs and project blogs (many-to-many communication). **Team blogs** are typically organized around formal work teams, and **project blogs** are organized around particular projects that are generally completed by temporary teams. Team and project blogs are excellent ways to post all the team's communications in a single place, such as updates, progress reports, problem-solving discussions, project timelines and goals, announcements, and a variety of other coordination tools. They are also a good place for success stories that shape organizational and team culture. It's important to note that blogs are called by many names depending on the platforms that organizations use. In popular team messaging platforms such as Slack, another common name for various blogs are *channels*.

Figure 10.9

Status Updates for Team Coordination

You can develop a reputation as a strong team player by using digital platforms to share information and make joint decisions.

©Kate Kunz/Glow Images; ©AbleStock.com/360/Getty Images; ©Photodisc/Getty Images; ©John A Rizzo/Pixtal/SuperStock

USE SHARED FILES TO COLLABORATE

Smart teams rely on shared files they post on a central platform (like Google Docs). This strategy overcomes the problems of emailing files back and forth by maintaining version control, allowing different people to edit at the same time, and hosting all important files in one location. As you share files with colleagues, consider the following tips:

- *Discuss with them the protocol for sharing and co-editing files.* Your team has a variety of decisions to make, including how to name documents; how to make, track, and manage edits; and how to respond to comments on the files.

- *Organize your files by project.* Unless you organize your files by project (or topic), shared files can become difficult to track and find. Discuss with your team members which folders and naming conventions you intend to use. Tagging your files is one way to help organize them.

- *Manage permissions.* Often, you'll keep sensitive, even confidential, information in shared files. Make sure you manage permissions and allow only the right people access to this information.

- *Add comments constructively and read your colleagues' comments carefully.* Simply writing "Great job!" isn't particularly helpful. Avoid generic comments; provide enough detail to help your colleagues. Notice in Figure 10.9 how a variety of teammates provide comments to Jeff's report draft. They complement Jeff *and* provide concrete suggestions to make his report even more valuable.

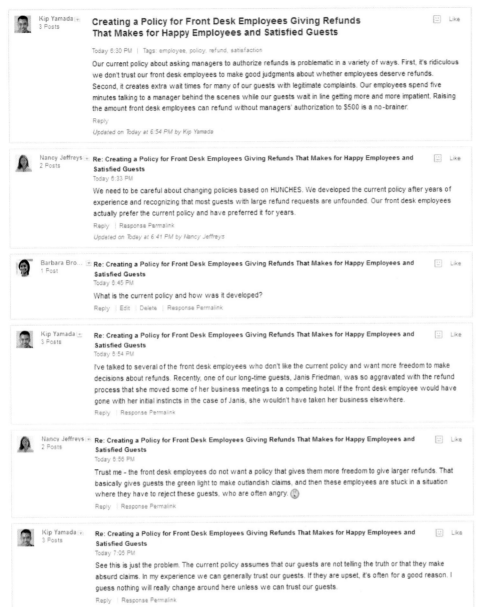

Figure 10.10

An Ineffective Example of a Forum Conversation

Online forums can be counterproductive when employees attempt to dominate the discussion.

©John A Rizzo/Pixtal/SuperStock; ©AbleStock.com/360/Getty Images; ©Photodisc/Getty Images

SOLVE PROBLEMS WITH DISCUSSION FORUMS

All internal digital platforms contain discussion forums for holding conversations between meetings. Some business professionals prefer forums over face-to-face meetings because forums allow them to make thoughtful, carefully prepared, and well-documented comments. Generally, introverts express themselves more easily in forums. So, using face-to-face meetings together with forums creates a work environment that brings out the contributions and best ideas of *all* team members. Help your teams avoid the following actions that hinder productive team communication:

- *Avoid leading posts.* Just as leading questions hinder listening in face-to-face communication, leading posts harm online discussions. Figure 10.10 displays an abbreviated discussion forum that is not effective. Take a few minutes to read it. One of the first things you'll notice is the leading subject line, which is nothing more than Kip's strong opinion. This immediately places the forum on the wrong trajectory.

- *Avoid ignoring competing points of views.* Many ineffective forums are the result of professionals sharing their own views but not acknowledging the views of others. You'll notice a variety of posts in the ineffective forum (Figure 10.10) where Kip and Nancy state their views but don't directly acknowledge one another's points. Professionals, even in forums, often "talk over" one another. This doesn't help Kip or Nancy influence others. It also discourages teammates from participating in the forum.

- *Avoid using strong or rigid language.* The goal is to explore one another's ideas and build solutions together. Strong and rigid language, however, signals that people are not open to new ideas. It can express *either-or options* ("the only way to . . ."), *finality*—implying the issue is not open to debate ("we already decided to . . ."), *exaggeration* ("the best way to . . ."), and *judgment* ("ridiculous"). If you sense that you or others are trying to "win the argument," stop and consider whether the direction of the discussion is helpful for your team and its goals.

- *Avoid blaming or complaining.* Complaining can drag down any conversation, including an online discussion. The major problem with complaining is dwelling on the inability to avoid negative outcomes. Blaming is similar to complaining in that it often places responsibility entirely on others, but it is more serious because it often also attacks others. In the ineffective forum, Kip and Nancy indirectly blame one another throughout the forum. Kip blames Nancy for not understanding the needs of front desk employees and guests. Nancy blames Kip for forming his conclusions based on hunches rather than careful research.

- *Avoid off-topic points.* The major value of forums is to create a space for targeted, specific conversations. A discussion that goes off topic (a) is unlikely to produce results; (b) will lose some participants; and (c) has less appeal as a reference in future conversations.

- *Avoid excessively short or lengthy posts.* Typically, posts that are too short show that participants aren't engaging the forum sufficiently. On the other hand, excessively lengthy posts often go unread. They also may signal that the writer is uninterested in a back-and-forth discussion with teammates.

- *Avoid sarcasm.* Sarcasm is usually misinterpreted on forums. One reason sarcasm doesn't work on forums is that it generally applies to a context at a shared moment. Since forums often run over days and weeks, this shared context at a point in time is missing.

Here are some positive strategies for making your forum an effective medium for producing better work:

- *State the purpose of the forum clearly.* The subject line for the forum should clearly lay out its purpose. In the effective forum in Figure 10.11, you can see that the forum subject is posed as a clear, specific question. Make sure the first few posts clearly describe why the issue is important and provide some background. This motivates other team members to participate.

- *Read your peers' comments completely and carefully.* You'll provide better responses and show that you care about your teammates. Your influence will then grow as others see your efforts to learn from them.

- *Use flexible, open, and inviting language.* You can express your views with confidence while also signaling that you want to hear from others. Using phrases such as *I think, I suggest,* or *perhaps we should* allows you to voice your opinions while staying open to those of others.

- *Build on the ideas of others and pose questions.* The best forums result from team members referencing and connecting each other's ideas. Posing questions will often help draw out the ideas of teammates.

- *Show appreciation for your teammates and their ideas.* You don't have to agree with everything your colleagues suggest to show appreciation. Find ways

Figure 10.11

An Effective Example of a Forum Conversation

You can contribute to effective online forums by involving all team members, validating their ideas, and supporting consensus-driven decisions.

©John A Rizzo/Pixtal/SuperStock; ©AbleStock.com/360/Getty Images; ©Photodisc/Getty Images

to see merit in their ideas. Use their names to show your interest in them individually. Assume that they are acting in the interest of the team and the organization.

- *Participate regularly.* First comers sometimes state their views and then never return. Latecomers may disrupt the process by entering the discussion after others have developed a consensus. If these latecomers go against the hard-earned consensus of the team, they cost the whole team time and morale. Consistent participation by each team member makes the process smooth and productive.

- *Meet in real time for touchy points.* Forums are excellent for fairly routine conversations. If the online discussion gets contentious or raises sensitive issues, schedule a time for the team to discuss the issues in real time. You'll accomplish much more in a real-time conversation and reduce the likelihood of misunderstandings.

- *Summarize and, as appropriate, identify next steps.* The purpose of most forums is to help a team arrive at solutions. At the end of the forum, summarize the discussion and identify actions your team will take. Participants should also evaluate their performance in the forum and ways to make the next one more effective.

LO10.4

Explain strategies to develop mass communications in digital environments.

Writing for External Audiences on Social Media

Increasingly, stakeholders expect to be given an inside view of organizations. One effective way of *telling the story* of your organization is through blog posts on a corporate website that are often linked to a variety of social networks such as Facebook, Twitter, LinkedIn, Instagram, and Pinterest. Also, many professionals now write blogs about their professional interests that are a powerful medium for personal branding. In this section, we'll discuss these two forms of writing blogs for external audiences.

WRITING POSTS FOR YOUR ORGANIZATION

Organizations' primary goal for running blogs is to create effective **public relations (PR)**. PR has been defined as "the management function that establishes and maintains mutually beneficial relationships between an organization and the various publics on whom its success depends."[19] In other words, PR is fundamentally about *building relationships* with employees, customers, communities, the media, and other stakeholders.

Many PR messages often draw positive attention to products and services, especially new, improved, or formally recognized for quality or effectiveness. They can also tout actions the company is proud of, such as corporate social responsibility efforts or charitable donations of time or money. Once you understand what the company wants to highlight and understand the strategy for doing so, you are ready to act much like a news reporter. You will gather accurate and reliable information that tells a compelling story of what the company has done.

In the press-release style, which still accounts for most written PR messages, the main components are a headline, a dateline, the PR story, some boilerplate, and contact information. The *headline* immediately captures the attention of stakeholders. Next, the *dateline* allows readers to identify when the story was released. Then, the *PR story*—whether it's announcing a product launch, an act of charity, a corporate event, or some other type of notable corporate activity—is written in third person in the *inverted pyramid style.* This means the story should answer the basic questions of *who, what, when, where,* and *why* quickly, within the first paragraph. It then provides supporting details—the second tier of the pyramid.

At the end of the PR story, a *boilerplate* or *positioning statement* briefly offers background about the company: the nature of its business, its products and services, its customers, and its unique selling position, meaning what distinguishes it from competitors. Typically, minor PR announcements are just 100 to 300 words, and major announcements are 500 to 800 words. You can see an example of this type of blog post in Figure 10.12.

Another common format for PR messages is the op-ed style. Traditionally, a corporate leader would write an opinion piece for a newspaper or other periodical, speaking in first person about a challenge or issue shared by the company and the public ("op ed" refers to the piece's location *opposite* the *editorial* page). Today the op-ed style is common on corporate blogs, where business leaders can regularly share their opinions and experiences. You can see an example in Figure 10.13.

WRITING POSTS FOR A PROFESSIONAL BLOG

Increasingly, business professionals have opportunities to build their personal brands with blog posts about their areas of expertise, using social media tools such as WordPress and Google's Blogger or networking platforms such as LinkedIn. While you can distinguish yourself on these external platforms, you can also write blog posts on internal digital platforms that help give you a reputation of expertise within your organization.

Figure 10.12 **A Press-Release Style Blog Post**

You can help your organization and build your own professional reputation at the same time by contributing to content for social media posts.

©Songbird839/Getty Images

MENU *The Prestigio*   **Find & Reserve**   **Meetings & Events**   **Reservations**

Blog>

The *Prestigio Market Restaurant* Adds Spice to the Menu

July 18, 2018
Posted by Kip Yamada

The award-winning Prestigio Market Restaurant just turned up the heat! Head Chef Fiona Nickerson unveiled three new menu items last week, each featuring a new combination of spices.

Chef Fiona spent the past six months working on these new menu items. The dishes include Coconut Curry Chicken, Szechuan Tofu, and Jamaican Jerk Wild Wings.

I asked Chef Fiona about trends in spicy foods. She explained, "We've seen an explosion of interest in spicy foods in the past few years. Not just jalapeños and red chile peppers but also anchos, Szechuan peppers, turmeric, coriander, and cumin."

Chef Fiona explained that each new dish is a fusion of ethnic dishes with local tastes. Coconut Curry Chicken combines Bengali-style curry with our area's famous love of coconuts. Szechuan Tofu is inspired by a Chinese-style bean curd dish with a mix of locally grown green beans and peppers.

The restaurant has always been famous for its wings. Chef Fiona beamed as she talked about the new Jamaican Jerk Wild Wings. "I think our wing lovers are going to love this dish. We marinate these wings overnight with a combination of jalapeños, thyme, black pepper, nutmeg, and a few other spices. It literally took us six months of daily trials to get this one just right!"

Last night I joined Louise and Jim Adams. Louise offered this assessment of the Coconut Curry Chicken: "The flavors are delicious. I loved it. Just the right kick!" Jim exclaimed his verdict on the Jamaican Jerk Wild Wings: "I try the wings wherever I go. I have never tasted anything quite like these wings. Just awesome!"

These new menu items are July Special Items, so they'll remain at 20 percent off for the rest of the month. To get a sneak peak, watch Chef Fiona work her magic on these dishes in this YouTube clip.

- -

The Prestigio Market Restaurant is open from 11 a.m. to 9 p.m. daily and serves a variety of delicious and healthy menu items. All fruits and vegetables are organic and sourced within 50 miles of the restaurant. You can contact Kip Yamada to arrange business events at the restaurant or contact the reservation desk for small group reservations.

Several strategies can increase the success of your own professional blog. First, develop a theme that readers easily recognize and that captures your areas of expertise or interests. Second, make sure your posts maintain a professional, fun, and helpful tone. Third, make sure your content is accurate. You can quickly gain a reputation as an expert with strong posts but seriously damage it with obvious mistakes. Most blog writers enhance their credibility by providing hyperlinks to their source or reference material. This helps readers make judgments about the quality of your posts.

Figure 10.13 An Op-Ed Style Blog Post

As you move into management roles, you'll often have opportunities to write op-ed style posts.
©RomoloTavani/Getty Images

MENU *The Prestigio* **Find & Reserve** **Meetings & Events** **Reservations**

Blog>

Green Meetings Make Us Leaner and Improve the Bottom Line

July 25, 2018
Posted by Andrea Garcia and Jeff Anderton

Meeting planners often ask us, "Do green meetings really make a difference?" One planner even commented to us, "I wonder if green meetings are like so-called 'low-fat' foods. They sound great but I'm still overweight."

We started implementing green meetings at the Prestigio a few years ago, and we can say definitively, *"Yes, green meetings make a difference."* As far as environmental impacts, we're leaner than ever. We're also passing major savings on to conference organizers.

With just a few simple measures, here's what we accomplished last year with green meetings:

- *We served water in pitchers rather than bottles.* We estimate we saved nearly 40,000 gallons of water as a result.

- *We helped meeting planners, at their request, use apps and e-reader formatted programs rather than printed conference schedules.* We estimate we saved roughly 800 trees.

- *We ensured that over 90 percent of produce in our restaurants was grown within 50 miles.* We estimate we significantly reduced our carbon footprint associated with food deliveries.

We've already started additional steps to make more dramatic impacts. Within the next year, we will replace all our vans with hybrid versions and require our vendors to meet green standards. Within two to three years, our hotel will be LEED certified. We anticipate overall drops in carbon emissions by almost 30 percent.

Some of these measures save money and others cost more. Overall, these measures drop conference costs significantly. Last year we priced green conferences 7 percent lower than non-green conferences. In fact, we estimate that the average green conference saved organizers more than $18,000.

Yes, green meetings make a difference. They're better for the environment and better for the wallet.

The Prestigio Hotel & Resort is a high-end resort committed to excellence in conferences, events, and other special occasions in an environmentally friendly, responsible way. You can learn more about conferences and events by contacting Barbara Brookshire.

Make sure your content is interesting and front-loaded. You usually have only 5 to 15 seconds to draw your readers in, so make sure you capture their interest immediately. Finally, stay responsive to your readers' comments. You can often learn what your readers are looking for from you by sifting through their comments.

Because so many styles exist for professional blogs, you should read the blogs of popular business and management bloggers to identify options that might work for you. You can see one example of a professional blog in Figure 10.14. Jeff Anderton, a marketing assistant at the Prestigio, has his own blog about digital marketing and customer loyalty. This blog can serve as a way for Jeff to continue developing professional

Figure 10.14 An Example of an Individual's Professional Blog

Consider whether you should develop your own professional blog to open new professional opportunities.

©Kate Kunz/Glow Images

The Digital Strategies and Customer Loyalty Blog

Home   **About**   **Past Blog Posts**

How Much Service and Content Should You Give Away for Free?

August 1, 2018
Posted by Jeff Anderton

About Jeff

I'm a marketing assistant at the Prestigio Hotel & Resort. I write about trends in digital marketing and customer loyalty. All views are my own.

Many software and consulting companies rely on a business model of giving away content and services. To make money, of course, these companies need paying customers. This business model is called *freemium* (combines the words *free* and *premium*). A well-known freemium company is LinkedIn. Most customers pay nothing for free profiles with a small proportion of customers paying for premium services.

In the recent *Harvard Business Review* article "Making 'Freemium' Work," Vineet Kumar provides an overview of the freemium business model. He presents the cases of LinkedIn, NYTimes.com, Spotify, and Dropbox. Kumar explains that freemium companies must figure out how to offer some features for free to attract new users, yet retain other features that are reserved for premium users. So, how do you do that? Kumar gives some hints but not any specific answers.

Over the past few weeks, I've read articles by many of the experts on freemium business models. They generally recommend the following strategies to find the "sweet spot" between offering too much or too little free content:

1. *Use the RIGHT MODEL.* Freemium expert Lincoln Murphy has examined this business model for nearly a decade and identified seven distinct freemium business models. Some companies even use more than one business model for various products and services. To know which model to use, freemium companies should know answers to the following questions: (a) Will the content or services remain free forever? (b) Will users or organizations purchase the content or services? (c) Is the primary purpose to get customers to upgrade or to get them to purchase other products or services (a cross-sell strategy)? (d) Is the base product intended to create an ecosystem? Without answering these questions carefully, companies may choose the wrong model and get the free/premium mix wrong.

2. *Keep track of the RIGHT METRICS.* One company that's mastered the mix between free and premium content is Breaking Into Wall Street, an educational service about landing a finance position. Its founder and president, Brian DeChesare, recently sat down for an interview with *Forbes* and mentioned all freemium companies must measure the following: (a) What is the cost of content creation? (b) How long will free content attract new customers? (c) What are the costs of updating free content? (d) What is the expected ROI on free content?

3. *Hire the RIGHT PEOPLE to oversee the process.* Among the most successful creators of a freemium company was David Sacks, founder and CEO of Yammer. He recently guest authored the article "When Freemium Beats Premium" for the *WSJ*. Sacks says that "a lot of effort, experimentation, and fine-tuning" are needed to succeed with freemium. So, yes, it's important to capture the right metrics. You need people who understand data. But, it's also important to hire people who embrace uncertainty and use a trial-and-error process to figure out what to give away for free and what to reserve for paid customers.

knowledge and to build a personal brand that will provide him with professional opportunities. When professionals create their own blogs, they often use phrases such as "all views are my own" to clearly show the content is not endorsed by their employers.

GENERAL GUIDELINES FOR USING SOCIAL MEDIA IN THE WORKPLACE

Of course, many communication outlets fall under the social media platform. Generally, you can apply the following strategies to any of them: (a) be an active contributor; (b) join communities; (c) focus on content; (d) make your content accessible; (e) make your messages authentic and friendly; (f) be responsive and help others; and (g) respect boundaries and avoid oversharing.

Be an active contributor. If your company or professional group has committed to using internal digital platforms and/or social networking platforms, make sure you contribute regularly and respond to the comments and work of others. As an example, for individual blogs, employees who gain the largest followings (and thus a reputation for thought leadership) make blog entries and other posts at least several times per month.

Join communities. Online communities are excellent places to network and participate with professionals in your organization and those with shared professional interests outside your organization. Some communities are built around committees, task forces, and teams with specific charges or tasks. Others, built around shared professional interests such as finance or project management, are often called *communities of practice* and allow you to share and learn from other professionals in your area. Yet other communities are focused on personal interests and hobbies. Actively participating in these communities can open up many professional and learning opportunities.

Focus on content. Blogs, forums, and even newsfeeds are collaborative tools. In other words, they are intended to help you work more effectively with your team members, other colleagues, and clients. The primary goal is not to entertain; it is to provide value to others and increase your professional, not social, credibility. The content of your posts should focus largely on your work projects, meetings, shared goals, experiences, and expertise and knowledge.

Of course, social media are called *social* for a reason, and including social content is good to a point. In high-performing teams, 60 to 70 percent of all comments are directly related to work, about 15 to 20 percent of comments are supportive of team members, and about 10 to 15 percent are primarily social.[20] This is also the case for business communication via internal digital platforms and other forms of social media. As a good rule of thumb, to support your professional goals, roughly 70 percent of your social media content should be directly related to work tasks, roughly 20 percent should be supportive of your colleagues and contacts, and roughly 10 percent should be social or fun.

Make your content accessible. To increase your influence, make your posts and comments easy to find later on. By naming, labeling, indexing, and tagging (applying keywords to your blogs and other posts) well, you help others find your information. Also consider using links to important files to help others open them immediately.

Make your messages authentic and friendly. Social media readers expect

FOCUS ON ETHICS
Using Social Media to Criticize a Competitor

As the new manager of an upscale seafood restaurant, you want to impress the owner by increasing business during the lunch hour. Your biggest competitor has a strong social media presence, including an active Facebook page and reviews on TripAdvisor and Yelp. You've eaten lunch at your competitor's restaurant and found the food and service mediocre, so you decide to create an anonymous profile on these social media platforms and say so, hoping your lukewarm review will drive business to your restaurant instead. After you notice an uptick in business, you consider creating additional anonymous profiles from which to criticize your competitor even more harshly.

CONSIDER THIS: Because you had a mediocre experience at your competitor's restaurant, was it ethical to say so online, even though your goal was to increase your own business? How ethical was it to post your comments anonymously? Would you be justified in issuing even harsher criticisms online, even though such criticisms were unfounded?

sincerity and truth. Your messages should not come off as spin and should not contradict who you really are. Be clear about your intentions. Your messages should also have a friendly tone. However, authenticity and friendliness do not mean sloppy writing or rudeness. Generally, avoid deleting comments to your posts except for unusual circumstances and avoid engaging in edit wars.

Be responsive and help others. One expectation of social networks is that you are a good member of the community. Respond positively to the requests of others and help when possible. As you gain a reputation for doing so, you can expect that other community members will respond and help you.

Respect boundaries and avoid oversharing. The many communication tools on internal digital platforms and/or social networks allow people to communicate with nearly anyone at nearly anytime from nearly any location about nearly anything. In other words, the division between professional and private lives is becoming increasingly blurred. However, oversharing can make you look domineering or self-centered. Set your own boundaries and stay observant about where your colleagues draw lines to preserve their lives away from work.

CHAPTER WRAP-UP

Effective writing benefits from attention to several important details. Here's a quick review of the chapter.

LO10.1 Recall principles for writing effective emails and digital messages.

- Use email for the right purposes.
- Ensure ease of reading.
- Show respect for others' time.
- Protect privacy and confidentiality.

- Respond promptly.
- Maintain professionalism and appropriate formality.

LO10.2 Describe how to effectively manage emotion in online communications.

- Reinterpret.
- Relax.
- Defuse.

LO10.3 Identify approaches to develop shared knowledge and make decisions in online forums and communities.

- Follow your company's social media guidelines.
- Organize your dashboard to control your communication and information flow.
- Create a complete and professional profile.
- Use blogs and status updates for team communication.
- Use shared files to collaborate.
- Solve problems with discussion forums.

LO10.4 Explain strategies to develop mass communications in digital environments.

- Write posts for your organization.
- Write posts for a professional blog.
- General guidelines for using social media in the workplace: (a) be an active contributor; (b) join communities; (c) focus on content; (d) make your content accessible; (e) make your messages authentic and friendly; (f) be responsive and help others; and (g) respect boundaries.

A LOOK BACK

Now let's return to the opening scenario. There are clear signals that Siddarth and Jerry are misusing email. The fact that they have emailed one another roughly 20 times over three days without resolving the issue shows they need an in-person, phone, or other real-time conversation to quickly do so. It's also clear Siddarth and Jerry are not effective at managing emotion. Jerry uses all caps to send a message ("PLEASE READ CAREFULLY!!!"), which most people would perceive as insulting. Siddarth makes a comment ("This is getting more and more confusing") that most people would perceive as blaming. It appears neither Siddarth nor Jerry has been attempting to reinterpret the other's messages objectively or relax to respond constructively, and neither is attempting to defuse the situation. While these mistakes may seem obvious, it's surprising how often professionals fall into this exact scenario.

KEY TERMS

active incivility   237
blog   242
cyber incivility   237
cyber silence   237
dashboard   241
defusing   239

flames   237
internal digital platform   240
microblog   242
negativity effect   237
neutrality effect   237
passive incivility   237

project blog   243
public relations (PR)   248
reinterpretation   238
relaxation   238
team blog   243

CHAPTER REVIEW QUESTIONS

1. Why do you think emails are used more often than messaging and texts for important business messages? **LO10.1**

2. What strategies can you use to ensure ease of reading in your emails and other digital communications? **LO10.1**

3. What strategies can you use to show respect for the time of others? **LO10.1**

4. Explain the neutrality effect and negativity effect in digital communications. What do they imply for the way you write digital messages? **LO10.2**

5. Explain the following components of constructively responding to uncivil digital messages: reinterpretation, relaxation, and defusing. **LO10.2**

6. What are some strategies for organizing a dashboard to help you work more efficiently with your teams? **LO10.3**

7. What do you think are some of the most important pieces of information for a professional profile on an enterprise social networking platform? LO10.3

8. When do you think you should use blogs in teams? LO10.3

9. What do you think are the primary challenges to running an effective forum? LO10.3

10. Which strategies do you consider most important when leading a forum? Explain. LO10.3

11. What elements of tone are most important for social media messages? LO10.4

12. What strategies can you use to build a credible online reputation? LO10.4

13. How can you use social media ethically from the perspective of your employer? LO10.4

SKILL-BUILDING EXERCISES

Evaluate Your Email (LO10.1)

Look at the email messages you've sent during the past week. Identify the strategies you use that are effective and three ways in which you can improve your email writing.

Evaluate a Professional Blog (LO10.4)

Choose a professional blog of interest to you. It could be a corporate or organizational blog or the blog of a business leader or other professional. Read a minimum of ten posts. Then, in one to two pages, respond to the following questions: What is the name and web address of the blog? What is the target audience for this blog? How does the content meet the needs of readers? Why would the target audience choose this blog over similar blogs? How does (do) the blog author(s) establish credibility? What type of online reputation does (do) the blog author(s) create? What design features make the blog effective? What three positive aspects of this blog could you apply to your own blog?

Evaluate the Tweets of Business Leaders (LO10.4)

View the recent tweets of two or three business leaders (you might consider looking for accounts of business leaders you're interested in). Then, write a short report about your observations of these business leaders' tweets. Include the following in your short report:

- Comparisons of the tweets of your chosen business leaders in terms of the following: (1) style and content of tweets, (2) frequency of tweets, and (3) goals of tweets.
- Three tips for business leaders when they create tweets.

Write a Professional Blog (LO10.4)

Considering your own career interests and the online reputation and personal brand you seek, write a blog about a business topic of interest to you that provides content valuable to others. With a specific audience in mind, post five original and insightful entries of about 700 to 1,000 words each. In each, consider applying the following formula: (a) one or two takeaway messages; (b) a catchy title and opening; (c) a winning tone—helpful, personalized, positive, informative, fun, and interesting; (d) hyperlinks to interesting articles or videos; (e) images if you'd like (not required); and (f) concise writing with fairly short paragraphs.

Manage Information Overload (LO10.1, LO10.2, LO10.3)

Go to the Information Overload Research Group's website (iorgforum.org). Read a research article, blog entry, or other content about a topic of interest. In three to five paragraphs, explain the following: (a) main points in the article, (b) your views of the main points, and (c) three strategies you will adopt to avoid information overload in the workplace.

Digital Sabbatical (LO10.1, LO10.2, LO10.3)

For 24 hours, avoid using your mobile device or a computer for any communication or accessing online information. (You might consider notifying your friends and family that you will be unavailable during this period.) Write a one- to two-page account of your experience. Consider including discussion about the following:

- How you felt going without communication (anxiety, relief, stress, peace, other).
- How you felt going without access to digital information (empowered, helpless, out of the loop, other).
- How you think going without digital communications affects your quality of life, productivity, and/or routines.
- Based on your experience, give two or three recommendations for professionals about handling digital communication and information.

ENDNOTES

1. Cardon, P. W. (2016, April 23). *The role of leadership communication and emotional capital in driving internal social media use.* Association for Business Communication Southeast/Midwest Regional Conference.

2. Morgan, N. (2002, August). Don't push that send button! *Harvard Management Communication Letter,* 4.

3. Bixler, S., & Dugan, L. A. (2000). *How to project confidence, competence, and credibility at work: 5 steps to professional presence.* New York, NY: Simon & Schuster.

4. Wright, G. (2009, July 30). Twitter with care: Web 2.0 usage offers few second chances. *Society for Human Resource Management* (online).

5. Washington, M., Okoro, E. A., & Cardon, P. W. (2014). Perceptions of civility for mobile phone use in formal and informal meetings. *Business and Professional Communication Quarterly, 77*(1), 52–64.

6. Langford, B. (2005). *The etiquette advantage: The unspoken rules for business success.* New York, NY: AMACOM.

7. Carnegie, D. (1981). *How to win friends and influence people.* New York, NY: Simon & Schuster.

8. Waldvogel, J. (2007). Greetings and closings in workplace email. *Journal of Computer-Mediated Communication, 12*(2), 456–477.

9. Byron, K. (2008). Carry too heavy a load? The communication and miscommunication of emotion by email. *Academy of Management Review, 33*(2), 309–327.

10. Byron, K. (2008). Carry too heavy a load? The communication and miscommunication of emotion by email. *Academy of Management Review, 33*(2), 309–327.

11. Alonzo, M., & Aiken, M. (2004). Flaming in electronic communication. *Decision Support Systems, 36,* 205–213.

12. Johnson, N. A., Cooper, R. B., & Chin, W. W. (2009). Anger and flaming in computer-mediated negotiation among strangers. *Decision Support Systems, 46,* 660–672.

13. Lim, V. K. G., & Thompson, S. H. T. (2009). Mind your e-manners: Impact of cyber incivility on employees' work attitude and behavior. *Information & Management, 46,* 419–425.

14. Lim, V. K. G., & Thompson, S. H. T. (2009). Mind your e-manners: Impact of cyber incivility on employees' work attitude and behavior. *Information & Management, 46,* 419–425.

15. Johnson, N. A., Cooper, R. B., & Chin, W. W. (2009). Anger and flaming in computer-mediated negotiation among strangers. *Decision Support Systems, 46,* 660–672.

16. Intel. (n.d.). Social media guidelines. Retrieved from *Intel* website at https://www.intel.com/content/www/us/en/legal/intel-social-media-guidelines.html.

17. Wright, S., & Zdinak, J. (2008). *New communication behaviors in a Web 2.0 world.* Boulogne-Bilancourt, France: Alcatel-Lucent.

18. Beal, A., & Straus, J. (2008). *Radically transparent: Monitoring and managing reputations online.* Indianapolis, IN: Wiley Publishing.

19. Schreiber, E. (2011, January 14). *Reputation.* Institute for Public Relations. Retrieved from http://instituteforpr.org/reputation.

20. Wheelan, S. A. (2014). *Creating effective teams: A guide for members and leaders* (5th ed.). Thousand Oaks, CA: Sage.

Learning Objectives

After reading this chapter, you should be able to do the following:

LO11.1 Name and define the primary forms of professional presentations.

LO11.2 Summarize four steps for identifying appropriate presentation topics.

LO11.3 Illustrate the strategies for analyzing an audience.

LO11.4 Explain the strategies for analyzing a speaking context.

CHAPTER 11

Major Goals for Presentations

Michelle Diep, a marketing associate at a fitness center, sighed as she glanced at the clock. It was nearly 1 a.m. and she was to give a 15-minute speech at a local Rotary club the next day. The club was composed of local professionals who met each week to learn more about the community and engage in service projects. The club's president had called about two weeks ago and said, "We'd love to have you stop by the club and tell us about the fitness center or health or whatever you want."

Michelle had thought it would be easy to come up with a good topic. Unfortunately, she still had no idea what she wanted to say.

LO11.1

Name and define the primary forms of professional presentations.

Know the Types of Professional Presentations

Acting students are taught to ask themselves, "What's my motivation?" when preparing for a performance. That question leads them to consider why their character should be saying or doing what's described in the scene. If the script calls for a character to appear aggressive toward others, for instance, a performer must know *why* the character is being aggressive to make his or her portrayal believable.

Preparing a professional presentation is no different. To be effective, you must begin by asking about your *own* motivation. Good speakers carefully consider the goals of the speeches they prepare. As we'll see in this section, we can speak with many different goals in mind, such as to inform, to persuade, to entertain, to introduce, or to make a group presentation or a special occasion speech. Those goals are not necessarily mutually exclusive; sometimes a speaker has more than one goal for the same speech. Just like actors who consider their characters' motivations, you can improve your performance as a speaker by identifying the goal or goals you want to accomplish in your speech.

SPEECHES TO INFORM

Allyson Lewis knows about informative speaking. As a professional consultant and executive coach, Lewis frequently speaks at conventions and corporate retreats on the topics of time management, productivity and efficiency, goal setting, and work/life balance. In each instance, her goal is to teach her listeners strategies they can use to maximize their effectiveness on the job.

The goal of an **informative speech** is to teach listeners something they don't already know. A refresher course for lifeguards, a retirement workshop for older adults, an employee meeting about a new policy, and a product demonstration at a trade fair are all examples of informative speaking. In each case, the speaker has knowledge on a particular topic that he or she wishes to impart to the audience. To do so successfully, the speaker must make the material interesting, clear, and easy for listeners to follow.

SPEECHES TO PERSUADE

Allyson Lewis, professional consultant and executive coach, is a frequent informative speaker.

©Seven Minutes, Inc.

After working for a pet supply company for more than three years, you believe your experience and current level of responsibility warrant an increase in your salary, so you meet with your supervisor to discuss your wishes. "Tell me why you deserve a raise," he says. Now, your task is to persuade him that you're worthy of a bigger paycheck.

Persuasion is the process of guiding people to adopt a specific attitude or enact a particular behavior. When we present a **persuasive speech**, we are therefore appealing to our listeners to think or act in a certain way. During a motivational halftime speech in the locker room, a basketball coach can persuade her team to play more effectively in the game's second half. During an inspiring commencement address, a celebrity or political figure can persuade new graduates to believe in themselves. In each of these instances, the speaker is attempting to lead listeners to think, believe, or act in a specific manner.

SPEECHES TO INTRODUCE

In March 2012, Hall of Fame football veteran and team vice president John Elway introduced Peyton Manning as the new starting quarterback for the Denver Broncos at a press conference in Colorado. During his speech, Elway spoke of Manning's previous

Denver Broncos vice president John Elway introduces new quarterback Peyton Manning.

©Justin Edmonds/Getty Images Sport/Getty Images

successes as well as his future potential with the Broncos, noting, "My goal is to make Peyton Manning the best quarterback to play the game."[1] At the conclusion of his remarks, Elway asked his listeners to welcome Manning to the stage.

Like Elway, many of us will give public presentations to introduce other people. When we make an **introductory speech**, our aim is often to inform listeners of the person's background and notable characteristics. Suppose you were introducing a new colleague to your project team at work. In your presentation, you might say a few words about the person's hometown, education, previous work experience, and hobbies or interests. Good speeches of introduction are usually short and focused on information listeners will find interesting.

We also speak to introduce ourselves. Perhaps you were called on to introduce yourself to your classmates on the first day of the academic term. If so, you may have informed your audience of your name, major, career goals, and reasons for taking the course. Here too, we want to select a few pieces of information our listeners will find interesting.

GROUP PRESENTATIONS

At times, you may be speaking as part of a group, and you will need to choose the most appropriate format for such a presentation. Sometimes the context dictates the format. Otherwise, you can choose a group oral report, a symposium, a colloquium, or a forum.

- *Group oral report:* Let's say your group has worked together to accomplish a project, investigate a question, or reach a decision. Perhaps it's up to you to deliver a speech on the group's behalf in the form of an **oral report**. Examples are a sales leader giving a pitch on behalf of her sales team, a wellness committee chair presenting requests to company leaders about the needs of employees,

SHARPEN YOUR SKILLS

Identifying Speaking Goals

Identify an influential leader from an industry in which you're interested, and search online for the text of one of his or her most notable speeches. Read the text and identify the speaking goal or goals you see reflected in the speech. Enumerate the goals in a blog post or journal entry.

and a work team member reporting the results of the team's latest project. The speaker (or speakers) may answer questions from listeners afterward, depending on the situation.

- *Symposium:* In a **symposium** format, each member of a small group makes an individual presentation, one after another, on a common topic. Let's say that as a resident adviser (RA) in your residence hall, you are part of a symposium about campus housing safety. Your group might feature five other RAs, each speaking about his or her most significant challenges and successes during the previous year. A moderator usually introduces each speaker and invites questions from the audience at the end.

- *Colloquium:* A **colloquium** is a speaking format in which members of a group discuss a predetermined topic with one another in front of an audience. Colloquium topics are often controversial, with speakers offering divergent points of view. For example, a nonprofit environmental organization might host a colloquium on the topic of genetically modified organisms, with the group consisting of scientists who have different perspectives on the topic. As in a symposium, a moderator typically oversees the session to ensure that everyone in the group receives equal time to speak. The difference between a symposium and a colloquium is that a symposium features individual speakers and presentations, whereas a colloquium is more of a group discussion. Although disagreement and debate among group members are often encouraged at a colloquium, the tone is expected to remain respectful.

- *Forum:* The most interactive format for a group presentation is a **forum**, in which members of the group and the audience offer comments and questions to one another. When considering a major policy decision, for instance, your company's board of directors might hold a forum to take comments and questions from the public. The board chair may enforce a time limit to ensure that everyone has an equal opportunity to speak. A forum can be held on its own, or it may follow an oral report, symposium, or colloquium.

In the workplace, many group presentations take place on **panels**, which are small groups of people brought together to discuss a specific topic. Organizations often hold events for just their employees, at trade shows and other industry events, or for customers. Panels can take many forms, including symposium-, colloquium-, or forum-style events. Symposium-style panels are common at industry events, for instance, wherein representatives of several companies—such as a pharmaceutical company, a software company, and a mining company—each speak on a similar topic, such as employee retention, digital marketing, or environmental sustainability. At conference or media events, colloquium-style panels commonly feature representatives of several organizations—say a tech company, a manufacturing company, and a government official—who offer diverse views on a company topic, such as the effect of big data on privacy or the role of tax incentives for companies.

Forum-style panels are extremely common in corporate settings. A group of managers might take input and questions from a group of its employees about a new parental leave policy, a group of nonprofit leaders might get guidance and feedback from a group of its funders about which programs to invest in, or a group of executives might get demands and questions from an organization's board members.

Group presentations are common in the business world.

©Photographee.eu/Shutterstock

PEOPLE **FIRST**

Writing a Memorable and Respectful Eulogy

IMAGINE THIS: Your long-time co-worker Brooke has passed away after an illness. Her parents are planning a memorial service that you and several colleagues will attend and they have asked you to deliver one of the eulogies.

Now, consider this: Despite not having written a eulogy before, you want to do the best job you can for your late friend and her family. How do you write a eulogy that is both memorable and respectful? Among the common challenges in this situation are that the audience is often emotional, you may be as well, and you will generally have a short period of time in which to prepare. Here are some strategies to help:

- Many successful eulogies combine serious commentary on the person's death with positive, even humorous memories from his or her life. Consider what you think will work best for the audience you expect. Remember that a eulogy doesn't have to be somber, just appropriate for the situation.

- Introduce yourself at the start of your eulogy and describe your relationship with the deceased. You could begin with how you met and go on to what you most appreciated about each other as colleagues and friends.

- Focus on the person's most positive qualities. Maybe you appreciated Brooke's loyalty to her family, her ambition and drive, and her love for animals. Include a brief story or two to illustrate these.

- Remember that the purpose of a eulogy is to comfort those who remain. Remind listeners how much they meant to Brooke and encourage them to share their fondest memories of her with one another.

- Keep your remarks brief. Many memorial services feature more than one eulogy, so if you are one of several speakers, plan to speak for no more than five minutes.

THINK ABOUT THIS:

If writing and delivering a eulogy seems daunting, what worries do you have about it? How can you overcome them?

SPECIAL OCCASION SPEECHES

On many occasions, we speak to give honor. Speaking at the 2015 funeral of Beau Biden—former Delaware attorney general and son of the U.S. vice president—younger brother Hunter said, "We will always be one family. You are at the center of the greatest love." His remarks were part of a **eulogy**, a speech made to honor the memory of people after their death and to comfort those who remain. We use eulogies and many other types of presentations to give honor to people, places, or significant points in history.

A eulogy is one of the most common types of speeches that give honor, yet many people find them intimidating to prepare. Take a look at the "People First" box for suggestions on putting together memorable remarks that are appropriate for the situation.

Many other situations call for a special occasion speech as well. At a social gathering such as a retirement ceremony for a colleague, it's common for particular guests to give a **toast**, a short speech of tribute to the person or people being celebrated. Most toasts offer comments on the honoree's positive qualities and congratulations on his or her accomplishments. Similarly, we might deliver a **speech of recognition** to honor someone who is receiving an award. Such presentations usually explain the criteria for the award and then identify the recipient by describing his or her achievements.

Speakers also give speeches to honor important places. In 2015, for instance, President Barack Obama delivered a **speech of dedication** to honor the Edward M. Kennedy Institute in Boston, Massachusetts. As is common during speeches of dedication, he spoke of the importance of the institute and the historic achievements of the man it honors. Perhaps the most famous speech of dedication in U.S. history was President Abraham Lincoln's Gettysburg Address, delivered during the Civil War in November 1863 to dedicate a new national cemetery for soldiers.

Finally, we can use speeches to honor significant points in history. On the sixteenth anniversary of the September 11 terrorist attacks on the United States, President Donald Trump gave a **speech of commemoration** at the Pentagon. He honored the memory of the victims and rescue workers who had lost their lives, and he reemphasized the United States' commitment to prosperity and security.

Keep in mind that many presentations have multiple goals. For instance, salespeople often attempt to persuade customers to buy a product by informing them of the item's positive features. The best man at a wedding might give a toast to honor the couple but also to entertain the guests with funny stories about the new spouses. Even if a speech has one primary goal, it can also have one or more secondary goals. Once you have identified the goal or goals for your presentation, you should think about an appropriate topic on which to speak. We'll examine that key step next.

LO11.2

Summarize four steps for identifying appropriate presentation topics.

Choose an Appropriate Topic

When you are invited to give a speech, you may be assigned a topic based on your specific knowledge—whether it's your understanding of cross-cultural business communication or your expertise in retirement planning, Internet marketing, or information security. At other times, however, you may select the topic for your speech. You can identify appropriate topics by following four steps:

1. Brainstorm to identify potential topics.
2. Identify topics that are right for you.
3. Identify topics that are right for your audience.
4. Identify topics that are right for the occasion.

We look at each step next, with examples.

BRAINSTORM TO IDENTIFY POTENTIAL TOPICS

The goal of brainstorming is to identify as many topics as possible before stopping to evaluate them.

©REDPIXEL.PL/Shutterstock

When no speech topic has been assigned, start by brainstorming to generate a list of potential topics. **Brainstorming** is a technique that encourages you to identify as many ideas as possible without stopping to evaluate them. You can use two questions to guide your brainstorming: what topics do you care about, and what topics are in the news?

What topics do you care about?   You could start by thinking about broad business topics by functional areas such as marketing or leadership (see Table 11.1). You might also ask yourself about the experiences, hobbies, beliefs, attitudes, values, and skills you have. How do you enjoy spending your time? What issues do you care about? Jot down as many topics as you can think of. Some of your topics might be questions; others might be statements. Don't stop to evaluate your ideas just

yet; for now, your goal is to generate as many ideas as possible. Your list might look something like this:

- Why does travel help you become a better marketer?
- How can you support colleagues on the autism spectrum?
- What are the most effective ways to save money during college?
- What do financial analysts do?
- How do companies use big data?
- How can you use social media to get a job?
- What are some tips for doing business in China?
- Should there be mandated parental leave?
- How do you get a small-business loan?
- What are the best ways to influence a stubborn boss?
- How should a small business develop a website?
- How do nonprofits fundraise?

Table 11.1 **Broad Topics by Business Discipline**

Marketing	Supply Chain Management/Operations
• Social media marketing	• Enterprise resource planning systems
• Brand management	• Sourcing and supplier management
• Marketing analytics	• Production planning
• Advertising	• Quality management
• Customer service	• Inventory management
• Business-to-business marketing	• Resource forecasting
• International marketing	
• Sales	*Information Systems/Technology*
• Product development	• Big data/business analytics
	• Cloud-based technologies
Finance/Accounting	• Social media policies
• Mergers and acquisitions	• E-commerce
• Auditing	• Technology adoption
• Risk management	• Artificial intelligence
• Banking and capital management	
• Corporate taxation	*Leadership/Management/Communication*
• Financial planning	• Business strategy
• International financial management	• Leadership styles
	• Personality
Human Resources	• Negotiation
• Talent management	• Organizational change
• Performance management	• Conflict management
• Employee recognition	• Crisis management
• Team development	
• Salary and benefit plans	*Ethics and Corporate Social Responsibility*
• Community management	• Sustainability
• Career paths	• Diversity
• Employee morale	• Compliance and governance
• Recruiting and hiring	• Transparency
	• Employee volunteering programs
	• Corporate philanthropy

As we consider next, you can also identify potential speech topics by looking at issues in the news.

What topics are in the news? Most of us have multiple sources of news available at all hours of the day and night. We can therefore turn to the news to see which topics might be of interest to audiences. A list of contemporary topics might look like this:

- Reduction of corporate tax rates
- Sexual harassment in the workplace
- Pros and cons of artificial intelligence and robotics
- Corporate crises (e.g., Facebook's misuse of users' data)
- Net neutrality
- Bitcoin
- Brexit
- National anthem protests in the NFL
- Mark Cuban

You can combine the list of topics you care about with the list of topics in the news to create a master list of potential topics. You'll then need to select one topic as the focus of your speech, being sure that it is appropriate for you, for your audience, and for the occasion.

IDENTIFY TOPICS THAT ARE RIGHT FOR YOU

When you are homing in on your presentation topic, first consider whether the topic is right for you. Ask:

- *What do I already know about this topic?* If you choose to speak about an issue with which you're already familiar, you will speak with credibility and confidence.
- *What do I need to learn about this topic?* Even if you're already familiar with your topic, you should still be willing to invest some time to ensure that your knowledge is up to date.
- *How much do I care about this topic?* Choosing a topic you care about will make preparing your speech more enjoyable, and your presentation will be more engaging for your listeners.
- *How valuable is the topic?* If you're going to the trouble of researching and preparing a speech, don't waste your energy on a trivial topic. Select something that is meaningful and valuable to you.

Answering those four questions won't always lead you toward the same topic. For instance, you might know a great deal about e-commerce, community management, or crisis communication, but you may care more about employee morale, diversity, or corporate philanthropy. Even if your answers to those questions don't lead you to a specific topic, they ought to narrow the field of potential topics. Once they do, there's another key question to consider: whether the topic is appropriate for your audience.

IDENTIFY TOPICS THAT ARE RIGHT FOR YOUR AUDIENCE

To give an effective speech, you need to select a topic that is right not only for yourself but also for your listeners. Once you have a potential topic in mind, ask:

- *How appropriate is this topic for my audience?* Topics that are appropriate for adults, for instance, may not be appropriate for a younger audience, and those that are appropriate for an audience of experts may not be for an audience of nonexperts.

CAREER TIP
When Giving Presentations, Be Yourself

Melinda Gates is the third most powerful woman in the world, according to the *Forbes World's 100 Most Powerful Women* list.[2] After a successful business career, she has spent the last several decades as one of the most active philanthropists in the world. The co-chair of the Bill and Melinda Gates Foundation, she works tirelessly to fight disease, increase prosperity, and support opportunities for women in the most vulnerable communities across the globe. Her ability to prepare and deliver speeches on catchy topics is one key to her success at generating support for her causes. For example, her most-watched TED Talk is called "What Nonprofits Can Learn from Coca-Cola."[3]

When Gates recently addressed college graduates, she said, "My best advice would be to be yourself." In the early 1980s, she was one of the only women at Microsoft with a technology background. She thought she had to adopt the "same style as all the men in the room." But she was so unhappy trying to mimic the behavior of others, she almost left the company. Ultimately, she pushed through several years of discomfort and learned to be herself. In the process, she developed her own unique leadership style and gained much more satisfaction at work.[4]

Melinda Gates, co-chair of the Bill and Melinda Gates Foundation
©Bloomberg/Getty Images

Gates's advice is important in many professional situations, especially in speech situations. Remember that, as you plan and develop presentations, your passion and authenticity are essential. Find ways to *be yourself* in this process, and you'll realize that your authenticity helps you connect with and influence others.

- *How much will my audience care about this topic?* If your listeners care about your topic, they will be more attentive and more likely to remember what you say.

We will return to ways to analyze your audience later in this chapter. For now, though, you'll want to ask yourself what topics are appropriate for the speaking occasion.

IDENTIFY TOPICS THAT ARE RIGHT FOR THE OCCASION

With your potential topic in mind, ask:

- *Why am I speaking?* Is your goal to inform or persuade? Are you introducing or honoring someone? Select a topic that will fit the primary goal of your speech.
- *What is the emotional tone of the event?* Is the occasion joyous and celebratory, such as a promotion ceremony? Is it somber, such as a memorial service? Is it formal but emotionally neutral, such as a stockholders' meeting? Make sure your topic fits the tone of the occasion.

After considering which topics are right for you, which are right for your audience, and finally which are right for the occasion, you should have a "short list" of excellent options from which to make your final selection.

TECH TIP
Alternatives to PowerPoint

In many work environments, PowerPoint slides have become the standard visual aid for presentations and meetings. Even if you're great at using them, you might consider other types of visual aids and props to add impact, creativity, or simply variety to your presentations.

- *Try other electronic slide and presentation software.* Consider trying Prezi, Google Docs, SlideRocket, 280 Slides, or other software packages to see what you're most comfortable with. Many presenters find that presentation software such as Prezi does not box them into bullet-point, linear presentations and provides more flexibility.

- *Use smartboards, whiteboards, or chalkboards.* Writing as you go with keyboards, markers, or chalk may allow you to engage your audience more effectively because you are presenting in the moment, avoiding the structure or order of electronic slides, and getting input from your audience. Drawing objects freehand may allow you to depict ideas more accurately and forcefully than the drawing tools in PowerPoint. Still, avoid spending too much time facing away from the audience.

- *Experiment with new presentation technologies.* Many new and emerging presentation technologies are *social.* For example, various options for conducting

Effective speakers consider many ways in which technology can aid their presentations.

©Andrey_Popov/Shutterstock

online polling during presentations—such as Presentain, Swipe, and ParticiPoll—allow you to incorporate feedback from your audience in your presentation. By experimenting with these technologies, you'll learn to tap into the incoming messages while also controlling your own message.

Analyze Your Audience

As CEO of India-based advertising and technology company InMobi, Naveen Tewari spends much of his time making public presentations. One day, he may be speaking to a group of advertising executives eager to learn about InMobi's success. The next day, his audience might be several dozen reporters at a press conference. Like other executives who give frequent public appearances, Tewari knows he must tailor each presentation to the audience if he is to speak effectively. He must understand who his listeners are and the situation they are in.

Savvy public speakers engage in **audience analysis**, which means thinking carefully about the characteristics of their listeners so they can address their audience in the most effective way. You'll want to ask questions such as the following:

How will audience members benefit from what I have to say? This is perhaps the single most important question you can use to guide you as you design your presentation. In particular, focus on benefits you can offer that fulfill an unmet need of your listeners.

What do listeners already know about my topic? Find out whatever you can about your audience members' knowledge level. The less they know about your topic, the more of your presentation time you should spend to inform them. Also, try to find out where they have gotten their information or perceptions about the topic. Knowing this allows you to deal more effectively with misinformation.

Naveen Tewari, CEO of
InMobi

©Mint/Getty Images

What are my listeners' chief concerns? Although you can take time to gather your thoughts when responding to someone's concerns in writing, in presentations and other face-to-face communications you must respond immediately. Find out what these issues are.

Who are the key decision makers? You want to earn the support of your whole audience, but some members are more powerful than others. For internal presentations, think about who has the most influence and authority to act on your ideas. For presentations to clients, customers, and prospects, identify the decision makers. Focus most of your attention on them.

What will appeal to my audience? Oral communications are well suited to conveying a strong emotional appeal because they create bonds between the speaker and the audience that can transfer to the topic of your speech. At the same time, you will be including a set of ideas you want your audience to appreciate analytically. Plan to make both emotional and analytical connections with your audience.

What is the learning style of my audience? **Visual learners** learn best from illustrations and simple diagrams that show relationships and key ideas. They also enjoy gestures and metaphors. Text-based PowerPoints do not appeal to them much, but slides rich in images and figures do help them respond to your message. **Auditory learners** prefer loud, clear voices and believe emotion is best conveyed through voice. Finally, **kinesthetic learners** need to participate in order to focus their attention on your message and learn best. They benefit from group activities, hands-on activities, or breaks at least every 20 minutes.

Another important part of audience analysis is taking account of listeners' **demographic characteristics**, which include their age, sex and sexual orientation, culture, socioeconomic status, physical and mental characteristics, and political orientation. If you don't know much about these, ask the person hosting your speech or someone who is familiar with your audience. You can then use what you know to identify issues, examples, opinions, and forms of evidence that are most relevant to your listeners.

As you do your homework about the audience, research the following demographic characteristics as thoroughly as possible.

AGE

Researchers have found important differences in attitudes depending on year of birth. Recall from Chapter 2 that people born during different time periods can have substantially different viewpoints on important social issues, such as the value of labor unions, the trustworthiness of the national news media, the role of religion in contemporary life, the acceptability of same-sex marriage, and so on.

Age also matters when a talk includes references to popular culture, and it influences audiences' facility with computer-mediated communication. Similarly, it can affect which forms of presentation will best grab and hold their attention. Younger adults often appreciate presentations that use multiple forms of media. When speaking to such groups, you may thus choose to incorporate music, multimedia slides, and video clips. Some older adults, however, may find the use of media distracting and prefer a no-frills presentation style.

SEX AND SEXUAL ORIENTATION

Effective speakers also consider the audience's sex composition. Although individual responses always vary, some research shows that men are often more interested than women in issues related to engineering, science, mathematics, and technology. Women, in contrast, are often more interested than men in social, artistic, and relationship issues.[5] These are broad generalizations that don't apply to every woman and man, and may even strike you as surprising or stereotypical, even though they are supported by research. In comparison, research shows that women and men are equally interested in many aspects of their working lives, including work hours, job security, and promotion opportunities.[6] If your audience is composed primarily of one sex or another, it may be best to tailor your presentation to appeal to their interests, if you have that option.

Especially when speaking to large, diverse audiences, effective presenters also bear in mind that listeners may vary in their sexual orientation. That matters because some forms of language reflect only the experiences of heterosexual people. Suppose a community business leader, speaking to an all-male audience at a men's retreat, encourages attendees to be mindful of the support they receive from their wives. To married heterosexual men, such a statement may sound like an important reminder to acknowledge the care and support their wives provide them on a daily basis. To men who are unmarried and/or gay, however, the statement may sound dismissive, because the word *wives* implies only female partners in legally recognized marriages. Were the speaker to encourage attendees to thank their "loved ones" instead, that statement would show greater sensitivity by including both legally recognized marriages and other committed relationships, whether with women or other men.

SHARPEN YOUR SKILLS

Audience Analysis

Select three very different audiences to whom you might speak, such as speaking to a group of immigrants about studying for citizenship, speaking to the board of trustees of a nonprofit organization about effective advertising strategies, and speaking to a tenth-grade class about careers in law enforcement. Working with a few other classmates, discuss the probable characteristics of each audience and articulate three ways you could adapt your speech to them.

CULTURE

The United States is among the most culturally diverse countries in the world.[7] As you may recall from Chapter 2, cultural groups can vary significantly in their perceptions of communication behaviors. Consequently, effective speakers take the cultural makeup of their audiences into account and speak in culturally sensitive ways. For instance, they avoid using words or phrases that insult, mock, or belittle cultural groups. Speakers who aren't culturally sensitive can cause offense even if they don't intend to do so. In February 2012, for instance, ESPN.com fired a staff writer for referring to Taiwanese American basketball player Jeremy Lin of the New York Knicks with the headline "Chink in the Armor."[8] Although the headline introduced a story about a Knicks loss to the New Orleans Hornets, many readers took offense at the word *chink,* which has been used as a racial slur to demean Asian Americans. ESPN.com took down the headline 35 minutes after posting it online and also suspended one of its sports anchors for using the phrase on air.

In a statement released after the incident, ESPN.com suggested that the headline was an honest mistake, not intended to cause offense.[9] Often, however, what matters is how comments are *interpreted* rather than how they are *intended.* Communicators who are insensitive to the way listeners or readers might interpret their remarks risk offending or alienating cultural groups in their audiences, even if their intentions are honorable. The risk of causing unintended offense is often heightened when speakers use humor inappropriately (see the "Focus on Ethics" box).

Effective speakers adapt to the cultural backgrounds and characteristics of their audiences.
©Phil Date/123RF

ECONOMIC STATUS

The United States is diverse not only culturally but also economically. According to the U.S. Census Bureau, approximately the same percentage of U.S. households earn below $10,000 per year as earn more than $150,000 per year.[10] Considering the economic status of your listeners can help you tailor your message to their priorities and experiences. For instance, wealthy listeners are often older, more educated, and more widely traveled.[11] They may be more likely to have certain markers of status, such as a home or an investment portfolio. Wealthy audiences are often politically conservative as well, so they may be more resistant to change.[12] In contrast, low-income audiences are often more liberal and more open to new ways of thinking. You can bear in mind such differences when choosing a speech topic. For instance, a speech on high-level investment strategies may not be well suited to a less wealthy audience, whereas a speech describing the stress of working two jobs might not be compelling to a wealthier one.

 FOCUS ON ETHICS

Questionable Humor

Your supervisor and mentor at work is getting ready to retire, and you have been asked to speak at her farewell party. A member of an ethnic minority, she frequently pokes fun at her own cultural background, so everyone at your workplace knows she is not offended by cultural humor even when the jokes are at her own expense. In addition, you know your audience expects your speech to be humorous and lighthearted rather than a serious tribute. You recall a joke your mentor recently made about her own culture, and you consider including it in your speech of recognition.

CONSIDER THIS: Even if you are positive the joke would not offend your mentor, what other ethical considerations should you make when deciding to tell it? Suppose you have the same ethnic and cultural background as your mentor, so the joke would be poking fun at you as well as her. Does that affect whether it is ethical to include it?

Before making a presentation, competent communicators learn as much as possible about the characteristics of their audience so they can tailor their remarks for maximum effectiveness. Consider an upcoming presentation and place a checkmark next to each applicable statement.

1. ____ My remarks and examples will be age-appropriate for all members of my audience.

2. ____ I have not included remarks dismissive of the experiences of listeners of a particular sex or sexual orientation.

3. ____ Nothing I plan to say is likely to be construed as culturally insensitive.

4. ____ I have ensured that my remarks are relevant for the economic status of my audience.

5. ____ My presentation is respectful of and will accommodate listeners with differing physical and mental capabilities.

6. ____ I have prepared my remarks so as not to cause offense to listeners of any particular political orientation.

Your goal should be to deliver a presentation that meets all these criteria. If you're unable to check any of these statements, review the section above for ways to make your presentation better adapted to your audience.

PHYSICAL AND MENTAL CAPABILITIES

Although many people function well despite physical or mental challenges, a speaker still must sensitively accommodate listeners' needs. If you're speaking to a group of retirees, for instance, many are likely to have impaired hearing or vision. To accommodate them, you need to speak clearly and at an appropriate volume, and your visual aids must be large enough to be seen easily. You may even need to describe your visual aids verbally for the benefit of those who cannot see them. You can appear insensitive if you don't consider your listeners' particular needs.

POLITICAL ORIENTATION

During the 2000 U.S. presidential election, the late journalist Tim Russert devised the method of dividing the country into "red states" and "blue states." Red states—such as Kansas, Texas, Utah, and Georgia—tend to support political candidates from the Republican Party because their populations are politically more conservative. Blue states—such as California, Illinois, Pennsylvania, and New York—usually support political candidates from the Democratic Party because their populations tend to be more liberal. A similar difference often also divides urban areas—which tend to be more liberal—from rural areas—which tend to be more conservative. Knowing whether your audience is primarily conservative, primarily liberal, or a mix of the two can help you tailor your message accordingly if your topic requires it.

Your listeners' political leanings will also affect how persuasive they judge your evidence to be. Liberals and conservatives alike are more readily persuaded by arguments from sources that lean the same way they do.

If you are able to gather at least some demographic information about your audience beforehand, you can use it to make your presentation more appropriate and more effective. The checklist in "The Competent Communicator" box will guide your efforts.

Consider the Speaking Context

As useful as it is to know the composition of your audience, it's equally helpful to consider the context of your speaking engagement: the audience's purpose, its size, the time available for your speech, the demands competing for your listeners' attention, and your audience's existing knowledge about your topic.

LO11.4
Explain the strategies for analyzing a speaking context.

PURPOSE

To maximize your effectiveness as a speaker, consider *why* your audience will come together to hear you. Will they choose to attend, or be required to? Will they anticipate being taught? Persuaded? Entertained? Is the context formal or informal? Is it joyous or somber? Those issues matter because they influence the behaviors your audience will expect from you.

Suppose you're leading a fire safety course that all new employees at your company are required to complete. In this situation, your listeners are probably expecting you to teach them what they need to know as efficiently as possible. Because they are not attending by choice, their motivation to pay attention is likely to be low. You can speak to them effectively by being clear, concise, and informative and by incorporating humor to lighten their experience.

SIZE

In general, the larger the group, the more formally structured you should make your presentation. If you're speaking to a company-sponsored youth group with only a dozen members, for instance, you might be most effective by behaving somewhat informally. You might choose to sit instead of stand, ask your listeners to introduce themselves, request audience participation in an activity, speak in an informal and conversational tone, and encourage your listeners to interrupt you with questions. None of those behaviors would be effective with an audience of 300, however. With that many listeners, activities and audience participation could easily become unmanageable, and an informal style of speaking would be inappropriate. Consider how you would feel, for example, if you were 1 of 300 people in the audience and the speaker asked each of you to introduce yourself.

AVAILABLE TIME

Have you ever been in a meeting in which time ran out but the speaker continued speaking anyway? To be effective, speakers must be aware of how long their presentations are supposed to last, and they must be realistic about how much material they can cover.

Suppose you're preparing a sales presentation about your financial firm's retirement planning products. If you have 45 minutes to speak, you might choose to discuss the 10 biggest mistakes people make when planning for retirement. If you have only 15 minutes, however, trying to cover the 10 biggest mistakes is probably a mistake in itself. In that context, you'll give a more effective speech by covering, say, the *three* biggest mistakes. Whatever the situation, your listeners are likely aware of how long your speech is supposed to last, and they may get restless and lose interest if you speak longer than you should. In contrast, if you can speak for slightly *less* than your allotted time, your audience is likely to be appreciative.

Some techniques work well with a small audience that would be ineffective with a large audience.

©kasto80/Getty Images

DISTRACTIONS

You probably know it's difficult to give anyone your undivided attention for very long. Your audience feels the same. Perhaps your speech is right before lunch, and your listeners are distracted by hunger. Maybe your microphone is faltering, and they can't hear you clearly.

You can address most such factors ahead of time if you're aware of them. If your speech is right before lunch, for instance, you can try to reschedule it for a time when your audience will be less distracted. If that's not an option, you can say to your listeners: "I know we're all eager to get to lunch, so if you'll give me your attention, I'll make my remarks as briefly as I can." Audiences will understand that certain factors, such as the time of your speech, may be beyond your control. They often will appreciate it, however, if you acknowledge their situation ("I know we're all eager to get to lunch") and pledge to do what you can to minimize their distraction ("I'll make my remarks as briefly as I can"). You can also avoid the distractions caused by malfunctioning equipment if you arrive early and test everything beforehand.

PRIOR KNOWLEDGE OF YOUR TOPIC

Finally, as suggested above, consider what your audience already knows about the topic of your speech. Armed with this information, you can avoid two mistakes: talking down to your listeners and talking over their heads. *Talking down* means telling people what they already know as if they didn't already know it. *Talking over people's heads* means assuming they have information or an understanding they don't actually have.

Let's say you're leading a workshop to teach college students about personal finance. If your listeners are business or accounting majors, they probably know the basics of how credit works, what a profit margin is, and how to reconcile a checking account statement. They would likely feel annoyed if you stopped to define a term such as *annual interest rate,* because they probably already know what that term means. You can cover more advanced topics with such an audience than you could with a group of students who lack training in the basics of finance. Many students without such training would feel frustrated if you used a term such as *annual interest rate* without defining it, because unlike the business students, they may not know what it means.

Tailoring your presentations to meet your listeners' needs and expectations requires considering not just who your listeners are but also what their situation is. Analyzing the audience and adapting your presentation to it can help you speak effectively and memorably.

CHAPTER WRAP-UP

Successful presentations benefit from careful planning and attention to detail. Here's a quick review of the chapter.

LO11.1 Name and define the primary forms of professional presentations.

- Informative speeches aim to teach listeners something they don't already know.
- Persuasive speeches appeal to listeners to think or act in a certain way.

- Introductory speeches inform listeners of a person's background and notable characteristics.
- Group presentations (including an oral report, symposium, colloquium, and forum) provide opportunities for groups of people to offer information or ideas.
- Special occasion speeches give honor and recognition to people, places, or significant points in time.

LO11.2 Summarize four steps for identifying appropriate presentation topics.

- Brainstorm to identify as many ideas as possible.
- Identify topics that are right for you and your background or expertise.
- Identify topics that are relevant and appropriate for your audience.
- Identify topics that are right for the occasion on which you are speaking.

LO11.3 Illustrate the strategies for analyzing an audience.

- Pay attention to who your listeners are, what they care about, and what their learning styles are.

- Take note of your listeners' demographic characteristics, including their age, sex, sexual orientation, culture, socioeconomic status, physical and mental characteristics, and political orientation.

LO11.4 Explain the strategies for analyzing a speaking context.

- Consider the reason why your audience is coming together to hear you speak.
- Pay attention to the size of the audience.
- Adapt to the time available for your speech.
- Take note of the demands competing for your listeners' attention.
- Attend to your audience's existing knowledge about your topic.

A LOOK BACK

Now, let's return to the opening scenario. Michelle has a speech the following day at a local community service club and has no idea what to say. She waited too long to start preparing and hasn't applied a systematic process. Instead of waiting until the last minute, she could have come up with some options fairly rapidly if she had identified the purpose of the presentation and applied the following process: (1) brainstorm potential topics; (2) identify topics that are right for her; (3) identify topics that are right for her audience; and (4) identify topics that are right for the occasion.

KEY TERMS

CHAPTER REVIEW QUESTIONS

1. When preparing a presentation, why is it useful to ask yourself about your motivation? **LO11.1**

2. What does a speaker attempt to accomplish in an informative speech? **LO11.1**

3. What must a speaker do with the material to give a successful informative speech? **LO11.1**

4. What does it mean to persuade someone? **LO11.1**

5. In an introductory speech, what is a speaker trying to accomplish? **LO11.1**

6. Compare and contrast an oral report, a symposium, a colloquium, and a forum. **LO11.1**

7. When might one give a special occasion speech? **LO11.1**

8. Where does a speaker present a eulogy? **LO11.1**

9. What is the goal of a toast? **LO11.1**

10. How are speeches of recognition, dedication, and commemoration similar, and how are they different? **LO11.1**

11. What does it mean to engage in brainstorming? Which two questions can guide your brainstorming about a speech topic? **LO11.2**

12. Why is it useful to consider which topics are right for you, your audience, and the occasion? **LO11.2**

13. What is audience analysis, and why is it valuable? **LO11.3**

14. How are visual, auditory, and kinesthetic learners different? How can you adapt your speaking style to each type of learner? **LO11.3**

15. Which demographic characteristics of an audience are advantageous to consider? **LO11.3**

16. In what ways might listeners' age, sex, or sexual orientation influence how you prepare or present a speech? **LO11.3**

17. Why is it useful to take into account listeners' culture, economic status, physical and mental capabilities, and political orientation when preparing or presenting a speech? **LO11.3**

18. How can you adapt your speech to the purpose of your presentation or the size of your audience? **LO11.4**

19. Why is it useful for a speaker to consider the available time and the listeners' distractions and prior knowledge when preparing a presentation? **LO11.4**

SKILL-BUILDING EXERCISES

Selecting an Appropriate Topic (LO11.2)

Suppose you've been invited to represent your company at a career fair for high school students, and you've been asked to make a 10-minute speech to the students who are attending. The choice of topic is left to you.

- Use the brainstorming technique to identify 10 or 12 potential topics.
- Narrow that list to 8 topics by considering which ones you know the most about.
- Narrow your remaining list to the 6 topics you think your audience of high school students would care most about.
- Narrow your remaining list to the 4 topics you consider most appropriate for the career fair.
- Finally, select the 2 topics from your list that you think are your best options. In a short paragraph, explain why these 2 topics are your best options.

Audience Analysis (LO11.3)

Suppose your supervisor at work is scheduled to deliver two key, high-profile speeches to large audiences next month. You know that the audience for the first speech will consist mainly of retired people of European American heritage and that the audience for the second speech will heavily comprise students from local universities.

- What are two (or more) pieces of advice you would give your supervisor about the speech to the retirees and the speech to the students, respectively?
- Imagine your supervisor has asked you to do some formal audience analysis before the speeches. Which

characteristics of the audiences will you seek to learn about, so that your supervisor can give the most effective speeches possible?

Introduce a Classmate (LO11.1, LO11.2)

Pair up with another student in class, and imagine that he or she is a new co-worker on your work team. Interview your classmate to find about his or her background and interests. Then, use what you learn to prepare a short speech in which you introduce your classmate to the rest of the class. Have your classmate do the same for you. Afterward, ask for feedback from other students or your instructor for ways to improve your introductory speech.

Practice a Special Occasion Speech (LO11.1, LO11.2)

Prepare either a speech of recognition, a speech of dedication, or a eulogy. Begin by writing a short paragraph describing the special occasion on which you might deliver such a speech, such as speaking at a colleague's retirement party, dedicating a new community center, or delivering remarks at a co-worker's memorial service. Based on the scenario you describe, prepare a 3- to 5-minute speech that would be appropriate for the occasion, taking note of the goals of each speech that are articulated in this chapter. Present your speech either to the rest of your class or to a small group of classmates or co-workers, and ask for constructive feedback.

Identifying Speaking Goals (LO11.1, LO11.3, LO11.4)

Imagine you're preparing to speak in front of your city council in favor of a proposal that would ban the use of plastic grocery bags in your community. Your primary argument is that because plastic grocery bags cannot be recycled, they are contributing to a growing litter problem in your city.

- Which type of speech (informative, persuasive, introductory, group, or special occasion) is called for in this situation?

- What specific steps could you take before your speech to analyze your likely audience for this event? How will you apply what you learn to your speech?

ENDNOTES

1. Breer, A. (2012, August 9). Peyton Manning's Denver Broncos built to win by John Elway. *NFL News*. Retrieved May 9, 2018, from http://www.nfl.com/news/story/0ap1000000047884/article/peyton-mannings-denver-broncos-built-to-win-by-john-elway.

2. Pomerantz, D., Shaddock, S., & Howard, C. (2017). The world's 100 most powerful women. *Forbes*. Retrieved from https://www.forbes.com/power-women/#224262025e25. The first and second most-powerful women on the list were Angela Merkel and Theresa May.

3. Gates, M. (2010, September). What nonprofits can learn from Coca-Cola. *TED*. Retrieved from https://www.ted.com/talks/melinda_french_gates_what_nonprofits_can_learn_from_coca_cola.

4. Ward, M. (2017, May 17). 3 things we learned from Sheryl Sandberg's Facebook Live with Melinda Gates. *CNBC*. Retrieved from https://www.cnbc.com/2016/10/07/lessons-from-sheryl-sandberg-facebook-live-with-melinda-gates.html.

5. Su, R., & Rounds, J. (2015). All STEM fields are not created equal: People and things interests explain gender disparities across STEM fields. *Frontiers in Psychology, 6*, 1–20; see also Lippa, R. A. (2010). Gender differences in personality and interests: When, where, and why? *Social and Personality Psychology Compass, 4*, 1098–1110; Su, R., Rounds, J., & Armstrong, P. I. (2009). Men and things, women and people: A meta-analysis of sex differences in interests. *Psychological Bulletin, 135*, 859–884.

6. Konrad, A. M., Ritchie, J. E., Lieb, P., & Corrigall, E. (2000). Sex differences and similarities in job attribute preferences: A meta-analysis. *Psychological Bulletin, 126*, 593–641.

7. United States Census Bureau. (2011, March 24). 2010 Census shows America's diversity. Retrieved December 8, 2017, from https://www.census.gov/newsroom/releases/archives/2010_census/cb11-cn125.html.

8. McNeal, G. S. (2012, February 18). ESPN uses "chink in the armor" line twice. Update: ESPN fires one employee, suspends another. *Forbes*. Retrieved May 9, 2018, from https://www.forbes.com/sites/gregorymcneal/2012/02/18/espn-uses-chink-in-the-armor-line-twice-did-linsanity-just-go-racist.

9. DeJohn, I., & Kennedy, J. (2012, February 20). Jeremy Lin headline slur was "honest mistake," fired ESPN editor Anthony Federico claims. *NY Daily News*. Retrieved May 9, 2018, from http://www.nydailynews.com/entertainment/tv-movies/jeremy-lin-slur-honest-mistake-fired-espn-editor-anthony-federico-claims-article-1.1025566.

10. DeNavas-Walt, C., & Proctor, B. D. (2014). *U.S. Census Bureau current population reports, P60–252: Income and poverty levels in the United States: 2014*. Washington, DC: U.S. Government Printing Office.

11. Zwick, R. (2013). Is the SAT a "wealth test"? The link between educational achievement and socioeconomic status. In R. Zwick (Ed.), *Rethinking the SAT: The future of standardized testing in university admissions* (pp. 203–216). New York, NY: Routledge.

12. Vo, L. T. (2012, October 1). How income divides Democrats, Republicans, and Independents. *Planet Money*. Retrieved May 9, 2018, from https://www.npr.org/sections/money/2012/09/26/161841771/how-income-divides-democrats-republicans-and-independents.

Learning Objectives

After reading this chapter, you should be able to do the following:

LO12.1   Illustrate purpose statements and thesis statements.

LO12.2   Identify the characteristics of main points and the options for arranging them in a speech.

LO12.3   Differentiate the goals of a compelling introduction and conclusion.

LO12.4   Explain the role of transitions in a speech.

CHAPTER 12

Planning and Crafting Presentations

Janis saw her colleague Vito across the room and walked over for a quick chat.

"Hey Vito, thanks for attending my speech at the finance seminar last week."

"Happy to be there. I thought that was a great speech and a great seminar. Great job, Janis!"

"Vito, do you mind telling me what you really think? Do you think it changed anyone's minds in the audience?"

Vito paused. "Well, yeah, I'm sure it influenced a lot of people."

Janis continued, "What message do you think it got across?"

Vito replied, "Janis, honestly I can't remember your presentation that well. There were so many speakers throughout the day. I just remember you did a great job."

Vito's difficulty recalling Janis's speech is actually not too surprising. Most speeches are mostly forgotten after a short period of time. What can you do to ensure people remember and are influenced by your speeches?

LO12.1

Illustrate purpose statements and thesis statements.

Articulate Your Purpose and Thesis

An old proverb says, "By failing to prepare, you are preparing to fail." Indeed, success in many endeavors relies on solid planning, and business speaking is no exception. One of the first steps in planning a successful speech is choosing the message. That is, once you've selected your topic, you must consider what you want to say about it.

Suppose your topic is doing business in Australia. You could use your presentation to teach your audience members about the nation's political climate or cultural history. You could try to persuade them to visit the country's securities exchange. You could entertain them with stories of U.S. businesspeople making the transition to Australian life. The point is that Australia is a broad topic you could address in many possible ways. To be effective, you'll need to narrow the scope of your speech by choosing what, in particular, you want to address. That process has two steps: clarifying the **specific purpose** of your speech—that is, the main goal for your presentation—and crystalizing the main message, or **thesis**, of your speech. Let's look at each step.

DRAFT A PURPOSE STATEMENT

We saw in Chapter 11 that a speech can have one of several *general* goals, such as to inform, to persuade, to introduce, and to give honor. The first step in preparing your speech is to identify your specific purpose.

Let's say your topic is web design. Consider the range of specific goals you might have. You could choose to describe the various web hosting services, demonstrate the process of cropping photos for a web page, or explain the similarities and differences between static and dynamic websites and argue that one is superior. You probably can't meet all these goals in the same speech, so you'll select one. You can articulate that specific goal in the form of a purpose statement. A **purpose statement** is a declaration of your *specific* goal for your speech. It expresses precisely what you want to accomplish during your presentation.

To draft a purpose statement, first identify your topic and your general goal. Sticking with your topic of web design, let's say your general goal is to inform. Next,

Drafting purpose and thesis statements is essential in planning your presentation.

©Viacheslav Iakobchuk/123RF

suppose you decide to teach your audience how to place advertisements on your website. Now you can articulate your purpose statement in this way:

Purpose statement: *Demonstrate the process of placing advertisements on a website.*

Suppose instead that you want to inform your audience about web page templates. You might express your purpose statement in this way:

Purpose statement: *Teach listeners the differences among five web page templates.*

Notice that each of these purpose statements reflects the general goal of your speech, which is to inform. At the same time, however, each makes your general goal more focused and specific.

What if your goal is to persuade rather than to inform? In that case, you will need to consider exactly what you want to persuade your listeners to think or do. Once again, you can use your purpose statement to make your general goal more specific. For example, you may want to persuade your listeners that dynamic web pages are more likely to attract business than static web pages. In that case, you might articulate your purpose statement in this way:

Purpose statement: *Persuade listeners that dynamic web pages are superior to static web pages.*

Or suppose you want to encourage listeners to use only standard type styles and fonts because they are easier to read. You might articulate your purpose statement in this way:

Purpose statement: *Persuade listeners to use only standard type styles and fonts on a website.*

Notice again that each purpose statement reflects the general goal—to persuade—but makes the goal specific.

What about other goals? Suppose you are asked to introduce the guest speaker at your company's midyear retreat. You could express your purpose statement in this way:

Purpose statement: *Introduce Denise McAdams by telling the story of how she and I first met.*

Finally, imagine you're giving a toast at your boss's retirement party. You might articulate your purpose statement in this way:

Purpose statement: *Bring recognition to my boss's career by describing her proudest accomplishments.*

A focused purpose statement can launch the creation of a great speech. It also makes it much easier to create a workable outline for your presentation. Indeed, your purpose statement will help you plan the content of your speech in ways we explore below.

To develop a strong purpose statement, follow these guidelines:

- *Be specific.* A purpose statement such as "Teach my audience about the steel industry" is vague because that industry has so many facets. It won't help you choose the content of your speech as effectively as a sharper, more specific purpose statement, such as "Teach my audience how Andrew Carnegie was instrumental in building the U.S. steel industry."

- *Be selective.* Focus your purpose statement on one specific goal for your speech. A statement such as "Persuade my listeners that government should provide universal health care and that the free market economy hurts working families" is too broad because it expresses more than one distinct purpose. Limiting your purpose statement to one goal will help you organize your speech effectively.

- *Be declarative.* Write your purpose statement as a directive to yourself, such as "Explain the most important steps in creating a Twitter account." Simply posing a question, such as "How does someone create a Twitter account?" doesn't indicate as clearly what you plan to accomplish in your speech.

CAREER TIP
Provide Value with Your Thesis

Nancy Duarte got a D in English and a C- in Speech Communication in college, yet she has risen to become among the most well-known and influential speech designers. She regularly coaches leaders and executives to deliver high-stakes speeches (she was the chief designer of speaking portions in Al Gore's Academy Award–winning documentary *An Inconvenient Truth*), speaks about how to influence others through presentations (her TED Talk "The Secret Structure of Great Talks" has been viewed more than 1.3 million times), and founded and leads one of the largest presentation-design firms in the country.

What's her secret? Providing value. She believes effective speeches must have a *big idea*, which means you take a position (your thesis statement) and explain why it matters (why it's valuable to your audience). No matter how well planned your speech or how polished your delivery, the most important metric of success is whether your audience found value in the speech. On an even broader level, providing value is the key to all work with clients. Nancy explains that the success of her firm is measured by whether clients are successful when they deliver speeches and whether they are happy with her team's work.

Nancy Duarte

©Peter DaSilva/The New York Times/Redux

SOURCES: Duarte, N. (2012). *HBR guide to persuasive presentations*. Boston, MA: Harvard Business Press; Cook, J. (n.d.). Nancy Duarte on failure, bootstrapping, and the power of better presentations. 99U. Retrieved from http://99u.com/articles/28337/nancy-duarte-on-failure-bootstrapping-and-the-power-of-presenting-better.

Now you're almost ready to begin constructing your speech. One task remains, however—to articulate the message you want to get across. You can express that message in the form of a thesis statement, as we'll see next.

DRAFT A THESIS STATEMENT

During the 2009 Super Bowl, the price of a 30-second television commercial was a staggering $3 million.[1] That high price prompted the Miller Brewing Company to run an advertisement lasting only 1 second, just long enough for the announcer to mention the name of the product. Suppose *you* had only *one sentence* in which to deliver an entire speech. What would your sentence be? What single specific message would you want your listeners to remember? You can answer that question by drafting a **thesis statement**.

Let's say you are preparing a presentation about the alternative medicine industry and your purpose statement is, "Teach about the effectiveness of herbal supplements." Before you develop your speech, consider what you want your takeaway message to be. You might articulate your message in this way:

> **Thesis statement**: *Although sales of herbal supplements are growing, medical research shows they are no more effective than placebos.*

As another example, suppose your topic is personal finance, and your purpose statement is "Persuade my listeners to invest in gold." You could convey your message in this way:

> **Thesis statement:** *Because gold prices rise even in a weak economy, investing in gold is a sound financial decision.*

Notice how each of those thesis statements expresses the *message* of the speech. That is, it identifies what you want your listeners to take away from your presentation. With a strong thesis statement, you'll find it much easier to construct the rest of your speech because you'll know exactly what to say to your audience.

To develop a strong thesis statement, follow these guidelines:

- *Be concrete.* Good thesis statements should be concrete, not vague or abstract. For an informative speech about socially responsible investing, a concrete thesis statement is "Millennial investors prefer to invest in companies with socially and environmentally responsible practices." In contrast, the thesis statement "Socially responsible investing is popular" is vague because it doesn't specify what socially responsible investing means or with whom it is popular.

- *Make a statement.* Frame your thesis statement as a sentence rather than a question. In a persuasive speech calling on customers to protect themselves against identity theft, the thesis statement "Using an identity protection plan is the most effective protection against identity theft" works well because it declares the point of your speech. In comparison, "What should people do to protect themselves against identity theft?" doesn't indicate the point you plan to make, only the topic you intend to discuss.

- *Be flexible.* Drafting your thesis statement will help you organize your outline and your research. Remain open, however, to revising it as you work. During your research, for instance, you may uncover details that warrant tweaking or even rewriting your thesis statement, so good public speakers stay open to that possibility.

- *Be truthful.* Ethical practice requires you to believe in the truth of your thesis statement so you don't knowingly mislead your audience. That doesn't just mean avoiding claims you know to be false. Also avoid exaggerating your claims beyond what the evidence warrants.

Table 12.1 presents examples of good thesis statements for three different speech topics. Armed with a topic, a purpose statement, and a thesis statement, you are ready to build your presentation. In the next sections, we'll explore the organization of a speech and see how to create a useful outline.

SHARPEN YOUR SKILLS

Purpose and Thesis Statements

Select a topic you find interesting. Write a purpose statement and thesis statement for an informative speech about that topic. Then write a purpose statement and thesis statement for a persuasive speech about the same topic. In a brief journal entry, describe how your purpose and thesis statements differ for the two speeches.

FOCUS ON ETHICS
When Exaggeration Becomes Deception

One of your first assignments as a new sales rep for a health and beauty products company is to prepare a presentation to persuade drugstores to carry your brand of antibacterial soap. While gathering evidence for your speech, you discover five studies that have tested the soap's effectiveness. In two studies, the soap was effective at killing only about 20 percent of the bacteria tested, and the other three studies showed nothing but negative results. You want to win the business, though, so you focus on the research that supports your argument and begin your sales pitch by claiming, "Clinical tests have repeatedly proven that our antibacterial soap is effective at killing dangerous household bacteria."

CONSIDER THIS: Given the evidence, would you consider this claim to be an example of exaggeration? In what ways is it truthful, and in what ways is it misleading? Even if everything in the claim is literally true, how might the claim still be considered deceptive?

Table 12.1 **Writing an Effective Thesis Statement**

Topic	Goal	Purpose Statement	Thesis Statement
Human rights for sexual minorities	To persuade	Persuade listeners that businesses should take a more proactive role in ensuring human rights for sexual minorities.	U.S. companies should refuse to do business in countries that impose capital punishment or life imprisonment for homosexual or bisexual behavior.
iPhone apps	To inform	Teach listeners about the most popular iPhone apps for personal finance.	Personal finance apps such as LearnVest and Level Money help users monitor their money, create budgets, prioritize their financial goals, and track their spending.
New high school library	To dedicate	Mark the opening of the new high school library and acknowledge the corporate sponsors who made it possible.	Thanks to the contributions of multiple business and community partners, a new high school library is now available to meet the needs of our students.

LO12.2

Identify the characteristics of main points and the options for arranging them in a speech.

Organize the Body of Your Speech

Even if you have a fascinating topic and a compelling thesis statement, your audience will quickly lose interest if your presentation lacks coherence and order. You may know this if you've had the experience of listening to a speaker who jumped from point to point and left you wondering where the speech was supposed to be going. Research shows that when speakers present material in an organized, coherent manner, their listeners are more motivated to learn,[2] take more detailed notes,[3] and recall more of the material than when the material is disorganized.[4]

This section focuses on organizing the body of the speech, where you make your specific points and subpoints. Later in the chapter, we will discuss ways to craft memorable introductions and conclusions, and to use transitions strategically.

DETERMINE YOUR MAIN POINTS

The body of your speech is the longest part of your presentation, because it is where you will deliver the substance of your message. To organize the body of your speech, identify the main points you want to address. A **main point** is a statement expressing a specific idea or theme related to the speech topic. Most speeches have between two and five main points; if you have more than five, your audience may have difficulty remembering them. As you'll see in this section, you want to ensure that your main points are written as complete sentences that are related, distinct, and equally important.

Main points should be written as complete sentences. Using complete sentences for your main points helps you think in complete thoughts and will assist you in rehearsing your speech for presentation.

Suppose you're preparing an informative speech about becoming a federal law-enforcement agent. Here's an example of how *not* to construct main points:

1. Prospective agents must be U.S. citizens.
2. How old do prospective agents have to be?
3. 20/20 eyesight.

Only the first and second points are complete sentences, and the second point is a question, not a statement. The third point is a sentence fragment. Compare them with a properly constructed set of points:

1. Prospective agents must be U.S. citizens.
2. Prospective agents must be between 21 and 37 years of age.
3. Prospective agents must have 20/20 eyesight.

These complete sentences are much better examples of how to construct main points.

Main points should be related.   Suppose you wanted to draft an informative speech about the FICO score—a widely used personal credit score calculated by the Fair Isaac Corporation—using the following purpose and thesis statements:

Purpose statement: *Describe the purpose and importance of FICO scores.*

Thesis statement: *FICO scores are a useful index of a person's creditworthiness.*

You might then propose the following main points:

Main point 1: *A FICO score is a number between 300 and 850 that represents an individual's creditworthiness.*

Main point 2: *A person's FICO score is calculated based on his or her payment history, debt burden, credit history, and other indicators of risk.*

Main point 3: *Most lenders use an applicant's FICO score as a factor when deciding whether to extend credit.*

Notice that the main points relate to one another because they all address the speech topic, the FICO score. The first main point defines what FICO scores are, the second indicates where they come from, and the third identifies why they matter. You don't want any of your points to seem out of place or unrelated to the topic of the presentation. For example, suppose you had proposed the following main points:

Main point 1: *A FICO score is a number between 300 and 850 that represents an individual's creditworthiness.*

Main point 2: *An individual's FICO score is based on his or her payment history, debt burden, credit history, and other indicators of risk.*

Main point 3: *The average U.S. adult now carries more credit card debt than ever before.*

The third main point may interest you, but it does not relate to the purpose statement and thesis statement of your speech. If you want to keep it in your outline, you need to expand your purpose and thesis statements to include information about average credit card debt. Otherwise, you are better off replacing the third main point with one that better relates to your topic.

Main points should be distinct.   Although they all address the same topic, each main point in the preceding example expresses a distinct idea: what FICO scores are, where they come from, and why they matter. Suppose you proposed the following main points:

Main point 1: *An individual's FICO score is based on his or her payment history.*

Main point 2: *An individual's FICO score is based on his or her debt burden.*

Identifying the right pattern for your speech will help you reach your purpose.

©alexsl/iStock/Getty Images

These two statements are probably not different enough to justify being separate points, so you can combine them into one main point:

Main point: *An individual's FICO score is based on his or her payment history and debt burden.*

Main points should be equally important. Ideally, you want to give each of your main points approximately the same amount of time, so they should all be equally important. Let's say you have three main points but plan to spend 95 percent of your time discussing the first two. In that case, perhaps you actually have only two main points, so you might delete the third. Or perhaps you aren't devoting sufficient time to the third point, in which case you should spend less time discussing the first two.

ORGANIZE YOUR MAIN POINTS STRATEGICALLY

In addition to being related, distinct, and equally important, your main points should be organized in a pattern that makes sense for your topic. Consider which of the following patterns might work best for your speech:

Arranging points by topic: When you adopt a **topic pattern**, you organize your main points to represent different categories. Let's say you are preparing an informative speech about the travel and tourism industry. You might include separate main points about different aspects of that industry, with an outline that looks like this:

1. Lodging operations
2. Transportation services
3. Food and beverage operations
4. Activities

If your points don't lend themselves to established categories, you can create categories of your own. In a speech about co-workers, for instance, you might distinguish various types of co-workers along these lines:

1. Good-time co-workers: those you always have fun with
2. Counselor co-workers: those with whom you share your problems
3. Downer co-workers: those who frequently put you in a bad mood
4. Connected co-workers: those who seem to know everything about everyone

Arranging points by time: A second option for organizing your main points is to use a **time pattern**, which means arranging them in chronological order. This option is particularly useful when you are describing the steps of a process, such as designing a business plan:

1. Describe your proposed business.
2. Conduct a market analysis.
3. Make financial projections.
4. Choose your management structure.

A time pattern is also useful when your main points describe a historical sequence of events, such as in this outline of a speech about the events leading to the decline of the mining industry:

1. The industry failed to incorporate innovations to make itself sustainable.
2. New technology took over functions that workers previously performed.

3. High-profile accidents raised awareness of how dangerous mining is.
4. The pool of applicants for mining jobs steadily declined.

Arranging points by space: A **space pattern** organizes your main points according to geographic or physical areas. In a speech about the effects of industry on the earth's atmosphere, you might arrange your points to cover the various atmospheric layers as they exist from the ground up:

1. Troposphere
2. Stratosphere
3. Mesosphere
4. Thermosphere
5. Magnetosphere

Arranging points by cause and effect: In a **cause-and-effect pattern**, you organize your points so they describe the causes of an event or a phenomenon and then identify its consequences. If you wanted to discuss the effects of acid rain, you could arrange your main points (and subpoints, which are described in the next section) in this way:

1. Causes of acid rain
   a. Natural causes, such as volcanic eruptions
   b. Human-made causes, such as industrial pollution
2. Effects of acid rain
   a. Effects on plants and wildlife
   b. Effects on surface waters and aquatic animals
   c. Effects on human health

Arranging points by problem and solution: A **problem-solution pattern** is similar to a cause-and-effect pattern, except that you are organizing your points so they describe a problem and then offer one or more solutions for it. Notice that pattern in this example of a speech about data breaches:

1. Data breaches are a substantial problem.
   a. Sensitive or confidential data has potentially been viewed or used by unauthorized individuals or entities.
   b. The prevalence of data breaches is increasing.
2. There are several steps you should take if you are a victim.
   a. You should change your passwords immediately.
   b. You should watch for suspicious email messages.
   c. You should check your credit reports for any discrepancies.

You can probably see why some ways of organizing your main points are likely to work better than others. Consider what your main points are and the way in which they are related to one another to select the organizational method that's best for your speech.

USE SUBPOINTS TO SUPPORT YOUR MAIN POINTS

As you explain each main point in your speech, you will typically make additional, more specific points to support it. Those supporting points are called *subordinate points*, or **subpoints**. Subpoints can clarify the meaning of a main point, provide examples, offer evidence, and elaborate on your argument. You will usually incorporate your supporting materials—such as quotations, definitions, and statistics—into your subpoints. You can have several subpoints for each main point, and your subpoints can even have subpoints of their own, which are sometimes called *sub-subpoints*.

Figure 12.1 **Complete Outline for a Speech**

Breaking your speech into main points, subpoints, and sub-subpoints helps organize your thoughts and improve the flow.

Specific purpose: Teach my audience about the practice of public relations.

Thesis statement: Public relations is the practice of creating and maintaining a favorable public image for an organization.

Main point 1: The practice of public relations relies on multiple tactics.

- **Subpoint 1.1:** Public relations professionals can use audience targeting.
    - **Sub-subpoint 1.1a:** An organization's target audience is identified.
    - **Sub-subpoint 1.1b:** Messages are tailored to the needs and priorities of that audience.
- **Subpoint 1.2:** Public relations professionals can use social media marketing.
    - **Sub-subpoint 1.2a:** Social media tools such as Facebook and Twitter can highlight an organization's favorable qualities.
    - **Sub-subpoint 1.2b:** Blogs provide more in-depth information about an organization's activities and attributes.
- **Subpoint 1.3:** Public relations professionals can use media events.
    - **Sub-subpoint 1.3a:** A media event is an activity conducted to generate media publicity.
    - **Sub-subpoint 1.3b:** Media events include news conferences, award ceremonies, and demonstrations of new products.

Main point 2: Public relations professionals build relationships with multiple stakeholders.

- **Subpoint 2.1:** Public relations professionals build relationships with the media.
    - **Subpoint 2.1a:** Public relations professionals connect regularly with traditional media outlets.
    - **Subpoint 2.1b:** Public relations professionals work with nontraditional media outlets such as influential bloggers and popular social media figures.
- **Subpoint 2.2:** Public relations professionals build relationships with non-media external stakeholders.
    - **Subpoint 2.2a:** Public relations professionals build sustainable relationships in the communities where their organizations are located.
    - **Subpoint 2.2b:** Public relations professionals inform and collaborate with policy-makers, including members of regulatory agencies and legislators.
    - **Subpoint 2.2c:** Public relations professionals form two-way communication channels with customers, clients, and the public at large.
- **Subpoint 2.3:** Public relations professionals build relationships with internal stakeholders.
    - **Subpoint 23a:** Public relations professionals provide news and announcements to employees.
    - **Subpoint 23b:** Public relation professionals create internal communication systems that ensure employees can share ideas and voice concerns with management.

Like main points, subpoints should generally be written as complete sentences and express only one idea at a time. Let's look at Figure 12.1 of a complete outline for a speech about public relations that includes subpoints.

In Figure 12.1, subpoints 1.1, 1.2, and 1.3 each provide more detailed examples of the claim made in main point 1. Sub-subpoints 1.1a and 1.1b provide more detailed examples of the claim made in subpoint 1.1.

In each case, the subpoints do their job of reinforcing or clarifying the points under which they fall. They therefore conform to the **rule of subordination**, a principle stating that the broadest, most important claims come first in the form of main points, and the lesser, more specific claims follow in the form of subpoints. This example also complies with the **rule of division**, which explains that whenever there is one subpoint, there must be at least one more.

Together, the main points and subpoints make up the heart of your speech. Surrounding the body of your speech will be its introduction and conclusion.

Creating a Compelling Introduction and Conclusion

LO12.3
Differentiate the goals of a compelling introduction and conclusion.

Regardless of the substance of your main points, the success of your presentation will depend heavily on your ability to introduce and conclude it in a compelling manner.

CRAFT A MEMORABLE INTRODUCTION

You get only one chance to make a good first impression. The same is true when you're preparing a speech. A good presentation starts with an introduction that accomplishes three goals: It captures your listeners' interest in your topic, it helps you build your credibility, and it previews the points you plan to make.

Capture your listeners' attention.   First, your introduction should grab your listeners' attention and arouse their interest in your topic. One way to accomplish that goal is to open with a story that will spark your audience's curiosity. Imagine a sales pitch that begins with the following:

> I was running late that morning, so I threw my belongings in my backpack and got ready to rush out of my house. I set my coffee on the kitchen counter while I searched frantically for my car keys. No sooner had I found them than I heard car alarms all around the neighborhood going off. I saw my coffee mug fall to the ground and shatter. I felt like I was standing on the back of a moving flatbed truck. Then, as quickly as it had started, it was over. It took me a few moments to realize I had just experienced my first earthquake.

That story would be an effective start to a sales pitch about earthquake preparedness because it begins with an easily relatable experience ("I was running late that morning"), describes unusual events (coffee cup shattering, floor shaking), and reveals the explanation for those events (an earthquake) only at the end.

Another way to spark your listeners' interest in your topic is to use statistics that illustrate its magnitude. Consider the following example from a speech for health insurance executives:

> Children in the United States are dealing with a growing problem, literally speaking. Over 9 million of them are overweight or obese. That's more people than the populations of Los Angeles, Chicago, San Antonio, and Detroit *put together.* Unfortunately, the problem is getting worse. In the past three decades, the childhood obesity rate has more than tripled for children aged 6 to 11. Obesity raises the risks of a range of health problems, including diabetes, hypertension, and heart disease. The annual cost of treating obesity-related disorders for children is nearly $150 million.

This introduction uses a few well-chosen statistics to illustrate the gravity of the problem of childhood obesity. It also provides an example to help the audience interpret the number of obese children. Simply saying obesity affects 9 million children may be ineffective if listeners aren't sure whether that's a large or small group. Explaining that the number exceeds the combined population of four major U.S. cities gives them a context for understanding its importance.

You get only one chance at a first impression for your speeches.

©Michail_Petrov-96/Getty Images

SHARPEN YOUR SKILLS

Finding and Using Statistics

Identify a topic for an informative speech, such as the student debt crisis, illegal immigration, or the worldwide digital divide. Locate three different statistics you could use in an introduction to generate interest in that topic. Then, write an introduction using these statistics.

In addition to using a story or a statistic to generate interest in your topic, you can use any of the following techniques:

* *Present a quotation.* Many speakers capture attention with a well-phrased quotation relevant to their topic—for instance: "As former U.S. senator Elizabeth Dole once said, 'Power is a positive force if it is used for positive purposes.'[5] Today, I'd like to discuss some of the many ways our organization can use power to improve the lives of others."

* *Tell a joke.* Opening your speech with a joke can be a particularly effective way to capture your listeners' attention, put them at ease, and generate positive feelings about you. Always make certain that your humor is appropriate for your audience and for the occasion and that it won't be interpreted as offensive.

* *Pose a question.* Beginning your speech with a question is a great way to get your audience thinking about your topic. You could ask something you want listeners to answer, such as "By show of hands, how many of you have ever been involved in a lawsuit?" You can also pose a *rhetorical question,* one you want your listeners to think about but not respond to—for instance: "Why do you suppose so many people struggle with work/life balance?"

* *Cite an opinion.* Provocative opinions from well-known people can also get your listeners' attention—for example: "Novelist Herman Melville once said that it is better to fail in originality than to succeed in imitation. In this presentation, I'll be exploring some of the reasons he may be exactly right."

* *Startle your listeners.* Saying or doing something unexpected or unusual can be an effective way to capture the attention of your audience. Begin your speech in a foreign language, for example.

* *Note the occasion.* Particularly if you are speaking to give honor to a person, place, or event, you can generate attention by noting the importance of the occasion—for instance: "We have come together today to honor the extraordinary career of our CEO as she begins her retirement."

* *Identify something familiar.* An excellent way to establish rapport with your listeners is to refer to something with which they are familiar. For example, "As I was driving in this morning, I was a little unsure of my directions, which simply said to 'turn left after the big red house.' Once I got to town, though, it made perfect sense!" By noting something with which your audience is familiar—in this case, the smallness of the town—you make a personal connection with your listeners.

* *Incorporate technology.* As you present a quotation or cite an opinion, show a photo of the person you're referencing. If you're telling a suspenseful story, play suspenseful music in the background.

Build your credibility.   A speaker's credibility is called his or her **ethos.** Ethos doesn't belong directly to a speaker; rather, judgments about a speaker's ethos belong to the audience. Therefore, your introduction is an opportunity to persuade your audience to find you credible.

Classical treatments of ethos give it three components.[6] You can think of them as three strategies for building credibility during your introduction:

1. *Wisdom:* Speakers are perceived as credible if they demonstrate their knowledge of or experience with the topics about which they speak. Suppose the topic of your speech is also your undergraduate major. You could mention that as a way to demonstrate your intellect and wisdom about that subject.

2. *Virtue:* Speakers who attain excellence are perceived as credible. The key to demonstrating such virtue is to highlight the quality of the work you put into your speech. For example, if you did exceptionally thorough research for your presentation, point that out. Did you make a special effort to land a key interview, for instance? If your listeners perceive that you care about the quality of the work you are presenting, they are likely to find you credible.

3. *Goodwill:* Speakers are perceived as credible if they seem to care about the audience. Speaking with sincerity will lead audience members to believe in your goodwill toward them. If listeners think you are being dishonest with them or attempting to mislead them, they are not likely to assume you are concerned about their well-being.

You don't necessarily have to highlight all three components—wisdom, virtue, and goodwill—in your introduction. Incorporating those most relevant to the circumstances of your speech will help you persuade your listeners that you are a credible speaker, one whose words deserve their trust. Figure 12.2 recaps the three components of ethos.

Preview your main points.   Once you have aroused your listeners' interest in your topic and highlighted your credibility, your final goal in the introduction is to preview the points you plan to make in your speech. A preview will help your listeners pay attention to the body of your speech by identifying ahead of time what they should listen for. Previews can be simple and straightforward, like the following example from a speech about business internships:

> Today I'd like to talk about the importance of providing internship opportunities for college students. First, I'll explain how participating in an internship helps students intellectually and professionally. Then I'll discuss the benefits that organizations experience when they offer internships. Finally, I'll offer some ideas for how our company can establish a strong and viable internship program.

Figure 12.2

Three Components of Ethos

Build your credibility by displaying virtue, wisdom, and/ or goodwill.

©Inspirestock Inc./Alamy Stock Photo

Notice that this preview clearly identifies the major ideas the speaker plans to address. It isn't necessary to explain or justify them during the preview; that's the purpose of the body of the speech. Rather, it's only necessary to identify the points you intend to make. If you put your preview at the end of your introduction, it will also serve as a lead-in to the body of your speech.

Some speeches focus on topics to which listeners will be sensitive, perhaps because they are uncomfortable or embarrassing to talk about. When you select such a topic as the focus of your speech, it's important to frame your introduction accordingly, as the "People First" box explains.

CREATE AN EFFECTIVE CONCLUSION

The conclusion is the last part of your speech that listeners will hear, and to be sure they remember you, you want it to stand out. Make sure that your concluding remarks accomplish four goals: signal the end of the speech, summarize your main points, create a memorable moment, and end with a call to action.

Signal the end of your speech.   The first goal of your conclusion is to signal to your audience that you are bringing your presentation to a close. You can do this verbally or nonverbally.

PEOPLE **FIRST**

Introducing a Sensitive Topic

IMAGINE THIS: Many potential speech topics can be somewhat sensitive for your audience. We tend to find some issues uncomfortable to think about, such as dealing with significant debt or end-of-life planning. Other topics can be embarrassing to talk about, such as having certain types of health problems. On occasion, a topic can be sensitive because of what is happening in the environment, such as speaking about suicide shortly after a co-worker has taken his own life.

Now, consider this: Just because a topic is sensitive doesn't mean you shouldn't choose it as the focus of your speech. However, it is helpful to take a "people first" approach by introducing that topic in a caring, sensitive way. Consider these strategies:

- Acknowledge that your topic is sensitive, and recognize why. One of the worst ways to introduce a sensitive topic is to ignore the fact that it's sensitive and hope your audience doesn't notice. Instead, be upfront with listeners: "I know it isn't easy to talk about being in debt. Owing a lot of money can be scary. Nonetheless, I plan to show how having a personal financial plan can ease the immediate stress on you and your family and allow you to anticipate a future that's debt-free."

- As always, preview what you plan to say, in this case especially so listeners know all your points will be relevant and worthy of their attention. In other words, you won't be asking them to think about an uncomfortable topic for trivial reasons.

- Try to avoid euphemisms, which are mild or indirect substitutes for terms we find too harsh or blunt. For instance, a health care professional talking about end-of-life planning might use the euphemism "kick the bucket" in place of "death." Although euphemisms can reduce audience discomfort, they can also trivialize the topic, reducing the impact of your speech.

We do listeners a disservice by sticking only to topics that are comfortable and "safe." Nonetheless, when you have chosen a topic that you expect to be sensitive for your audience, it helps to introduce that topic in a caring and competent manner.

THINK ABOUT THIS: In what situations might you be called upon to speak about a particularly sensitive topic? What can you do to manage your own discomfort about that topic? Why is it beneficial to introduce such topics in a conscientious, caring manner?

Verbal statements are direct ways to begin concluding your speech. You might make a transition statement, such as

- *In conclusion . . .*
- *In summary . . .*
- *As I bring my speech to a close . . .*

Nonverbal behaviors like these can also signal that you are nearing the end of your presentation:

- If you have moved around during the speech, return to the physical place where you began.
- Slow your speaking rate and lower the pitch of your voice.
- Smile and noticeably pause at the end of your last point.

Provide a summary of your main points. Besides signaling the end of your speech, your conclusion should summarize your central message. Effective speakers often repeat their thesis statement and then summarize the main points they made in support of it.

Suppose you're concluding an informative speech about the dramatic increase in U.S. consumers declaring bankruptcy. How might you summarize? Here's one example:

> As I've explained, personal bankruptcies are on the rise in the United States for three primary reasons. First, consumer debt as a percentage of personal income is growing. Second, people are paying more money out of pocket for medical expenses not covered by insurance. Finally, changes in bankruptcy laws have made the process of declaring bankruptcy easier than before. Although bankruptcy exposes people to some significant limitations, more and more people are deciding to pursue it.

This conclusion begins with the primary idea of the speech, that personal bankruptcies are increasing in the United States. It then repeats the three main points of the speech (the growing amount of consumer debt, the rising costs of health care, the changes in bankruptcy laws) and restates the central idea even more strongly (more and more people are filing for bankruptcy). By accomplishing these three tasks, the conclusion clearly and powerfully summarizes the central message.

Create a memorable moment.   You can probably think of movies that had memorable endings; although you may not recall every detail of the plots, you remember how they ended. Creating a *memorable moment* in your conclusion will similarly help your listeners remember your presentation.

One strategy is to end with humor. If your concluding lines make the audience laugh, they are likely to remember your speech—and remember it positively. Another option is to return to a story you told earlier and provide further details. For instance, if you spoke of someone affected by the issue you're addressing, your conclusion could describe how the person dealt with the issue and how he or she is doing now.

Finally, many great speeches end on an emotionally dramatic note. In 2009, on the steps of the U.S. Capitol Building in Washington, DC, Barack Obama concluded his inaugural address with this dramatic appeal:

> America, in the face of our common dangers, in this winter of our hardship, let us remember these timeless words. With hope and virtue, let us brave once more the icy currents, and endure what storms may come. Let it be said by our children's children that when we were tested, we refused to let this journey end, that we did not turn back nor did we falter. And with eyes fixed on the horizon and God's grace upon us, we carried forth that great gift of freedom and delivered it safely to future generations. Thank you, God bless you, and God bless the United States of America.

Whether you use humor, surprise, or drama, creating a memorable moment in your conclusion will help ensure that your audience remembers your presentation.

End with a call to action.   Whether your purpose is to inform or persuade, you'll often conclude with a direct appeal to your audience to take action. For example, if you're showing your audience how to build a website, you might conclude with a statement such as "You can learn more tips about driving traffic to your website at my blog. If you take out your phone, you can sign up right now for my free online newsletter." Or, if you're talking about FICO scores, you might end with advice such as "By law, all U.S.

Chris Anderson, head of TED Talks, suggests that making a call to action is an effective way to conclude a speech.

©Brent N. Clarke/Getty Images

TECH TIP

Using Technology to Improve Your Nonverbal Communication

Throughout the speech and presentation chapters, you read about various ways to use nonverbal communication to reach your presentation goals. But can you really change or improve your nonverbal communication? The answer is yes! Before you ever give a speech in front of an audience, you can record it on your own webcam or cell phone so you can observe yourself and make some adjustments to your content and delivery.

Watch your video at least three times. The first time, focus only on content. Is your speech well organized, does it flow, and does it hold your attention? The second time is to focus on your vocal qualities—are you speaking too quickly

or slowly, in monotone, or with enough volume? Then, with the audio turned off, watch yet again to observe your facial expressions, gestures, and body movements. Consider including someone else—a professor, peer, or trusted friend—to help you identify your strengths and weaknesses in nonverbal communication.

In the past few years, rapid advances in artificial intelligence have made computer-assisted forms of evaluating nonverbal communication more reliable and helpful. There are already several commercially available products of this kind, such as PitchVantage. It's likely this type of tool can help you throughout your career.

---

citizens are entitled to free credit reports each year. I've placed a handout on the back table with several easy ways to get your free credit reports. Please grab one of the handouts on your way out and take control of your personal creditworthiness."

LO12.4

Explain the role of transitions in a speech.

Using Transitions Effectively

Now that you have crafted your introduction, main points, and conclusion, you need to tie them all together in an effective manner. A **transition** is a statement that logically connects one point in a speech to the next, giving it a satisfying flow. Some transitions are full statements that provide previews and internal summaries of the material. Others are single words or phrases, called "signposts," that help distinguish one point from another. Finally, many nonverbal behaviors can signal transitions.

SOME TRANSITIONS PREVIEW AND INTERNALLY SUMMARIZE

One type of transition is a **preview transition**, a statement alerting listeners that you are about to shift to a new topic. Notice how each of the following examples previews a change of topic:

- *Next, I'd like to discuss recent innovations in management recruiting.*
- *Let's now turn our attention to the financial implications of managed care.*

As you can see, previews need only be short statements that do not yet present any new information. By signaling a change of topic, they help your listeners track where you are in your speech.

A second type of transition is the **summary transition**, a statement that briefly reminds listeners of points you have already made. For example:

- *As we've seen, some salespeople lack adequate training and resources to accomplish their sales goals.*
- *So far, we have discussed two different business accounting methods: cash accounting and accrual accounting.*

Notice that each statement simply reminds listeners about what they have learned so far and signals that those points are complete, meaning you are about to move on to a new one.

Table 12.2 **Follow Along: Some Effective Signposts**

Specific Function	Examples
Compare or contrast points	*On the other hand . . .* *In contrast . . .* *Similarly . . .*
Indicate a sequence of events	*First . . . Second . . . Third* *Primarily . . .* *Now . . . then . . .* *Finally . . .*
Provide explanation	*For instance . . .* *To illustrate . . .* *In other words . . .*
Emphasize importance	*Most important . . .* *Remember that . . .* *Above all . . .*
Show cause and effect	*If . . . then . . .* *Consequently . . .* *Therefore . . .*
Give additional examples	*Likewise . . .* *In a similar way . . .* *As a second example . . .*
Summarize	*Finally . . .* *As I've explained . . .* *In summary . . .*

It is possible to combine summaries and previews. Many speakers will use a summary when they are finishing a point and then use a preview to start the next point. For instance:

- *At this point, we have covered the early life and education of Mark Zuckerberg. Next, let's examine the events that led to his founding of Facebook.*

SOME TRANSITIONS ARE SIGNPOSTS

Previews and summaries are typically full sentences, but you can also use single words or phrases to distinguish one point in your presentation from another. Such words and phrases (such as "for example" and "on the other hand") are known as **signposts** because they serve as signs to help listeners follow the path or outline of your speech.

As you'll see in Table 12.2, signposts can serve several specific functions, including comparing or contrasting points, indicating a sequence of events, providing an explanation, and emphasizing the importance of a point. The signposts that will work best for your presentation will depend on the particular points you intend to make.

SOME TRANSITIONS ARE NONVERBAL

In addition to using verbal transitions, you can also help listeners follow your speech by incorporating specific nonverbal behaviors, including

- *Body movement:* Unless you are standing behind a podium during your speech, use the available space to move around during your presentation. You can highlight transitions from one point to the next nonverbally by changing where you are standing as you discuss each point.

Speech Preparation Checklist

Use this checklist to ensure you have completed each required step in preparing an effective speech. Read each of the following statements and indicate whether the statement is true or false by placing a checkmark in the appropriate column.

	True	False
1. I have drafted a purpose statement reflecting the specific goals of my speech.	____	____
2. I have written a thesis statement summarizing the principal message of my speech.	____	____
3. I have created an introduction that generates interest and previews my main points.	____	____
4. I have organized my speech around related, distinct, and equally important main points.	____	____
5. I have written all my main points as complete sentences.	____	____
6. I have adopted an organizational pattern appropriate to the message of my speech.	____	____
7. My subpoints observe both the rule of subordination and the rule of division.	____	____
9. I have used transitions throughout my speech to preview and review.	____	____
9. My speech includes material that attests to my credibility.	____	____
10. I have crafted a conclusion that signals the end of my speech, summarizes my main points, and creates a memorable moment.	____	____

If you checked false for any of these steps, you may want to go back and complete them before making your presentation.

- *Vocal inflection:* Inflection refers to variation in the pitch and volume of your voice. You can increase your volume and pitch to emphasize that a specific point is very important. As you prepare to transition between points, let your volume and pitch drop as you conclude one point and then rise again as you begin the next point.

Nonverbal communication can be used to transition from one point to another as well as to highlight key points.

©Sergey Nivens/123 RF

- *Pauses:* The brief silence of a pause is an effective way to signal that you have finished your current point and are about to start the next one. You can also pause for effect, such as after you've made a very important statement that you want your listeners to think about before you move on.

- *Gestures:* You can use hand movements to punctuate your speech. If you intend to present three main points in the body of your presentation, you might signal the start of your first, second, and third points by holding up one, two, or three fingers, respectively. If you're comparing two arguments, you might hold out your right hand and say "on the one hand . . ." and then hold out your left as you say "on the other hand . . ."

Nonverbal transition behaviors are generally effective only to the extent that they seem natural rather than staged. As you rehearse your speech, practice using movement, inflection, pauses, and gestures until they feel natural. When you can incorporate these behaviors without consciously thinking about them, they are likely to look and seem natural to your audience.

Effective transitions ensure that the shifts from one part of your speech to the next don't seem abrupt. You want all the parts to fit together seamlessly so your listeners can easily follow your presentation from start to finish.

"The Competent Communicator" box provides a handy checklist for preparing a speech.

CHAPTER WRAP-UP

Careful planning and preparation are the keys to effective presentations. Here's a quick review of the chapter.

LO12.1 Illustrate purpose statements and thesis statements.

- Draft a purpose statement that is specific, selective, and declarative.
- Draft a thesis statement that is concrete, sentence-based, flexible, and truthful.

LO12.2 Identify the characteristics of main points and the options for arranging them in a speech.

- Determine your main points.
- Organize your main points strategically.
- Use subpoints to support your main points.

LO12.3 Differentiate the goals of a compelling introduction and conclusion.

- Craft a memorable introduction by capturing your listeners' attention, building your credibility, and previewing your main points.
- Create an effective conclusion by signaling the end of your speech, providing a summary of your main points, creating a memorable moment, and ending with a call to action.

LO12.4 Explain the role of transitions in a speech.

- Use transitions to preview and internally summarize.
- Use transitions as signposts.
- Use nonverbal transitions.

A LOOK BACK

Now, let's return to the opening scenario. Janis asked Vito about his reactions to a speech she gave one week ago, and it turned out that Vito couldn't even remember it. Busy schedules and information overload confront so many professionals that unless a speech is extremely well crafted, it will be forgotten. If Janis were to apply the principles of successfully speech planning, Vito would likely recall her speech a week later. Specifically, Janis would spend hours or even days crafting and polishing a specific and compelling thesis. She would repeat the thesis in the speech several times for impact, including in the preview and the conclusion. She would come prepared with an attention-getter that was closely connected to her thesis, making it even more memorable. She would come prepared with main points and subpoints that reinforced the thesis over and over. In short, taking the time to identify your purpose, carefully craft a specific and compelling thesis, and develop supporting content will help you deliver speeches that will influence others.

KEY TERMS

CHAPTER REVIEW QUESTIONS

1. How are a specific purpose and a thesis similar? How are they different? **LO12.1**

2. Which strategies should a speaker follow when drafting a strong purpose statement? **LO12.1**

3. Which guidelines are useful for drafting a strong thesis statement? **LO12.1**

4. What is the function of a main point? **LO12.2**

5. Why is it useful to write main points that are complete sentences, related, distinct, and equally important? **LO12.2**

6. What kinds of main points would lend themselves to a topic pattern? **LO12.2**

7. When is using a time pattern valuable? **LO12.2**

8. Which types of main points would benefit from a space pattern? **LO12.2**

9. How are a cause-and-effect pattern and a problem-solution pattern different? **LO12.2**

10. Why are subpoints useful? **LO12.2**

11. What are the rule of subordination and the rule of division? Why is each rule valuable? **LO12.2**

12. What characteristics make an introduction memorable? Which strategies can you use to make your introduction a memorable one? **LO12.3**

13. How can you demonstrate the three components of ethos? **LO12.3**

14. Why is it valuable to preview your main points in an introduction? **LO12.3**

15. What are the four functions of an effective conclusion? **LO12.3**

16. Why is it helpful to use transitions? **LO12.4**

17. What is the difference between a preview transition and a summary transition? **LO12.4**

18. What are the various functions of signposts? **LO12.4**

19. How can nonverbal behavior function as a transition? **LO12.4**

SKILL-BUILDING EXERCISES

Planning Attention-Getters (LO12.3)

Identify a potential purpose and thesis you could use for a presentation. Then describe how you could use each of the following attention-getting devices:

- Tell a story
- Provide a memorable statistic
- Present a quotation
- Tell a joke
- Pose a question
- Cite an opinion
- Startle your listeners
- Note the occasion
- Identify something familiar
- Incorporate technology

Evaluate the Introduction and Conclusion of a Business Speech (LO12.3)

Find a speech by a business, government, or nonprofit leader on YouTube or another site. Respond to the following questions:

- How effectively did the speaker gain attention? Explain. What could he or she have done differently?
- How well did the speaker build credibility? Be specific. What could he or she have done differently?

- How effectively did the speaker preview the main points?
- How well did the speaker conclude the speech? What aspects of the speech did he or she emphasize? What could he or she have done more effectively in the conclusion?

Interviewing a Business Professional about Planning for Presentations (LO12.1, LO12.2, LO12.3)

Interview a business professional about best practices in planning business presentations. Write four to five paragraphs about the interview and address the following issues:

- Developing an effective purpose and thesis (professionals will often use a phrase like takeaway *message* or *main message* when referring to the thesis).
- Adapting the presentation to the needs and preferences of the audience.
- Using attention-getters to engage the audience in the opening moments.
- Preparing examples and support for key ideas.

Creating a Presentation Outline (LO12.1, LO12.2, LO12.3)

Create a presentation outline that contains the following:

- Purpose and thesis
- Attention-getter

- Main points and subpoints
- Topic pattern (topics, time, space, cause-and-effect, problem-solution)

Evaluate a Business Presentation for Purpose, Thesis, Organization, and Topic Pattern (LO12.1, LO12.2, LO12.3, LO12.4)

Find a speech by a business, government, or nonprofit leader on YouTube or another site. Watch the presentation and evaluate the following:

- Purpose
- Thesis

- Organization (main points and subpoints)
- Topic pattern (topics, time, space, cause-and-effect, problem-solution)
- Aspects that could be improved: Explain at least three ways in which the speech could be improved in terms of its purpose, thesis, organization, and topic pattern.

ENDNOTES

1. Reuters. (2008, May 6). Super Bowl 30 second ads to cost $3 mln in 2009: Report. Retrieved July 16, 2017, from http://www.reuters.com/article/us-nbc-superbowl-idUSN0644484220080506.

2. Comadena, M. E., Hunt, S. K., & Simonds, C. J. (2007). The effects of teacher clarity, nonverbal immediacy, and caring on student motivation, affective, and cognitive learning. *Communication Research Reports, 24*, 241–248.

3. Titsworth, B. S. (2004). Students' notetaking: The effects of teacher immediacy and clarity. *Communication Education, 53,* 305–320.

4. Houser, M. L. (2006). Expectancy violations of instructor communication as predictors of motivation and learning: A comparison of traditional and nontraditional students. *Communication Quarterly, 54,* 331–349; see also Chesebro, J. L. (2003). Effects of teacher clarity and nonverbal immediacy on student learning, receiver apprehension, and affect. *Communication Education, 52,* 135–147.

5. Elizabeth Dole, speech to the 300 Group, London, November 15, 1989.

6. See, e.g., Reynolds, N. (1993). Ethos as location: New sites for discursive authority. *Rhetoric Review, 11,* 325–338.

Learning Objectives

After reading this chapter, you should be able to do the following:

LO13.1 Determine when supporting material is needed in a presentation and which type of supporting material is appropriate.

LO13.2 Evaluate the quality of supporting material.

LO13.3 Compare and contrast various information-gathering techniques.

LO13.4 Summarize strategies for maximizing the effectiveness of presentation aids.

LO13.5 Describe strategies for using supporting materials ethically.

CHAPTER 13

Finding Support for Your Presentation Goals

Kevyn finished his presentation about digital commerce in China and invited the audience to ask questions. A woman in the front row asked, "You mentioned that about 90 percent of Chinese managers use the Alibaba platform. Where did you hear that and do you think it's a reliable figure?"

Kevyn replied, "I found that figure online and it's pretty much the same figure you'd get anywhere."

A man near the back raised his hand and inquired, "Do you have any recommendations of books we can read to learn more about how to succeed in China's online market?"

Kevyn paused. Then he admitted, "I'm not aware of any books about this topic, but there are a lot of articles online."

The audience continued to ask questions about where to find reliable information about digital commerce in China. The longer the question-and-answer period went on, the more Kevyn realized how weak the support for his presentation was.

LO13.1

Determine when supporting material is needed in a presentation and which type of supporting material is appropriate.

Understand Where and Why You Need Support

Especially when your goal is to inform or to persuade, you will require supporting material to back up the claims you make in your presentation. Finding supporting material is not necessarily difficult. However, as you will see in this section, to use it effectively you need to identify places in your speech where you need support, determine the type of support you require, and evaluate the quality of the material you find.

IDENTIFY PLACES WHERE YOU NEED RESEARCH SUPPORT

Before locating supporting material for your speech, you must know where you need it. Consult your outline to identify where you are making points that require or would benefit from supporting data. For instance, you need to provide research support whenever you make a factual claim. Recall from Chapter 3 that a factual claim is a statement asserting that something is objectively true. Each of the following statements is a factual claim because it argues that something is true in an objective sense, even though the claim may not actually *be* true:

- Flying is the safest mode of transportation.
- Chinese is the most commonly spoken language in the world.
- Solar power alone is not capable of meeting the U.S. energy demand.
- Islam is the world's most widespread religion.

We distinguish factual claims, which are claims about what *is* true, from opinions, which are statements of belief about what *ought to be* true. The statement "Every person should learn to speak Chinese" is an opinion, because it conveys what the speaker believes *should be*. The speaker might argue persuasively for that opinion and even cite opinions of political scientists or expert linguists as support. He or she cannot cite evidence showing that the statement is true and factual, however, because opinions are never true or false in an objective sense.

The first step in gathering support for your presentation is to determine which claims require supporting evidence.

©Mimagephotography/Shutterstock

In contrast, the statement "Chinese is the most commonly spoken language in the world" is a factual claim, because it is either true or false no matter how the speaker thinks or feels about it. To locate effective supporting material, therefore, start by identifying the types of claims you intend to make, and then search for appropriate material to support each one.

DETERMINE THE TYPE OF SUPPORT YOU REQUIRE

Your options for supporting your speech claims include definitions, examples, statistics, quotations, and narratives. As we'll see, different types of claims require different types of support.

- *Definitions:* When your speech focuses on a concept that may be unfamiliar to your audience—or one that can have multiple meanings—you can support your use of that concept by defining it explicitly. In a presentation about advertising strategies, you might say "According to the American Association of Advertisers, an infomercial is a commercial that is similar in appearance to a news broadcast or talk show." By identifying the source of your definition, you give that definition credibility.

- *Examples:* Another way to help your audience understand a concept is to offer examples of it. Suppose you're giving an informative speech about industrial espionage. Even if your listeners understand in principle what industrial espionage is, they may benefit from hearing specific examples, which might include the 1993 accusations of espionage against Volkswagen[1] and the 2009 accusations against the Hilton hotel chain.[2]

- *Statistics:* Statistics are numbers—usually identified through research—that you can use to support your claims. If your focus is on strategies for combating teen pregnancy, for instance, you might support the importance of that topic in this way: "According to the Centers for Disease Control, the United States has the highest rate of teen pregnancy among all industrialized nations. Nearly 250,000 babies are born each year to mothers aged 15 to 19, and almost two-thirds of those pregnancies are unintended."[3] By providing such statistics, you support your claim that teen pregnancy is a significant issue. Because some statistics are more reliable than others, however, it is always important to identify their source. The next section will give you some hints for assessing the trustworthiness of your statistics.

- *Quotations:* Quotations from people who are recognized experts on your topic can serve as valuable supporting material. Suppose your presentation is about the 2014 outbreak of the Ebola virus in West Africa. To address the question of whether the first case of Ebola infection in the United States would cause a similar epidemic, you might say, "As Tom Freiden, director of the Centers for Disease Control and Prevention, has noted, 'The bottom line here is that I have no doubt that we will control this importation or this case of Ebola so that it does not spread widely throughout this country. There's no doubt in my mind, we will stop it here.'"[4] As with definitions and statistics, it is critical to your credibility that you identify the source of the quotation and his or her qualifications for speaking on that topic.

- *Narratives:* Many speakers use narratives—such as personal stories or testimonies—to support their claims. If you're speaking about the benefits of investing in a tax-sheltered annuity to a group of individuals considering doing the same, you might relate stories of individuals who have invested and

Many speakers use narratives to make their presentations compelling and memorable.

©Matej Kastelic/Alamy Stock Photo

experienced benefits to their retirement portfolio. When speaking about something that is personally relevant to you, you may also elect to share a story or testimony of your own. Narratives can be especially compelling for listeners because they often make a topic feel personal in a way that examples or statistics do not.

EVALUATE SUPPORTING MATERIAL

Not all supporting material is equally valuable. You'll want to find the best possible supporting material, and that means checking carefully for three particular characteristics: credibility, objectivity, and currency.

Consider the source's credibility. As you learned in Chapter 3, information has credibility if it is believable and trustworthy. To be credible, supporting material must come from a trustworthy source. A source is convincing if experience, training, and expertise give its claims more authority than the claims of others.

Suppose your speech focuses on the mental health of people in senior corporate leadership positions. Which of the following statements do you think has more credibility?

- *According to Wikipedia, the stress of high-level corporate management elevates the risk of anxiety and depression.*
- *According to a report from the U.S. Surgeon General, the stress of high-level corporate management elevates the risk of anxiety and depression.*

These statements make exactly the same claim. The first statement attributes the claim to Wikipedia, a website that anyone—regardless of his or her credentials—can edit (except in some limited cases). The second statement attributes the claim to the U.S. Surgeon General, a recognized national authority on public health. As such an authority, the Surgeon General is a more credible source to cite on matters of health than Wikipedia. Note, however, that the health information on Wikipedia isn't necessarily inaccurate. Rather, the Surgeon General—because of his or her professional training and medical expertise—is a more trustworthy source of medical information.

Besides coming from an appropriate source, credible supporting material often also includes statistics that enumerate an effect. As mentioned before, statistics are simply numbers that you can use to help make a point more informatively. Imagine that you're speaking to a consumer group about safe driving, and you want to argue that talking on a cell phone while driving is dangerous. Which of the following statements makes that point more credibly?

- *According to the National Safety Council, talking on a cell phone while driving increases the chances of a collision.*
- *According to the National Safety Council, talking on a cell phone while driving increases the chances of a collision by 400 percent.*

The second statement specifies *how much* the risk of collision increases when the driver uses a cell phone. Without such support, your listeners won't know whether cell phone use poses a relatively minor risk—which may cause them to ignore your point—or a significant risk—which may cause them to pay close attention.

Evaluate the source's objectivity. When you are evaluating the potential usefulness of supporting material, consider how objective the source is. A source is **objective** to the extent that it presents information in an unbiased fashion. In contrast, sources are **subjective** when they offer information in a manner that supports only their favored position on an issue. That distinction matters because many people will consider data from subjective sources to be less trustworthy.

Let's say you're preparing a speech about the financial crisis that gripped the United States in the early 21st century and the subsequent recovery. Which is a more objective source to cite—a university study published in a journal of economic science, or the documentary *Capitalism: A Love Story*, written and directed by controversial filmmaker Michael Moore? To what extent is each source objective? Most people would consider the university study to be more objective because in scientific research, conclusions must be dictated by the data. That is, regardless of what researchers *want* to be true, they can claim only what their data tells them. Moreover, a researcher's work is heavily scrutinized and reviewed before being published in an academic journal. The scientific process demands objectivity. In contrast, Hollywood movies such as Moore's do not require objectivity. The purpose of most movies—even documentaries—is to entertain, not to provide objective facts. That doesn't necessarily mean that statements made in a movie are untrue, only that movies are more subjective than academic studies.

When you are evaluating a source's objectivity, also consider the extent to which that source has a political or financial interest in the content of the message. A report on the effectiveness of childproof locks is likely to be more objective if issued by a government agency than by a manufacturer of childproof locks. The reason is that the latter group has a financial interest in reporting that the locks are effective, whereas the former group is less likely to lean toward any particular outcome. Likewise, the report would be considered less objective if it were funded, or otherwise facilitated, by someone with a political or financial interest in the outcome. In 2015, for instance, it was reported that Harvard University climate scientist Dr. Wei-Hock Soon had published research denying the widely accepted notion that rising greenhouse gas emissions cause climate change. His research was funded almost entirely by the coal and fossil fuel industry, however, which has a financial stake in avoiding blame for climate change. This conflict of interest rightly calls the objectivity of Dr. Soon's work into question.[5]

Hollywood movies—even documentaries—are rarely as objective as scientific studies.

©Paramount Vantage/Kobal/ Shutterstock

Check the source's currency.   A final consideration when selecting supporting material is the currency of the information. Information that was produced or published recently is likely to be more up to date than older information. Using recent supporting material is particularly important when you're speaking about issues that change continually, such as technology and world politics.

Suppose you're developing a speech about how people communicate online. Which of the following sources would provide better supporting material?

Lea, M., & Spears, R. (1992). Paralanguage and social perception in computer-mediated communication. *Journal of Organizational Computing, 2*, 321–341.

Pang, A., Shin, W., Lew, Z., & Walther, J. B. (2018). Building relationships through dialogic communication: Organizations, stakeholders, and computer-mediated communication. *Journal of Marketing Communications, 24*, 68–82.

A key first step in evaluating the quality of supporting material is to distinguish what matters from what does not. Suppose you have identified a book you want to use as supporting material in your speech about government regulation of communication technology. Read each of the following statements and indicate which ones would *enhance* the quality of your supporting material by placing a checkmark next to those.

1. ____ The author of the book is a well-known celebrity.

2. ____ The book was published three months ago.

3. ____ The book presents the results of scientific research.

4. ____ The publisher of the book is a political watchdog group that campaigns against government regulation.

5. ____ The book's author has an advanced degree in communication technology.

6. ____ All the research described in the book was published before 2005.

7. ____ The book's author has 250,000 Twitter followers.

8. ____ The book presents its arguments logically, and without biased or inflammatory language.

For a contemporary topic such as government regulation of communication technology, high-quality supporting material needs to have credibility, objectivity, *and* currency. The characteristics on this list that would enhance the quality of your supporting material are 2, 3, 5, and 8. Items 1 and 7 have to do with the author's popularity, which doesn't necessarily relate to his or her credibility. Item 4 suggests that the book may be biased toward a particular conclusion, and item 6 suggests that the book's material may be outdated.

Because of its more recent publication date, the second article would clearly provide more up-to-date information than the first. Given how rapidly computer-mediated communication technology develops, having the most recent information to support the points in your speech will be very advantageous.

As you search for appropriate supporting material, remember that credibility, objectivity, and currency are all important, but they are not necessarily equally important for all topics. When preparing a talk on the history of the Motion Picture Production Code, which governed movie content in the United States from 1930 to 1968, for instance, you may find the credibility of your sources to be more important than their currency, because the facts about movie regulation history don't change as rapidly as the facts about, say, computer-mediated communication. If you're speaking about the safety of a newly developed treatment for muscle pain, then the objectivity of your supporting material may be paramount, to ensure that the facts you present are as unbiased as possible.

How good are you at evaluating the quality of supporting material? Take a look at "The Competent Communicator" box to assess your ability.

SHARPEN YOUR SKILLS

Finding Credible Websites

Consider the claim "Government regulation hurts businesses." Find three websites that offer data either supporting or refuting that claim. For each site, address the following questions: (1) Who created the site, and does that person or group have a reason to want this claim to be true or false? In making that evaluation, consider whether the person or group would benefit financially or politically if their argument were true. (2) What kind of data are presented? Are they the results of an academic study or merely the observations of an opinionated source? Based on your responses to those questions, write a short paragraph explaining which of the three websites is the most credible and why.

Know Where to Find Information

When planning a speech, you'll often find it helpful to consult various sources for information or guidance. You may already have used some or all of these sources to prepare papers or other class assignments, and they can be just as valuable when you are developing a speech. In this section, we'll look at several potential sources of good supporting material.

LO13.3

Compare and contrast various information-gathering techniques.

WEBSITES

The Internet puts a wealth of information at your fingertips, and it can be an invaluable source of supporting material if you use it responsibly. One of the Internet's greatest assets as a source of supporting material is also its greatest liability, and that is the sheer volume of information it can provide. It's unlikely you will fail to discover something useful for your speech, but the breadth of information can seem overwhelming. Particularly if you are searching for material on a popular topic, such as fashion or environmental activism, you could easily identify thousands of websites after just a few moments of searching. As we'll see, however, it's easy to narrow the parameters of an Internet search so that you identify only specific types of information.

Many public speakers use one or more of three kinds of websites when searching online for supporting material: general search engines, research search engines, and website-specific searches. The broadest of these, the **general search engine**, is a website that allows you to search for other websites containing information about a topic you specify. For instance, if you type "sexual harassment" into google.com, that search engine will produce a list of nearly 40 million other websites offering information about the topic.

In most cases, using a general search engine will identify a wide range of sources. Some may be helpful to you, and others may not. Among the 40 million websites about sexual harassment, for instance, are bound to be thousands that feature individuals' stories of dealing with harassment in their places of work. Those may or may not be useful sources of supporting material for the claims you want to make in your speech. You can reduce the number of websites identified in a search by submitting more terms to the search engine. For instance, if you type "sexual harassment laws in the workplace" into google.com, the search will identify approximately 6,600 websites. That's still an enormous number—and, once again, many sites are likely not to be useful to your search—but it is considerably fewer than the 40 million sites your original search identified. However, if you know ahead of time that you want to look specifically for published research on your topic, you may prefer to use a research search engine.

A **research search engine** doesn't scan the Internet as broadly as a general search engine but instead looks only for research that has been published in books, academic journals, and other periodicals. If you type "sexual harassment" into Google Scholar (scholar.google.com), the search will identify approximately 400,000 sources reporting published research on the topic. In many instances, the publications are available to read online. Other research search engines include Microsoft Academic (academic.microsoft.com) and PubMed (ncbi.nlm.nih.gov/pubmed).

Finally, you can do a website-specific search, which means confining your search to specific websites that you know will contain the information you're seeking. To find information about sexual harassment, for instance, you could consult the website for

Google Scholar is one of the most popular research search engines online.

Source: Google Inc.

the U.S. Equal Employment Opportunity Commission, www.eeoc.gov. That page provides information about the laws and regulations related to sexual harassment, types of harassment, prohibited practices, and guidance for managing instances of harassment. Similarly, you could consult the websites of various organizations to examine their sexual harassment policies. For example, you might find online the sexual harassment policy for the U.S. Department of State or for the aerospace company Boeing.

Websites are extraordinary research tools, but they aren't your only option. Books, periodicals and nonprint materials, databases, personal observations, and surveys can also provide many useful resources to help you prepare a speech.

BOOKS

Books are another invaluable resource for research. Books include both fictional and nonfictional works, as well as reference volumes such as dictionaries and encyclopedias. With a bit of searching, you are likely to find books containing information about almost any speech topic you could choose.

In a library, each book has a unique catalog number—its "call number"—that helps you locate the book on the library shelf. Most libraries allow you to search their catalog by author, subject, title, and/or publisher so you can easily locate the book you want. Figure 13.1 gives an example of a book's listing in a library's online catalog.

You can also find and read many books online. The website books.google.com allows you to search books by title, author, or subject and lets you survey a book's content. More than 25 million books have already been scanned into the system's database, making it a valuable resource for finding books relevant to your topic.

Most books can also be purchased online, through vendors such as amazon.com and barnesandnoble.com. Many are available in either print or digital formats, allowing you to read the material in whichever manner suits you best.

Figure 13.1

A Book Listing

An example of a catalog entry for a book.

Author	Duckworth, Angela
Title	Grit: The power of passion and perseverance
Publisher	New York, NY: Scribner
Copyright year	2016
Call number	BF637.S8 D693 2016
Description	Xv, 333 pages : illustrations ; 24 cm
ISBN	9781501111105
Subject	Success – Perseverance (Ethics) – Expectation (Psychology) – Diligence
Contents	Showing up – Distracted by talent – Effort counts twice – How gritty are you? – Grit grows – Interest – Practice – Purpose – Hope – Parenting for grit – The playing fields of grit – A culture of grit

CAREER TIP
Read Lots of Books

Oprah Winfrey is among the most popular people in the world due to her authentic and inspirational media presence, global philanthropic efforts, and immense business success. She believes books built the foundation for her career. In her 2004 Global Humanitarian Award acceptance speech at the United Nations, she explained, "Books allowed me to see a world beyond the front porch of my grandmother's shotgun house and gave me the power to see possibilities."[6] Elsewhere, she has stated, "Books were my path to personal freedom."[7] It's not surprising that one of her most influential efforts over the past few decades has been *Oprah's Book Club.*

Like Oprah, many business, nonprofit, government, and other leaders credit books with opening their eyes to new possibilities and sparking new ideas. In fact, many leaders read several hours each day to continue learning. Even as your career becomes busy and hectic, find ways to read every day and include book reading as part of your regimen. For instance, you might set aside 20 minutes a day when you can read without distraction. Consider carrying a book with you so you

Oprah Winfrey, an avid reader
©Tinseltown/Shutterstock

can read during "down times," such as while riding the bus or sitting in a waiting room. Read what interests you, and set goals for yourself, such as reading one new book each month.[8] Developing a strong reading habit can keep you inquisitive and curious and provide you with new perspectives about the challenges you face in your professional and private life.

PERIODICALS AND NONPRINT MATERIALS

Periodicals are materials that are published on a regular basis, such as magazines, newspapers, and scientific journals. Newspapers are often published daily, whereas magazines might be published weekly or monthly, and journals are typically published quarterly. Because they appear on a recurring basis, periodicals generally provide more current information than books do. Thus, if you're preparing a speech about the economy, you will find more recent information in *The Wall Street Journal*, a daily financial newspaper, than in a book published several months ago.

Nonprint materials are audiovisual resources such as sound recordings, movies, and photographs. Many libraries have extensive collections of records, videotapes, CDs, DVDs, and photographs that patrons can check out. You can use nonprint materials both as sources of research and as audiovisual aids to enhance your presentation.

Finally, for making older resources available to users, most libraries also have collections of print materials stored on microfilm, a photographic medium that stores reproductions of books and periodicals on film at a greatly reduced font size. Transferring printed materials to microfilm both preserves the materials and conserves storage space. With a special viewer, you can read materials on microfilm and even print them in their original font size.

DATABASES

A **database** is an electronic storehouse of specific information that you can search. Using a research database is much like using a research search engine. The major difference is that databases tend to be narrower and more specialized; most are focused on specific academic disciplines. Comindex is a database for communication studies, for instance; PsycINFO is for psychology, Sociological Abstracts for sociology, ERIC for education, and Business Source Elite for business.

Many college and university libraries offer access to databases on their websites, but you can also visit your library in person and ask for help. One of a library's most valuable assets is its staff of trained professionals who can help you navigate the library's resources. If you are uncertain where to begin searching for supporting material, don't be afraid to ask a library staff member for help.

PERSONAL OBSERVATIONS

When you think of doing research, you may think only about locating information that already exists. However, an additional option is to do original research by gathering information yourself. One way is by observing a phenomenon and taking notes about what you see and hear.

Let's say you were preparing a speech about the practice of handing out printed advertising leaflets on a college campus, and you wonder whether women or men are more likely to take such leaflets when offered. To learn about the topic, you might spend a few hours watching people on your college campus. You could sit close to the area where salespeople offer printed advertisements to passersby, and you could observe and take note of how people respond. For example, you could record what percentage of male and female passersby accept the leaflets when offered, as opposed to refusing them.

As part of your speech, you might describe how you conducted your observations and what you found:

> To observe people's reactions to being offered advertising leaflets, I spent two hours in a busy spot on campus during a weekday, when several salespeople were offering such advertisements to passersby. Within two hours, I observed almost 100 offers of leaflets and some stark differences in the way people responded. Specifically, women were much more likely to accept the leaflets than reject them. Men, on the other hand, were equally likely to reject or accept. I also noticed that approximately 18 percent of all passersby who accepted a leaflet threw it away within 45 seconds.

Observing social behavior is one way to gather information.

©slobo/E+/Getty Images

When using personal observations as supporting material, remember that your observations may not accurately reflect the behaviors of the population at large. After observing people for two hours at one place on one college campus, you could not say with certainty that *all* women and men differ in their response to advertising leaflets. You could, however, use this personal observation in conjunction with other forms of data, such as findings from behavioral research, to illustrate how patterns of behavior are enacted in a local environment.

In addition to collecting your own personal observations, you can also use observations made by others as supporting material. Perhaps you're drafting a speech about working in Venice, Italy, and you want to describe how people travel the city's many canals on boats called gondolas. Even though you haven't visited Venice yourself, you might base your description on the personal observations of your friend who spent a semester studying there. For additional material, you could also consult the personal observations of other visitors by reading their travel blogs or Facebook pages.

SURVEYS

Personal observation is a good way to collect original data, but it is effective only if the topic is directly observable, such as public behavior on a college campus or tourist travel on a gondola. What if you want to learn about something you cannot directly observe, such as people's attitudes, beliefs, or histories? To learn about those topics, you can conduct a **survey**, which means collecting data by asking people directly about their experiences.

SHARPEN YOUR SKILLS

Informal Interviewing

Select a current issue on which people's opinions vary, such as how the government should address unemployment. Conduct informal interviews with two or three family members, co-workers, and classmates in which you ask what people's opinions are on the issue and why they hold those opinions. When interviewing others, it is useful to ask all respondents the same questions, and in the same order. As you conduct each interview, try to keep your own opinions private so you don't influence what others say. Write a paragraph describing the results of your interviews, which could be one form of evidence you use in a speech.

One method of surveying people is to interview them. As we discussed in Chapter 9, an *interview* is a structured conversation in which one person poses questions to which another person responds. Some interviews are brief, making use of a few questions that probe the person's experiences. Others are in-depth conversations in which the respondent speaks in great detail about his or her experiences. Many interviews take place in a face-to-face setting, but you can also conduct them over the telephone, via text messaging or email, or in an online chat room.

A second method of surveying people is to distribute a **questionnaire**, a written instrument containing questions for people to answer. Like interviews, questionnaires help you learn about people's attitudes, preferences, values, and experiences. You might survey students at your school about their use of the campus health service or their preferences for community arts and entertainment. Let's say you discovered that 87 percent of students have visited your campus health service within the previous six months. You could use that information to argue for expanding health services for students.

Compared to interviews, questionnaires have the advantage of allowing you to collect data from a large number of people efficiently. Using a questionnaire, for instance, you could collect data from every student in your communication course in the same amount of time it might take you to interview one person. The disadvantage is that you usually cannot get the detailed answers possible in an interview, and you cannot follow up a questionnaire response by saying, for instance, "Can you tell me more about that?" For those reasons, surveys that include data from both in-depth interviews and questionnaires are often more informative than those that rely on only one method.

Because Internet research, library research, personal observations, and surveys all differ in the depth and breadth of information they provide, it's often to your advantage to use more than one of these when you're preparing a speech.

Mastering Presentation Aids

LO13.4
Summarize strategies for maximizing the effectiveness of presentation aids.

The Home Shopping Network (HSN) airs infomercials for everything from jewelry and handbags to steam cleaners and computers. The speakers in infomercials don't simply *tell* you about their products—they also *show* you what the products are and how they work. They may demonstrate the products in use, show photographs of the sizes and colors in which they are available, or present video-recorded testimonials from satisfied customers. They may also display the item name, dimensions, and price on the television screen. Their sales strategies center on **presentation aids**, which consist of anything used in conjunction with a speech or presentation to stimulate listeners' senses. Presentation aids help the viewing audience understand the products those HSN presenters are pitching.

You can similarly incorporate presentation aids into your speech to make it memorable and engaging for your listeners. Many speakers use presentation aids to display supporting evidence for their claims and to help their audiences follow their points. In this section, we look first at the benefits of using presentation aids and then at the electronic and nonelectronic forms available. Finally, we focus on some tips for choosing and using presentation aids effectively.

PRESENTATION AIDS CAN ENHANCE YOUR SPEECH

Although presentation aids take time and energy to prepare, research shows that using them properly can dramatically enhance a presentation. They work by improving at least three audience responses—attention, learning, and recall.

Presentation aids improve attention. One benefit of using presentation aids is that the audience will pay more attention.[9] Most listeners can think much faster than you can talk, so if all they have to attend to are your words, their minds will likely wander. Incorporating one or more presentation aids will better hold their attention.

Presentation aids improve learning. A second benefit of using presentation aids is that the audience will learn more from the speech. One reason is that they are paying closer attention, as we just considered. Another is that most people learn better when more than one of their senses is engaged. If the speaker incorporates materials that activate the listeners' sense of sight, hearing, touch, or smell, listeners will take in more from the presentation than if they are only listening to the speaker's words.[10]

Presentation aids improve recall. Listeners will also remember more of what is said if the speaker incorporates presentation aids. One study compared listeners' recall of material from a speech that included visual aids to recall from one that did not. Three hours after the speech, audience members recalled 85 percent of the content if visual aids were used but only 70 percent if not. The difference was even more striking three days later, when listeners exposed to visual aids still remembered 65 percent of the content, compared to only 10 percent for the others.[11] A later study found that listeners exposed to visual aids remembered 85 percent of the material immediately after a presentation and 71 percent after four weeks.[12]

You have several options to choose from when selecting presentation aids, from simple demonstrations with samples and props, to hand-drawn charts and graphics, to multimedia presentation software.

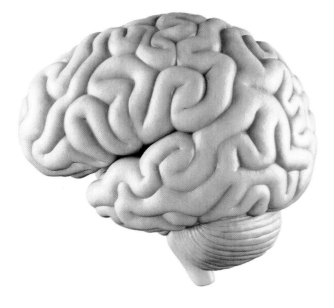

Models can be excellent low-tech presentation aids.

©eranicle/123RF

LOW-TECH PRESENTATION AIDS

Some of the most engaging presentation aids are decidedly low tech. As we explore in this section, you can make presentation aids from objects, flavors, textures, odors, handouts, and even people.

Use relevant objects. Almost any physical object can be an effective presentation aid if it is relevant to your topic and if it can be incorporated easily and safely. If your speech is about the role of a notary public, you might bring in a notary stamp—the stamp placed next to a notary's signature on official documents—to use as a visual aid. If you're speaking about the French clothing industry, you could bring several different pairs of high-heeled shoes to demonstrate the French influence on women's footwear.

If it isn't feasible to bring the actual object you want to show your listeners, you may be able to bring a *model*, which is a representation of the object. Suppose you're explaining how the human brain is divided into four different lobes. Instead of bringing an actual brain to use as a visual aid, you can bring a plastic model that pulls apart to show where the lobes are located.

You can also use objects to demonstrate processes. Let's say your goal is to explain how to set up a LinkedIn profile. Rather than simply telling your listeners what to do, you could bring a computer whose screen is projected on a wall so everyone can see it and set up an online profile as you describe the process. That way, your listeners hear your description and see the process at the same time.

Before incorporating any object into your speech, consider whether it will be feasible for the space in which you're speaking. Make sure it is large enough to be seen by everyone in your audience but not so large that it dominates your presentation. Check with your instructor or the person in charge of the venue before bringing any type of object that might be considered dangerous or unsanitary, such as a weapon, a power tool, a hot plate, or a live animal. Some school policies prohibit having such objects on campus; the same is often true for workplaces and rented venues such as conference centers.

Add flavors, textures, and odors. You can also use presentation aids to appeal to your listeners' senses of taste, touch, and smell. For example, a speech about the citrus fruit industry might incorporate slices of orange, lemon, tangerine, and grapefruit that your audience can sample. A presentation about interior design might use swatches of different types of carpeting or upholstery fabric that your listeners can feel. If you're speaking about marketing men's cologne, you might bring fragrance samples for your audience to smell. Presentation aids that appeal to our senses can be an effective way of demonstrating your speech points and can be especially engaging for audience members with impaired vision or hearing, for whom audio-visual aids can be less useful.

Utilize handouts. Another type of nonelectronic presentation aid is a handout. Most handouts are copies of written material that listeners can keep after the speech is over. They are especially effective when you want your listeners to have more information than you can reasonably address during your presentation. When incorporating a handout, make certain to bring enough copies for everyone in the audience. If you need your listeners to see your handout while you're speaking, distribute it at the beginning of your speech. If not, distribute it at the end so it doesn't distract listeners while you're speaking. As the "Tech Tip" box describes, handouts can also be created and distributed digitally. If your audience includes listeners who are visually impaired, you might also create an audio recording of the information on your handouts.

Incorporate people. Finally, you can use people—including yourself—as presentation aids. Suppose your speech is about the Chinese martial art of tai chi. You might choose to show your audience some of the fundamental movements of tai chi by either performing them yourself or having someone else do so. Similarly, if you are speaking about the procedure for measuring blood pressure, you might perform a blood pressure test on someone to demonstrate the technique. In both cases, using a person as a presentation aid is more engaging than showing your audience photographs or video recordings, because your demonstration is live.

TECH TIP
Using Digital Handouts

Increasingly, the boundaries between physical and digital are blurring, and handouts are a good example. You can easily send digital handouts to audience members' phones or other mobile devices, avoiding excessive printing and providing more data if you wish. Digital handouts may even be more convenient or permanent for your audience members.

Here are several issues to consider before you opt to use digital handouts: (1) *Can you distribute the digital handouts at the right moment?* One major advantage of handouts is that you can distribute them at the right point in a speech or presentation so they are most influential and least distracting. (2) *Can you distribute digital handouts that are easy to read?* Many handouts are difficult to read on mobile phones or tablets. If this is the case, you might opt for physical handouts. (3) *Will all audience members be able to access the digital handout quickly?* Although nearly all professionals carry mobile devices, software issues, user proficiency, and limited cellular or wi-fi access might reduce the effectiveness of a digital handout.

Tips for Staying Healthy

- Get enough sleep.
- Eat a healthy diet.
- Take a multivitamin.
- Avoid smoking.
- Exercise daily.

Figure 13.2

An Effective Text Slide

A text slide presents information in the form of words, such as with a quote or a bulleted list.

MULTIMEDIA PRESENTATION AIDS

Technology provides a wealth of opportunities for creating interesting and memorable computer-mediated presentation aids. Presentation software programs allow speakers to integrate many different kinds of presentation aids into a unified display. In this section, we'll look at the use of text slides, graphic slides, video, and audio.

Use text slides.   One form of electronic presentation aid is a **text slide**, an electronic display of text to accompany a speech. Perhaps you are already familiar with presentation software for creating text slides, such as Microsoft PowerPoint, Apple Keynote, Google Slides, or Prezi. Text slides often take the form of bulleted lists of words or phrases relevant to the presenter's topic.

Effective text slides are clear and brief. Notice, for instance, that the slide in Figure 13.2 doesn't go into detail about how much sleep a person should get or what a healthy diet should include. That detail is for the speaker to present. The slide itself should give only enough information to introduce each new point. We'll continue the discussion about maximizing the effectiveness of presentation aids later in this chapter.

Use graphic slides.   Another practical electronic presentation aid is a **graphic slide**, the electronic display of information in a visually compelling format that can enhance listeners' attention. Graphic slides include

- *Tables:* A *table* is the display of words or numbers in a format of columns and rows. It is a particularly effective option when you want to compare the same information for two or more groups. For instance, Figure 13.3 compares starting salaries for high school and college graduates in various fields. This simple illustration makes it easy to spot large and small differences.
- *Charts:* A *chart* is a graphic display of numeric information. Like a table, it is also useful for comparing data between two or more groups. Whereas a table presents the actual text or numbers being compared, a chart converts numbers

into a *visual* display. Three types of charts are common. A **pie chart**, seen in Figure 13.4, is a graphic display in the form of a circle divided into segments, each of which represents a percentage of the whole; for example, a pie chart could illustrate the percentages of people around the world who practice various religions. A **line chart**, shown in Figure 13.5, is a graphic display in the form of a line or lines that connect various data points; for example, a line chart could illustrate the percentage of U.S. children living in poverty in various years. Finally, a **bar chart**, in Figure 13.6, depicts numbers as bars on a graph, such as the percentages of people in various parts of the world who regularly use the Internet.

Average Starting Salaries
Source: *Wall Street Journal, January 12, 2017.*

Field	High School Graduate	College Graduate
Sales	$21,000	$38,500
Health care	$28,500	$52,000
Law enforcement	$46,500	$47,000
Event planning	$19,000	$24,750

Figure 13.3

A Table Slide

A table slide presents words or numbers in a format of columns and rows.

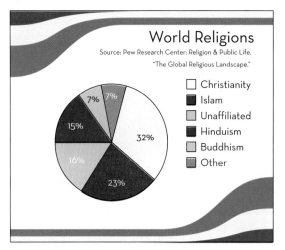

Figure 13.4

A Pie Chart

A pie chart is a graphic display in the form of a circle divided into segments.

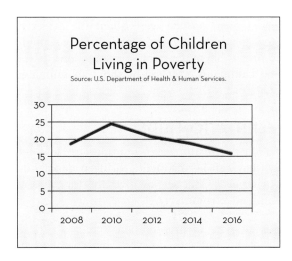

Figure 13.5

A Line Chart

A line chart is a graphic display in the form of a line or lines that connect various data points.

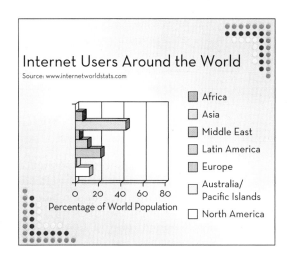

Figure 13.6

A Bar Chart

A bar chart depicts numbers as bars on a graph.

Figure 13.7

A Picture Slide

A picture slide presents a photograph or drawing.

©Glow Images

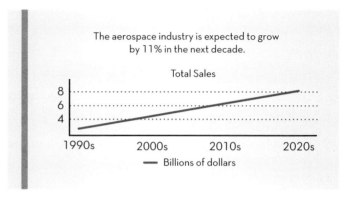

Figure 13.8

Assertion-Evidence Approach

In the assertion-evidence approach, a claim is presented with text and then supported with a visual element, such as a graph or photo.

- *Pictures:* Visual images can be very provocative, so many speakers use pictures as presentation aids. You can embed drawings or photographs directly into a slideshow. For instance, Figure 13.7 illustrates the use of a photograph in a presentation about Central America.

One option that combines the features of a text slide and a graphic slide is to use the assertion-evidence approach, in which a claim is presented as a heading and then a photo, graph, or other evidence supporting that claim is presented next. This approach focuses on building a presentation around messages rather than just topics and supporting those messages with visual elements rather than bulleted lists. You can see an example of this design in Figure 13.8.

Use video and audio.   Text and graphic slides are excellent options for displaying information, but there may be occasions when you want your audience to listen to or see an audio or a video recording. If your speech were about the career of entrepreneur and Apple co-founder Steve Jobs (who died in October 2011), you might have your audience watch or listen to one of his many public presentations. If you were pitching a proposed advertising campaign, you might show an animated storyboard or play the jingle you intend to use.

CHOOSING AND USING PRESENTATION AIDS

If they are used well, presentation aids can greatly enhance a speech. However, if they are not incorporated correctly, they can be distracting or even dangerous, greatly diminishing the effectiveness of a speech. This section gives tips for choosing and using presentation aids for maximum effectiveness.

Remember the goal.   No matter what type of presentation aids you choose, remember they are meant to *aid* your speech. They should never themselves become your focus. Instead, they should be used as accessories, embellishing your delivery but not overpowering it. Your listeners' primary focus should be on you and what you have to say.

Consider the context. Think about which presentation aids will work best for your audience, the layout of the room, and the resources available to you. Pay particular attention to these factors:

- *The size and arrangement of the room:* Make sure everyone will be able to see, hear, touch, taste, or smell the presentation aids you plan to use. If you're creating a slideshow presentation, use a font large enough for everyone to read comfortably. Before your speech, try your presentation aids in the space where you'll be speaking and confirm that every listener will be able to take advantage of them.
- *The time available for the speech:* Be certain you'll have adequate time to set up your presentation aids before you begin. Also, be sure you don't have too many slides to get through in the time allotted for your speech. This is an excellent reason to rehearse your speech with your visual aids, as discussed below.
- *The resources available:* Establish beforehand that you will have everything you need to make your presentation aids work, such as an accessible outlet, a power cord that reaches it, a projector and screen, and so on. Particularly in an unfamiliar room, don't take anything for granted. Double-check that you will have everything you need.

Strive for simplicity. Choose or create presentation aids that are as simple and straightforward as possible so your listeners will pay attention to their content instead of their form. For example, develop slides that are clean and uncluttered. Stay away from sound effects, fancy transitions, and pictures or photographs that are irrelevant to the content of the slide; these distracting features can reduce your listeners' ability to learn.

Prioritize simplicity in your timing as well. Present a presentation aid only when you are ready to use it; then turn it off or put it away. In this way, you will keep your audience's focus on your words and delivery.

Practice with your presentation aids. Practice advancing from slide to slide in your multimedia presentation—manually or with a remote control—so you can do so effortlessly and without awkward pauses. Practice speaking in the direction of your listeners instead of facing your slideshow while you talk. Rehearsing with your slideshow is also a good way to ensure you don't have too many slides for your allotted time. If you plan to use models, people, or other types of presentation aids, practice using those aids in your speech so that you can display and discuss them with ease.

Have a backup plan. Regardless of the type of presentation aid you plan to use, something can always go wrong that will prevent you from using it. You might misplace the USB drive containing your slides, or the computer on which you planned to run it might crash. The light bulb in your projector could burn out, the room's wi-fi could fail, or the person who was to demonstrate tai chi moves might get sick and cancel.

Think through everything that might go wrong and devise a backup plan. Bring a laptop computer or tablet containing your slideshow in case you forget your USB drive or the room's wi-fi fails. Copy your handouts a day or two before your speech. Learn the tai chi moves well enough to demonstrate them yourself if you have to. Being prepared to respond to such contingencies will help your speech succeed under any circumstances.

LO13.5

Describe strategies for using supporting materials ethically.

Using Supporting Material Ethically

Now that you have your supporting material and presentation aids, how do you use that material ethically and responsibly, to ensure that you aren't causing your audience harm or committing intellectual theft?

CAUSE NO HARM

The first rule of using supporting materials ethically, especially presentation aids, is to ensure that they don't cause your audience any harm. To that end, stay away from horrifying or disgusting photographs, audio or video recordings with profane or offensive language, and objects that produce dangerously loud sounds or noxious fumes. Using those sorts of presentation aids is unethical because it places your listeners in danger of being hurt, either physically or emotionally.

If you must use a potentially harmful aid in your speech, explicitly warn your audience about it at the beginning of your presentation and again right before you introduce it. For instance, if you're speaking about your organization's humanitarian response to a recent terror attack and feel you should include a photograph of the scene, tell your listeners beforehand that your photograph includes graphic depictions of victims who are injured or dead, so that your listeners have the option to look away.

DON'T COMMIT INTELLECTUAL THEFT

Although incorporating material from other sources is perfectly acceptable, you must avoid committing intellectual theft when you do so. A common form of intellectual theft is **plagiarism**, the use of information from another source without giving proper credit to that source. You plagiarize, that is, when you misrepresent someone else's words or ideas as your own, which is what you are doing when you fail to say where they come from. Intellectual theft also occurs as **copyright infringement**, the unauthorized use of materials protected by copyright such as photos or works of art. To use such material, you must gain the permission of the copyright holder and usually also give proper recognition of the source. As acts of academic and professional dishonesty, plagiarism and copyright infringement are subject to serious punishment and should always be avoided.

Intellectual theft can take several forms. When people prepare speeches, they may commit intellectual theft in at least three different ways. Understanding each will help you avoid plagiarism or copyright infringement when you put together a public presentation.

Using supporting material responsibly requires avoiding plagiarism and other forms of intellectual dishonesty.

©wavebreakmedia/Shutterstock

- **Global theft** means stealing your entire speech from another source and presenting it as if it were your own.
- **Patchwork theft** occurs when you copy words from multiple sources and put them together to compose your speech. Suppose you took large sections of your introduction directly from a magazine article, portions of your main points straight from a website, and the bulk of your conclusion verbatim from a television show. Even if you wrote portions of your speech to tie these stolen pieces together, you would still be committing plagiarism because you are passing off someone else's words as your

FOCUS ON ETHICS

Using Online Material Responsibly

Your manager has assigned you the task of compiling a written report on a new start-up company with the potential to compete for your business. You do some searching online and find a highly informative description of the company, its founder, and its business philosophy—exactly the details your manager wants to know. You figure that because the Internet doesn't technically *belong* to anyone, the way a book or newspaper does, it is fine to copy passages from this online description and paste them into your report word for word.

CONSIDER THIS: In what ways might this action be considered unethical? Why doesn't the source from which you are copying matter in a consideration of the ethics of your actions? Instead of copying and pasting passages from the online description, what is the more ethical way to use this material?

own. Similarly, if you download images from the Internet and include them in your presentation slides, because the images are protected by copyright, you are also committing patchwork intellectual theft.

- **Incremental theft** means failing to give credit for small portions of your speech—such as a phrase or paragraph—that you did not write. It is entirely acceptable to quote other people's words in your speech, but it is essential that you use a **verbal footnote**, a statement giving credit for the words to their original source. For example, you might say, "According to an April 2018 edition of *Forbes*, . . ." or "As former Hewlett-Packard CEO Carly Fiorina once noted, . . ." If you are using the person's words exactly as he or she wrote them, say "quote" when you begin reciting the quoted passage and "end quote" when you have finished, and make sure to cite the source.

Intellectual theft is a serious offense.   Those who commit intellectual theft are stealing someone else's work and committing academic dishonesty by passing that work off as theirs. Colleges and universities enforce codes of student conduct that prohibit plagiarism and copyright infringement and identify punishments such as failing grades, suspension, or even expulsion for offenders. Being found guilty of intellectual theft can also cast doubt over your credibility in the future. Professional associations in the communication discipline, including the National Communication Association and the International Communication Association, condemn plagiarism and copyright infringement as serious professional offenses.[13]

Given the amount of information readily available online, some students are tempted to commit plagiarism in their speeches and papers because they believe the likelihood of getting caught is low. To combat plagiarism, however, instructors at many colleges and universities now employ plagiarism-prevention software, such as SafeAssignment, iThenticate, or Turnitin. These programs check the text of speeches and papers against a wide variety of sources online, and they clearly identify passages of text that have been copied verbatim from another source, making it increasingly easy to spot plagiarism. For that reason alone, it is worth ensuring that you properly cite your sources and clearly identify any verbatim quotes in the speeches you prepare.

Imagine how you would feel if someone at your workplace committed intellectual theft by taking credit for something *you* had written. You would certainly be justified in feeling as though this person had stolen from you and cheated you out of receiving proper credit for your work. For tips on how to handle such a delicate situation gracefully, see the "People First" box.

PEOPLE **FIRST**

Reacting to Intellectual Theft

IMAGINE THIS: Each member of your work team has been assigned the task of drafting new marketing strategies for an upcoming product line. You spend much of the week and most of your weekend writing your report, and you are excited about the ideas you have formulated. Because each person on your team is compiling his or her material on a shared drive, you have been able to see the ideas your colleagues have come up with, and they have seen yours. When it comes time to report individually on the strategies you've each drafted, you are shocked to hear your colleague present two of your own ideas as though they were his.

Now, consider this: Because you have been able to see each other's material, you know your colleague did not come up with these ideas independently. Rather, he simply took credit for your work. In this situation, it is natural to feel angry, even infuriated. You came up with the ideas, after all, yet your colleague is getting the glory. How might you react to this situation in a way that makes your frustration known but still preserves your relationships with those involved?

- As much as you may want to call out your colleague immediately, that is seldom the best response. In this moment, you are feeling angry, cheated, and perhaps hurt. These emotions cloud your judgment and make it difficult to think clearly or act professionally, so your first strategy should be to take some time to calm down.

- Instead of accusing your colleague of stealing your ideas, tell him you noticed that he used some of your ideas in his presentation, and ask him whether that was intentional. Asking questions instead of making accusations puts the burden on your colleague to explain why he did what he did. Bear in mind the possibility that his action was an honest mistake; in that case, asking questions about it gives him space to apologize.

  - Ask your colleague what he is willing to do to set things straight. For instance, you might suggest that he make clear to the rest of your team that some of the ideas in his presentation were actually yours.

  Approaching your colleague in this way may not solve the issue, but it shows respect, professionalism, and a willingness to put people above hurt feelings. From time to time, most of us will feel unfairly treated by a co-worker, and our frustration is compounded when we believe that unfair treatment was intentional. Nonetheless, professionals rise above their anger and attempt to manage the situation in a calm and respectful manner.

THINK ABOUT THIS:

How do you feel when others take credit for your work? Have you ever taken credit for someone else's work, either inadvertently or on purpose? How did that person react?

The Internet provides resources to help students avoid intellectual theft. Table 13.1 describes three such websites you might find useful when you prepare a speech.

Table 13.1 Avoiding Intellectual Theft: Some Helpful Websites

Website	Materials
www.plagiarism.org	Types of plagiarism; instructions for citing sources; frequently asked questions about plagiarism
https://owl.english.purdue.edu/owl/resource/589/1	Specific tips for avoiding plagiarism; an exercise to identify properly cited sources
https://paragondigital.com/blog/how-to-avoid-copyright-infringement	Instructions for avoiding copyright infringement when using photos and images found online

Supporting material is key to an effective and engaging presentation. Here's a quick review of the chapter.

LO13.1 Determine when supporting material is needed in a presentation and which type of supporting material is appropriate.

- Factual claims should be distinguished from opinions, as they often benefit from different forms of supporting material.
- Definitions explain concepts that are unfamiliar to your audience.
- Examples help illustrate the topic or thesis of your presentation.
- Statistics are numbers that can help you support your claims.
- Quotations from experts can serve as valuable supporting material.
- Narratives are personal stories or testimonies that can support your claims.

LO13.2 Evaluate the quality of supporting material.

- Supporting material has credibility if it is believable and comes from a trustworthy source.
- Supporting material is objective to the extent that it presents information in an unbiased fashion.
- Supporting material has currency if it is up to date.

LO13.3 Compare and contrast various information-gathering techniques.

- Websites, including general search engines and research search engines, are invaluable sources of supporting material.

- Books, periodicals, and nonprint materials can all provide useful information.
- A database is an electronic storehouse of specific information that you can search.
- Conducting personal observations and surveys can be extremely useful ways of gathering supporting material.

LO13.4 Summarize strategies for maximizing the effectiveness of presentation aids.

- Presentation aids can improve audience attention, learning, and recall.
- Some of the most engaging presentation aids are low tech, including objects, flavors, textures, odors, handouts, and people.
- Multimedia presentation aids, including text slides, graphic slides, video, and audio, can allow speakers to integrate many different stimuli into a unified display.
- When choosing and using presentation aids, it is helpful to remember your goal, consider the context, strive for simplicity, practice with your presentation aids, and have a backup plan.

LO13.5 Describe strategies for using supporting materials ethically.

- The first rule of using presentation aids ethically is to ensure that they cause no harm to your listeners.
- Ensure that you are not committing intellectual theft in the form of plagiarism.
- Remember that intellectual theft can take several forms, including global theft, patchwork theft, and incremental theft, and that it is a serious offense.

A LOOK BACK

Now, let's return to the opening scenario. Kevyn gave a presentation about digital commerce in China. The presentation seemed fine until the audience started asking questions. Because audience members were likely considering how to invest in the Chinese market, they had pointed questions that focused on the reliability of information and where to find additional details. Kevyn showed that he hadn't carefully selected supporting material for his presentation and wasn't prepared to provide guidance about where to get reliable information. In other words, his presentation was relatively superficial. Were Kevyn adequately prepared, he would have provided only credible information and would have known exactly where it came from. He would have relied on diverse sources of information, and he would have been prepared to tell audience members where to get additional data.

bar chart   315

copyright infringement   318

database   310

general search engine   307

global theft   318

graphic slide   314

incremental theft   319

line chart   315

objective   304

patchwork theft   318

pie chart   315

plagiarism   318

presentation aid   312

questionnaire   311

research search engine   307

subjective   304

survey   311

text slide   314

verbal footnote   319

CHAPTER REVIEW QUESTIONS

1. How should you determine the type or types of support you require for a speech? LO13.1

2. When are definitions, examples, statistics, quotations, and narratives each likely to be useful? LO13.1

3. Why are credibility, objectivity, and currency valuable? Under what conditions is one of these characteristics more or less important than the others? LO13.2

4. What is the difference between an objective source and a subjective source? When is one type superior to the other? LO13.2

5. When doing research online, what advantages does a research search engine provide, compared to a general search engine? LO13.3

6. What is a periodical, and how does it differ from nonprint material? LO13.3

7. Which databases are particularly relevant for your academic discipline? LO13.3

8. What are the advantages of conducting a personal observation? What are the disadvantages? LO13.3

9. To collect original data, when might you conduct an interview, and when might you use a questionnaire? What are their relative advantages? LO13.3

10. In what ways can using presentation aids enhance your speech? LO13.4

11. What are some examples of low-tech presentation aids? LO13.4

12. What are the various types of slides you might use as presentation aids? What kind of data is each designed to present? LO13.4

13. When choosing presentation aids, what considerations should you take into account? LO13.4

14. How can presentation aids cause unintentional harm to your audience? LO13.5

15. What is the difference between global, patchwork, and incremental intellectual theft? LO13.5

16. Why is intellectual theft considered a serious offense? LO13.5

SKILL-BUILDING EXERCISES

Examine Objectivity and Currency (LO13.2)

Choose an issue of importance to you, such as diversity in the workplace or job growth in the medical sector. With another student, do a search for sources on that topic using scholar.google.com. Look at the first ten sources identified, and, working independently from each other, evaluate each source for its objectivity and its currency. Each of you should select the one source that you think provides the strongest combination of objectivity and currency and be able to explain why. Then, compare your answers and reasoning with each other.

Design a Questionnaire (LO13.3)

Suppose you want to collect original data from students at your school about their perceptions of companies that recruit on campus. Generate five specific questions you want to ask. For each, determine whether the question is open-ended (inviting broad, multi-word responses) or closed-ended (inviting a short, specific answer such as "yes" or "no"). For closed-ended questions, generate the list of potential answers from which students can select. Type up your questionnaire in a document or on a web page, and then ask your instructor to evaluate it.

Conduct a Personal Observation (LO13.3)

Select a behavior that is publicly observable at your workplace, on your campus, or in a public setting. An example could be the behavior of contributing to a donation drive, such as those stationed outside stores and restaurants during the holiday season. Find a place to observe this behavior unobtrusively—that is, without being obvious. For one hour, make notes about what you observe. For instance, you might observe that people are more likely to put money in a donation jar if they are by themselves than if they are in a group, or that younger people are more likely to contribute than older people. Write up your findings in a brief report, and then speculate as to how your observations might have been different at a different location or time of day.

Experiment with Different Types of Charts (LO13.4)

Search your college website for information on the demographic characteristics of the study body, such as the proportions of each sex, nationality, and/or ethnic group it includes. Represent your findings in a pie chart, then a line chart, and finally, a bar chart. Which of those formats do you think an audience would find most visually appealing, and why? Create a text slide to report your assessments.

Collect Multiple Forms of Evidence (LO13.2, LO13.3)

Pick a topic relevant to your current or future work goals. For that specific topic, identify one definition, one example, one statistic, one quotation, and one narrative that you might include as supporting material in your presentation.

Evaluate a Speaker's Use of Supporting Material (LO13.1, LO13.2, LO13.5)

Watch and listen to a speaker representing an industry in which you are interested. As you observe the speech, take careful notes about (1) what claims the speaker made, and (2) what type of evidence he or she provided in support of those claims. Was the speaker using statistics? Examples? Narratives? How well did each piece of supporting material match the claim it was intended to support? Write up your evaluation in a brief report.

ENDNOTES

1. *The Baltimore Sun.* (1996, December 3). General Motors vs. Volkswagen industrial espionage: Former GM executive who became VW president accused. Retrieved May 31, 2018, from http://articles.baltimoresun.com/1996-12-03/news/1996338063_1_gm-general-motors-lopez.

2. Hernandez, B. (2009, April 21). Hilton gets subpoena in Starwood's industrial espionage lawsuit. *CBS News Money Watch.* Retrieved May 31, 2018, from https://www.cbsnews.com/news/hilton-gets-subpoena-in-starwoods-industrial-espionage-lawsuit.

3. Martin, J. A., Hamilton, B. E., & Sutton, P. D. (2017). *Births: Final data for 2015. National vital statistics report* (Vol. 66, no. 1). Hyattsville, MD: National Center for Health Statistics.

4. Tom Frieden, CDC Director, quoted in Moran, J. M. (2014, September 30). CDC confirms first case of Ebola in US. *Fox News Health.*

5. Goldenberg, S. (2014, February 21). Work of prominent climate change denier was funded by energy industry. *The Guardian.* Retrieved May 31, 2018, from https://www.theguardian.com/environment/2015/feb/21/climate-change-denier-willie-soon-funded-energy-industry.

6. Kniffel, L. (2011, May 25). Reading for life: Oprah Winfrey. *American Libraries Magazine.* Retrieved from https://americanlibrariesmagazine.org/2011/05/25/reading-for-life-oprah-winfrey.

7. Weller, C. (2017, July 20). 9 of the most successful people share their reading habits. *Business Insider.* Retrieved from http://www.businessinsider.com/what-successful-people-read-2017-7/#oprah-winfrey-4.

8. Cowles, G. (2018). How to tap your inner reader. *The New York Times.* Retrieved May 31, 2018, from https://www.nytimes.com/guides/year-of-living-better/how-to-tap-your-inner-reader.

9. Alley, M. (2003). *The craft of scientific presentations: Critical steps to succeed and critical errors to avoid.* New York, NY: Springer.

10. Kim, D., & Gilman, D. A. (2008). Effects of text, audio, and graphic aids in multimedia instruction for vocabulary learning. *Educational Technology & Society, 11,* 114–126.

11. Zayas-Baya, E. P. (1997). Instructional media in the total language picture. *International Journal of Instructional Media, 5,* 145–150.

12. Houts, P. S., Witmer, J. T., Egeth, H. E., Loscalzo, M. J., & Zabora, J. R. (2001). Using pictographs to enhance recall of spoken medical instructions II. *Patient Education & Counseling, 43,* 231–242.

13. See, e.g., International Communication Association. (n.d.). Mission statement. Retrieved May 31, 2018, from https://www.icahdq.org/page/MissionStatement.

Learning Objectives

After reading this chapter, you should be able to do the following:

LO14.1 Compare and contrast the four styles of delivering a presentation.

LO14.2 Explain how to use visual and vocal cues effectively.

LO14.3 Summarize the psychological, physical, and behavioral effects of stage fright.

LO14.4 Describe strategies for managing public speaking anxiety and using it to a speaker's advantage.

LO14.5 Explain how to maintain presence and confidence while speaking.

CHAPTER 14

Rehearsing and Delivering Successful Presentations

Kalani paced slowly back and forth behind the podium. People were slowly trickling into the 50-person-capacity room for her conference presentation. She pulled out her notes and tried to review them one more time. Just three more minutes to go. Kalani was happy to see her colleague Paul sit in the second row. Unfortunately, she also saw her colleague Jessica enter the room. It seemed like Jessica was always critical of Kalani's work.

Kalani stepped up to the podium to begin her presentation. Her mouth felt dry. She looked at Jessica. Now even more nervous, she looked down at her notes for help and began speaking. By avoiding looking at her audience altogether, she made it through her presentation. As she concluded, she heard the weak applause and thought, "I never want to volunteer for a speech again."

Most professionals, especially early in their career, suffer through painful moments like this. What can you do to overcome anxiety and present with confidence and impact?

LO14.1

Compare and contrast the four styles of delivering a presentation.

Choose Your Delivery Format

As you learned in the chapter on choosing, developing, and researching a topic, people prepare speeches for many different reasons, such as to inform, to persuade, to entertain, to introduce, and to give honor. No matter *why* you're speaking, however, you have various options for *how* to deliver your speech. In this section, we examine four basic styles of delivery: impromptu, extemporaneous, scripted, and memorized. Because each style has specific benefits and drawbacks, you'll want to consider which works best in the context in which you are speaking.

SOME SPEECHES ARE IMPROMPTU

An **impromptu speech** is one you deliver on the spot, with little or no preparation. Suppose you're meeting with your project team at work and your manager asks you to share your marketing ideas with the group. If she had mentioned a week ago that she wanted you to speak at the meeting, you might have used that time to consider your message and prepare your remarks. Instead, she expects you to speak without the benefit of planning. Making an impromptu speech requires you not only to think spontaneously about what you want to say but also to organize your thoughts quickly into a set of speaking points. If you are already a bit apprehensive about public speaking, it can be a challenge.

When you're called on to deliver an impromptu speech, these hints can help you succeed:

- *Don't panic.* A pang of fear is a normal response, but it needn't prevent you from speaking well. Take a deep breath and tell yourself, "I can do this." Remember that you wouldn't be asked to speak if you didn't have something worthwhile to say.
- *Think in threes.* Whatever the topic of your impromptu speech, identify three points you want to make about it. Ask yourself "What three things do I want my audience to know?" Make these the three main points of your speech. If you include more than three points, it will be harder for your listeners—and you—to remember them all.
- *Draw on what's already happened.* Consider what else has been said or done in the context you're in and make reference to it. For example, you might begin your speech by responding to someone else's earlier observations or end by commenting on the occasion or the audience.
- *Be brief.* Fortunately, because impromptu speeches are spontaneous, people usually expect them to be short. Make your points concisely, provide a brief conclusion, and thank your audience for listening.

Although impromptu speaking can be stressful, it is certainly possible to do it well. As with many communication skills, you'll get more comfortable with it the more you practice.

SHARPEN YOUR SKILLS

Drafting Three Speaking Points

Suppose you were asked to deliver an impromptu speech addressing the question, "Why should businesspeople in the United States learn more about cultural diversity?" Identify three points you would make in such a speech.

SOME SPEECHES ARE EXTEMPORANEOUS

One benefit of giving an impromptu speech is that listeners believe your words are genuine or from the heart because you didn't have time to prepare them in advance. Another style of delivery that gives you that advantage—but also allows you some planning time—is the extemporaneous style. An **extemporaneous speech** is a prepared speech rehearsed to *sound* as though it is being delivered spontaneously.

Preparing to speak extemporaneously relies on the steps we examined in earlier chapters: constructing purpose and thesis statements; organizing your speech with an introduction, main points and subpoints, transitions, and a conclusion; creating a working outline; and drafting a set of speaking notes. Using your speaking notes, you can practice making your speech sound off the cuff or not heavily prepared. As an extemporaneous speaker, you want to communicate in a natural, conversational manner—to give the impression that you are simply *talking with* your listeners instead of *formally addressing* them. Analyzing and understanding your audience (see Chapter 11 on choosing, developing, and researching a topic) will help you relate to your speakers as effectively as possible.

Extemporaneous speaking offers some advantages over other styles of delivery. Because extemporaneous speakers use minimal notes, they can maintain audience eye contact, which helps their listeners engage. They can also speak in a more relaxed tone than if they were reading a script. Yet using speaking notes helps ensure that extemporaneous speakers won't forget their main points or lose their place.

Despite those important advantages, the extemporaneous style of delivery is not the best option in every situation. For instance, if a speech *must* last a specified period of time, such as on a television show or in a podcast, it is safer to read from a script that has been timed to fit that period. The extemporaneous style can also be challenging if the speech must have perfect grammar and no informalities, or if large sections must be exactly worded. These occasions call for the use of a script.

SOME SPEECHES ARE SCRIPTED

Unlike an extemporaneous speech, a **scripted speech** is composed word for word in a manuscript and then read aloud exactly as written. Scripted speeches are particularly common when the exact wording is crucial or when the speech must fit within a predetermined time frame. For instance, politicians often deliver scripted speeches before large audiences, such as the president does when delivering the State of the Union speech every year. The manuscript of the speech is projected onto a teleprompter in such a way that only the speaker can see it. Similarly, television news

Many business leaders, such as Apple's Tim Cook, use extemporaneous speeches to introduce new products and services. These speeches are carefully prepared but are delivered to appear spontaneous, conversational, and relaxed.

©Justin Sullivan/Getty Images

Leaders, such as IBM's Gini Rometty, often use scripted speeches at important events when the exact wording is crucial or when the speech must fit within a predetermined time frame.

©Chesnot/Getty Images

anchors read the day's stories word for word from a manuscript projected next to the cameras they are facing. A reporter or elected official must also ensure that facts are presented accurately, and going off script risks mistakes that can damage the speaker's credibility.

Many people opt for scripted speeches when they are nervous about speaking. Perhaps you've noticed that it is easy to become distracted when you're nervous. Distraction can cause you to stumble over your words or forget parts of what you want to say. Having a manuscript with all your words in front of you can be comforting, because it seems to ensure that you will always know exactly what you want to say.

Scripted delivery has some clear disadvantages, however. First, it often takes much more time and energy to prepare scripted than impromptu and extemporaneous speeches. Not only must you create a detailed outline for a scripted speech—as you would for an extemporaneous speech—but you also must then compose every part of the speech word for word. That process can be time-consuming, particularly when you generate several drafts.

Second, unless you are using a teleprompter, delivering a scripted speech requires you to manipulate a manuscript. If you were to drop it or shuffle the pages, you could lose your place. Even if you're reading from an iPad or tablet, your scrolling from page to page can distract your listeners. Finally, because you use your voice differently when you read aloud than when you engage in conversation, reading a speech can make you sound stiff or uninteresting rather than energetic and sincere. The best way to deal with that challenge is to practice reading your speech while varying your tone, volume, and speaking rate as you would during a conversation. In that way, you can help ensure that your speech doesn't *sound* read, even if you are reading it.[1]

SOME SPEECHES ARE MEMORIZED

Many talks, such as this TED Talk by Shonda Rhimes, are memorized to allow the speakers to gesture and maintain contact while maintaining complete control of the content.

Source: *TED Conferences, LLC*

Perhaps you like the control over your words that a scripted speech gives you, but you can't use or don't want to use a manuscript. In that case, you probably want to give a **memorized speech**, a speech you compose word for word and then deliver from memory. When you don't have to handle a script or set of notes, you can gesture naturally and maintain an effective level of eye contact with listeners, behaviors that can enhance your credibility as we'll see later in this chapter. Going "noteless" also frees you to move around while you speak.

Like scripted speeches, memorized speeches are useful when the time frame is limited. In political debates, for instance, candidates are often allowed only a certain number of minutes for their opening and closing statements. They usually prepare and rehearse memorized speeches that conform to those time limits.

Like all forms of delivery, memorized speeches have some drawbacks. One is that, like scripted speeches, they take a good deal of time and energy to prepare. Not only must you write the speech itself, you must also commit it to memory, which can be a challenge especially if it is relatively long. Another drawback is that

Table 14.1 Benefits and Drawbacks of Four Styles of Delivery

Style	Benefits	Drawbacks
Impromptu	Requires little preparation. Often makes the speaker sound genuine.	Lack of opportunity to prepare can be stressful. Thinking on the spot can be difficult.
Extemporaneous	Provides the speaker with notes while making the speech sound spontaneous.	Takes time to prepare. Difficult to do well under strict time constraints or if perfect grammar is required.
Scripted	Provides maximum control over the verbal content. Ensures the speaker always knows what to say.	Takes much time to prepare. Use of a manuscript can be distracting for speaker and audience.
Memorized	Allows high control over verbal content. Requires no notes, so speaker can use natural gestures and maintain eye contact.	Requires considerable effort to write and memorize. Can sound insincere. Speaker's memory can fail during delivery.

memorized speeches can come across as overprepared and highly formal. As a result, they may not sound as sincere as impromptu or extemporaneous speeches often do. You can overcome that disadvantage by rehearsing to make your speech *seem* as though you are presenting it for the first time.

A third disadvantage of giving a memorized speech is that your memory can fail. If you ever encounter that problem, the best way to recover is to improvise. Consider what you were saying right before your memory failed and then speak extemporaneously about it. Improvising for even a few moments may jog your memory, allowing you to resume your memorized speech without anyone's noticing that you temporarily forgot your words.

As summarized in Table 14.1, each style of delivery provides specific benefits but entails certain drawbacks. To succeed at any of these forms of delivery, however, you must first learn how to manage public speaking anxiety, our next topic.

RECORDED SPEECHES

Business professionals increasingly record their presentations to live stream to remote audiences and/or distribute via social media and other channels. Often, these recorded presentations are watched by more people online than in person. As a result, recorded presentations present a significant opportunity for many professionals. Whenever your presentations are recorded, you should think carefully about the benefits and drawbacks of impromptu, extemporaneous, scripted, and memorized styles for online audiences.

Business professionals rarely choose recorded *impromptu* presentations. While you may come across as genuine, you risk *going on the record* with unplanned or poorly formulated messages. A common exception involves panel discussions. Still, most professionals come prepared with talking points to keep them focused. Professionals should choose recorded *extemporaneous* speeches for energizing, promotional, and informational situations, often with friendly audiences. For example, most product launches should come across as exciting, engaging, and spontaneous. Professionals should choose recorded *scripted* speeches for highly consequential, precision-oriented, and serious occasions. For instance, leaders often record scripted messages during crises to ensure they demonstrate urgency and provide precise information. Finally, professionals should choose recorded *memorized* speeches for audience-centric, schedule-driven situations. For example, TED Talks generally involve speakers who connect deeply with their audiences but must stick to a well-choreographed schedule.

Rehearsing Effective Delivery

LO14.2

Explain how to use visual and vocal cues effectively.

Think about the most memorable speech you can recall hearing. What makes it stick in your mind? Perhaps it's partly what the speaker said, but what you probably remember most is the speaker's delivery. After all, we don't usually read other people's speeches—instead, we watch and listen to them. As we considered in Chapter 5, most of us pay more attention to the way people look and sound than to what they say. An effective speech therefore requires an effective delivery. We can categorize the behaviors of effective delivery as either visual elements or vocal elements. We can also note some of the ways in which speakers' cultural norms affect the styles of delivery they prefer.

VISUAL ELEMENTS AFFECT DELIVERY

Humans have a strong tendency to evaluate a situation—including a speech—according to what they see. This section describes how you can use visual cues like facial expression, eye contact, posture and body position, gestures, and personal appearance to your advantage.

Use appropriate facial expressions.   Recall from Chapter 3 that the face communicates more information than any other nonverbal channel. Research further indicates that two qualities of your facial expression are particularly important for an effective speech. The first is the degree to which they match the tone of your words. When your words are serious, your facial expression should be serious as well. You should smile when telling positive stories and express concern when telling troubling stories. Doing so creates *congruence* between your facial expressions and your verbal message that makes your audience more inclined to believe what you're saying.[2]

The second effective quality of your expressions is their ability to vary over the course of your speech. Presenting the same expression throughout your speech may cause listeners to tune you out. Speakers who vary their facial expressions—as long as they do so in ways that are appropriate to their words—are seen as competent and credible.[3]

Maintain eye contact.   A second element of effective delivery is eye contact. Inexperienced presenters often stare at the floor or the ceiling while speaking. Their subconscious is saying, "If I can't see my listeners, they can't see me." In contrast, looking your audience in the eye can make you feel vulnerable, because it acknowledges that your listeners are evaluating you.

Effective speakers know that maintaining eye contact with their listeners is extremely important, however.[4] Imagine carrying on a face-to-face conversation with someone who never looks you in the eye. You would likely get the impression that the person isn't interested in you or perhaps isn't being honest with you. Your listeners will probably form the same impressions of you if you don't look them in the eye while speaking.[5]

Of course, it's not necessary to stare at your listeners. Rather, you should make eye contact with one person in your audience, hold it for a moment, and then make eye contact with another audience member. Focus on one section of the audience at a time. Look at people in the front row for a minute or two and then direct your eye contact to those in the back corner or in the middle of the group. Try to make eye contact with each person at least once during your speech. When you look your listeners in the eye, you come across as confident and believable even if you feel nervous.[6]

Be aware of posture and body position.   Whether you're sitting or standing during your speech, it's important to adopt a posture that is relaxed but confident. Slouching or hanging your head will make you appear uninterested in interacting

CAREER TIP
Smile

Sir Richard Branson is the charismatic and energetic founder of the Virgin Group, a group of companies in travel and leisure, music and entertainment, financial services, and even aerospace, among other industries. Aside from his immense business success, Branson is known for his philanthropy, humanitarianism, and commitment to employees. He is among the most widely followed executives on social media. For example, he has roughly 13 million followers on Twitter who enjoy the career advice and motivational quotes he dispenses.

Branson often talks about the importance of smiling. He has said, "When somebody smiles at you, it is immediately clear whether the smile is genuine or forced. You can tell if the person's eyes shine and their whole face lights up, or if their lips simply upturn a little. You can tell if the person is happy and sharing their happiness with you. . . . Next time something really makes you smile, share it with the person next to you."[7] Branson's advice applies to many

Sir Richard Branson
©Facundo Arrizabalaga/Epa/Shutterstock

communication situations, including speaking: by smiling with others, you can display your authenticity and share your enthusiasm.

with the audience. Instead, keep your back straight, your shoulders square, and your head up. That posture makes you appear strong, composed, and in control.[8]

You should also be aware of your body movement and position, particularly if you're standing. First, make sure you stand facing your listeners. That advice may seem obvious, but it is particularly easy to forget if your speech incorporates visual aids. When presenting a slideshow, for instance, some speakers turn away from the audience and talk to the screen. They not only seem like they are ignoring their audience; they're also making it difficult for listeners to hear them. A better approach is to stand alongside the screen so you are still facing your audience, and to turn your head—instead of your whole body—when you need to see the next slide.

Depending on the size and layout of the room in which you're speaking, you may also have the option of walking around during your speech. Even if you're presenting a slideshow, you can use a remote-control clicker to advance your slides while you walk around. Moving around can make your presentation more visually interesting to your audience than standing in one spot, and natural gestures can also help the audience understand what you are saying, as Chapter 12's discussion of nonverbal signposts suggested.[9]

If you are able to move around during your speech, make your movements appear casual but deliberate. Move slowly to one position, stay there for a few minutes, and then move slowly to another spot. A particularly good time to move from one place to another is during a transition in your speech, because your change in position will correspond to a change in your remarks. You want to avoid random movement, which will suggest you are simply expending nervous energy. Similarly, avoid movement that looks contrived or unnatural, such as circulating continuously around three specific spots. If you can move in a natural and relaxed manner, you will hold your listeners' attention and enhance your credibility.

Use appropriate gestures. Gestures are movements of the hands, arms, or head that express meaning. Most of us gesture naturally as we converse with other people, and the use of conversational gestures also enhances the effectiveness of a speech.[10]

There are three pointers about gestures to keep in mind. First, gestures should look spontaneous rather than planned. Spontaneous gestures naturally follow what you are saying and thus appear well connected to your verbal message. Planned gestures, in contrast, appear contrived and insincere. Perhaps the best way to keep your gestures from looking planned is not to plan them but to let them arise naturally from the words you're speaking. Even if you do rehearse your gestures, follow the advice in the chapter on organizing and finding support for your speech by rehearsing them until they look and feel natural.

A second key factor is that gestures should be appropriate in number. Some speakers, especially when they're anxious, gesture almost constantly because the motion helps them to get rid of excess nervous energy. If you've ever listened to such a speaker, however, you know that using too many gestures can distract an audience and make it difficult for listeners to concentrate on the speaker's words. While some speakers show nervousness by overdoing gestures, others become physically tense and barely gesture at all. As a result, they appear stiff and rigid. Effective speakers, then, use a *moderate* number of gestures—not too many, not too few.

Finally, gestures should be appropriate in size for your proximity to the audience. If your listeners are relatively close to you, as in a conference room or a small classroom, you should use gestures similar to those you would use in face-to-face conversations. The same is true if you are speaking to your audience via a webcam; you'll want to keep your gestures somewhat small so they are easily captured by the camera. If you are farther away from your listeners, as in an auditorium, using larger, more dramatic gestures is appropriate so that your audience can see them.

Pay attention to personal appearance. A final visual element of an effective delivery is personal appearance—clothing, accessories, and grooming. Of course, your appearance should be appropriate for your audience and for the occasion on which you're speaking. Dress to match the formality of—or to be slightly more formal than—your listeners' appearance. The more your personal appearance reflects theirs, the more they will perceive you as similar to them, and that perception enhances your credibility.[11] In contrast, dressing far more formally or far less formally than your listeners will lead them to see you as more of an outsider.

Jewelry and accessories should complement your clothing but not attract attention. Long, flashy earrings or multiple bracelets that clang together whenever you move

Savvy speakers dress for the occasion. Leaders, such as Mark Zuckerberg, are aware of the formality of the situation.

When you're getting ready to present a speech, use this checklist to make sure you have given adequate attention to your personal appearance. Read each of the following statements and indicate whether the statement is true or false by placing a checkmark in the appropriate column.

	True	False
1. My clothing is far more formal than that of my audience.	——	——
2. I am wearing jewelry that makes noise when I move.	——	——
3. I am dressed far more casually than my listeners are.	——	——
4. My appearance is unkempt.	——	——
5. I am wearing accessories that will attract attention.	——	——
6. My clothing is similar to what my listeners will be wearing.	——	——
7. I look well groomed.	——	——
8. Everything I am wearing is clean.	——	——
9. I'm not wearing any flashy jewelry.	——	——
10. I believe my appearance will make the impression I want to make.	——	——

As you might guess, you should answer "false" to the first five items and "true" to the second five. If any of your answers are otherwise, you may want to recheck your personal appearance before your speech to ensure you are making the visual impression on your listeners that you intend to make.

your arm will distract your audience. Effective speakers also know it's important to be well groomed when giving a speech. You can use the checklist in "The Competent Communicator" box to ensure you've attended adequately to your personal appearance before presenting a speech.

Your facial expressions, eye contact, posture and body position, gestures, and personal appearance all influence the effectiveness of your speech by affecting what your audience *sees*. However, effective delivery also relies on what your audience *hears*.

VOCAL ELEMENTS AFFECT DELIVERY

Several elements of the voice influence the way people understand and evaluate what the speaker says. Here we'll examine the influence of rate, volume, pitch, articulation, and fluency in effective speech delivery.

Consider the rate of your speech. Your speech rate is simply the speed at which you speak. In normal conversation, most U.S. adults speak approximately 150 words per minute.[12] Studies find, though, that speaking at a faster rate makes a speaker seem more persuasive[13] and more credible.[14] The explanation may be that speakers who speak quickly appear to be in command of what they're saying, whereas slower speakers sound less sure of themselves.

There are two important caveats about speaking rate, however. The first is that it is possible to speak *too* fast. If you speak unusually fast, your listeners may not understand your message but may instead simply focus on how fast you're talking. The second caution is that you should adapt your speaking rate to your audience.

Speaking at a brisk rate may work well with most audiences, but you'll likely need to speak more slowly to be understood if your audience is composed of young children, older adults, people with developmental disabilities, or people who don't speak your language fluently.

Determine the appropriate volume. Vocal volume is the loudness or softness of the voice. The appropriate volume for your speech depends on several factors, such as the size of your audience, the size of the room, and whether you're using a microphone. Just as you would in a face-to-face conversation, you want to ensure that you are speaking loudly enough for your listeners to hear you but not so loudly as to make them uncomfortable. In general, you will speak more loudly if you have a large audience than a small one, but if you are using a microphone, you need only speak at a normal conversational volume to be heard. If you know you'll be using a microphone for an upcoming speech, practice with it ahead of time if you can.

Effective speakers also vary their volume during their speech to create certain effects. They may speak more loudly when making particular points to express enthusiasm or conviction. They may speak softly to create a serious tone or to encourage the audience to pay close attention. Varying your vocal volume will add variety to your speech and help keep your listeners engaged in it.

Be aware of pitch. Vocal **pitch** is a measure of how high or how low the voice is. Every voice, whether naturally high, medium, or low, typically has a range of pitches it can produce. When speakers are nervous, their vocal pitch becomes higher than normal. High-pitched speech often makes the speaker sound nervous and unsure, whereas a deeper pitch may convey greater confidence. If you focus on relaxing while you speak, your voice may also relax, allowing you to speak at a deeper pitch.

Perhaps more important than pitch itself is the variation in pitch you use while speaking. Speakers who vary their pitch sound energetic and dynamic and are judged by others as friendly[15] and caring.[16] In contrast, those who speak in a monotone voice, with little or no variety in pitch, often come across as tired or annoying.[17] Just as effective speakers vary their volume to create certain effects, so too do they vary their pitch to hold their listeners' attention.

Employ good articulation. **Articulation** is the extent to which the speaker pronounces words clearly. A speaker who mumbles has poor articulation, which makes it difficult for listeners to understand what he or she is saying. In contrast, a speaker with good articulation enunciates each word clearly and correctly.

You can improve your articulation by avoiding five common articulation problems:

- *Addition* is caused by adding unnecessary sounds to words. For example, a person might say "real-ah-tor" instead of "real-tor" or "bolth" instead of "both."
- *Deletion* occurs when a speaker omits part of a word sound, usually at the beginning or end of the word. Someone may say "frigerator" instead of "refrigerator," or "goin'" instead of "going."
- *Transposition* means reversing two sounds within a word. Examples include saying "hunderd" instead of "hundred" and "perfessor" instead of "professor."
- *Substitution* is caused by replacing one part of a word with an incorrect sound. A person might say "Sundee" instead of "Sunday" or "wit" instead of "with."
- *Slurring* occurs when a speaker combines two or more words into one. "Going to" becomes "gonna" and "sort of" becomes "sorta."

Articulation errors such as these aren't necessarily problematic when they occur in face-to-face conversations. Many of us are so used to committing such errors in our everyday communication that we don't even notice them. In a speech, however, poor articulation can damage the speaker's credibility.

Ensure good fluency. Whereas articulation refers to the speaker's clarity, **fluency** refers to the smoothness of the speaker's delivery. Speeches that are fluent have an uninterrupted flow of words and phrases. There is a smooth rhythm to the delivery, without awkward pauses or false starts. In contrast, disfluent speeches are characterized by the use of filler words, such as "um," "uh," and "like," and by the unnecessary repetition of words. Researchers have known for some time that people who speak with fluency are perceived as more effective communicators than people who do not.[18]

Speaking with fluency is a particular challenge for individuals who stutter. **Stuttering** is a speech disorder that disrupts the flow of words with repeated or prolonged sounds and involuntary pauses.[19] Stuttering usually strikes individuals early in life and can significantly impair their ability to communicate.[20] With treatment, many can overcome their stuttering before reaching adulthood. For those who do not, ongoing speech therapy can often help improve the fluency of speech, even if it doesn't eliminate stuttering entirely.[21] Former U.S. vice president Joe Biden, actors Samuel L. Jackson and Emily Blunt, singer Chris Martin, sportscaster Bill Walton, and golfer Tiger Woods are among many famous people who have dealt with stuttering and gone on to lead successful lives in the public sphere.

Rate, volume, pitch, articulation, and fluency aren't the only vocal elements of an effective speech delivery, but they are among those most noticeable to listeners. Paying attention to them as you speak will help you sound confident and credible.

CULTURAL NORMS AFFECT PREFERRED DELIVERY STYLES

Although the visual and vocal elements we just described often accompany speech performances that are considered effective in U.S. culture, speakers with other cultural backgrounds may prefer different delivery styles.[22] For example, many Asian cultures teach students to behave modestly and quietly, especially around people of higher status such as teachers, which can make delivering a speech in a classroom setting especially uncomfortable for Asian American students. Similarly, whereas U.S. audiences generally appreciate speeches that are organized linearly—so that each topic flows logically into the next—norms in some Asian cultures value more circular presentations in which the speaker comes back to the same point multiple times.

Cultural norms can affect the content of a speech as well as its delivery. Many in the United States enjoy speeches that identify a problem and then persuade listeners to adopt a particular solution to it. Political speeches often take that form, for instance. Some Arab cultures, however, regard problems as "severe twists of fate that cannot be solved," making speakers from those cultures less likely to adopt the problem-solving model common among many U.S. speakers.[23]

When listening to speakers whose cultural backgrounds differ from your own, remember that their cultural norms and values may lead them to prefer styles of speaking that are unfamiliar to you. Because competent speakers work to adapt their behaviors to their listeners' expectations, they also respect the diversity of ways in which people around the world are taught to express themselves.

Managing Public Speaking Anxiety

Every few years, the Gallup organization polls U.S. adults about what they most fear. In a survey of more than a thousand people, the most commonly mentioned item was snakes—and the second was public speaking.[24] Incidentally, the fear of death didn't make the top ten list, a finding suggesting that some respondents were more afraid of giving a speech than they were of dying. That reality once prompted comedian Jerry Seinfeld to joke that at a funeral, most people would rather be in the casket than giving the eulogy.

All joking aside, public speaking can be a terrifying prospect for people who suffer from **public speaking anxiety**, sometimes also called *stage fright:* nervousness or fear brought on by performing in front of an audience. As you'll learn in this section, public speaking anxiety is a type of stress that affects individuals psychologically, physically, and behaviorally.[25] It can sometimes be debilitating, causing people to deliver poor performances. Fortunately, you can learn to use stage fright to your advantage by overcoming some of its problematic effects.

PUBLIC SPEAKING ANXIETY IS A COMMON FORM OF STRESS

LO14.3

Summarize the psychological, physical, and behavioral effects of stage fright.

The anxiety or fear that many people feel before giving a speech or performing in front of a crowd is a form of stress. **Stress** is the body's reaction to any type of perceived threat. You may feel stress, for instance, when you think about an upcoming visit to the doctor, when you sit down to take a final exam, or when you are laid off from a job. Although those are different situations, each poses some type of threat, whether it's to your physical health, academic record, or financial well-being. Scientists use the term **stressor** to refer to events that cause the body to experience stress.

As communication scholar James McCroskey has documented, public speaking is a common stressor.[26] Research indicates that the anxiety associated with public speaking affects more than one in five adults,[27] a figure that has remained stable for the last four decades.[28] Public speaking stress is so common, in fact, that many scientific experiments about stress purposely use a public speaking activity to elevate participants' stress levels.[29]

Although public speaking may not threaten a person's physical, academic, or financial well-being as do other stressors, many people feel that it threatens their emotional well-being. For instance, they might worry about experiencing embarrassment, disapproval, or ridicule if their speech doesn't go well. For them, giving a speech can be just as stressful as many more serious threats.

One speaking situation that can be particularly stress-inducing is having to take a position you know some members of your audience will disagree with or even be offended by. For some suggestions on how to handle that task, check out the "People First" box.

When we feel stress, our body reacts in ways that affect us psychologically, physically, and behaviorally. Let's examine how those components of the stress response are related to public speaking anxiety.

Psychological effects of public speaking anxiety. Public speaking anxiety represents a specific form of **anxiety**, a feeling of worry and unease. Communication scholars Ralph Behnke and Chris Sawyer devoted much of their careers to studying the anxiety associated with public speaking. One of their most important findings is that anxiety often begins long before speakers stand in front of an audience. According to Behnke and Sawyer, many people experience **anticipatory anxiety**, which is the worry they feel when looking ahead to a speech.[30] Perhaps you can recall feeling worried or stressed when you learned you would have to make a speech in class or at work. Anticipatory anxiety usually decreases as individuals begin preparing their speeches, probably because preparation gives them a sense that they can control their performance.[31] Then, just before delivering the speech, anxiety peaks as people feel the pressure to perform.

Not every speech will evoke the same level of anxiety. For instance, you've probably found that you're less anxious when speaking about a topic you understand well

PEOPLE **FIRST**

Addressing the "Elephant in the Room"

IMAGINE THIS: As a spokesperson for a nonprofit organization focused on peace and diplomacy, you are currently preparing a persuasive speech for a public forum in which you will argue that the United States should cease military interventions in foreign countries. The position of your organization is that the United States should respect cultural diversity instead of imposing its customs and forms of government on other cultures. In particular, you plan to claim that the 2003 invasion of Iraq, and the war that followed, were unjustified. You know, however, that a few members of your audience will be military veterans who have done tours of duty in the Middle East. You recognize that your remarks could be considered offensive to them, as well as to other audience members who support the military or have veterans in their families, but you aren't sure whether or how to address this.

Now, consider this: This situation can create an "elephant in the room," which refers to a context in which an obvious truth is being ignored because it would be awkward to acknowledge. In this case, people in your audience may realize there are veterans present who could be offended by your words. This creates an uncomfortable situation for your listeners as well as for you. To avoid having an "elephant in the room," consider these strategies:

- Acknowledge the issue instead of ignoring it. In this case, you might say "I realize we have some veterans in the audience today, and many of us may have military members or veterans in our families. I certainly understand that some of them may disagree

with the position I'm taking." Audiences often grow increasingly uncomfortable the longer the elephant is ignored.

- Make clear that your opposition is not to military members themselves. To defuse tension, you might offer praise for active duty or military veterans. You can then be clear that your opposition is to government policies that direct military action, not to the troops who carry out those orders.

- Whenever you disagree with a sizeable proportion of your audience, point out that people on both sides of the issue feel strongly about their positions. Then, focus on what you believe you have in common: "We may not agree on government policies for military action, but I think we can all agree that it's important to respect the sacrifices of our women and men in uniform and to avoid putting them in harm's way whenever we can."

By acknowledging conflicts of opinion, treating the opposing side with respect, and focusing on your similarities instead of just your differences, you can reduce the stress such situations create.

THINK ABOUT THIS:

Why is it less stressful to acknowledge an elephant in the room than to ignore it? How does it put "people first" to deal with the elephant respectfully?

---

than one that is less familiar. The reason is that having a command of your topic gives you confidence in what you're saying. Delivery style also appears to affect how much anxiety people experience about public speaking. One study found that speakers had the most anxiety when anticipating an impromptu speech, less when anticipating an extemporaneous speech, and least when anticipating a scripted speech.[32]

People vary with respect to how many of the psychological effects of speaking anxiety they experience. Those who are outgoing,[33] uninhibited,[34] intellectually sophisticated,[35] and not prone to worry[36] typically experience the lowest levels. Women in one study had higher levels of anticipatory anxiety than did men[37]—perhaps a reflection of differences in the ways women and men react physically to stressful situations.[38]

Physical effects of public speaking anxiety. Try to recall a time when you experienced stress. Perhaps your heart beat faster, you breathed more heavily, and you perspired more than normal. Other physical changes were occurring outside your conscious awareness. Your body was producing more stress hormones, for instance, and the pupils of your eyes were dilating. Those physical effects of stress are part of the body's **fight-or-flight response**, a reaction that helps prepare the body either to confront the stressor (through a fight) or to avoid it (by fleeing the situation).[39] Your heart and breathing rates increase to get more oxygen to your muscles so you have more energy for either fighting or fleeing. You perspire more to keep from overheating. Your stress hormones temporarily increase your strength, and your pupils dilate so that you can take in as much visual information about the situation as possible.[40] In these ways, the physical effects of stress enable you to deal with it as effectively as possible.

Public speaking anxiety produces many of the same physical stress reactions, including increased heart rate and blood pressure and elevated stress hormones.[41] These are also similar to the effects of other forms of stage fright, such as people might experience before acting in a play or dancing in a recital. One study found that people training to be professional musicians experienced increases in heart rate and stress hormones when they performed in front of an audience, as opposed to when practicing on their own.[42] Even college instructors sometimes experience anxiety before they teach.[43] Fears of making a mistake and being embarrassed can invoke physical stress for anyone performing in front of a crowd, including public speakers.

Like psychological anxiety, stress varies from person to person in the level experienced when speaking in public. Some studies have demonstrated, for example, that individuals with a strong tendency to worry experience more physical stress when anticipating, preparing, and delivering a speech than do non-worriers.[44] Moreover, those who react strongly to other stressful situations tend to experience highly elevated stress during a speech.[45] There are also some sex differences in public speaking stress. Although women report more psychological anxiety about public speaking than men do, research shows that men experience more physical stress overall while delivering a speech. In particular, men demonstrate greater elevations in stress hormones[46] and blood pressure,[47] although women appear to experience greater elevations than men do in heart rate.[48]

Behavioral effects of public speaking anxiety. In addition to its psychological and physical effects, public speaking anxiety also influences the way people behave.[49] You can probably recall from your own experience how you act when you're nervous. Perhaps you fidget or pace. Maybe you find it difficult to speak. Researchers have been examining those and other behavioral effects of anxiety for several decades.[50] Their work indicates that public speaking anxiety—as well as other forms of stage fright—affects behavior in at least five separate domains:

- *Voice:* Public speaking anxiety often causes the voice to quiver or sound tense—or to sound higher than normal.[51]
- *Mouth and throat:* People experiencing public speaking anxiety often swallow and clear their throat more frequently than normal.
- *Facial expression:* Muscle tension in the face causes a general lack of expression and eye contact. It can also make the face twitch slightly.
- *General movement:* Public speaking anxiety frequently causes people to fidget or engage in random movement. It can also cause them to pace, sway, or shuffle their feet.
- *Verbal behavior:* People experiencing public speaking anxiety often stutter more than usual. They also increase their use of filler words, such as "um" or "uh," and they are more likely to forget what they want to say.[52]

As we'll discover in the next sections, the psychological, physical, and behavioral effects of speaking anxiety can inhibit your ability to speak effectively, but speaking anxiety can also *improve* your performance if you know how to manage it successfully.

PUBLIC SPEAKING ANXIETY CAN BE DEBILITATING

When public speaking anxiety is particularly intense, it can become debilitating—that is, it can overwhelm people and prevent them from speaking or performing effectively. Like a deer caught in the headlights, people with debilitating speaking anxiety can become immobilized and unable to deliver their speech, even if they have rehearsed extensively. More intense forms of social anxiety can even affect people economically, in the form of lost productivity and increased health care costs.[53]

Debilitating public speaking anxiety often causes two distinct sensations. The first is that your mind seems to go blank, and the second is that you are motivated to try to escape the situation. In the grip of intense stage fright, you become distracted by your body's efforts to manage the emotion you are feeling, and you can easily forget words or information you would readily remember under normal circumstances.[54]

We've seen that stressful events often trigger a fight-or-flight response, so you may not be surprised to learn that the second sensation sometimes triggered by debilitating anxiety about public speaking is an urge to escape.[55] Because stress and fear make you perceive that your well-being is threatened, you want to get away to protect yourself from harm.[56] If you feel intensely nervous about giving a speech, for example, you may find yourself wishing you could postpone the speech or trying to get it over with as quickly as possible. You may also avoid eye contact with your listeners as a subconscious way to escape their attention.

It's difficult to speak effectively when your mind goes blank and you feel the urge to escape. Just because speaking anxiety *can* have those debilitating effects, however, doesn't mean that it *must*.

MAKING PUBLIC SPEAKING ANXIETY AN ADVANTAGE

Although speaking anxiety is common, you can learn to turn it to your advantage. This section offers six pieces of advice for making it your friend.

Accept public speaking anxiety as a normal response.   When you are working to become a better speaker or performer, you might be inclined to focus on trying to eliminate your public speaking anxiety. You may reason that if it inhibits your ability to perform well, it makes sense to get rid of it. Such efforts would be largely wasted, however. All forms of fear, including speaking anxiety, are deeply rooted in humans' ancestral experiences. The fear response is largely innate, and although people who perform frequently in front of audiences usually become less nervous over time, this visceral response rarely goes away entirely. Thus, rather than trying to eliminate it, accept it as a normal part of the performance experience. In fact, speaking anxiety can even help you perform better than you would if you didn't feel nervous. Next we'll show you how.

Focus your nervous energy.   Recall that the stress of public speaking causes bodily changes—including elevated heart rate, breathing rate, and stress hormone levels—that increase your energy stores. That energy boost is meant to help you deal effectively with a threatening situation. You can train yourself to focus your nervous energy on the goal of giving the best speech possible rather than letting it distract you.

LO14.4

Describe strategies for managing public speaking anxiety and using it to a speaker's advantage.

You can use a variety of strategies to turn anxiety into an advantage.

©recep-bg/Getty Images

TECH TIP
Practicing Speeches with Virtual Reality or Augmented Reality

Practicing your speeches and presentations in virtual reality (VR) or augmented reality (AR) may sound complicated, but it's relatively straightforward with some inexpensive, easy-to-use tools. For example, with a VR headset such as Google Cardboard (starting around $10; many other VR headsets are available to use with your mobile phone), you can get a variety of free or inexpensive apps—including Samsung's #BeFearless, VirtualSpeech, and AncientC's Public Speaking Simulator—that allow you to practice giving speeches in different situations. These apps continue to become more lifelike with simulated audiences. VR apps are also being developed with many other communication situations. Consider trying them to overcome nerves and improve your communication skills.

Many people find it helpful to rehearse a speech with a virtual audience.

©Purestock/SuperStock

Just as many athletes try to get psyched up before a game so they have more energy to channel toward their performance, so, too, can you use your nervousness to energize your speech.

Visualize a successful performance.   A technique that often helps individuals perform well, even if they are experiencing anxiety, is **visualization**: developing a specific mental image of winning or giving a successful performance.[57] Practice visualization by closing your eyes and imagining yourself delivering an expert speech.

As you visualize, see yourself giving your entire speech in a confident and relaxed manner. Research shows that people who visualize a successful speech performance experience less speaking anxiety and fewer negative thoughts when they actually deliver their speeches, compared to people who don't use visualization.[58]

Desensitize your fear.   People generally avoid what they fear. For instance, if you're afraid of flying, you will tend not to fly. The more you avoid flying (or something else you're afraid of), however, the scarier it often seems. In contrast, when people face their fears and encounter the situations that frighten them, they often realize these aren't as scary as they once seemed; your fear of flying may lessen after you have taken a flight and experienced a safe take-off and landing. You will gradually feel less and less afraid each time you fly.

The process of confronting frightening situations head-on is called **desensitization**, and it can significantly reduce the anxiety individuals experience about all sorts of fears, including public speaking.[59] The more you practice speaking in front of people, the less frightening public speaking will become, because over time you will become desensitized to it.

Practice in virtual reality.   One way to desensitize yourself to public speaking anxiety is to take every opportunity you have to speak in public, even if the prospect scares you. Remind yourself that you're facing your fears so you can overcome them, and you will be stronger and more confident after each speech.

Another way to desensitize yourself to the anxiety of public speaking is to practice speaking in front of a computer-generated audience. Then deliver speeches to that virtual audience before you deliver them to real-life listeners. In the safety of a computer-mediated environment, you will gain practice in the public speaking context. Research has shown that practicing with an online audience can help desensitize you to public speaking anxiety.[60]

Stay positive. Finally, approach the delivery of your speech with a positive, optimistic attitude. Tell yourself that you can—and will—succeed. This positive self-talk can be difficult, particularly if you're very nervous or have had negative experiences with previous performances. It's helpful for two reasons, however. First, positive thoughts and emotions help relieve the negative physical effects of stress.[61] Therefore, you'll approach your speech in a more relaxed manner than you otherwise would. Second, recall from the chapter on perceiving that negative thoughts can turn into a self-fulfilling prophecy, causing you to have a poor performance simply because you expect to. Approaching your speech with an optimistic attitude, in contrast, can encourage the behaviors that will help you succeed.

In summary, public speaking anxiety is a common experience that can either inhibit or enhance your ability to give an effective speech. The key is knowing how to manage it and make it work to your advantage. Yet even if you feel nervous about delivering a speech, you don't have to look or sound nervous. In the next section, you'll discover how to deliver a speech so you come across as calm and confident in the eyes of your audience.

Creating Presence and Projecting Confidence

LO14.5
Explain how to maintain presence and confidence while speaking.

When it's time to speak, you can adopt several strategies to create presence and project confidence, including getting comfortable with your audience, choosing words that focus on people, staying flexible and calm, using the room to your advantage, and involving your audience during and after the speech.

GET COMFORTABLE WITH YOUR AUDIENCE

Getting comfortable with your audience will help you speak more confidently, and your ability to put your audience at ease will increase their confidence in you. Here's how.

Engage with audience members before starting your presentation. One of the best ways of relaxing immediately before your presentation is to speak with audience members. Greet them at the door, walk around the room, engage in small talk, and find other ways to break the ice and help you and your audience members warm up to each other.

Focus on friendly faces at first, to gain composure and confidence. Inevitably, the presence of some audience members will make you more nervous than others. It may be a critical boss, a skeptical client, a person you often disagree with, or someone who intimidates you for other reasons. In the opening moments of your presentation, when you are most apt to suffer from nervousness, look at those in the audience with whom you are most friendly. This will help calm you during those important first moments.

Make your audience comfortable and be sensitive to their unique needs. Always learn as much about your audience as possible and be perceptive to their unique needs. For example, you might learn that many audience members have poor eyesight or poor hearing. Distributing easy-to-read handouts may help those who can't view slides well. If you think some audience members may have impaired hearing, make sure to use the microphone at all times and annunciate clearly. Avoid being distracted when you see some audience members looking at their phones. It's not uncommon for those with hearing impairments to use their mobile phones to control volume in their hearing aids. As you consider the comfort of your audience members (without drawing attention to any unique needs), you'll naturally develop a better connection and rapport with them.

CHOOSE WORDS THAT FOCUS ON PEOPLE

If you make your speech about people, your audience members are more likely to trust your commitment to them and others: People like to hear about people. Also, a strong people-focus will allow you to liven up dry facts and statistics. It generally increases your confidence when you make a real connection with your audience members. Try the following ways to make your speech about people.

Make people the subject of your sentences. Especially when you present numerical information, using people as the subjects of your sentences humanizes your presentation. Notice the distinctions between the less effective and more effective examples in Table 14.2.

Table 14.2 **Making People the Subject of Your Sentences**

Less Effective	More Effective
The survey showed just 43 percent of respondents believe that annual reviews are accurate indicators of performance.	Jeff, Steve, and I developed the survey after holding focus groups with our employees to learn about their views of annual reviews. Of the 223 employees who took the survey, just 43 percent believed that annual reviews are accurate indicators of performance.
Explanation: This statement is compelling but dry and impersonal to some audience members.	**Explanation:** This statement is more compelling because it introduces the people who designed the survey based on what they heard from employees, and the larger group of employees who ultimately took the survey.

Table 14.3 **Introducing Colleagues by Name**

Less Effective	More Effective
I'll be presenting research conducted by the HR team.	*Our HR team, including Jeff Brody and Steve Choi, spent the last two months gathering information about annual reviews and continuous reviews. We've talked to HR directors at other companies, software vendors who provide new continuous review tools, and our own employees. Today we'll share this research with you.*
Explanation: This statement is good but could be improved by elaborating on who the members of the HR team are and why they're positioned to provide good advice.	**Explanation:** This statement is stronger, with its focus on the members of the HR team and why they are positioned to provide strong advice.

Table 14.4 **Using Names of Audience Members**

Less Effective	More Effective
It's common for managers to continue conducting annual performance reviews, even though they think there should be better ways of evaluating and motivating performance.	*Just before we started the meeting this morning, Cynthia, John, and I were chatting about annual performance reviews. They each mentioned great managers they knew here in this company who conduct annual performance reviews as a matter of routine but don't think they work. These managers believe there should be better ways of evaluating and motivating performance.*
Explanation: This statement is good but is not personalized. It is essentially a "faceless" comment that may be less persuasive because it doesn't talk about real people.	**Explanation:** This statement makes the point in a personalized, relatable manner. It shows the presenter is connected to the experiences of the audience.

Introduce colleagues and refer to them by name during your presentation. By naming members in your organization or other relevant people, you help your audience members feel they are getting to know these important individuals (see Table 14.3).

Use names of audience members as appropriate. When you know the names of those in your audience, consider using their names from time to time to personalize your presentation (see Table 14.4).

STAY FLEXIBLE AND CALM

Presentations rarely go as planned. Knowing your content perfectly will help you adapt to unexpected circumstances. Maintaining a flexible approach will help you think on your feet for unanticipated events. Consider the following ways of staying flexible.

Arrive early. Arriving early lets you notice any surprises in terms of equipment, room layout, or people in attendance. You may then be able to make adjustments before the presentation begins. When presenting in a place you've never been to before, arrive at least an hour or two early.

Focus on the needs of your audience. Some presentations can get off course when audience members raise questions or make comments. If you are preoccupied with your own agenda only, you can become flustered or disorganized if someone poses a question. Be ready to adapt to the immediate needs of your audience so you can quickly modify your presentation based on their requests. If you spend time anticipating possible questions, you will generally be prepared to answer them at any point in your presentation and segue back into your speech.

When you lose your place, don't panic.   All presenters inevitably lose their train of thought from time to time. When this happens, you can try a few strategies. One is simply to pause until you regain your composure and your line of thinking. Within a few seconds, you will often get back on target. What seems like an eternity to you will be but a short pause to audience members. Many audience members will not even notice you lost your place. Another strategy is to repeat the last statement you made (five or six words). Doing so will help you regain your thought process.

Never tell your audience things haven't gone as expected.   Many presenters instinctively tell the audience when, say, needed technology has failed or handouts have been misplaced. Resist the urge to mention these mishaps. To many audience members, it sounds like excuse-making and detracts from your key messages and/or your credibility. Most audience members will never know anything out of the ordinary has happened if you simply proceed with slightly modified plans.

Always have a plan B.   If you have electronic slides to display, be prepared for the projector not to work and to speak without them. If you spot factual problems in your handouts at the last moment, be prepared to present without them. Know ahead of time how you'll present under these situations.

Know what your key messages are.   You can often leave out parts of your presentation as necessary with little change in impact as long as you know your three or four key messages and accentuate them throughout your presentation.

USE THE ROOM TO YOUR ADVANTAGE

You will inevitably present in rooms of various sizes and layouts. Generally, you connect with your audiences best if you position yourself close to them and establish eye contact. Consider the following advice.

Position yourself where people can see you easily.   Walk around the room before your presentation to check the vantage points that various audience members will have. Now you know where you can stand to get the most eye contact with your audience. Also, think about how you can be closest to them. If your audience members have taken all the back seats and left the front seats empty, move closer to them to reduce the spatial barrier. Or, politely ask them to move forward to the front of the room.

Move around but avoid distracting the audience.   During presentations of more than five to ten minutes, you can keep the audience more engaged by moving around the room. This draws the focus to you and allows you to gain spatial proximity with most of your audience members at some point during your presentation. However, some movements can be distracting. For example, excessive pacing may show that you're nervous. Or, since you will likely be standing and your audience members will likely be seated, getting too close may make them feel that you are hovering over them.

Use podiums and tables strategically.   Many rooms are set up with podiums or tables, where presenters can place notes and other materials. Standing behind a podium or table can help you project authority and add to the formality of the presentation. If you do use a podium to achieve these goals, make sure you stand upright.

Avoid leaning on or gripping the podium, which indicates nervousness. Also, consider whether a podium, table, or other object placed between you and your audience creates a barrier to connection. If you stand in front of the podium or table, you can get closer to your audience physically. As a result, you may achieve a more friendly, accessible, and casual tone.

ENGAGE YOUR AUDIENCE

Good speakers engage the audience as much as possible without getting off message and taking too much time. A few ways to interact with your audience include fielding questions during the presentation as well as mingling and following up with audience members afterward.

Field questions.   Many of your presentations will include a question-and-answer (Q&A) portion. You may ask for questions at the conclusion or invite them throughout. When you take questions, you show you are interested in your listeners' real concerns and needs. You also have an opportunity to clarify points you may have misstated or omitted. Of course, fielding questions carries a number of risks: Your audience members may ask you difficult ones and may even get you off topic. The solution is to reinforce your key messages while also addressing the needs of your questioners. Practice the following strategies to make the Q&A go as smoothly and effectively as possible:

Pause before answering.   This gives you time to reflect and quickly develop the best response. It also gives the impression that you are thoughtful. In some cases, you may feel under pressure during questioning. Pausing helps you stay calm and collected.

Be honest.   During questioning, many presenters are so committed to supporting their own positions that they respond with exaggeration or with excessive confidence. This is a mistake. Admit when you do not know the answer. Explain that you would like to get an answer to the question and seek an opportunity to continue the conversation later on. Notice in Table 14.5 less effective and more effective responses when the speaker doesn't have a firm answer to a question.

Table 14.5 **Be Honest**

Less Effective	More Effective
Q. *I know you've said that managers will like this new system, but you haven't really talked about what managers wouldn't like about the system. For me, I'd worry about this system eroding my authority to ask for real changes, especially if other employees are giving so much positive feedback. So, don't you think this could actually upset some managers?*	
A. I guess that I haven't really heard that concern yet. I think that managers might have a concern like that initially, but as they continue using the system they'll notice they are actually empowered rather than having their authority eroded.	**A.** I'm not prepared to give a good answer to that question right now, but I think we certainly need to address it. Perhaps the HR team can ask some of our contacts at companies using continuous reviews to tell us their experiences with the challenges that managers face with these systems. If it's okay with you, the HR team and I will get some answers to your question and email the entire senior management team within a week.
Explanation: This response glosses over the fact that she is not informed enough to give an accurate answer. Although she attempts to put a positive spin on the problem, she may appear dismissive of some listeners' genuine concerns.	**Explanation:** The speaker states that she is uncertain. However, she demonstrates a willingness to get the answer from reliable sources and promises to provide that information within a week. Overall, she gains credibility with her up-front, helpful response.

Table 14.6 **Show Appreciation**

Less Effective	More Effective
Q. *Do you think there's a risk that because the feedback is public, managers and employees will avoid sharing their candid and real views of one another's performance?*	
A. Actually, the system allows private feedback so that . . .	**A.** That's a good question. We talked to four or five HR directors who have implemented continuous reviews, and they each initially had this concern. In practice, employees and managers use the private feedback feature when they offer negative or sensitive feedback.
Explanation: This is a good, rational response but could be improved with additional validation of the questioner.	**Explanation:** By briefly validating the importance of the question, the speaker is able to demonstrate that she relates directly to this concern and that her company is committed to facilitating this communication. The response is strong rationally and emotionally.

Table 14.7 **Be Concise**

Less Effective	More Effective
Q. *You've mentioned a few success stories at Peakster Computing. Could you mention some examples at other companies you've talked to?*	
A. Sure. I could give you lots of examples. Let me tell you about three other companies . . . (continues on for three to four minutes largely repeating the same key points).	**A.** Momentarily, I'll distribute a handout with more comprehensive information from our research. The handout provides cases for four companies we worked with, so you'll be able to see that the results at Peakster Computing are quite similar to those at the other three companies.
Explanation: By providing such a lengthy answer, the speaker may inadvertently disengage some of her audience members who have already gotten her key points.	**Explanation:** In this brief response (roughly 20 seconds), the speaker provides new information (that will be in a handout) and touches on but does not belabor key take-away points. This response has broad appeal since it allows audience members to locate additional results from other companies.

Show appreciation.   Fielding questions allows you to develop an emotional bond with the questioner. You can do so by sincerely showing thanks, recognizing the importance of the question, and otherwise validating the questioner, as the speaker does in the more effective example in Table 14.6.

Be concise.   Short responses are effective for several reasons. First, the question may be of interest to just one or a few of your audience members. Second, the longer your response, the more likely you are to stray from your key messages or excessively repeat them. As a rule of thumb, keep most responses to between 20 and 45 seconds. Pay close attention to your audience members during Q&A to see whether they are remaining interested and engaged. Read Table 14.7 to compare less and more concise responses.

Reframe the question to match your agenda.   You should have fairly clear objectives for your presentation. When your listeners ask questions that could derail your agenda, find ways to tactfully reframe the conversation in favor of your objectives, as the speaker does in Table 14.8.

Table 14.8 Reframe the Question to Match Your Agenda

Less Effective	More Effective
Q. *I'm quite skeptical that our company will get the dramatic results you've suggested. Do you really think a software program will help us reduce employee turnover?*	
A. Well, actually, I can't guarantee anything. But I can tell you with certainty that these types of software platforms have made dramatic differences in each company we've talked to. I think we'll have similar results here.	**A.** I think it's fair to say that we can reduce employee turnover by focusing on performance in a more positive and motivating way. What we've learned from these other companies is that they used the software successfully because they created a culture of performance where managers and employees are giving one another more frequent, more positive, and more candid feedback. This energizing environment is what reduced employee turnover. So, I'd say creating this culture with the help of these software tools will help us reduce employee turnover.
Explanation: This question challenges the basic premise that technology (a software platform) can make a difference. It may raise the same doubt among other audience members as well. While the response is true, it fails to reframe the question in a way that focuses on how managers and employees help each other.	**Explanation:** This response reframes the conversation by emphasizing how managers and employees encouraging one another to improve is the key driver of lower employee turnover. This response is successfully reframed to address the questioner's real concern: Technology isn't the solution.

Mingle and follow up.   When you complete your presentation, your work is not complete. In most cases, this is a good opportunity to work the room, further connecting with your audience. You can get additional feedback and discuss future endeavors with your listeners.

Similarly, in the days following the event, you can reach out to your audience members. Follow up on any promises you made about providing additional information. If possible, send a quick email note to thank people for attending. Set in motion steps that turn a one-time presentation into an ongoing professional relationship.

CHAPTER WRAP-UP

Following the principles and suggestions for rehearsing and delivering presentations will lead to a successful outcome. Here's a quick review of the chapter.

LO14.1 Compare and contrast the four styles of delivering a presentation.

- An impromptu speech is delivered on the spot, with little or no preparation.
- An extemporaneous speech is prepared ahead of time and rehearsed to sound as though it is being delivered spontaneously.
- A scripted speech is composed word for word in a manuscript and then read aloud exactly as written.
- A memorized speech is composed word for word and then delivered from memory.

- Some speeches are recorded in order to live stream to remote audiences and/or distribute via social media and other channels.

LO14.2 Explain how to use visual and vocal cues effectively.

- Your facial expressions should match the tone of your words and create congruence with your verbal message.
- Eye contact with your audience can make you come across as confident and believable to your audience.
- Your posture and body position should be relaxed but confident.
- Your gestures should appear spontaneous, appropriate in number, and appropriate in size.

- Your personal appearance should be appropriate for your audience and for the occasion.
- You should adopt effective vocal cues in terms of rate, volume, pitch, articulation, and fluency.

LO14.3 Summarize the psychological, physical, and behavioral effects of stage fright.

- Many people suffer from public speaking anxiety, which is a form of stress.
- Many speakers experience anticipatory anxiety.
- Many speakers experience physical effects such as elevated stress levels, faster heart beat, heavier breathing, and perspiration.
- Many speakers experience behavioral effects of stage fright such as a quivering or higher-pitched voice, dry mouth and throat, tense or twitchy facial expressions, random movements, and an increase in stuttering or use of filler words.

LO14.4 Describe strategies for managing public speaking anxiety and using it to a speaker's advantage.

- Accept public speaking anxiety as a normal response.
- Focus your nervous energy.
- Visualize a successful performance.
- Desensitize your fear.
- Practice in virtual reality.
- Stay positive.

LO14.5 Explain how to maintain presence and confidence while speaking.

- Get comfortable with your audience.
- Choose words that focus on people.
- Stay flexible and calm.
- Use the room to your advantage.
- Engage your audience.

A LOOK BACK

Now, let's return to the opening scenario. What could Kalani have done differently to deliver a more successful presentation? Kalani likely suffers from public speaking anxiety. She should take time to consciously reduce the effects of this anxiety. She should accept it as a normal response, focus her nervous energy, visualize a successful performance, and desensitize. From the opening scenario, we can also see several mistakes that likely increased her anxiety and reduced her ability to speak confidently and connect with her audience. Rather than mingling with the audience members as they entered, she stayed back behind the podium. Rather than focusing on the friendly face in the audience (her colleague Paul), she focused on the intimidating face in the audience (her colleague Jessica). Had she gotten more comfortable with her audience and focused on Paul as she was gaining eye contact with the audience, she likely could have presented with much more confidence.

KEY TERMS

CHAPTER REVIEW QUESTIONS

1. What are the advantages and drawbacks of impromptu, extemporaneous, scripted, and memorized speeches? **LO14.1**

2. Why is it important for facial expressions to match your message? **LO14.2**

3. What are some reasons people tend to avoid eye contact when speaking? **LO14.2**

4. Why do effective speakers moderate their gestures? **LO14.2**

5. How does the distance from the audience impact how speakers should gesture? **LO14.2**

6. What factors should you consider when choosing attire and accessories to wear when giving a speech? **LO14.2**

7. What are the benefits and drawbacks of speaking more rapidly? **LO14.2**

8. How can you avoid articulation problems? **LO14.2**

9. What are some ways culture impacts speech norms? **LO14.2**

10. What are common reasons for public speaking anxiety? **LO14.3**

11. How can you make your listeners more comfortable when taking a position they may disagree with? **LO14.3**

12. What are common psychological, physical, and behavioral reactions associated with speech anxiety? **LO14.3**

13. How can speakers use anxiety to their advantage? **LO14.4**

14. What are some ways you can get comfortable with your audience? **LO14.4**

15. Describe strategies for making people the focus of your presentations. **LO14.5**

16. Describe strategies for effectively fielding questions during or after your presentation. **LO14.5**

SKILL-BUILDING EXERCISES

Evaluating a Corporate Presentation (LO14.5)

Go online and find a business presentation that interests you and that includes a Q&A. You can generally find presentations easily on company websites (usually in the Media, Newsroom, or Investors sections), YouTube, or business websites (e.g., CNBC). Evaluate the presentation and include the following in your analysis:

- How effectively did the speaker make people the subject of sentences?
- How effectively did the speaker refer to others by name?
- Did the speaker pause before answering questions?
- Did the speaker show appreciation for questions, even when they were challenging?

- Did the speaker respond to questions concisely enough?
- Did the speaker come across as credible as he/she responded to questions?

Assess Public Speaking Anxiety (LO14.3, LO14.4)

Take James McCroskey's Personal Report of Public Speaking Anxiety (PRPSA)[62] assessment:

Directions: Below are 34 statements that people sometimes make about themselves. Please indicate whether or not you believe each statement applies to you by marking whether you:

Strongly Disagree = 1; Disagree = 2; Neutral = 3; Agree = 4; Strongly Agree = 5.

_____ 1. While preparing for giving a speech, I feel tense and nervous.

_____ 2. I feel tense when I see the words "speech" and "public speech" on a course outline when studying.

_____ 3. My thoughts become confused and jumbled when I am giving a speech.

_____ 4. Right after giving a speech I feel that I have had a pleasant experience.

_____ 5. I get anxious when I think about a speech coming up.

_____ 6. I have no fear of giving a speech.

_____ 7. Although I am nervous just before starting a speech, I soon settle down after starting and feel calm and comfortable.

_____ 8. I look forward to giving a speech.

_____ 9. When the instructor announces a speaking assignment in class, I can feel myself getting tense.

_____ 10. My hands tremble when I am giving a speech.

_____ 11. I feel relaxed while giving a speech.

_____ 12. I enjoy preparing for a speech.

_____ 13. I am in constant fear of forgetting what I prepared to say.

_____ 14. I get anxious if someone asks me something about my topic that I don't know.

_____ 15. I face the prospect of giving a speech with confidence.

_____ 16. I feel that I am in complete possession of myself while giving a speech.

_____ 17. My mind is clear when giving a speech.

_____ 18. I do not dread giving a speech.

_____ 19. I perspire just before starting a speech.

_____ 20. My heart beats very fast just as I start a speech.

_____ 21. I experience considerable anxiety while sitting in the room just before my speech starts.

_____ 22. Certain parts of my body feel very tense and rigid while giving a speech.

_____ 23. Realizing that only a little time remains in a speech makes me very tense and anxious.

_____ 24. While giving a speech, I know I can control my feelings of tension and stress.

_____ 25. I breathe faster just before starting a speech.

_____ 26. I feel comfortable and relaxed in the hour or so just before giving a speech.

_____ 27. I do poorer on speeches because I am anxious.

_____ 28. I feel anxious when the teacher announces the date of a speaking assignment.

_____ 29. When I make a mistake while giving a speech, I find it hard to concentrate on the parts that follow.

_____ 30. During an important speech I experience a feeling of helplessness building up inside me.

_____ 31. I have trouble falling asleep the night before a speech.

_____ 32. My heart beats very fast while I present a speech.

_____ 33. I feel anxious while waiting to give my speech.

_____ 34. While giving a speech, I get so nervous I forget facts I really know.

Scoring: To determine your score on the PRPSA, complete the following steps:

- *Step 1:* Add scores for items 1, 2, 3, 5, 9, 10, 13, 14, 19, 20, 21, 22, 23, 25, 27, 28, 29, 30, 31, 32, 33, and 34.
- *Step 2:* Add the scores for items 4, 6, 7, 8, 11, 12, 15, 16, 17, 18, 24, and 26.
- *Step 3:* Complete the following formula: PRPSA = 72 − Total from Step 2 + Total from Step 1. Your score should be between 34 and 170. If your score is below 34 or above 170, you have made a mistake in computing the score. Your overall anxiety level is on the following scale: High >= 131; Moderate = 98–131; Low <= 98.

Create a plan to use anxiety to your advantage: After completing the PRPSA assessment, answer the following questions.

- What did you learn about your own public speaking anxiety by taking this assessment? Categorize your stage fright or nervousness in terms of psychological, physical, and behavioral effects.
- What three strategies can you adopt to use anxiety to your advantage? Be specific about how to apply these strategies and how each strategy addresses specific types of stage fright or nervousness.

Evaluating an Effective Presentation (LO14.1, LO14.2, LO14.5)

Think about a recent presentation you attended in which the speaker was successful at delivery. In three to five paragraphs, describe why it was effective. Include the following aspects in your analysis:

- What was the general approach to the presentation (impromptu, extemporaneous, scripted, or memorized)? How did this approach match goals of the presentation?
- How effectively did the speaker employ nonverbal communication?
- How effectively did the speaker employ verbal qualities (such as articulation, tone, and pitch)?
- How effectively did the speaker project confidence?

Video Recording Your Presentation (LO14.1, LO14.2, LO14.5)

Record one of your presentations and then do the following:

A. Immediately following your presentation, draft your basic impressions of your performance.
B. Watch the video recording three times as follows:

- On the first viewing, observe the overall impact of your presentation.
- On the second viewing, turn off the volume and observe your nonverbal behaviors.
- On the third viewing, close your eyes and listen. Pay attention to the speed, volume, pitch, variety, and enthusiasm in your voice.

After completing steps A and B above, answer the following questions about your presentation:

- How effective was your opening?
- How effective was your nonverbal communication (e.g., voice quality, eye contact with audience)?
- How effective was the content of your presentation (e.g., relevance to audience, logical order, impact)?
- How persuasive was your presentation?

- How well did you connect with your audience?
- Overall, name two major strengths and two major weaknesses of your presentation.
- If you were going to deliver this same presentation again, what three adjustments would you make?
- What are the two presentation skills you believe you most need to improve? Explain.

ENDNOTES

1. See Schwanenflugel, P. J., Hamilton, A. M., Kuhn, M. R., Wisenbacker, J. P., & Stahl, S. A. (2004). Becoming a fluent reader: Reading skill and prosodic features in the oral reading of young readers. *Journal of Educational Psychology, 96*, 119–129.

2. Knapp, M. L. (2009). *Lying and deception in human interaction.* Boston, MA: Pearson.

3. Mehu, M., Mortillaro, M., Bänziger, T., & Scherer, K. R. (2012). Reliable facial muscle activation enhances recognizability and credibility of emotional expression. *Emotion, 12*, 701–715.

4. Yokoyama, H., & Diabo, I. (2012). Effects of gaze and speech rate on receivers' evaluations of persuasive speech. *Psychological Reports, 110*, 663–676.

5. van Straaten, I., Holland, R. W., Finkenauer, C., Hollenstein, T., & Engels, R. C. M. E. (2010). Gazing behavior during mixed-sex interactions: Sex and attractiveness effects. *Archives of Sexual Behavior, 39*, 1055–1062.

6. Vincze, L. (2009). Gesture and gaze in persuasive political discourse. *Multimodal Signals: Cognitive and Algorithmic Issues, 5398*, 187–196.

7. Branson, R. (2017, December 22). *A smile is the universal welcome.* Retrieved from https://www.virgin.com/richard-branson/smile-universal-welcome.

8. See de Gelder, B., de Borse, A. W., & Watson, R. (2015). The perception of emotion in body expressions. *Wiley Interdisciplinary Reviews: Cognitive Science, 6*, 149–158.

9. Munhall, K. G., Jones, J. A., Callan, D.E., Kuratate, T., & Vatikiotis-Bateson, E. (2004). Visual prosody and speech intelligibility: Head movement improves auditory speech perception. *Psychological Science, 15*, 133–137.

10. Goldin-Meadow, S., & Alibali, M. W. (2013). Gesture's role in speaking, learning, and creating language. *Annual Review of Psychology, 64*, 257–283.

11. Elsbach, K. D. (2004). Managing images of trustworthiness in organizations. In K. M. Roderick & K. S. Cook (Eds.), *Trust and distrust in organizations* (pp. 275–292). New York, NY: Russell Sage Foundation.

12. Wolvin, A. D. (Ed.). (2010). *Listening and human communication in the 21st century.* Chichester, England: John Wiley & Sons.

13. Jones, C., Berry, L., & Stevens, C. (2007). Synthesized speech intelligibility and persuasion: Speech rate and non-native listeners. *Computer Speech & Language, 21*, 641–651.

14. Simonds, B. K., Meyer, K. R., Quinlan, M. M., & Hunt, S. K. (2006). Effects of instructor speech rate on student affective learning, recall, and perceptions of nonverbal immediacy, credibility, and clarity. *Communication Research Reports, 23*, 187–197.

15. Rockwell, P., & Hubbard, A. E. (1999). The effect of attorneys' non-verbal communication on perceived credibility. *Journal of Credibility Assessments and Witness Psychology, 2*, 1–13.

16. Ray, G. B. (1986). Vocally cued personality prototypes: An implicit personality theory approach. *Communication Monographs, 53*, 266–276.

17. Miley, W. M., & Gonsalves, S. (2003). What you don't know can hurt you: Students' perceptions of professors' annoying teaching habits. *College Student Journal, 37*, 447–455.

18. Miller, G. R., & Hewgill, M. A. (1964). The effect of variations in nonfluency on audience ratings of source credibility. *Quarterly Journal of Speech, 50*, 36–44.

19. Brundage, S. B., & Hancock, A. B. (2015). Real enough: Using virtual public speaking environments to evoke feelings and behaviors targeted in stuttering assessment and treatment. *American Journal of Speech-Language Pathology, 24*, 139–149.

20. Reilly, S., Onslow, M., Packman, A., Wake, M., Bavin, E. L., Prior, M., . . . Ukoumunne, O. C. (2009). Predicting stuttering onset by the age of 3 years: A prospective, community cohort study. *Pediatrics, 123*, 270–277.

21. Guitar, B. (2013). *Stuttering: An integrated approach to its nature and treatment* (4th ed.). San Diego, CA: Lippincott, Williams & Wilkins.

22. Kragh, S. U., & Bislev, S. (2005). Universities and student values across nations. *Journal of Intercultural Communication, 9*, 48–63.

23. Stewart, E. C., & Bennett, M. J. (1991). *American cultural patterns: A cross-cultural perspective.* Yarmouth, ME: Intercultural Press. Quote is from page 155.

24. Gallup, G. (Ed.). (2001). *The 2001 Gallup poll: Public opinion.* Lanham, MD: Rowman & Littlefield.

25. Pull, C. B. (2012). Current status of knowledge on public-speaking anxiety. *Current Opinion in Psychiatry, 25*, 32–38.

26. McCroskey, J. C. (2009). Communication apprehension: What we have learned in the last four decades. *Human Communication, 12*, 157–171.

27. Ogden, J. S. (2010). *Public speaking anxiety, test anxiety, and academic achievement in undergraduate students.* Unpublished

master's thesis, College of Education, Bucknell University. Retrieved from http://digitalcommons.bucknell.edu/masters_theses/51.

28. Heimberg, R. G., Stein, M. B., Hiripi, E., & Kessler, R. C. (2000). Trends in the prevalence of social phobia in the United States: A synthetic cohort analysis of changes over four decades. *European Psychiatry, 15,* 29–37.

29. Kirschbaum, C. (2015). Trier social stress test. In I. P. Stolerman & L. H. Price (Eds.), *Encyclopedia of psychopharmacology* (pp. 1755–1758). Berlin, Germany: Springer-Verlag.

30. Behnke, R. R., & Sawyer, C. R. (1998). Conceptualizing speech anxiety as a dynamic trait. *Southern Communication Journal, 63,* 160–168.

31. Benke, R. R., & Sawyer, C. R. (1999). Milestones of anticipatory public speaking anxiety. *Communication Education, 48,* 165–172.

32. Witt, P. L., & Behnke, R. R. (2006). Anticipatory speech anxiety as a function of public speaking assignment type. *Communication Education, 55,* 167–177.

33. MacIntyre, P. D., & Thivierge, K. A. (1995). The effects of speaker personality on anticipated reactions to public speaking. *Communication Research Reports, 12,* 125–133.

34. Freeman, T., Sawyer, C. R., & Behnke, R. R. (1997). Behavioral inhibition and the attribution of public speaking state anxiety. *Communication Education, 46,* 175–187.

35. MacIntyre, P. D., & Thivierge, K. A. (1995). The effects of speaker personality on anticipated reactions to public speaking. *Communication Research Reports, 12,* 125–133.

36. Mladenka, J. D., Sawyer, C. R., & Behnke, R. R. (1998). Anxiety sensitivity and speech trait anxiety as predictors of state anxiety during public speaking. *Communication Quarterly, 46,* 417–429.

37. Behnke, R. R., & Sawyer, C. R. (2000). Anticipatory anxiety patterns for male and female public speakers. *Communication Education, 49,* 187–195.

38. Ordaz, S., & Luna, B. (2012). Sex differences in physiological reactivity to acute psychosocial stress in adolescence. *Psychoneuroendocrinology, 37,* 1135–1157.

39. Catterall, W. A. (2015). Regulation of cardiac calcium channels in the fight-or-flight response. *Current Molecular Pharmacology, 8,* 12–21.

40. Floyd, K., Mikkelson, A. C., & Hesse, C. (2007). *The biology of human communication* (2nd ed.). Florence, KY: Thomson.

41. Roberts, J. B., Sawyer, C. R., & Behnke, R. R. (2004). A neurological representation of speech state anxiety: Mapping salivary cortisol levels of public speakers. *Western Journal of Communication, 68,* 219–231.

42. Arch, J. J., & Craske, M. G. (2006). Mechanisms of mindfulness: Emotion regulation following a focused breathing induction. *Behaviour Research and Therapy, 44,* 1849–1858.

43. Fredrikson, M., & Gunnarsson, R. (1992). Psychobiology of stage fright: The effect of public performance on neuroendocrine, cardiovascular, and subjective reactions. *Biologial Psychology, 33,* 51–61.

44. Witt, P. L., Brown, K. C., Roberts, J. B., Weisel, J., Sawyer, C. R., & Behnke, R. R. (2006). Somatic anxiety patterns before, during, and after giving a public speech. *Southern Communication Journal, 71,* 87–100.

45. Finn, A. N., Sawyer, C. R., & Behnke, R. R. (2009). A model of anxious arousal for public speaking. *Communication Education, 58,* 417–432.

46. Bouma, E. M. C., Riese, H., Ormel, J., Verhulst, F. C., & Oldehinkel, A. J. (2009). Adolescents' cortisol responses to awakening and social stress: Effects of gender, menstrual phase and oral contraceptives. The TRIALS study. *Psychoneuroendocrinology, 34,* 884–893.

47. Traustadóttir, T., Bosch, P. R., & Matt, K. S. (2003). Gender differences in cardiovascular and hypothalamic-pituitary-adrenal axis responses to psychological stress in healthy older adult men and women. *Stress, 6,* 133–140.

48. Heponiemi, T., Keltikangas-Järvinen, K., Kettunen, J., Puttonen, S., & Ravaja, N. (2004). BIS-BAS sensitivity and cardiac autonomic stress profiles. *Psychophysiology, 41,* 37–45.

49. See Russell, J. J., Moskowitz, D. S., Zuroff, D. C., Bleau, P., Pinard, G., & Young, S. N. (2011). Anxiety, emotional security and the interpersonal behavior of individuals with social anxiety disorder. *Psychological Medicine, 41,* 545–554.

50. Clevinger, T., & King, T. R. (1961). A factor analysis of the visible symptoms of stage fright. *Speech Monographs, 28,* 296–298.

51. Giddens, C. L., Barron, K. W., Byrd-Craven, J., Clark, K. F., & Winter, A. S. (2013). Vocal indices of stress: A review. *Journal of Voice, 27,* 390.e21–390.e29.

52. Bulleted list was adapted from Table 1 of Mulac, A., & Sherman, A. R. (1974). Behavioral assessment of speech anxiety. *Quarterly Journal of Speech, 60,* 134–143.

53. Acaturk, C., Smit, F., de Graaf, R., van Straten, A., ten Have, M., & Cuijpers, P. (2009). Economic costs of social phobia: A population-based study. *Journal of Affective Disorders, 115,* 421–429.

54. Beatty, M. J., Heisel, A. D., Lewis, R. J., Pence, M. E., Reinhart, A., & Tian, Y. (2011). Communication apprehension and resting alpha range asymmetry in the anterior cortex. *Communication Education, 60,* 441–460.

55. Moons, W. G., Eisenberger, N. I., & Taylor, S. E. (2010). Anger and fear responses to stress have different biological profiles. *Brain, Behavior, and Immunity, 24,* 215–219.

56. Williams, C. (2012). Performance anxiety and the fight or flight syndrome. *Journal of Literature and Art Studies, 2,* 551–558; Porges, S. W. (2009). The polyvagal theory: New insights into adaptive reactions of the autonomic nervous system. *Cleveland Clinic Journal of Medicine, 76* (Suppl 2), S86–S90.

57. Ayres, J., & Hopf, T. (1992). Visualization: Reducing speech anxiety and enhancing performance. *Communication Reports, 5,* 1–10.

58. Ayres, J., Hopf, T., & Ayres, D. M. (1994). An examination of whether imaging ability enhances the effectiveness of an intervention designed to reduce speech anxiety. *Communication Education, 43,* 252–258.

59. Docan-Morgan, T., & Schmidt, T. (2012). Reducing public speaking anxiety for native and non-native English speakers: The value of systematic desensitization, cognitive restructuring, and skills training. *Cross-Cultural Communication, 8,* 16–19.

60. Jönsson, P., Wallergård, M., Österberg, K., Hansen, Å, M., Johansson, G., & Karlson, B. (2010). Cardiovascular and cortisol reactivity and habituation to a virtual reaility version of the Trier Social Stress Test: A pilot study. *Psychoneuroendocrinology, 35,* 1397–1403.

61. Garland, E. L., Fredrickson, B., Kring, A. M., Johnson, D. P., Meyer, P. S., & Penn, D. L. (2010). Upward spirals of positive emotions counter downward spirals of negativity: Insights from the broaden-and-build theory and affective neuroscience on the treatment of emotion dysfunctions and deficits in psychopathology. *Clinical Psychology Review, 30,* 849–864.

62. McCroskey, J. C. (n. d.). *Personal Report of Public Speaking Anxiety (PRPSA).* Retrieved from http://www .jamescmccroskey.com/measures/prpsa.htm; McCroskey, J. C. (1970). Measures of communication-bound anxiety. *Speech Monographs, 37,* 269–277.

GLOSSARY

A

abilities Skills and knowledge we can apply to accomplishing work tasks, such as using accounting software or conducting marketing surveys.

accommodating style Conflict style that reflects a high concern for the other party but a low concern for the self.

acquired diversity Differences gained through experience, such as customer service experience, retail experience, or engineering experience.

action-oriented style Listening style that looks for organization and precision.

active incivility Direct forms of disrespect (being condescending or demeaning, saying something hurtful).

active listening As defined by Michael Hoppe, "a person's willingness and ability to hear and understand. At its core, active listening is a state of mind. . . . It involves bringing about and finding common ground, connecting to each other, and opening up new possibilities."

agenda A list of items to be discussed at a meeting.

ambiguous language Language that we can interpret to have more than one meaning.

anticipatory anxiety The worry many people feel when looking ahead to giving a speech.

anxiety A feeling of worry and unease.

appraisal interview A discussion between an employee and a manager or supervisor to discuss the employee's performance and goals.

articulation The extent to which a speaker pronounces words clearly.

artifacts The objects and visual features within our environment that reflect who we are and what we like.

association The psychological bonding that occurs between people and their ideas.

attributes Personal traits or characteristics.

attribution An explanation of an observed behavior; the answer to the question "Why did this occur?"

audience analysis Thinking carefully about the characteristics of listeners so the speaker can address the audience in the most effective way.

auditory learner A learner who prefers loud, clear voices and believes emotion is best conveyed through voice.

autocratic style Leadership style in which the leader views himself/herself as having both the authority and the responsibility to take action on behalf of the group.

autonomy face Our need to avoid being imposed on by others.

avoiding style Conflict style that demonstrates low concern for both the self and the other party.

B

bar chart A chart that depicts numbers as bars on a graph, such as the percentages of people in various parts of the world who regularly use the Internet.

blog A discussion website on which posts are arranged chronologically, similar to a journal format.

brainstorming A technique that encourages participants to identify as many ideas as possible without stopping to evaluate them.

C

cause-and-effect pattern A pattern that organizes the points in a speech so they describe the causes of an event or a phenomenon and then identify its consequences.

channel A type of communication pathway used to convey a message. May include face-to-face, email, text message, or voice mail, among others.

chronemics The way we use time.

chronological résumé Résumé that presents the information grouped by work and education over time.

cliché Word or phrase that was novel at one time but has lost its effect due to overuse.

closed-ended question Question that prompts a brief, specific answer.

closed-mindedness The tendency not to listen to something with which we disagree.

co-culture Group of people who share values, customs, and norms related to mutual interests or characteristics besides their national citizenship.

cognitive complexity The ability to consider a variety of explanations and understand a given situation in multiple ways.

collaborating style Conflict style that represents a high concern for the needs of both sides in a conflict.

collectivistic culture A culture in which people are taught that their primary responsibility is to their families, their communities, and their employers.

colloquium A speaking format in which members of a group discuss a predetermined topic with one another in front of an audience.

communication apprehension Anxiety or fear about communicating with others.

communication competence The ability to communicate in ways that are effective and appropriate in a given situation.

competence face Our need to be respected—to have others acknowledge our abilities and intelligence.

competing style Conflict style that represents a high concern for our own needs and desires and a low concern for the other party.

competitive interrupting The practice of using interruptions to take control of the conversation.

compromising style Conflict style that reflects a moderate concern for everyone's needs and desires. Both parties give up something in order to gain something.

connotative meaning The ideas or concepts a word suggests in addition to its literal definition.

consensus Achieved when a group has identified an acceptable plan of action that all or most group members can support, even if that specific plan isn't everyone's preference.

content dimension The literal information being communicated by a message.

content-oriented style Listening style that hones in on intellectual challenges.

context The physical and psychological environment in which a message is communicated.

coordination meeting Meeting that primarily focuses on discussing tasks, roles, goals, and accountabilities.

copyright infringement The unauthorized use of materials protected by copyright such as photos or works of art.

counseling interview An interaction aimed at supporting an individual through a personal problem.

credibility The extent to which others perceive us to be competent and trustworthy.

critical listening Listening with a goal of evaluating or analyzing what is being heard.

cross-functional (team) Team that includes members from various functional backgrounds, such as finance, marketing, and operations.

cultural centrism The belief that our own culture is superior and the correct lens from which we judge other cultures.

culture The totality of learned, shared symbols, language, values, and norms that distinguish one group of people from another.

cyber incivility The violation of respect and consideration in an online environment based on workplace norms.

cyber silence Nonresponse to emails and other digital communications.

D

dashboard The front page when an employee logs in to an internal digital platform, which operates as his/her communication and information hub.

database An electronic storehouse of specific information that you can search.

decode To interpret a message.

defamation Language that harms a person's reputation or gives that person a negative image.

defuse (an uncivil email) Focus on task-related facts and issues in your reply.

democratic style Leadership style in which the leader engages as many people as possible in decision making.

demographic characteristics Characteristics that include age, sex and sexual orientation, culture, socioeconomic status, physical and mental characteristics, and political orientation.

denotative meaning The literal meaning of a word—the way a dictionary defines it.

desensitization The process of confronting frightening situations head-on.

dialect Language variation shared by people of a certain region or social class.

disassociation A process by which professionals accept critiques of their ideas without taking them personally or becoming defensive.

disclaimer Statement, usually offered at the beginning of a message, that expresses a speaker's uncertainty, such as "I could be wrong about this, but. . . ."

downward communication Communication that flows from superiors to subordinates.

dynamic Constantly changing and evolving.

E

emotional intelligence A person's ability to "perceive and accurately express emotions, to use emotion to facilitate thought, to understand emotions, and to manage emotions for emotional growth."

empathic listening Listening that involves trying to identify with the speaker by understanding and experiencing what he/she is thinking or feeling.

empathy The ability to be "other-oriented" and understand other people's thoughts and feelings.

encode When formulating a message, putting an idea into the form of language or a nonverbal behavior that the receiver can understand.

EQ Stands for *emotional quotient;* a person's level of emotional intelligence.

ethics Guides us in judging whether something is morally right or wrong.

ethnicity A person's perception of his/her ancestry and heritage.

ethos A speaker's credibility.

eulogy A speech made to honor the memory of people after their death and to comfort those who remain.

exit interview An interview with an employee leaving an organization; usually includes describing both positive and negative aspects of the job, his/her supervisors, and the organization.

explicit rules Rules that have been clearly articulated as direct expectations for communicative behavior.

extemporaneous speech A prepared speech rehearsed to sound as though it is being delivered spontaneously.

extraversion A personality trait shared by people who are friendly, assertive, and outgoing with others.

F

face Our desired public image.

face needs Important components of our desired public image.

face-threatening act An act that hinders the fulfillment of one or more of our face needs.

facework The behaviors we use to project our desired public image to others.

facial display Facial expression; a form of nonverbal communication.

facilitator Individual who acts from a neutral position to get each person to participate in the conversation and ensure that each agenda item is properly discussed.

factual claim An assertion that can be verified with evidence and shown to be true or false.

feedback A receiver's various verbal and nonverbal reactions to a message.

fellowship face The need to have others like and accept us.

feminine culture A culture in which people tend to value nurturing behavior, quality of life, and service to others, all stereotypically feminine qualities.

fight-or-flight response A reaction that helps prepare the body either to confront the stressor (through a fight) or to avoid it (by fleeing the situation).

flames Emails or other digital communications with "hostile intentions characterized by words of profanity, obscenity, and insults that inflict harm to a person or an organization."

fluency The smoothness of a speaker's delivery.

formal address term Term that indicates the listener is of higher status than the speaker, such as "Sir" and "Ma'am."

formal professional networks Types of professional relationships that generally have clear lines of authority and reporting structures, shoulder standard sets of responsibilities, and require accountability to other members of the network.

formality The protocols, rules, structure, and politeness associated with formal professional networks.

forming stage Team members focus on gaining acceptance and avoiding conflict.

forum A format in which members of the group and the audience offer comments and questions to one another.

functional résumé Résumé that presents the information in terms of key skills.

fundamental attribution error The tendency to attribute other people's behaviors to internal rather than external causes.

G

gender A social and psychological variable that characterizes a person's identity as feminine, masculine, or androgynous (a combination of masculine and feminine traits).

general search engine A website that allows you to search for other websites containing information about a topic you specify.

gesticulation The use of arm and hand movements to communicate.

glazing over Daydreaming; actually listening to the speaker, but allowing your mind to drift.

global theft Stealing an entire speech from another source and presenting it as if it were your own.

graphic slide The electronic display of information in a visually compelling format that can enhance listeners' attention.

groupthink Occurs when team members seek unanimous agreement despite their individual doubts.

H

halo effect A strong predisposition to attribute positive qualities to physically attractive people.

haptics The study of the way we use touch to communicate.

hearing The sensory process of receiving and perceiving sounds—listening is about creating meaning from what we hear.

hedge Words that introduce doubt into a speaker's message, such as "I guess I feel we should . . ."

hesitation Term that introduces pauses into speech, such as "um" and "well."

high-contact culture A culture in which people usually stand or sit fairly close to one another and touch one another frequently.

high-context culture A culture in which people are taught to speak in an indirect way, and that maintaining harmony and avoiding offense are more important than expressing their true feelings.

high-power-distance culture A culture in which people believe that certain individuals or groups deserve more power than others, and that respecting power and privilege is more important than promoting equality.

hypothetical question Question that describes a realistic situation and asks you to speculate about how you would react.

I

I-statement A statement that claims ownership of what a communicator is feeling or thinking.

identity Our own stable perceptions about who we are; also called our *self-concept.*

image management The process of behavioral adjustment to project a desired image.

implicit rules Rules that almost everyone in a certain social group knows and follows, even though no one has formally expressed them.

impromptu speech A speech that is delivered on the spot, with little or no preparation.

incremental theft Failing to give credit for small portions of your speech—such as a phrase or paragraph—that you did not write.

individualistic culture A culture in which people believe their primary responsibility is to themselves.

informal communication Communication that is generally less bound by protocols, rules, structure, and politeness, typically found in informal professional networks.

informal professional networks Voluntary professional connections—such as friendships formed with co-workers—rather than formal reporting structures.

information overload The state of being overwhelmed by the huge amount of information taken in every day.

informational interview An interview with a successful and accomplished professional to seek out career advice.

informational listening Listening to learn.

informative speech A speech whose goal is to teach listeners something they don't already know.

inherent diversity Differences in traits such as age, gender, ethnicity, and sexual orientation.

intensifier Word such as "very" and "really" that heightens the importance of other words.

internal digital platform Platform provided by most organizations to organize communication among employees; may include many tools, including a dashboard, blogs, and discussion forums.

interpretation After noticing and classifying a stimulus, assigning it an interpretation to figure out its meaning for you.

interview A structured conversation that focuses on questions and answers.

intimate distance The zone people willingly occupy with only their closest and most intimate friends, family members, and romantic partners; ranges from 0 to approximately 1½ feet.

introductory speech A speech whose goal is to inform listeners of the person's background and notable characteristics.

introversion A personality trait shared by people who are shy, reserved, and aloof.

J

Johari window A visual representation of the self as composed of four separate parts.

K

kinesics The study of movement, including the movement of walking.

kinesthetic learner A learner who needs to participate in order to focus his/her attention on the message and learn best.

L

laissez-faire style Leadership style in which the leader rarely interacts with employees, gives them little feedback on job performance, and generally trusts others to make the right decisions.

language A structured system of symbols, in the form of words, used for communicating meaning.

lateral (horizontal) communication Communication among peers or colleagues with relatively equal positions in the organization.

libel A defamatory statement made in print or some other fixed medium, such as in a photograph or on a website or blog.

life story A way of presenting ourselves to others that is based on our self-concept but is also influenced by other people.

line chart A graphic display in the form of a line or lines that connect various data points.

listening The active process of making meaning from another person's spoken message.

loaded language Language that consists of words with strongly positive or negative connotations; also called *trigger words.*

low-contact culture A culture in which people keep great amounts of personal space between themselves and touch one another infrequently.

low-context culture A culture in which people are expected to be direct, to say what they mean, and to use language that is specific and concrete.

low-power-distance culture A culture in which people believe that all individuals are equal and that no one person or group should have excessive power.

M

main point A statement expressing a specific idea or theme related to the speech topic.

masculine culture A culture in which people tend to cherish stereotypically masculine values, such as ambition, achievement, and the acquisition of material goods.

memorized speech A speech that is composed word for word and then delivered from memory.

message Consists of verbal and/or nonverbal behaviors to which people give meaning.

metacommunication Communication about communication.

microblog Short comment that typically contains just a few sentences; also called *status update.*

minutes (meeting) Should include the date and time of the meeting, team members present, decisions, key discussion points, open issues, and any action items, the people undertaking them, and related deadlines.

monochronic (concept of time) Concept of time as a commodity.

N

nationality A person's status as a citizen of a particular country.

negativity effect Effect causing people to perceive messages as negative that are meant to be neutral.

networking A proactive approach to building professional relationships to achieve shared company, career, and professional development goals.

neutrality effect Effect causing people to perceive messages with an intended positive emotion as neutral.

noise Anything that interferes with a receiver's ability to encode or decode a message.

nonverbal communication Messages that include those behaviors and characteristics that convey meaning without the use of words.

norming stage The team arrives at a work plan, including the roles, goals, and accountabilities.

O

objective (source) A source that presents information in an unbiased fashion.

oculesics The study of eye behavior, as a separate nonverbal channel.

open-ended question Question that invites a broad range of answers.

opinion Expression of a personal judgment or preference that can be agreed or disagreed with but that is not true or false in an absolute sense.

oral report A speaking format in which one person gives a speech or presentation on the group's behalf.

organization The classification of information according to its similarities to and differences from other things we know about.

outgroup homogeneity effect The tendency to think members of other groups are all the same.

P

panel A small group of people brought together to discuss a specific topic.

passive incivility Using emails for time-sensitive messages rather than more direct and efficient forms of communication, or not acknowledging or replying to emails.

patchwork theft Copying words from multiple sources and putting them together to compose a speech.

people-oriented style Listening style that consists of finding common interests with others and discerning their emotions and interests.

perception The process of making meaning from what we experience in the world around us.

perceptual set A predisposition to perceive only what we want or expect to perceive.

performing stage Team operates efficiently toward accomplishing its goals.

personal distance The distance people typically maintain with their friends and relatives; extends from 1½ to about 4 feet.

persuasion The process of guiding people to adopt a specific attitude or enact a particular behavior.

persuasive interview A conversation intended to affect someone's belief, opinion, or behavior.

persuasive speech A speech whose goal is to appeal to listeners to think or act in a certain way.

phonological rules Language rules that deal with the correct pronunciation of a word; they vary from language to language.

pie chart A graphic display in the form of a circle divided into segments, each of which represents a percentage of the whole.

pitch A measure of how high or how low the voice is.

plagiarism The use of information from another source without giving proper credit to that source.

polychronic (concept of time) Concept of time as more holistic and fluid and less structured.

post-trust era The current climate in which people overwhelmingly view businesses as operating against the public's best interests and the majority of employees view their leaders and colleagues skeptically.

powerful speech A style of speaking perceived as active and assertive.

powerless speech A style of speaking that is perceived as passive and timid.

pragmatic rules Language rules that help us interpret statements.

presentation aid Anything used in conjunction with a speech or presentation to stimulate listeners' senses.

preview transition A statement alerting listeners that the speaker is about to shift to a new topic.

primacy effect A principle that says that first impressions are critical because they set the tone for all future interactions.

probing question Question that requests more detail on an answer you have already provided.

problem-solution pattern A pattern that organizes the points in a speech so they describe a problem and then offer one or more solutions for it.

problem-solving interview An interview that helps participants understand the nature of a problem and identify potential solutions.

problem-solving meeting Meeting that usually includes brainstorming about how to address and solve a particular work problem.

project blog Blog that is organized around a particular project that generally is completed by a temporary team.

projected cognitive similarity The tendency to assume others share our cultural norms and values.

proxemics The scientific study of spatial use.

pseudolistening Pretending to pay attention to someone but not really listening.

public distance Distance that applies when someone is giving a speech or performing in front of a large audience. The purpose is to keep the presenter far enough away from the group that he/she is comfortable and visible to everyone. Public distances are usually 12 to 25 feet or greater, depending on the circumstance.

public relations (PR) Defined as "the management function that establishes and maintains mutually beneficial relationships between an organization and the various publics on whom its success depends."

public speaking anxiety Nervousness or fear brought on by performing in front of an audience; also called *stage fright*.

purpose statement A declaration of the specific goal for a speech. It expresses precisely what the speaker wants to accomplish during the presentation.

Q

questionnaire A written instrument containing questions for people to answer.

R

race Differences in sets of physical characteristics—such as bone structure and the color of skin, hair, and eyes—that have often been presumed to have a biological or genetic basis.

rapport A sense of harmony, goodwill, and caring among people.

rebuttal tendency The propensity to debate a speaker's point and formulate a reply while that person is still speaking.

receiver The person who decodes, or interprets, a message.

recency effect A principle that says that the most recent impression we have of a person's communication is more powerful than our earlier impressions.

reinterpretation Adjusting your initial perceptions by making more objective, more fact-based, and less personal judgments and evaluations.

relational dimension The signals in messages about the nature of the relationship in which they're shared.

relaxation Releasing and overcoming anger and frustration so that you can make a more rational and less emotional response.

research search engine A search engine that doesn't scan the Internet as broadly as a general search engine but instead looks only for research that has been published in books, academic journals, and other periodicals.

rule of division Principle stating that whenever there is one subpoint in a speech, there must be at least one more.

rule of subordination A principle stating that the broadest, most important claims in a speech come first in the form of main points, and the lesser, more specific claims follow in the form of subpoints.

S

scripted speech A speech that is composed word for word in a manuscript and then read aloud exactly as written.

selection The process by which our mind and body help us isolate certain stimuli to pay attention to.

selection interview A conversation intended to help the interviewer choose the most appropriate person for a position, an assignment, a promotion, or an award.

selective attention Listening only to what we want to hear and ignoring the rest.

self-concept Our own stable perceptions about who we are; also called our *identity*.

self-esteem Our subjective evaluation of our value and worth as a person.

self-fulfilling prophecy A situation in which a prediction causes people to act and communicate in ways that make it come about.

self-monitoring Being aware of our own behavior and its effects on others.

self-serving bias The tendency to attribute our successes to stable, internal causes and our failures to unstable, external causes.

semantic rules Language rules that dictate the meaning of individual words.

sender The source of an idea when formulating a message.

service-oriented interview A conversation meant to help a customer with a product or service he/she has purchased.

sex A genetic variable that determines whether someone is born male, female, of another sex, or of an indeterminate sex.

sexuality Describes the sex or sexes to which a person is romantically or sexually attracted; also called *sexual orientation*.

shared story Combines everyone's experiences, perspectives, and goals into a shared approach to work.

signpost A single word or phrase that distinguishes one point in a presentation from another.

slander A defamatory statement made aloud, within earshot of others.

social distance Distance used with customers, casual acquaintances, and others to convey more formal, impersonal interaction; ranges from about 4 to 12 feet.

society Group of people who share the same culture.

socioeconomic status (SES) A measure of a person's financial and social position relative to that of others.

solicited cover letter A cover letter for an open position that a company advertises.

space pattern A pattern that organizes the main points in a speech according to geographic or physical areas.

specific purpose (of speech) The main goal for the presentation.

speech of commemoration A speech given to honor a significant point in history.

speech of dedication A speech given to honor important places.

speech of recognition A speech given to honor someone who is receiving an award.

STAR method An approach to telling success stories; stands for Situation–Tasks–Actions–Results.

stereotype A generalization about a group or category of people that can have a powerful influence on the way we perceive others and their communication behavior.

storming stage Team members open up with their competing ideas about how the team should approach work.

story Each person's version of past interactions or explanation of business successes and failures.

stress The body's reaction to any type of perceived threat.

stressor An event that causes the body to experience stress.

stuttering A speech disorder that disrupts the flow of words with repeated or prolonged sounds and involuntary pauses.

subjective (source) A source that offers information in a manner that supports only the source's favored position on an issue.

subpoints Supporting points in a speech; also called *subordinate points*.

summary transition A statement in a speech that briefly reminds listeners of points you have already made.

survey Collecting data by asking people directly about their experiences.

survey interview An interaction aimed at gathering information.

symbol Representation of an idea.

symposium A speaking format in which each member of a small group makes an individual presentation, one after another, on a common topic.

syntactic rules Language rules that govern the order of words within phrases and clauses.

T

tag question Question at the end of a statement that asks for listener agreement, such as "Okay?" and "Don't you agree?"

team blog Blog that is typically organized around a formal work team.

team culture A team's set of shared perceptions and commitment to collective values, norms, roles, responsibilities, and goals.

text slide An electronic display of text to accompany a speech.

thesis (of speech) Crystalizes the main message of a speech.

thesis statement A one-sentence version of the message in a speech.

time pattern A pattern that arranges the main points in a speech in chronological order.

time-oriented style Listening style that emphasizes efficiency.

toast A short speech of tribute to the person or people being celebrated.

topic pattern A pattern that organizes the main points of a speech to represent different categories.

transition A statement that logically connects one point in a speech to the next, giving it a satisfying flow.

2-D diversity The presence of both inherent diversity and acquired diversity.

U

uncertainty avoidance The extent to which we try to avoid situations that are unstructured, unclear, or unpredictable.

unsolicited cover letter A cover letter that states your interest in working for a company that is not actively requesting job applications.

upward communication Communication that flows from subordinates to superiors.

V

validating Recognizing others' perspectives and feelings as credible or legitimate.

verbal communication The use of words to communicate.

verbal footnote A statement giving credit for words to their original source.

virtual team Team composed of employees who rarely see one another in person and are usually geographically dispersed.

visual learner A learner who learns best from illustrations and simple diagrams that show relationships and key ideas.

visualization Developing a specific mental image of winning or giving a successful performance.

vocalics Characteristics of the voice, such as having a high, breathy voice or a deep, booming one; talking very fast or loudly; having an accent; or speaking with a particular tone in the voice to suggest irritation, amusement, or boredom; also called *paralanguage*.

Y

you-statement A statement that shifts responsibility for thoughts and feelings to the other person.

INDEX

Page numbers in **bold** indicate definitions of key terms. The italicized *f* and *t* following page numbers indicate figures and tables, respectively.

Facilitators, **158**
Factual claims, **57**–58, 81, 302–303
Feedback, **8**, 8*f*, 81, 133, 136
Fellowship face, **119**
Feminine culture, **34**
Ferrazzi, Keith, 146, 162
Field, Tiffany, 36–37
Fight-or-flight response, **338**, 339
Finality, expressions of, 246
Flames, **237**
Fluency, **335**
Follow-up, 222–223, 223*f*, 347
Formal address terms, **60**
Formal communication, 10
Formality, **10**, 37, 332
Formal professional networks, **10**
Forming stage of team development,
        129, 129*f*, 145*t*
Forums, 245–247, 245*f*, 247*f*, **262**
Forward feature, 233
Fried, Jason, 241
Functional résumés, **187**–188, 190–191*f*
Fundamental attribution error, **111**

G

Gait, 62
Gates, Melinda, 267
Gay, 29
Gender, **29**
Gender roles, 38
General Electric (GE), 133, 136
General search engines, **307**
Generational identity, 30–31
Generation Xers, 30
Gesticulation, 5, 6, **62**, 296, 332
Gettysburg Address, 264
Gift giving customs, 36
Giver mentality, 198
Glassdoor.com, 211
Glazing over, **86**, 89*t*
Global theft, **318**
Goal setting, 176–177, 176*f*
Goffman, Erving, 119
Goldschmidt, Myra, 118–119
Golen, Steven, 86
Goodwill, as component of ethos, 291, 291*f*
Google, 60, 132, 209, 307, 308
Grammar checks, 235, 236
Graphic slides, **314**–316
Greeting customs, 35–36, 63
Group presentations, 261–262
Groupthink, 133, **140**–142

H

Hall, Edward T., 37
Halo effect, **64**
Handouts, 313, 314
Haptics, **63**
Harassment, 63, 307–308
Harvard Negotiation Project, 164
Hayakawa, Samuel, 55, 56*f*
Hearing, **76**, 79–80. *See also* Listening
Hedges, **60**

Heen, Sheila, 164
Hesitations, **60**
Heterosexuality, 29
High-contact culture, **36**–37
High-context culture, **32**–33
High-morale organizations, 235, 237*f*
High-power-distance culture, **33**–34, 40
Hofstede, Geert, 32, 34
Holacracy, 138
Home Shopping Network (HSN), 311–312
Homosexuality, 29
Honesty, 345, 345*t*
Hoppe, Michael, 12
Horizontal (lateral) communication, 10
Houston, Drew, 130
Hsieh, Tony, 163
HSN (Home Shopping Network), 311–312
Humor, 271, 290, 293
HURIER model of effective listening, 79–82, 79*t*
Hypothetical questions, **212**

I

Identity, 61, **112**
Identity needs, 4
Iguodala, Andre, 109
Illegal questions, 217–219, 218*t*
Image management, **116**–120
Implicit rules, **4**–514
Impromptu speeches, **326**, 329, 329*t*, 337
Incremental theft, **319**
Individualistic culture, **32**, 38, 105–106, 139
Informal communication, **10**
Informal interviews, 311
Informal professional networks, **10**
Informational interviews, **178**–179
Informational listening, **82**, 90–91, 143
Informational needs, 4
Information overload, **85**–86, 89*t*, 143
Informative speech, **260**, 280–281, 285,
        286, 293
Ingham, Harry, 112
Inherent diversity, **133**
InMobi, 268, 269
Inspirational listening, 83
Instrumental needs, 4
Integrity, 12
Intel, 240
Intellectual theft, 318–320, 320*t*
Intelligence, emotional, 15*t*, 17, 166, 216, 239
Intensifiers, **60**
Interaction constructs, 104
Internal digital platforms, 240–247
        blogs on, 242–243, 243*f*
        dashboard organization, 241
        defined, **240**
        discussion forums on, 245–247, 245*f*, 247*f*
        guidelines for, 240
        profile on, 242, 242*f*
        shared files for collaboration on, 244
        status updates on, 242–243, 244*f*
Internal loci, 110
International Communication Association, 319
Internet, supporting materials from, 306–308
Interpersonal perception, 103
Interpretation, 80–81, 103*f*, **104**–105

Positioning statements, 248
Post-millennials, 30
Post-trust era, **12**
Posture, 330–331
Power distance, 33–34, 40
Powerful speech, 59–**60**
Powerless speech, **60**
PowerPoint, 268, 269, 314
Pragmatic rules, **54**
Presentation aids, 311–317
  backup plan for, 317, 344
  benefits of, 312
  defined, **312**
  graphic slides, 314–316
  handouts, 313, 314
  learning style and, 269
  low-tech, 312–313
  multimedia, 314–316
  overview, 311–312
  practicing with, 317
  selection and use of, 316–317
  text slides, 268, 314, 314*f*
  video and audio, 316
Presentations, 259–274. *See also* Audiences; Speeches; Supporting
    materials
  distractions during, 274
  follow-up to, 347
  group, 261–262
  purpose of, 264, 273
  question-and-answer portion of, 345–347*t*
  time available for, 273, 317
  topic selection for, 264–267, 265*t*
  types of, 260–264
Press-release style blogs, 248, 249*f*
Preview transitions, **294,** 295
Primacy effect, **106**–107, 109, 109*f*
Principle of facial primacy, 61
Priority flags, 233
Privacy. *See* Confidentiality
Probability, 92–93
Probing questions, **212**
Problem-solution patterns, **287**
Problem-solving interviews, **206**
Problem-solving meetings, **155**
Productive time of workdays, 155, 155*f*
Professional development events, 179
Professional networks, 10–11, 198
Profiles, 196, 242, 242*f*
Project blogs, **243**
Projected cognitive similarity, **43**
Proofreading, 186, 186*t*, 194, 235, 236
Proportionality, 61
Proxemics, 36–37, **63**–64
PR (public relations), 248
Pseudolistening, **83**–85, 89*t*
Psychological constructs, 104
Psychological noise, 8, 83
Public distance, **37,** 64
Public relations (PR), **248**
Public speaking anxiety, 335–341
  behavioral effects of, 338
  debilitating cases of, 339
  defined, **336**
  management of, 339–341

physical effects of, 338
prevalence of, 335–336
psychological effects of, 336–337
PubMed, 307
Pupil size, 61–62
Purpose statement, **280**–282

Q

Questionnaires, **311**
Questions
  closed-ended, 212
  hypothetical, 212
  illegal, 217–219, 218*t*
  interviewee-generated, 219–220, 220*t*
  open-ended, 212
  during presentations, 345–347*t*
  probing, 212
  reframing, 346, 347*t*
  rhetorical, 290
  tag questions, 60
Quotations, 290, 303

R

Race, **27**
Radical transparency, 163
Rapport, **12,** 145, 290
Rate of speech, 333–334
Readability statistics, 236
Reading habits, 309
Rebuttal tendency, **86**–87, 89*t*, 143
Recall, 312
Receivers, **8,** 8*f*
Recency effect, **107,** 109, 109*f*
Recorded speeches, 329–330
Reference lists, 192, 193, 194*f*
Reference/referent, 54, 55*f*
Reframing questions, 346, 347*t*
Regional differences, 31, 56
Reinterpretation, **238**
Relational dimension of messages, **5**
Relational needs, 4
Relaxation, **238**
Religious beliefs, 29–30, 30*t*
Reply all feature, 234
Research search engines, **307**
Response strategies, 81–82, 212–216, 217*t*
Résumés, 180–194
  action verbs for, 182–184*t*
  checklist for, 187
  chronological, 187–189*f*
  cliché avoidance on, 184
  distinguishing information on, 186, 186*t*
  electronic screening of, 189–192
  fudging facts on, 185
  functional, 187–188, 190–191*f*
  irrelevant detail removal on, 184, 185*t*
  layout for, 186–187
  message structure for, 180–181
  proofreading, 186, 186*t*, 194
  quantification of accomplishments on, 183, 184–185*t*
  reference list for, 192, 193, 194*f*
  tone, style, and design of, 182–187